ESSENTIALS OF

TEXAS
POLITICS

ESSENTIALS OF

TEXAS
POLITICS
TENTH EDITION

RICHARD H. KRAEMER

Professor Emeritus of Government
University of Texas at Austin

CHARLDEAN NEWELL

Regents Professor Emerita of
Public Administration
University of North Texas

DAVID F. PRINDLE

Professor of Government
The University of Texas at Austin

Australia • Brazil • Canada • Mexico • Singapore • Spain
United Kingdom • United States

THOMSON
WADSWORTH

Essentials of Texas Politics, **Tenth Edition**
*Richard H. Kraemer, Charldean Newell,
and David F. Prindle*

Editor in Chief: P. J. Boardman
Executive Editor: Carolyn Merrill
Associate Development Editor: Rebecca Green
Editorial Assistant: Patrick Rheaume
Technology Project Manager: Inna Fedoseyeva
Marketing Manager: Janise Fry
Marketing Assistant: Kathleen Tosiello
Senior Marketing Communications Manager:
   Tami Strang
Project Manager, Editorial Production: Marti Paul
Creative Director: Rob Hugel
Art Director: Maria Epes
Print Buyer: Nora Massuda

Permissions Editor: Bob Kauser
Production Service: International Typesetting
   and Composition
Text Designer: Cynthia Bassett, Denise Davidson
Copy Editor: Joan Flaherty
Illustrator: International Typesetting and Composition
Cover Designer: Denise Davidson
Cover Photo: "Natural Bridge of Texas," ©2005
   Jay H. Wilbur
Cover Printer: Thomson West
Compositor: International Typesetting and
   Composition
Printer: Thomson West

Printed in the United States of America
1 2 3 4 5 6 7 11 10 09 08 07

Library of Congress Control Number: 2006908560

ISBN-13: 978-0-495-00679-4
ISBN-10: 0-495-00679-3

Thomson Higher Education
10 Davis Drive
Belmont, CA 94002-3098
USA

For more information about our products,
contact us at:

Thomson Learning Academic Resource Center
1-800-423-0563

For permission to use material from this text or
product, submit a request online at
http://www.thomsonrights.com.

Any additional questions about permissions can be
submitted by e-mail to
thomsonrights@thomson.com.

CONTENTS

4   Political Parties   66

5   Voters, Campaigns, and Elections   89

7   The Governor and State Administration   150

PREFACE

In Texas, as in the rest of the United States, government and politics are important aspects of life. Government includes public institutions and policies, and politics encompasses political behavior and action. Both touch our daily lives in many ways. Getting a driver's license, being charged extra pennies when we buy a hamburger, arranging for water service at home, paying tuition—in all of these routine actions we deal with government. In addition to the big concerns such as Operation Iraqi Freedom, finding ways to shore up a sagging economy, and electing a president, government encompasses many of the little things in our lives.

Texas continues to be a dynamic and fascinating state. Many readers of this book were not yet born when the first edition was published in 1980. Then, the book described the one-party, Democrat-dominated state and a budget rooted in the oil and gas industry. The Texas population was a little over 11 million. Now, the state has about 23 million residents, more than double the 1980 figure. Republicans have moved from being a decidedly minority party to a dominant force. Oil and gas revenues now fuel less than 2 percent of the state budget. The state's biennial budget has risen from $16.8 billion to more than $139 billion.

Other aspects of government and politics have not changed much at all. The Texas Constitution is still a patchwork of detailed provisions and numerous amendments—in fact, more each year—rather than a streamlined document. Business and economic interests continue to be the dominant influences on the legislature. And the executive branch and the courts are both still hodgepodges of agencies and different courts that confuse most citizens. Both change and the lack of it make studying Texas politics interesting.

There are three themes that the reader will encounter in *Essentials of Texas Politics*, tenth edition. The over-riding theme is a comparison of the reality of Texas government and politics to the democratic ideals of participation, majority rule, protection of minority rights, and equality before the law. Throughout, the authors ask whether a particular political action or institution serves the general public interest or only narrow private interests.

The authors are political scientists trained to be analysts, not merely observers, of politics. Our mission is not to offer a defense or apology for the present system but to identify the differences between governmental practices and the sense of fair play and equity expected in a democratic system. Thus, we point out where the system works well, but we also examine the faults of the system and suggest changes.

A second theme is increasing conservatism even in a state that has always been conservative. The Democrats have long been divided into liberal and conservative wings, with the term *conservative* mainly meaning protection of business interests and a paternal attitude toward ethnic minorities and the poor. The Republicans seem headed toward a division between economic conservatives and social conservatives.

Because political ideologies are so different among the various political factions and because the ethnic and racial composition of the state is changing rapidly, a third theme is that of conflict. We particularly call attention to conflicts among the rich, the poor, and the middle class; among and between Anglos, Mexican Americans, and African Americans; among ideologies; and among religious traditions.

Essentials is a short book, and we cannot provide a comprehensive, in-depth analysis of all things political in Texas. We hope, however, that we can pique the interest of students to learn more about government and politics in the Lone Star State and can help them understand how much state and local governments affect them every day. The book is supplemented by an online site, which includes "A Research Guide to Texas Politics" as well as various instructor's aids. To access these resources, please go to http://www.thomsonedu.com/politicalscience/kraemer. This companion website for both students and instructors includes a description of how students will use the book in their Texas government and politics course, and explains new features in the textbook. For students, we provide learning objectives, flashcards, and multiple-choice practice quiz questions.

We want to thank our colleagues across the state who reviewed the tenth edition and made valuable comments to aid us in revising the book. They are Robert Glen Findley, Odessa College; John Glassford, Angelo State University; and Dr. H. Ibrahim Salih, Texas Wesleyan University. Although space limitations and occasional conflicting recommendations made it impossible to incorporate all of their suggestions, we did include most of the ideas proposed.

We appreciate colleagues and students at our own institutions who have given us their observations, constructive criticisms, and expertise. Also, we thank the many elected officials, legislative staff members, and state agency staff members who provided us with information, clarification, and graphics material. We particularly thank Ben Sargent, winner of the 1982 Pulitzer Prize for editorial cartooning, for again graciously permitting the use of his outstanding cartoons. And we thank Angie Prindle for practical and moral support. Of course, any errors of fact or interpretation are ours alone.

1

THE CONTEXT OF TEXAS POLITICS

If I owned Hell and Texas, I'd rent out Texas and live in Hell.

General Philip H. Sheridan
Fort Clark, 1855

I wasn't born in Texas, but I got here as fast as I could.

On earth as it is in Texas.

Bumper stickers noticed on Texas vehicles in the early years of the twenty-first century.

All government is bad, including good government.

Edward Abbey
The Journey Home, 1977

INTRODUCTION

Much has changed between the 1850s, when General Sheridan made his well-known evaluation of Texas, and the modern period, in which Texans often proclaim their state patriotism with bumper stickers. In 1855 Texas was poor and offered few comforts to a soldier assigned to garrison an outpost against Indian raids. Today, Texas is the nation's second most populous state, is 84 percent urban, and leads the country in consuming energy and producing semiconductors, among other distinctions. Yet in some ways the state has changed little since Sheridan's era. Texas is a mix of old and new.

Habits of thought and behavior evolved to meet the problems of the nineteenth century, when Texas was settled by Americans of Western European background. Old habits persist today, despite serious problems created in the latter decades of the twentieth century and the early years of the twenty-first. As Texans prepare to meet the problems of the present and future, they have to ask themselves if the habits and institutions they have inherited are up to the job.

The first topic of this chapter is a list of the most important principles of democratic theory and an explanation of why it is vital to understand them. Next is a discussion of Texas as one among fifty states in a federal system and as an actor in the international arena. Following that is an exploration of some of the social and political attitudes that are of historical importance in the state. Next is a discussion of the economy of Texas and the way it interacts with the state's political system. As an introduction to some topics later in the book, we summarize the origin and distribution of the people of Texas. Finally, we present a brief outline of the agenda for the remainder of the book.

TEXAS AS A DEMOCRACY

Part of the task of this book is to discuss the concept of **democracy** and evaluate the extent to which Texas measures up as a democratic state. A democracy is a system of government, the legitimacy of which is based on the people's participation. **Legitimacy** is the belief people hold that their government is moral, fair, and just and that therefore they should obey its laws. According to the moral theory underlying a democratic system of government, because the people themselves (indirectly, through representatives) make the laws, they are morally obligated to obey them.

There are many implications of this theory, and we will explore a number of them. Because the people must have some way to participate in the government, free elections, in which candidates or parties compete for the citizens' votes, are necessary. There must be some connection between what a majority of the people want and what the government actually does. Nevertheless, majorities must not be allowed to deny certain rights to minorities, such as the right to vote, the right to be treated equally under the law, and the right to freedom of expression.

In a well-run democracy, politicians debate questions of public policy honestly, the media report the debate in a fair manner, and the people pay attention to the debate and then vote their preferences consistent with their understanding of the public interest. Governmental decisions are made on the basis of law, without anyone having an unearned advantage. In a badly run or corrupt democracy, politicians are dominated by special interests but seek to hide the fact by clouding public debate with irrelevancies and showmanship. The media do not point out the problems because they themselves are either corrupt or lazy, and the people fail to hold either the politicians or the media accountable because they do not participate or because they participate carelessly and selfishly. In such a corrupt system, governmental decisions are made on the basis of special influence and inside dealing. A good democracy, in other words, is one in which government policy is arrived at through public participation, debate, and compromise. A bad democracy is one in which mass apathy and private influence are the determining factors.

All political systems based on the democratic theory of legitimacy have elements of both good and bad. No human institution—no family, or church, or government—is perfect, but it is always useful to compare a real institution to an ideal and judge how closely the reality conforms to the ideal. Improvements come through the process of attempting to move the reality ever closer to the ideal. Although many of them could not state it clearly, the great majority of Americans, including Texans, believe in some version of democracy. That being so, it is possible to judge our state government (as it is also possible to judge our national government) according to the extent to which it approximates the ideal of a democratic society; from that evaluation, it is possible to indicate the direction that the political system must move in order to become more fully democratic. In this book we frequently compare the reality of state government to the ideal of the democratic polity and ask readers to judge whether there is room for improvement in Texas democracy.

As indicated, one of the major causes of shortcomings in democratic government, in Texas as elsewhere, is private influence over public policy. Ideally, government decisions are made to try to maximize the public interest, but too often they are made at the behest of individuals who are pursuing their own interests at the public's expense. This book often explores the ways that powerful individuals try to distort the people's institutions into vehicles for their own advantage. It also examines ways that representatives of the public resist these selfish efforts to influence public policy. Part of the political process, in Texas as in other democracies, is the struggle to ensure that the making of public policy is truly a people's activity rather than a giveaway to the few who are rich, powerful, and well connected.

TEXAS IN THE FEDERAL SYSTEM

This book is about the politics of one state. Just as it would be impossible to describe the functions of one of the human body's organs without reference to the body as a whole, however, it would be misleading to try to analyze a state without reference to the nation. The United States has a **federal system**. Its governmental powers are shared among the national and state governments. A great many state responsibilities are strongly influenced by the actions of all three branches of the national government (executive, judicial, and legislative).

The way politics in Texas interacts with politics at the national level is well illustrated by the experience of Justice Priscilla Owen of the state supreme court. After earning a law degree from Baylor University in 1977, she was in private practice until 1994. That year she was elected to the state's highest civil court in the Republican sweep. On the court, she earned high marks from fellow Republicans for fair-mindedness and intelligence. President George W. Bush nominated her to a federal judgeship in 2001. The American Bar Association gave her its highest rating, and she was supported in editorials by newspapers as diverse as the (generally liberal) *Washington Post* and (generally conservative) *Wall Street Journal*.

Under the federal Constitution, however, presidential judicial nominees must be ratified by the U.S. Senate. During her confirmation hearings in 2002, Democrats held a one-vote majority in the Senate, and therefore a one-vote majority on the Judiciary Committee. Democrats had no quarrel with Owen's intelligence or fair-mindedness, but they strongly objected to her conservative ideology (see Chapter 4). They attacked her Texas Supreme Court rulings and dissents, portraying her as too pro-business, too anti-consumer, and, in particular, too anti-abortion (for an account of Owen's role in one particularly contentious abortion ruling, see Chapter 8).

Despite Republican protests that Owen was being "attacked with orchestrated deceptions, distortions, and demagoguery," the Judiciary Committee rejected her nomination on a straight party-line vote, 10 to 9. Owen's decisions within Texas determined her experience in national politics.

As national politics changed, however, so did Owen's fortunes. In the November 2002 elections, Republicans won majority control of the U.S. Senate and therefore control of its Judiciary Committee. As soon as Congress reconvened in January 2003, President Bush renominated Owen to the federal bench. Senate Democrats successfully blocked the nomination with a filibuster for two years, but in May of 2005 the full Senate confirmed Owen to the federal bench by a vote of 56 to 43.

Sources: Chuck Lindell, "Senators Reject Owen for Appeals Court Seat," *Austin American-Statesman*, September 6, 2002, A; Chuck Lindell, "31 Rejected Judicial Picks Are Renominated by Bush," *Austin American-Statesman*, January 8, 2003, A11; John Council and T. R. Goldman, "Senate Showdown Ends with Owen Confirmation," *Texas Lawyer*, V. 20, #13, May 30, 2005, 5.

Education, for instance, is primarily a responsibility of state, not federal, government. Yet the U.S. Congress influences Texas education policy with many laws that direct the state to govern the schools in a certain way and with promises of money in return for taking some action. The U.S. Supreme Court has often forced Texas schools to stop something they were doing—prayers in the classroom, for example. It has also made it necessary for them to do things they did not want to do—integrate racially, for example. Finally, the U.S. president makes many decisions that help or hinder the state in its pursuit of its own educational objectives. For example, in 2001, at the urging of President Bush, Congress passed the No Child Left Behind Act, which established national education standards to which all the schools in all the states would have to conform.

The federal government makes an impact on Texas government in several areas:

1. Nearly one-third of state revenue each year comes from federal grants (see Chapter 10).
2. The U.S. Supreme Court oversees the actions of the state government and, historically, has forced the state to make many changes in its behavior, especially in regard to civil rights and liberties (see Chapter 8).
3. Congress allocates many of the "goodies" of government—military bases, veterans' hospitals, highways, and the like—that have a crucial impact on the state's economy.
4. Congress also mandates the state government to take actions, such as making public buildings accessible to physically disabled people and instituting background checks on gun purchasers, that force the Texas legislature to raise and spend money.

5. When Congress declares war or the president sends troops to a foreign con- flict without a declaration of war, Texans fight and die. The president has many discretionary powers, such as cutting tariffs on imported goods and releasing federal disaster relief funds, that leave their mark, for good or ill, on the state's economy.

7. When the Federal Reserve Board raises or lowers interest rates, it constricts or stimulates Texas's economy along with the economies of the other forty-nine states. The changes thus created powerfully affect both the amount of money the state legislature has to spend and the allocation of resources.

8. National institutions also have an impact on Texas in regard to what they fail to do. For decades, for example, the federal government neglected the levee system that was supposed to protect New Orleans from the waters of the Mississippi River and Lake Pontchartrain. When Hurricane Katrina caused the levees to fail in 2005, flooding the city, Texas communities were forced to accommodate the needs of thousands of Louisiana refugees.

Texas politics is thus both a whole subject unto itself and a part of a larger whole. Our focus is on Texas in this book, but there are frequent references to actions by national institutions and politicians.

TEXAS IN THE INTERNATIONAL ARENA

Although the United States Constitution forbids the individual states to conduct independent foreign policies, Texas's shared border with Mexico has long exer- cised an important effect on its politics. Not only are many Texas citizens of Mexican (and other Latin) backgrounds, but the common border of Texas and Mexico, the Rio Grande, flows for more than 800 miles through an arid countryside, a situation that almost demands cooperation over the use of water. Furthermore, with the passage of the North American Free Trade Agreement (NAFTA) in 1993, Texas became impor- tant as an avenue of increased commerce between the two countries. Interstate Highway 35, which runs from the Mexican border at Laredo through San Antonio, Austin, the Dallas/Fort Worth metroplex, and north to Duluth, Minnesota, has become so important as a passageway of international trade that it is sometimes dubbed "the NAFTA highway." As a result of its geographic proximity, Mexico is an important factor in the Texas economy and Texas politics, and vice versa.

One of many examples from the early years of the twenty-first century illustrates the interconnections of Texan and Mexican politics. The example is drawn from the criminal justice system, which at first glance might seem to be a matter of wholly internal interest to Texas. On the contrary, even such a subject as the state's execution of a murderer can have an international impact.[1]

In 1988, Javier Suarez Medina shot to death a Dallas police officer while the offi- cer was conducting an undercover drug sting. There was no doubt about Medina's guilt because he was immediately apprehended by other police officers—the perfect open-and-shut, smoking-gun-in-the-hand arrest. But things were not so simple as they first appeared. Medina, as became clear later, had been born in Mexico. Because of his foreign nationality, under the Vienna Convention of Consular Relations of 1963,

YOU DECIDE

Should Texas Have a Foreign Policy?

As the world economy has become more integrated, the leaders of Texas, like the leaders of other states, have attempted to establish institutions to coordinate and encourage trade. Texan efforts in this area have been particularly enthusiastic in regard to Mexico. The state opened a trade office in Mexico City in 1971, helped establish the Border Governors' Conference in 1980, and began the Texas–Mexico Agricultural Exchange in 1984. Texas governors now have special advisers on the economy and politics of foreign countries, and they travel to visit foreign politicians in the hopes of increasing commerce between their state and foreign countries.

In its attempts to establish regular relationships with foreign countries, Texas comes close to having a state "foreign policy." But is it wise for a state, as opposed to the United States national government, to be so deeply involved in foreign affairs?

Pro	Con
⇨ The Constitution does not forbid states to enter into voluntary, informal arrangements with foreign governments, and the 10th Amendment declares that anything not forbidden to the states is permitted.	⇨ A major reason that the independent states came together to form the union in 1787 was so they could stop working at cross purposes in foreign policy and present a united front to the world. That is why Article I, Section 10 of the Constitution says that "No state shall . . . enter into any Agreement

local authorities were supposed to notify the Mexican consul and allow that country to assist Medina with his defense. However, Medina gave conflicting and confusing statements as to his nationality, claiming at various times that he came to El Paso when he was three-years-old, he came when he was seven, or he was born in that city. Partly because of their confusion as to his nativity and partly, no doubt, because of their intense desire to punish a cop-killer, neither the Dallas police department nor the state ever contacted the Mexican consulate. Medina was tried, convicted of murder, and sentenced to die by lethal injection.

While Medina sat on death row, however, his case came to the attention of Mexican officials. They launched a campaign to persuade the state to re-try him, this time complying with the requirements of the consular treaty. The case became a patriotic cause in Mexico, with all that country's politicians feeling bound to try to

Pro

⇨ The Logan Act of 1799 prohibits U.S. citizens from "holding correspondence with a foreign government or its agents, with intent to influence the measures of such government in relations to disputes or controversies with the United States."

⇨ If states (and cities) are allowed to compete for business with foreign countries, their rivalry will cause them to lower standards of labor and environmental protection.

⇨ If all fifty states have independent relations with foreign countries, it will cause confusion and chaos between the federal government and those countries.

Con

or Compact . . . with a foreign Power . . ."

⇨ Most state foreign policy initiatives, such as Texas's trade agreements with Mexico, deal with friendly relations, not disputes.

⇨ Since when is competition a bad thing? If citizens want to keep labor unions strong and the environment clean, they should vote for candidates who will support such policies.

⇨ As the example of Javier Suarez Medina illustrates, Texas's domestic actions already have an impact on relations with foreign countries. It would be better to acknowledge this fact frankly and make state policy with the conscious intent of furthering the state's interests.

Source: Julie Blase, "How U.S. States Became Global Actors: Texas–Mexico Relations and the Trend of Internationally Active States," Ph.D. dissertation, University of Texas at Austin, 2003.

make Texas officials reverse the conviction or, at least, commute Medina's sentence to life in prison.

In 2002 Mexican President Vicente Fox made a personal crusade of the Medina case. He appealed to the Texas Board of Pardons and Paroles, Governor Rick Perry, and President George W. Bush to stop or postpone the execution. Fox had been the most pro–U.S. (and pro-capitalist) president in Mexico's history. In numerous visits to this country, and to Texas, he had attempted to forge personal and institutional bonds that would allow the United States and Mexico to overcome their historic suspicion of each other. He thus had good reason to think that his intervention might sway some important person to re-think Medina's scheduled execution. If he had been able to affect the decisions of Texas's government in such a visible way, it would have enormously helped his popularity in Mexico. In turn, his enhanced power would have been a good thing for the United States in general and for Texas in particular.

Nevertheless, all national and state individuals and institutions politely ignored Fox. Medina was executed on August 14, 2002. Fox was scheduled to visit Texas and to meet President Bush at his ranch in Crawford in late August of that year. However, the Mexican president's inability to affect the Medina case was, from his point of view and from his country's point of view, an insult that could not be ignored. Fox cancelled the visit. His office issued a statement that "it would be inappropriate to carry out this trip to Texas given these lamentable circumstances." Relations between the two countries, which had been on the upswing after decades of hostility, immediately turned around and became more tense.

After Medina's execution, there were still fifty-one Mexican nationals on death row in the United States, many of them in Texas. In 2004 the International Court of Justice in The Hague, Netherlands, found that the United States had violated its treaty obligations and ordered the Mexicans re-tried. In response, in 2005 the administration of President George W. Bush withdrew from the protocol of the treaty that gave the international court jurisdiction in such cases. Shortly afterward, however, in a puzzling development, the administration announced that it would *comply* with the ruling. In a hearing on one Mexican's suit before the U.S. Supreme Court, the federal government lawyers informed the justices that Bush would require the states to re-hear the cases of all the Mexican prisoners. The Court then tossed out the lawsuit as premature. This series of maneuvers left the legal principles in a muddle: were or were not the states required by the national treaty to give alien defendants access to the assistance of their countries' consuls? That question promised to be the source of a rich controversy in the coming years.

To sum up, although Texas leaders are trying very hard to establish good business relations with Mexico (see box), they resist the Mexicans' desire to see their nationals treated with the respect supposedly guaranteed by international agreement. Thus, the actions of Texas's criminal justice system, and its elected politicians, have repercussions on relations between the United States as a whole and a foreign country. The political choices Texans make have consequences far beyond their own borders.

THE TEXAS POLITICAL CULTURE

Like the other forty-nine states, Texas is part of a well-integrated American civil society. It is also a separate and distinctive society with its own history and political system.

Culture is the product of the historical experience of a people in a particular area. Our political system is the product of our political culture. **Political culture** is a shared system of values, beliefs, and habits of behavior in regard to government and politics. Not everyone in a given political culture agrees with all of its assumptions, but everyone is affected by the beliefs and values of the dominant groups in society. Often, the culture of the majority group is imposed on members of a minority who would prefer not to live with it.

Not all Texans have shared the beliefs and attitudes that are described here. Especially, as is discussed in more detail in Chapter 3, African Americans and Mexican Americans have tended to be somewhat separate from the political culture of the dominant Anglo majority. Nevertheless, both history and political institutions have imposed clear patterns on the assumptions that most Texans bring to politics.

Part of the larger American political tradition is a basic attitude toward government and politicians that was most famously expressed in a single sentence attributed to the revolutionary leader and president, Thomas Jefferson: "That government is best which governs least." Jefferson's aphorism is a summary of a political philosophy called conservatism that has dominated Texas politics in the twentieth century.

The term *conservative* is complex, and its implications change with time and situation. In general, however, it refers to a general hostility to government activity, especially in the economic sphere, and a complementary faith in the judgment of businesspeople. Most of the early White settlers came to Texas to seek their fortunes. They cared little about government and wanted no interference in their economic affairs. Their attitudes were consistent with the popular values of the Jeffersonian Democrats of the nineteenth century: the less government, the better; local control of what little government there was; and freedom from economic regulation, or laissez-faire. Texas conservatism minimizes the role of government in society in general and in the economy in particular. It stresses an individualism that

In practice, laissez-faire in Texas has often been pseudo (false) laissez-faire. Entrepreneurs don't want government to regulate or tax them, and they denounce policies to help society's less fortunate as "socialism." But when they encounter a problem that is too big for them to handle, they do not hesitate to accept government help. A good example is the city of Houston. Its leaders praise their city as the home of unrestrained, unaided free enterprise. In fact, however, Houston has historically relied upon government activity for its economic existence. The ship channel, which connects the city's port to the sea and thereby created it in an economic sense, was dredged and is maintained by government. Much of the oil industry, which was responsible for Houston's twentieth-century boom, was sustained either by state regulation by the Railroad Commission or by the federal government's selling facilities to the industry cheaply, such as occurred with the Big Inch and Little Inch pipelines. Billions of dollars of federal tax money have flowed into the area to create jobs in the space industry (the Johnson Space Center and NASA).

Houston's business leaders have not resisted such government action on their behalf; quite the contrary. It is only when government tries to help ordinary people that the business community upholds the banner of laissez-faire.

Source: Joe R. Feagin, *Free Enterprise City: Houston in Political-Economic Perspective* (New Brunswick, NY: Rutgers, 1988), passim.

maximizes the role of businesspeople in controlling the economy. Like Edward Abbey, quoted at the beginning of this chapter, most Texans have suspected, historically, that even good government is bad. To a Texas conservative, a desirable government is mainly one that keeps taxes low.

Consistent with the emphasis on pseudo laissez-faire is a type of Social Darwinism, the belief that individuals who prosper and rise to the top of the socioeconomic ladder are worthy and deserve their riches, while those who sink to the bottom (or, having been born there, stay there) are unworthy and deserve their poverty. Social Darwinists argue that people become rich because they are intelligent, energetic, and self-disciplined, and those who become or remain poor do so because they are stupid, lazy, and/or given to indulgence in personal vices. Socio-economic status, they argue, is the result of the "survival of the fittest."[2]

Of course, a person's success in life frequently is the result of personal behavior and qualities of character. But it also often depends on many other factors, such as education, race and ethnicity, proper diet, medical care, the wealth and education of one's parents, and luck. Nonetheless, Social Darwinism continues to dominate the thinking of many Texans. They strongly resist the idea that government has an obligation to come to the aid of society's less fortunate. This hostility to government aid to the needy has resulted in many state policies that mark Texas as a state with an unusually stingy attitude toward the underprivileged. For example, among the fifty states, in 2003 Texas ranked forty-fifth in its average monthly welfare payments to poor families and forty-sixth in its per capita spending on welfare.[3]

Historically, the conservatism of the Texas political culture was enhanced and modified by the fact that Texas was originally a slave-owning state. After their defeat in the Civil War of 1861 to 1865, and the emancipation of the slaves, Whites in Texas and the ten other states of the defunct Confederacy made a determined effort to prevent the freed African Americans from assuming full citizenship. For many decades, Whites in Texas and the other states of the Old South denied a significant number of their citizens full economic, social, legal, and political rights. In the case of Texas, this racist exclusion from equality was extended to Mexican Americans. Southern Whites, until recent decades, were not only economically conservative in the sense of opposing government activity on behalf of the poor, they were also socially conservative in

Cartoonist Ben Sargent pokes fun at the Texas tradition of bragging about the state while he criticizes one consequence of Texas's conservative political culture: its habit of paying little attention to the environmental consequences of economic development.

SOURCE: Courtesy of Ben Sargent.

the sense of opposing government activity, whether federal or state, on behalf of the civil rights of the minority population. In Texas, it is now conventional to speak of non-Hispanic Whites as "Anglos," but the difference in nomenclature does not hide a continuity in historical experience.

Time, immigration from Northern states, and federal government activity have significantly altered the racist Old South political culture in Texas and other former Confederate states. African Americans and Mexican Americans now have the unquestioned right to vote. Minority citizens run important businesses, campaign for and sometimes win public office, and teach at major universities. Yet traces of the Old South culture remain, and more important, the state is still experiencing the political fallout from its Old South heritage. Although the dominant Anglo culture is still generally conservative, minority citizens tend to be influenced more strongly by another attitude toward government known as liberalism.

Liberals commonly accept government activity—especially on behalf of the less fortunate—as a good thing. Although conservatives have dominated Texas politics through most of its history, liberals have occasionally been elected to public office and liberal ideas have sometimes been adopted as state policy. The conflict between liberalism and conservatism underlies much political argument in the United States. Chapter 4 explores the way these two ideologies have sometimes formed the basis for Texas politics and speculates on the way changes in the state's population may affect its ideological quarrels.

ECONOMY, TAXES, AND SERVICES

When General Sheridan made his harsh evaluation of Texas in 1855, the state was poor, rural, and agricultural. In the twentieth century, however, its economy was transformed, first by the boom in the oil industry that began with the discovery of the great Spindletop oil field in 1901, then by its diversification into petrochemicals, aerospace, computers, and many other industries. Metropolitan areas grew along with the economy, and the state became the second most populous in the nation.

Political culture, however, has not changed as rapidly as the state's population and economy. The influence of its conservative culture is evident in the treatment Texas affords to business and industry. In 1996 a private firm conducted a nationwide survey to determine how favorable a "business climate" each of the states had created. North Carolina was found to have the most favorable business climate, and Texas was second.[4] Using a different set of measures in 2004, *Congressional Quarterly* ranked Texas as the state with the fourteenth greatest "economic momentum."[5]

A "favorable business climate" and "economic momentum" in the short run are identified with low taxes, weak labor unions, cheap labor, and little regulation by government, but in the long run these policies may weaken the thing they are designed to nurture. Other observers are less admiring of the Texas economy and less optimistic about its future.

For example, the Corporation for Enterprise Development (CFED) is a private organization that grades each state in terms not only of its economic health at any one time but also of its capacity for positive growth. In 2002 the CFED flunked the Texas economy as a whole, giving it a D in "earnings and job quality," an F in "equity," an F in "quality of life," and a D in "resource efficiency." The CFED commented that "a theme of inequality throughout the state. . . the disparity between the wealthy and the poor. . ." augured poorly for Texas's future. In contrast to Texas, the CFED reported that its "honor roll" states of Colorado, Connecticut, and Maryland were pursuing public policies that ensured them a brighter economic outlook. In 2005 the CFED again flunked Texas on its "Assets and Opportunity Scorecard," faulting the state in particular for its educational and health care systems.[6]

Part of the substance of this textbook is the discussion of the way the politics of Texas reflects "a theme of inequality." Some chapters analyze the sources of unequal politics; some portray its consequences in terms of public policy. Always, the implications of inequality for democratic legitimacy are major topics. The overall contours of public policy in the Lone Star State can be illustrated in a preliminary way by comparing Texas to its forty-nine sister states on some important spending and taxing measures. As Table 1.1 shows, when its fiscal policies are compared with those of the other states, Texas government is revealed as small and cheap. Overall, on the basis of per capita spending, Texas has one of the least active governments in the United States. Its spending on welfare measures and the arts ranks near the bottom. On education spending it ranks about in the middle. On no type of public policy does Texas spend an unusually large amount, when compared to other states.

The way Texas raises its money is also noteworthy. As we would expect from its spending record in Table 1.1, it has very low taxes. It is important to note, however, that compared to other states the Texas tax structure is relatively regressive—that is, it falls unusually heavily on the poor and unusually lightly on the rich. In Chapter 10 these points are explored in greater detail. For now, it is sufficient to point out the way that state taxing figures bear out the "theme of inequality" emphasized by the CFED.

TABLE 1.1

Texas's Rank among States in Expenditure and Taxation

Category	Year	Rank
a. Per capita state and local government expenditures	2002	49
b. Per capita state and local education spending	2002	19
c. Per capita state and local welfare spending	2002	46
d. Average welfare (TANF) payments	2003	45
e. Per capita Medicaid spending	2002	42
f. Per capita spending on state arts agencies	2004	46
g. Per capita spending on public health	2004	45
h. Per capita spending on water quality	2004	49
i. Per capita state and local tax revenue	2002	42
j. Tax rate on high income families	2003	45
k. Progressivity of state and local taxes	2003	43

SOURCES: Items a through f and i through k from Kendra A. Hovey and Harold A. Hovey, *CQ's State Fact Finder 2005: Rankings Across America* (Washington, DC: *Congressional Quarterly*, 2005), 187, 216, 318, 311, 255, 91, 148, 168, and 170; items g and h from John Young, "It's Texas vs. Mississippi in a Race to the Bottom," *Austin American-Statesman*, March 8, 2005, A11.

The points at issue here—private influence over public policy, inequality, inactive government—would be of little interest to anyone except political scientists if Texas were a paradise for its citizens. Historically, Texans have had a very strong state patriotism and have earned a reputation throughout the rest of the country for proclaiming their state the best, the most charming, the prettiest, the healthiest, and the friendliest place to live in the United States. Perhaps Texas is the friendliest, but on attributes that are easier to measure, the state scores as something less than a utopia. As Table 1.2 illustrates, on a variety of calculations of quality of life, Texas ranks poorly in relation to other states. It has high crime and poverty rates, the health of its citizens is not good, the educational attainment of its children is questionable, its air is unclean, and so on. Whether Texas's low ranking on quality-of-life measures is a cause of, a consequence of, or unrelated to the state's weak, inactive government is a matter for political debate. Liberals would argue that an inactive government causes low quality of life. Conservatives would argue that Table 1.2 measures the wrong things, that it fails to show Texas's improvement over the years, or that it neglects to take into account Texas's social problems, which are worse than those in other states. It is part of the purpose of this book to supply information to students on this question, to help them make up their own minds.

Whatever students' conclusions about the debate, it is evident that the greatest accomplishment of Texas government through the twentieth century was to keep taxes low for its more affluent citizens. As the twenty-first century progresses, Texas citizens may wonder if that is enough.

TABLE 1.2

Texas's Rank in Measures of Quality of Life

Category	Year	Rank
a. Crime rate	2003	5
b. Poverty rate	2001	9
c. "Condition of children index"	2004	36
d. Health ranking	2004	35
e. Percentage of population obese	2003	12
f. Percentage of population covered by health insurance	2003	50
g. Average SAT scores	2004	23 (of 25)
h. Average proficiency in reading, eighth grade	2003	36
i. Average proficiency in math, eighth grade	2003	30
j. Air pollution emissions	2001	1
k. Drinking water quality	2003	44
l. "Livability index"	2003	36

SOURCES: Items a, c, d, e, g, h, i, j, and k from Kendra A. Hovey and Harold A. Hovey, *CQ's State Fact Finder 2005: Rankings Across America* (Washington, DC: *Congressional Quarterly*, 2005), 268, 309, 242, 247, 207, 205, 204, 97, 95; item b is from state comptroller's Web site in 2002, listed at the end of this chapter (the ranking is from 2001 because as of 2005 the Web site had been discontinued); item f is from *The Book of the States* (Lexington, Kentucky: The Council of State Governments, 2005), 555; item j is from the Web site www.morganquitno.com [the "livability index" was created by combining a number of indicators of well-being; the "most livable" state was Minnesota, the least livable was Mississippi].

THE PEOPLE OF TEXAS

In many ways Texas is the classic American melting pot of different peoples, although it occasionally seems more like a boiling cauldron. The state was originally populated by various Native American tribes. In the sixteenth and seventeenth centuries the Spaniards conquered the land, and from the intermingling of the conquerors and the conquered came the *mestizos,* persons of mixed Spanish and indigenous blood. In the nineteenth century Western European immigrants wrested the land from the heirs of the Spaniards. They often brought with them black slaves. Soon waves of immigration arrived from Europe and Asia, and more mestizos came from Mexico. The inflow continued into the twenty-first century, with Vietnamese creating the state's first large Asian American community.

One of the best ways to observe the changing Texas melting pot is to follow developments in recent U.S. censuses. Once per decade, the national government makes an accounting of the population of all fifty states. The methodology of the census is a hot political topic because its results create the basis for distributing money from many federal programs and also for allocating seats in both the U.S. House of Representatives and the state legislatures. Critics of the census charge that it misses millions of poor people, especially those for whom English is not the first language. Both the 1990 and 2000 censuses were the subject of political wrangling, and the final figures of each eventually had to be ratified by the courts.

Table 1.3 shows the official 1980, 1990, and 2000 census figures for Texas. The increase in population indicated in the table entitled Texas to two additional seats in the U.S. House of Representatives after 2000, bringing the state's total to 32.

Besides the overall increase in population of 22.8 percent in the final decade of the twentieth century, the most significant fact revealed by the 2000 census was the rapid increase in Texas's Hispanic population. Whereas Hispanics—the great majority of whom in Texas are Mexican or Mexican American—constituted 21 percent of the state's population in 1980 and 26 percent in 1990, by 2000 they totaled 32 percent, and their percentage continued to grow. The other important minority group, African Americans, comprised 11.5 percent of the state's citizens, a percentage that

TABLE 1.3

The Texas Population: 1980, 1990, and 2000

Ethnic group	1980	1990	2000	Percentage of total
Anglo (non-Hispanic, White)	9,350,299	10,291,680	10,933,313	52.4
African American	1,710,175	2,021,632	2,404,566	11.5
Hispanic* or Latino (of any race)	2,985,824	4,339,905	6,669,665	32.0
Other	200,528	378,565	844,276	4.1
Total	14,229,191	16,986,510	20,851,820	

* The great majority of Hispanics in Texas are Mexican American or Mexican.

SOURCES: For 1980 and 1990, 1992–1993 Texas Almanac and State Industrial Guide (Dallas: A. H. Belo Corp., 1991); for 2000, see the U.S. Census Web site, listed at the end of this chapter.

has not changed appreciably since 1980. Meanwhile, the non-Hispanic White population ("Anglos"), which used to be a large majority, dropped to 52.4 percent in 2000.[7]

The Census Bureau also makes estimates, based on extending trends, between the end-of-decade years during which it takes a full national population count. In 2005 it estimated that the percentage of Anglos had dropped to 49.8 percent of the Texas population. For the first time, Anglos constituted less than majority, although they were still the largest minority. If present immigration and birth/death trends continue, however, Hispanics will almost certainly be a majority of the Texas population by 2040.[8] Moreover, partly because of the rapid growth of its Latino population, the Texas population as a whole is enlarging faster than the total of most other states. As a result, Texas is expected to gain another two or three Congressional seats in the U.S. Congress after the 2010 census.

The distribution of population in Texas shows evidence of three things: the

The 2000 census portrayed a Texas in transition. Among other revelations was the fact that only 62 percent of its population had been born in the state. A continuing influx of immigrants, many of them from outside the American South, had many ramifications for Texas, some of them political, some of them not. Among the latter was the decline of traditional Texas dialects, from the deep-South drawl of the piney woods of the east to the nasal "twang" of the residents farther west. Although many older citizens continue to speak in a "Texas" accent, more and more residents of the state come from somewhere else, and sound like it. In fact, nearly one-third of Texans speak a language other than English at home. Spanish is by far the most common non-English language spoken, but about 7 percent speak Vietnamese, Chinese, Hindi, or some other Asian language.

Sources: Terry Wallace, "Could the Urban Influx of Outsiders Take the Twang out of Texas?" *Denton Record-Chronicle,* March 24, 2002, A6; "Portrait of Our Nation," *Austin American-Statesman,* June 9, 2002, E1; Gaiutra Bahadur, "Census Survey Confirms Texas' Growing Diversity," *Austin American-Statesman,* August, 7, 2001, A1.

initial patterns of migration, the influence of geography and climate, and the location of the cities. The Hispanic migration came first, north from Mexico, and to this day is concentrated in South and West Texas. Likewise, African Americans still live predominantly in the eastern half of the state. Also, as one moves from east to west across Texas, annual rainfall drops by about 5 inches per 100 miles. East Texas has a moist climate and supports intensive farming, while West Texas is dry and requires pumping from underground aquifers to maintain agriculture. The overall distribution of settlement reflects the food production capability of the local areas, with East Texas remaining far more populous. Cities developed at strategic locations, usually on rivers or the seacoast, and the state's population is heavily concentrated in the urban areas.

THE POLITICAL RELEVANCE OF POPULATION

The division of the Texas population into Anglos, Mexican Americans, and African Americans reflects political realities. All citizens are individuals, form their own opinions, and have the right to choose to behave as they see fit. No one is a prisoner of his or her group, and every generalization has exceptions. Nevertheless, it is a long-observed fact that people in similar circumstances often see things from similar points of view, and it therefore helps to clarify political conflict to be aware of the shared similarities.

Although in this book, Anglos, Mexican Americans, and African Americans are often discussed as groups, there is no intent to be unfair to individuals. Historically, both minority groups have been treated badly by the Anglo majority. Today, the members of both groups are in general less wealthy than are Anglos, although this situation, like others, is evolving with the Texas economy. With the historical pattern of economic differences has come political conflict. As explained in Chapters 3, 4, and 5, Mexican Americans and African Americans tend to hold more liberal political opinions and identify more with the Democratic Party than do Anglos.

One trajectory for Texas politics would be that the growing minority population will make it more liberal, a possibility we discuss in detail in Chapter 5. Yet population changes do not always have the effects we might have expected. For example, as many northerners, attracted by the opportunities in the Texas economy, have moved to the state over the last several decades, they might have been expected to dilute the traditional "southern" conservatism of the Anglo population. But it has not happened. As we discuss in Chapter 4, if anything, it appears that Texans have become more, not less, conservative over the last four decades.

As the minority population increases in size relative to the Anglo population, its greater liberalism may make itself felt, sooner or later, in the voting booth. Or changes in the composition of the population may confound expectations, as they sometimes have in the past. Texas's changing mix of population therefore may or may not modify its politics. We discuss some of the possible—but not certain—consequences of these potential changes at several points in this book.

THE AGENDA OF THIS BOOK

The following chapters examine how Texans organize and operate politically to attempt to deal with their present social and economic problems and to plan for the future. Every chapter compares the reality of Texas politics to the democratic ideal and asks readers to decide how defensible the reality is. The book considers, in order, the Texas Constitution and then the inputs of politics: the state's important interest groups, the activities of political parties, and the individual voter within the context of campaigns and elections. The next subject is the institutions of state government—the legislature, the executive branch, and the judiciary. A discussion of local government within Texas follows. Finally, we present an analysis of the outputs of politics—public policy—with one chapter examining several issues facing Texas and another devoted entirely to an analysis of state finance.

SUMMARY

This chapter begins with a summary of democratic theory, which holds that the legitimacy of a government rests upon the citizens' participation; its announced intention is to contrast the ideal of democracy and its practice in Texas. The topic then shifts to the way the Lone Star State is situated within the American federal system and the way its policies may have an impact on its relations with foreign countries, particularly Mexico. The discussion then turns to political culture and some implications of the general conservatism that has dominated Texas through much of its history. An examination of census data leads to the conclusion that Texas has a large and ethnically diverse population that continues to grow and change. Because minority citizens tend to have different political values than Anglo citizens, the state's changing population has implications for the present and future of its politics.

STUDY QUESTIONS

1. Could a king with absolute power be the head of a legitimate government? Why or why not?
2. Briefly describe political conservatism and liberalism.
3. Would you say that the Texas political culture, as described in the text, is dominant in your family? Why or why not? In your community? Why or why not?
4. In general, what has been Texas's historical policy toward business (the economy)? Toward taxes? Toward welfare?
5. Would you say that the evidence supports the opinion that Texas is a better place to live than other states? On what evidence do you base your opinion?
6. Why is the decennial census so important to Texas politics? Historically, "minority" ethnic groups now constitute a growing majority of the Texas population. What effects might this have on the state's politics and government?

SURFING THE WEB

Visit the companion site for this book:

http://www.thomsonedu.com/politicalscience/kraemer

You can access facts about Texas history at the "Lone Star Junction" Web site by logging on to the site and then clicking on any of several icons. The site is:

http://www.lsjunction.com/

To access more facts than anyone could use from the U.S. Census, log on to:

http://www.census.gov/

To find out more about the Corporation for Enterprise Development and examine its ratings of all the states, log on to:

http://www.cfed.org

Although the state comptroller's office Web site no longer features the "Texas: How We Stand" comparison of Texas with other states, it still contains a wealth of information on economics and other topics:

http://www.window.state.tx.us

NOTES

1. The information in the following account comes from Michael Graczyk, "Parole Board Refuses to Stop Man's Execution," *Austin American-Statesman*, August 14, 2002, B6; Susan Ferriss, "Execution Leads Fox to Scrap Trip," *Austin American-Statesman*, August 15, 2002, A1; Adam Liptak,

"U. S. Says It Has Withdrawn from World Judicial Body," *New York Times,* March 10, 2005, A14; Linda Greenhouse, "Bush Decision to Comply with World Court Complicates Case of Mexican on Death Row," *New York Times,* March 29, 2005, A14; "Mexican's Death Row Appeal Is Rejected," *Austin American-Statesman,* May 24, 2005, A5.

2. For a description and evaluation of Social Darwinism in American culture, see Carl N. Degler, *In Search of Human Nature: The Decline and Revival of Darwinism in American Social Thought* (New York: Oxford University Press, 1991), and Richard Hofstadter, *Social Darwinism in American Thought,* revised edition (Boston: Beacon Press, 1955).

3. Kendra A. Hovey and Harold A. Hovey, *CQ's State Fact Finder 2005: Rankings Across America* (Washington, DC: *Congressional Quarterly,* 2005), 307, 318.

4. Steve Brown, "Texas No. 2 on List of Best Business Sites," *Dallas Morning News,* October 2, 1996, D1.

5. Hovey and Hovey, op. cit., 71.

6. The CFED's state rankings, and a discussion of how they were created, can be found on its Web site: www.cfed.org.

7. The information in this paragraph is based on U.S. Census figures, and Mark Babineck, "Hispanic Majority Seen in Texas by 2030s," *Austin American-Statesman,* January 12, 2002, B6; Chris Kelley, "Minorities on Pace to Be Texas Majority by 2005," *Dallas Morning News,* January 27, 2001, A1.

8. Alicia A. Caldwell, "Census: More Than Half of Texans Are Minorities," *Austin American-Statesman,* August 11, 2005, B1; Steve H. Murdock, Steve White, Md. Nazrul Hoque, Beverly Pecotte, Xuihong You, and Jennifer Belkan, *The New Texas Challenge: Population Change and the Future of Texas* (College Station: Texas A & M, 2003), 27.

2

THE CONSTITUTIONAL SETTING

A political power is inherent in the people, and all free governments are founded on their authority, and instituted for their benefit.

Article 1 Texas
Constitution

It is very doubtful whether man is enough of a political animal to produce a good, sensible, serious and efficient constitution. All evidence is against it.

George Bernard Shaw
Irish dramatist

INTRODUCTION

Since its ratification in 1788, the Constitution of the United States has been used frequently as a model by emerging nations. State constitutions, however, seldom enjoy such admiration. Indeed, the Constitution of the State of Texas is more often ridiculed than praised because of its length and its outdated, unworkable provisions.

Texas is far from the only state whose constitution draws such criticism. The political circumstances that surrounded the writing of the national **Constitution** differed considerably from those existing at the times when the constitutions of the fifty states, especially the states of the old Confederacy, were written. State constitutions tend to be very rigid and to include too many details. As a result, we find that Texas and many other states must resort to frequent **constitutional amendments**, which are formal changes in the basic governing document. In federal systems, which are systems of government that provide for a division and sharing of powers between a national government and state or regional governments, the constitutions of the states complement the national constitution. In the United States specifically, the state constitution cannot conflict legally with the U.S. Constitution. Article VI of the U.S. Constitution provides that the Constitution, laws, and treaties of the national government take precedence over the constitutions and laws of the states. Nevertheless, state constitutions are important because state governments are responsible for many of the basic programs and services, such as education, that affect citizens daily. A major difference between the U.S. and Texas constitutions is the generality of the national document and the statute-like specificity of the state charter.

The basic purposes of all constitutions are the same. This chapter examines those purposes, then outlines the development of the several Texas constitutions, elaborates the principal features of the state's current document, and illustrates the problems that have led to numerous amendments and revision efforts.

PURPOSES OF CONSTITUTIONS

The first purpose served by a constitution is to give *legitimacy* to the government. A government has legitimacy when the governed accept its acts as moral, fair, and just and thus believe that they should obey its laws. This acceptance cuts two ways, however. On the one hand, citizens will allow government to act in certain ways that are not permitted to private individuals. For example, citizens cannot legally drive down a city street at 60 miles per hour, but police officers may do so when pursuing wrongdoers. On the other hand, citizens also expect governments not to act arbitrarily; the concept of legitimacy is closely associated with lawful limits on governmental behavior. If a police officer sped down a city street at 90 miles per hour just for the thrill of doing so, this behavior would fall outside the bounds of legitimacy.

What citizens are willing to accept is conditioned by their history and political tradition and by their civic culture. In Texas and the rest of the United States, democratic practices including citizen participation in decision making and fair processes are a part of that history and culture.

The second purpose of constitutions is to *organize government.* Governments must be structured in a way that makes it clear who the major officials are, how they are selected, and what the relationships are among those charged with basic governmental functions. And again, to some extent, the American states have been guided by the national model. Both national and state constitutions incorporate **separation of powers** with a system of **checks and balances** to ensure that each branch of government can be restrained by the others. In reality, we have separate institutions and defined lines of authority that lead to a sharing of power more than to a literal separation of powers. For example, passing bills is thought of as a legislative function, but the governor can veto a bill, and the courts can declare a bill unconstitutional.

The Constitution of the United States expressly grants certain powers to the national government and implies a broad range of additional powers through Article I, Section 8, the "necessary and proper clause." This clause, also known as the "elastic clause," enables Congress to execute all its other powers by providing broad authority to pass needed legislation. Thus, *granting specific powers* is the third purpose of constitutions. The powers not explicitly or implicitly granted to the national government were reserved for the people or for the states by the 10th Amendment. As the national Constitution has been developed and interpreted, many powers actually exist concurrently at both the federal and state levels of government—for example, the power to assess a tax on gasoline. Within this general framework, which continues to evolve, the Texas Constitution sets forth specific functions for which the state maintains primary or concurrent responsibility. Local government, criminal law, and regulation of intrastate commerce are among the diverse activities over which the state retains principal control.

American insistence on the fourth purpose of constitutions, *limiting governmental power*, reflects the influence of British political culture, our ancestors' dissatisfaction with colonial rule, and the extraordinary individualism that characterized our national development during the eighteenth and nineteenth centuries. The most famous and important limitations on governmental power are the guarantees of individual rights found in the national Bill of Rights. In Texas, the conservative political tradition resulted in a heavy emphasis on limiting government's ability to act. For example, the governor has only restricted power to remove members of state boards and commissions except by informal techniques such as an aggressive public relations campaign against a board member.

As we assess the degree to which democratic theory is actually applied in practice, one measure is how well a constitution accomplishes all these purposes. A constitution that only organizes government and assigns power could be very undemocratic because it could allow for arbitrary governmental action. A constitution that provided only for limiting government power, even though that single purpose might be enough to achieve legitimacy, would still fall short since government would be unable to act effectively on behalf of the citizens.

TEXAS CONSTITUTIONS

The United States has had two fundamental laws: the short-lived Articles of Confederation and the present Constitution, which was written in 1787. Texas is currently governed by its sixth constitution, ratified in 1876. The fact that the 1876 constitution had five predecessors in only forty years illustrates the political turbulence of the mid-1800s in Texas. Table 2.1 lists the six Texas state charters.

TABLE 2.1

Constitutions of Texas

Constitution	Dates
Republic of Texas	1836–1845
Statehood	1845–1861
Civil War	1861–1866
Reconstruction	1866–1869
Radical Reconstruction	1869–1876
State of Texas	1876–present

Texas was under the formal governance of Spain for 131 years, although only San Antonio and El Paso received any attention because the rest of the colony was sparsely populated. It became a Mexican state for 15 years after Mexico declared its independence from Spain in 1821. Paramount among several events that led Texians—as they were called—to seek their independence was the assumption of power in Mexico by Antonio López de Santa Anna in 1834, the temporary incarceration of Texas colonizer Stephen F. Austin, and the exercise of greater control over Texans.

Texans issued a Declaration of Independence on March 2, 1836, stating that "the people of Texas do now constitute a Free, Sovereign, and Independent Republic, and are fully invested with all the rights and attributes which properly belong to independent nations. . . ." After a brief but bitter war with Mexico, Texas gained independence on April 21 following the Battle of San Jacinto. Independence was formalized when the two treaties of Velasco were signed by President López de Santa Anna of Mexico and President David Burnet of Texas on May 14, 1836. By September, the Constitution of the Republic of Texas, drafted shortly after independence was declared, had been implemented. Major features of this charter paralleled those of the U.S. Constitution, including election of a president and a congress; however, unlike the U.S. Constitution, the document also guaranteed the continuation of slavery.

The United States had been sympathetic to the Texas struggle for independence. Nevertheless, Texas's admission to the Union was postponed for a decade because of northern opposition to the admission of new slave states. After nine years of nationhood, Texas was finally admitted to the Union. The Constitution of 1845, the "Statehood Constitution," was modeled after the constitutions of other southern states. It was regarded as one of the nation's best at the time. The 1845 constitution not only embraced democratic principles of participation but also included many elements later associated with the twentieth-century administrative reform movement and was a very brief, clear document.[1]

The Constitution of 1845 was influenced by Jacksonian democracy, named for President Andrew Jackson. Jacksonians believed in an expansion of individual participation in government, at least for white males.[2] Jackson's basic beliefs ultimately led to the spoils system of appointing to office those who had supported the victors in the election ("to the victors belong the spoils"). Jacksonian democracy also produced long ballots with almost every office up for popular vote, short terms of office, and the expansion of voting rights. Thus, while participatory, Jacksonianism was not flawless.

When Texas joined the Confederate States of America in 1861, its constitution was again modified. This document, the Civil War Constitution of 1861, merely altered the Constitution of 1845 to ensure greater protection for the institution of slavery and to declare allegiance to the Confederacy.

Texas was on the losing side of the Civil War and was occupied by federal troops. President Andrew Johnson ordered Texas to construct yet another constitution. The 1866 document declared secession illegal, repudiated the war debt, and abolished slavery. However, it did not provide for improving conditions for African Americans. In other words, the only changes made were those necessary to gain presidential support for readmission to the Union.

Because Texas was an independent republic when the United States annexed it, the annexation agreement reflected compromises by both the state and national governments. For example, Texas gave up its military property but kept its public lands. The national government refused to assume the state's $10 million debt but provided that four additional states could be carved out of the Texas territory should the state desire such a division.

In the 1990s, a radical group calling itself the Republic of Texas contended that Texas remains a nation and that the United States illegally annexed Texas in 1845. Pursuing this belief, members of the movement harassed state officials in a variety of ways, including filing liens against the assets of public agencies and regularly accusing state officials of illegally using their powers.

Radical postwar congressional leaders were not satisfied with these minimal changes in the constitutions of southern states. They insisted on more punitive measures.

In 1868–1869, a constitution that centralized power in the state government provided generous salaries for officials, stipulated appointed judges, and called for annual legislative sessions was drafted. It contained many of the elements that present-day reformers would like to see in a revised state charter. However, because the constitution was forced on the state by outsiders in Washington and by carpetbaggers—northerners who came to Texas with their worldly goods in a suitcase made out of carpeting—white southerners never regarded the document as acceptable. They especially resented the strong, centralized state government and the powerful office of governor that were imposed on them. Moreover, because all former rebels were barred from voting, the 1869 Constitution was adopted by Unionists and African Americans. Ironically, this constitution least accomplished the purpose of legitimacy—acceptance by the people—but was the most forward-looking in terms of granting power and organizing government.

The popular three-term governor Elisha Pease resigned in the fall of 1869 after the radical constitution was adopted. After a vacancy in the state's chief executive office that lasted more than three months, Edmund J. (E. J.) Davis was elected governor and took office at the beginning of 1870. The election not only barred the state's Democrats and traditional Republicans, both conservative groups, from voting but also exhibited a number of irregularities. Davis was an honest man, but the radical state charter, Davis's Radical Republican ties, and his subsequent designation as provisional governor by President Ulysses Grant combined to give him dictatorial powers.[3]

THE PRESENT TEXAS CONSTITUTION

Traditionally Democratic and conservative Texans began to chafe for constitutional revision as soon as the Democrats regained legislative control in 1872. An 1874 reform effort passed in the Texas Senate but failed in the House. This constitution would have provided flexibility in such areas as the ways in which tax dollars could be spent and terms of office. It also would have facilitated elite control and a sellout to the powerful railroads, which were hated by ordinary citizens because of their pricing policies and corruption of state legislators.[4]

In 1875 the legislature called a constitutional convention, and 90 delegates were elected from all over the state. In the 1870s, farming and ranching dominated the state's economy, and one particular farmers' organization, the Grange, was a dominant force during the convention. The elected delegates overwhelmingly reflected a rural conservatism that embodied a belief in white supremacy and a strong emphasis on the constitutional purpose of limiting government. Other factors at work during the convention included Jacksonian democracy, the like-mindedness of the delegates, and a general lack of faith in government. The administration of Governor E. J. Davis contributed greatly to this cynicism.

Accordingly, the new constitution, completed in 1875, emphasized curbing the powers of government. The governor's term was limited to two years, a state debt ceiling of $200,000 was established, salaries of elected state officials were fixed, the legislature was limited to biennial sessions, and the governor was allowed to make very few executive appointments.

When this document went to the people of Texas for a vote in February 1876, it was approved by a margin of 136,606 to 56,652; 130 of the 150 Texas counties registered approval. The 20 counties that did not favor the new charter were urban areas. Understandably, modern critics of the Texas Constitution are also primarily urban because the constitution does little to help solve the problems of the state's cities.

General Features

The Texas Constitution of today is very much like the original 1876 document, in spite of numerous amendments, including major changes in the executive article. It consists of a preamble and 17 articles, with each article divided into subsections.

The Lone Star State can almost claim the record for the longest constitution in the nation. Only the constitution of Alabama contains more words than the roughly 93,000 in the Texas charter.[5]

Overall, the Texas Constitution reflects the factors, outlined earlier, that influenced the constitutional convention. It embodies the state's conservative political tradition. Changes in the national Constitution, both by amendment and by judicial interpretation, have necessitated alterations of the state constitution, although "deadwood" provisions—those that cannot be made operational and that conflict with federal law—remain. The public has voted on 616 proposals to amend the constitution, with the result that 439 amendments had been added by the middle of 2006 (Table 2.2). These amendments, necessary because of the basic document's restrictiveness, have produced a state charter that is poorly organized and difficult

TABLE 2.2

Texas Constitutional Amendments, 1879*–2002

Decade	Proposed	Adopted	Cumulative total
1870s–1880s	16	5	5
1890s	15	11	16
1900s	20	10	26
1910s	35	9	35
1920s	26	12	47
1930s	45	34	81
1940s	35	25	106
1950s	43	33	139
1960s	84	55	194
1970s	67	44	238
1980s	99	88	326
1990s	80	64	390
2000s through 9/06	51	49	439
Total through 9/06	616	439	439

* The first amendment to the 1876 Texas Constitution was adopted in 1879.

SOURCE: Compiled by C. Neal Tate and Charldean Newell.

to read, let alone interpret—even by the courts.[6] In effect, the constitution is both fundamental law and a legislative code—that is, it incorporates provisions that in other states are usually found in statutes. Such matters as state university capital funding (buildings and equipment, for example), the creation of hospital districts, and the land program for veterans are all found in the constitution.

Specific Features

The Texas Constitution is similar to the U.S. Constitution in many ways, particularly the way in which the purposes of organizing and limiting government and legitimacy are addressed. That is, each government has executive, legislative, and judicial branches. Each has a system of shared powers. Each includes provisions against unequal or arbitrary government action, such as restricting freedom of religion. The two documents are less alike in terms of providing power to government—the national Constitution is much more flexible in allowing government to act than is the state document. Texas legislators, for example, cannot set their own salaries or determine when their business is finished and adjournment is appropriate.[7] Details of these features can be found in the later chapters of this book.

Bill of Rights. Similar to the Bill of Rights in the U.S. Constitution, Article I of the Texas Constitution provides for equality under the law; religious freedom, including separation of church and state;[8] due process for the criminally accused; and freedom of speech and of the press. The state constitution further provides protection for the mentally incompetent and several specific guarantees, such as a prohibition against deporting an individual from the state, among the thirty protections cited in the document. It includes an Equal Rights Amendment for all Texans.

Citizen opinion generally supports the U.S. and Texas bills of rights. However, just as the public sometimes gets upset with the U.S. Bill of Rights when constitutional protections are afforded to someone the public wants to "throw the book at"—an accused child molester, for example—Texans sometimes react against the protections provided in the state constitution. A 1992 Texas Poll revealed that if given a chance to vote on the Bill of Rights today, "a significant number of Texans would balk at several sweeping protections—including the rights to assemble and protest, to hold unpopular beliefs, and to bear arms."[9] Nevertheless, several modern efforts to revise the constitution have failed to modify protections such as freedom of speech and press and protection against unreasonable searches and seizures found in Article I.[10]

Following the terrorist attack on the World Trade Center in New York City in 2001, many Americans have been willing to sacrifice some protections to help prevent further acts of terrorism, a willingness that has engendered national debate on the conflict between homeland security and civil rights and liberties. Support for such intrusions on basic civil liberties has been dwindling, however.[11] Because homeland security issues involve racial and ethnic profiling, Texas, with its very diverse population, could be affected more than some other states.

Separation of Powers.   Like the national Constitution, the state charter divides governmental functions among three branches: the executive, the legislative, and the judicial. The national government divides power between the nation and the states as well as among the three branches. Providing for a sharing of power should ensure that one branch cannot become too powerful. Article II outlines the separation of institutions, and the articles dealing with the individual "departments"—as these branches are labeled in the state constitution—develop a system of checks and balances similar to those found in the national Constitution. Examples of these checks include the governor's power to veto acts of the legislature and the legislature's power to impeach a governor.

Legislative Branch.   The Texas Legislature, like the U.S. Congress, consists of a senate and a house of representatives. The legislative article (Article III) establishes a legislative body, sets the qualifications for membership, provides its basic organization, and fixes its meeting times. This article also sets the salary of state legislators. A 1991 constitutional amendment created an Ethics Commission whose powers include recommending legislative salaries, but the recommendation must be approved by the voters. The Ethics Commission has made no such recommendation. Until it does, a $7,200 annual salary prevails.

Rather than emphasizing the positive powers of the legislature, the article spells out specific actions that the legislature cannot take, reflecting the fear of strong government brought about by Reconstruction. For example, the U.S. Constitution gives Congress broad powers to make any laws that are "necessary and proper." In contrast, rather than allowing lawmaking to be handled through the regular legislative process, the Texas Constitution forces state government to resort to the process of constitutional amendment. Another illustration is that adding to the fund maintained by the state to help veterans adjust to civilian life by giving them good deals on the purchase of land requires an amendment. So does changing the percentage of the state budget that can be spent on public welfare.

Article III also sets limits on legislative procedure. It stipulates that the legislature may meet in regular session only every two years. It also specifies the number of days for introduction of bills, committee work, and floor action, although the governor, to permit early floor action, can declare an emergency.

Executive Branch. Little similarity exists between provisions for the executive branch in Texas's charter and those in the national Constitution. The U.S. Constitution provides for a very strong chief executive, the president, and creates only one other elective office, the vice president, who runs on a ticket with the presidential candidate. Article IV of the state constitution

The 76th Legislature in 1999 proposed seventeen amendments to the Texas Constitution. One of the most interesting ones was Proposition 1, which established a procedure for succession to the lieutenant governor's office. Amid wide speculation that Governor George W. Bush might be the next U.S. president, the state wanted to ensure an orderly procedure if Lieutenant Governor Rick Perry moved up to the governor's office. The amendment established a procedure whereby the members of the Senate would elect one of their own members to act as lieutenant governor. The individual would remain a member of the Senate. Even before the vote on the amendment, political speculation began about which senator might be catapulted into the very powerful position of lieutenant governor and, thus, presiding officer of the Senate. Bush, of course, was elected president in 2000 and re-elected in 2004. Although Perry quickly took to the role of governor and successfully ran for that office, Bill Ratliff, the senator selected, did not find the lieutenant governor's role to his liking and chose not to seek election to that position in 2002.

provides that the governor is the "chief executive" of the state. However, the state constitution requires that, like the governor, the citizens elect people to fill the following positions:

- The lieutenant governor, who presides over the Texas Senate
- The comptroller (pronounced con-TROL-ler) of public accounts, who collects the state's taxes and determines whether enough revenue exists to fund the state budget and who keeps the state's money
- The attorney general, who is the state's lawyer
- The commissioner of the General Land Office, who protects the state's environment and administers its vast public lands
- Members of the Texas Railroad Commission, who regulate intrastate transportation and the oil and gas industry

Furthermore, statutory laws require that the agriculture commissioner and members of the State Board of Education be elected. Thus, quite unlike the president, who appoints most key federal executives, the governor is saddled with five other elected executives and two key elected policy-making boards. He or she has no formal control over these individuals.

The result is that Texas has a "disintegrated" or "fragmented" executive branch; that is, the governor has little or no control over other elected officials or most state agencies. Most of the more than 231 state agencies (the number for the 2006–2007 budget year, excluding separate campuses of community colleges and programs housed in the offices of elected executives) receive policy direction from a board or commission that is largely independent of the chief executive. Thus, we see that the executive article, like the legislative one, is overly specific and creates roadblocks to expeditious governmental action. When government is burdened with too many restrictions, it cannot act quickly, even when citizens need a fast response. The governor, however, does have significant legislative powers through control of special sessions and through the veto.

Judicial Branch.   The national judicial system is clear-cut—district courts, appeals courts, the U.S. Supreme Court—but the Texas judicial system is not at all clear. There are three distinctive features of the judicial article of the state constitution. First, a rather confusing pattern of six types of courts is established. The picture is further complicated by two supreme courts, one each for civil (Supreme Court) and criminal (Court of Criminal Appeals) matters.

Second, each level of trial court has concurrent, or overlapping, jurisdiction with another level; that is, either level of court may hear the case. Additionally, there are trial courts established by statute that have different jurisdictions from those established by the constitution. For example, constitutional county courts have concurrent jurisdiction with justice of the peace courts in civil matters involving $200 to $5,000. County courts-at-law overlap district courts in civil matters up to $100,000. Although the legislature can adjust the jurisdiction of statutory courts, constitutional court authority can be altered only by constitutional amendment. Furthermore, the minimum dollar amounts stated in the constitution reflect economic values of the nineteenth century. In an era of multimillion-dollar lawsuits, having a district court—the chief trial court of the state—hear a case when the disputed amount is $1,000 or less detracts from the more significant trial work of that court.

Third, qualifications of judges are stated so as to allow those with no legal training to be eligible for a justice of the peace or county court bench.[12] The problem of judicial qualifications is aggravated by the fact that judges are elected in Texas, so that, on occasion, vote-getting ability may be more important than the ability to render judgments. In the national government, the president appoints all federal judges, who must be confirmed by the Senate.

Local Government.   The Texas Constitution assigns considerable power to units of local government, especially municipalities. Local governments fall into three categories: counties, municipalities, and special districts. The constitution gives these governmental units varying degrees of flexibility. Counties, often regarded as administrative and judicial arms of the state, are most restricted. They are saddled with a commission form of government that combines executive and legislative authority and is headed by a judge. The powers vested in them and the services they offer are fragmented.

Cities whose population is 5,000 or more may become home-rule units of government. **Home rule** allows a city to write its own charter and make changes in it without legislative approval; general-law cities must operate under statewide statutes. The major constitutional handicaps for cities are the ceilings imposed on tax rates and debt and the limitations on the frequency of charter amendments.

Special districts are limited-purpose local governments that have taxing authority. The legislature generally authorizes the creation of special districts, although some water and hospital districts have been created by constitutional amendment and some by administrative agencies. School districts are the best-known type of special district.

Suffrage.   The provisions on voting and the apportionment of legislative bodies are interesting because many of them clearly conflict with federal law, which itself continues to evolve as the legal/political philosophies of federal judges change. For example, Article VII of the Texas Constitution still contains references to 21 as the minimum voting age although citizens can now vote at 18. As mentioned earlier, such provisions are known as "deadwood" because they cannot be made operational. In some cases, stopgap measures have been passed by the legislature to achieve compliance with federal law, but the retention of these constitutional provisions is certainly confusing.

Amendments.   The framers of a constitution cannot possibly anticipate every provision that should be included. Consequently, all constitutions specify a procedure for amendment. In Texas, proposals for amendment may be initiated during a regular or special session of the legislature, and an absolute two-thirds majority—that is, 100 House and 21 Senate members—must vote to submit the proposed changes to the voters. The governor cannot veto a proposed amendment. The legislature also specifies the date of the election at which an amendment is to be voted on by the public.

Whenever possible, amendments are placed on the ballot in general elections to avoid the expense of a separate, called election. Only a simple majority of those citizens who vote—that is, half plus one—is needed for ratification, making it rather easy to add amendments.

CONSTITUTIONAL REVISION

Need for Reform

On the whole, state constitutions are long, restrictive, inclusive, and confusing and need frequent amendment to permit the provision of necessary services as well as to keep pace with contemporary needs. State constitutions tend to reflect the concerns of people with vested interests, who prefer the "security blanket" of constitutional inclusion to the insecurity of being left at the mercy of legislatures with changing party alignments, political persuasions, and political concerns.

The Texas document especially illustrates the problem of having to legislate by constitutional amendment because of the rigidity of the constitution. For example, in recent years amendments have included everything from legalizing bingo for church and fraternal organizations to allowing an East Texas farmer to keep the land he had bought almost fifty years earlier in spite of a technical defect in the title to the property, to eliminating the tax on leased cars not primarily used to produce income.

The constitutional amendment election of November 2005 illustrates that the amendment process is often used instead of legislation, is highly political, and focuses on the specific.

Nine proposals were advanced concerning railroad finance, a ban on gay marriage, economic development not constituting debt, conditions for denying bail, defining rates for commercial loans, altering the membership of the State Commission on Judicial Conduct, lines-of-credit with reverse mortgages, land title relinquishments in Smith and Upshur Counties, and easing the length of terms on regional mobility commissions. The proposals concerning interest rates and terms on mobility commissions failed. The others passed. All of these joint resolutions focused on issues that in most states would have been matters of statutory law, not constitutional law.

One issue overshadowed the others: the provision that marriage consists only of the union of one man and one woman and that prohibits any subdivision from altering that status. The so-called "gay marriage" proposal was very controversial. Because it was badly drafted, it may well affect other relationships and could deter some highly skilled people from wanting to work in the state if for no other reason than its intent is clearly to discriminate against one category of people. Moreover, it was redundant because a ban on same-sex marriage already existed in statute. Conservative Texas, however, was caught up in the national frenzy of reaction against more liberal states attempting to provide for marriage among same-sex couples.

Nevertheless, citizens often have little or no interest in constitutional revision. Like the legislators who would have to propose the constitutional overhaul, they are more concerned about the issues that regularly beset the Texas political system—education, insurance rates, health care, highways, air quality, and so on. Too, most Texans—at least those who turn out to vote—are politically conservative and prefer the basic governing document that they know to one that could cause socio-political and economic changes that they would not like.

Constitutions, like all laws, are political. What one group advocates may be strongly opposed by other interests. For example, should an amendment absolutely prohibiting a state income tax be added to the constitution, individuals who do not like income taxes would be satisfied, but governmental agencies, including colleges and universities, could suffer dire financial consequences because virtually all the other tax sources are already in use.

Nevertheless, the advocates of **constitutional revision**, although not always agreeing on what the change should be, tend to focus on the following provisions of the current constitution:

1. *The biennial legislative session.* As state politics and finance become more complex, the short legislative sessions, held only every other year, become more of a handicap to developing long-range public policy.
2. *The judicial system.* The Texas judicial system, as previously discussed, is characterized by multiple layers of courts with overlapping jurisdictions. Many reform advocates would like to see the establishment of a streamlined, unified judicial system that ordinary citizens could understand.
3. *The disintegrated/fragmented executive branch.* The executive branch is characterized by a multiplicity of elected officials and policy-making boards. Reformers suggest an executive branch modeled on the national executive—that is, a single elected official and a series of executive departments responsible to that official. Democratic theory requires that citizens be able to understand how to influence the agents of government. In a system in which one can reasonably

ask, "Who's in charge here?" citizens have a hard time ensuring that they will be represented in or even heard by government.

4. *County government.* County government's structure and its lack of power to pass ordinances mean that counties cannot readily respond to problems, which is especially troublesome in urban counties. Reform advocates suggest that county government be streamlined and given at least limited ordinance power.

5. *Detailed provisions in the constitution.* For example, each time more funding is needed for welfare payments or the veterans' land program, a constitutional amendment must be passed. Thus, another area for reform is removing from the constitution details that are better left for statutory law, which can be changed more readily as situations demand.

Recent Reform Efforts

Attempts to modernize the Texas Constitution have been made from time to time since its adoption in 1876. Serious interest in constitutional change was evident in 1957–1961, 1967–1969, and 1971–1974, and to some extent in 1991–1993 and 1999, but the only reform effort that actually resulted in an opportunity for the electorate to decide on a new document came in 1975.

1971–1974. A 1972 constitutional amendment authorized the 63rd Legislature to convene itself as a constitutional convention. The Texas Constitutional Revision Commission, created by the same amendment, provided a detailed study of the state constitution that served as the basis for new constitutions proposed in 1974 and 1975.

The constitutional convention was quickly labeled the "Con-Con." The proposal drafted by the convention was defeated when two issues—parimutuel (that is, race-track) betting and right-to-work, which is an anti-union provision—were introduced that became the red herrings for foes of reform. They brought opposition from religious conservatives opposed to gambling and from organized labor opposed to the continuation of right-to-work. These and other groups made enough legislators skittish to prevent a favorable decision in the legislature (1974 was an election year). The proposal died without ever reaching the voters.

1975.   Interest in constitutional reform remained high. When the 64th Legislature convened in January 1975, constitutional revision was a principal issue. Senate Joint Resolution (SJR) 11 (with amendments) emerged as the vehicle for accomplishing constitutional change. Although the legislature did not adopt all of the changes suggested by the 1973 revision commission, legislators did draw heavily on that work.[13] Highlights of SJR 11 included annual legislative sessions, a streamlined judicial system, modernization of county government, elimination of such details as the welfare ceiling, more power for the governor coupled with a limit of two terms, property tax relief, and a tax on petroleum refining.

Powerful interests lined up on both sides of this proposed constitutional reform, with vested economic interests and emotionalism acting as important components of the struggle for ratification of the document. Those whose interests were already protected in the constitution did not want to risk change; those who wanted equal protection or who simply wanted a more workable document eagerly sought change. In spite of the efforts of most state officials to convince the voters of the worth of the proposed state charter, the entire proposal was defeated by a two-to-one margin on November 4, 1975. Governor Dolph Briscoe, fearful of higher taxes and government expansion, and county officials, fearful for their jobs, helped bring about the defeat. Texans clearly preferred the old, lengthy, familiar document to one they saw as possibly promoting more spending and allowing greater governmental power.

1991–1993.   In 1991 Senator John Montford drafted a proposed new constitution for introduction during the 1993 legislative session. The Montford proposal included such features as the following:

- Six-year terms for senators and four-year terms for House members, coupled with a limit of two consecutive terms for a senator and three for a House member
- A 60-day budget session of the legislature in even-numbered years
- Empowerment of the legislature to meet to reconsider bills vetoed by the governor
- The only elected executives to be the governor, lieutenant governor, and comptroller, each with a limit of two terms
- Simplification of the court system and a provision of nonpartisan elections
- Creation of five regional university systems, all of which would share the Permanent University Fund (PUF)
- Ordinance power for counties, subject to local voter approval[14]

As is so often the case, immediate problems such as the budget shortfall, school finance, and the inability of the prison system to cope with the volume of state prisoners crowded out constitutional revision in 1993. Additionally, the author of this proposal subsequently became head of Texas Tech University until 2001. Thus, the proposal lost its leading advocate.

After the 1997 legislative session, Representative Rob Junell, chair of the powerful House Appropriations Committee, expressed interest in constitutional reform. Junell liked some of the Montford ideas, particularly reducing the number of elected officials, including making judges subject to gubernatorial appointment. He was joined by Senator Bill Ratliff, chair of the equally powerful Senate Finance Committee. Their proposal included the following items:

- Six-year terms for senators and four-year terms for House members
- Limiting the elected executives to the governor, lieutenant governor, comptroller of public accounts, and attorney general
- Providing for an Executive Department that would consist of specified department heads, excluding elective officials and reporting to the governor
- Simplification of the court system, with judges to be appointed by the governor
- Establishing the possibility of a veto session for the purpose of reconvening to consider whether to override the governor's veto

One of the thorniest constitutional problems was the determination by state courts that the Texas public education system did not provide "efficient and effective" education for all students. From 1989 to 1993, the legislature struggled to produce a funding scheme to equalize public education that was acceptable to the courts. Tax schemes in 1997 put such funding in the spotlight again. In 2003 new problems of educational equity again created a focus on school funding, and the issue remained unresolved by April 2006.

SOURCE: Courtesy of Ben Sargent.

Known as HJR 1 and SJR 1 in the 76th Legislature in 1999, the Junell–Ratliff proposal was withdrawn from committee in late April when the sponsors realized that their resolution had no chance of being considered by the full House or Senate. Opposition was widespread among both the Democratic and Republican state party organizations, the Texas AFL-CIO, and various other interest groups. Long-time political reporter Sam Attlesey characterized the demise of the proposal as due to "a lack of interest, excitement or crisis in state government."[15]

Twenty-nine states have constitutions newer than Texas's, and twelve have state charters written since 1950. Yet in spite of the occasional difficulty of governing under the present state charter, only the League of Women Voters has shown a long-term concern for constitutional revision, joined by sporadic media interest in reform.[16] Recent sessions of the legislature have faced too many problems demanding immediate solutions to allow legislators to give any consideration to a new constitution. Furthermore, many citizens fear that change may be for the worse rather than for the better, and special interests want to preserve what they already have embodied in the state charter. This conservative stance, reflecting once again the state's traditionalism, is encouraged by the major economic forces in the state.

YOU DECIDE

Should Texas Convene a Constitutional Convention?

The Texas Constitution was ratified in 1876. By mid-2006, it had been amended 439 times and is now more than 93,000 words in length. The average for all fifty states is 133 amendments and 35,554 words. California, the only state with a population larger than that of Texas, has a constitution with 513 amendments and 54,645 words. The constitution of New York, the third largest state, has 216 amendments and 51,700 words. Should Texas convene a constitutional convention to draft a new state charter?

Pro

The present state constitution

⇨ is antiquated.

⇨ conflicts with the national constitution.

⇨ protects special interests.

⇨ reflects agrarian interests and thus does not meet the needs of an urban state.

⇨ is far too specific.

⇨ needs frequent interpretation.

⇨ poorly organizes government.

Con

The U.S. Constitution is 89 years older than the Texas Constitution, proving that age is an asset for constitutions. The state constitution should not be revised, in order to avoid

⇨ increasing partisanship that could create a political disaster.

⇨ a process likely to be an expensive exercise resulting in stalemate.

⇨ fixing something that "ain't broke."

⇨ giving more authority to counties, which are already inefficient.

⇨ giving government, especially the governor, too much power.

⇨ creating litigation stemming from a comparison of the old and the new.

⇨ unneeded changes in governmental institutions.

SUMMARY

Texans were so unhappy with Reconstruction government that, given the opportunity to draft and ratify a new constitution in 1876, they concentrated their attention on two of the four purposes of constitutions: legitimacy and limiting government. The intent of the framers was to curb governmental power. Thus they largely ignored the importance of assigning sufficient power to governmental officials, and they subverted the purpose of organizing government by creating a fragmented set of institutions and offices designed to diffuse authority. Although this approach limits government, it also makes citizen participation more difficult because Texas's government is confusing to most people.

Lacking the farsightedness of the framers of the U.S. Constitution, the authors of the Texas charter produced a restrictive document that sometimes impedes the development and implementation of needed policies and programs. By the middle of 2006, lawmakers and the public have had to resort to amending the Texas Constitution 439 times to make possible programs that otherwise would have been consigned to legislative dreamland. In one sense, the element of democratic theory that holds that public input into policy is important is well satisfied by such a practice, but policies are very hard to modify once they are written into the constitution. Dynamic public issues such as funding for water quality, prison expansion, insurance regulation, and public education could be handled more smoothly without the cumbersome amendment process. Now, if a policy proves to be ineffective, only another amendment can resolve the problem.

The most cumbersome and/or unnecessarily restrictive provisions in the 1876 constitution, with their consequences, are summarized in the following list:

- The governor, although held responsible by the public for overall state leadership and the actions of state agencies, in reality has little direct control over most major policy-making offices, boards, and commissions.
- The legislature is caught between the proverbial "rock and a hard place." Constantly criticized by the citizenry for poor performance, it is operating in the stranglehold of poverty-level salaries, short and infrequent sessions, and innumerable restrictions on legislative action.
- Texas judges are well aware of the lack of cohesiveness in the judicial system, but they are virtually powerless to provide simpler, more uniform justice because of the overlapping and parallel jurisdictions of the state's courts and the lack of effective supervision of the whole judicial system.
- County governments, even when county commissioners have relatively progressive attitudes, are restricted by their constitutional structure and scope.
- In spite of frequent amendments, the Texas Constitution still does not conform to current federal law.
- The 439 amendments exacerbate rather than improve the poor organization of the charter, making it even more difficult for laypersons to read.

Four modern legislatures have shown an interest in constitutional revision; two devoted time and energy to reform efforts. But the electorate still lacks sufficient understanding of and interest in the shortcomings of the present constitution to be intent on constitutional change. Citizens are also far too concerned about state taxes, public education, social services, crime and punishment, and many other pressing issues to give constitutional revision much attention. Although the current constitution "creaks and groans," the state still takes care of its business. A successful revision effort will have to wait until the citizens of Texas are more aware of the pitfalls of the present state charter and more convinced of the need for change. For now, "if it ain't broke, don't fix it" prevails.

STUDY QUESTIONS

1. What are the four purposes of constitutions? Which ones are most reflected in the Texas Constitution? Which ones are least reflected? Can you add to the examples stated in the chapter.
2. How many constitutions has Texas had? Why have there been so many? Do you think there needs to be yet another one? Why or why not?
3. Why is the Texas Constitution amended so frequently? What types of interests are involved when constitutional change is advocated?
4. What similarities and differences between the U.S. and Texas Constitutions do you see?
5. Do you think that you, personally, could get interested in constitutional revision? Why or why not?

SURFING THE WEB

Visit the companion site for this book:

http://www.thomsonedu.com/politicalscience/kraemer

View the entire Texas Constitution:

http://www.capitol.state.tx.us/txconst/toc.html

Click on "Legislation–Amendments" for amendments proposed in the most recent legislative session:

http://www.capitol.state.tx.us/

Type in "Constitution" to see articles on the various constitutions of the state:

http://www.tsha.utexas.edu/handbook/online

Click on "Voter Information" then download the latest Voters' Guide prepared by the Texas League of Women Voters. It includes a neutral analysis of constitutional amendments on the ballot:

http://www.lwvtexas.org/

NOTES

1. See, for example, Fred Gantt, Jr., *The Chief Executive in Texas: A Study in Gubernatorial Leadership* (Austin: University of Texas Press, 1964), 24.

2. The Jacksonians supported slavery and devised an Indian policy that led to the brutal treatment of Native Americans.

3. Jim B. Pearson, Ben Procter, and William B. Conroy, *Texas, The Land and Its People,* 3rd ed. (Dallas: Hendrick-Long, 1987), 400–405; *The Texas Almanac,* 1996–1997 (Dallas: *Dallas Morning News,* 1996), 499.

4. Historical perspectives are based on remarks of John W. Mauer, "State Constitutions in a Time of Crisis: The Case of the Texas Constitution of 1876," Symposium on the Texas Constitution, sponsored by the University of Texas Law School and the *Texas Law Review,* October 7, 1989.

5. The Alabama Constitution had approximately 340,000 words as of 2005. This and other comparative information can be found in *The Book of the States, 2005 Edition,* vol. 37 (Lexington, KY: Council of State Governments, 2005), 10.

6. A full discussion of poorly organized sections and provisions in conflict with federal law can be found in *Reorganized Texas Constitution without Substantive Change* (Austin: Texas Advisory Commission on Intergovernmental Relations, 1977).

7. The definitive study of the Texas Constitution is Janice C. May, *The Texas State Constitution, A Reference Guide* (Westport, CT: Greenwood, 1996).

8. Article I, Section 4, stipulates acknowledgment of the existence of a Supreme Being as a test for public office; however, this provision is not enforced because it violates the U.S. Constitution.

9. Todd J. Gillman, "Bill of Rights Might Face Tough Ride Now," *Dallas Morning News*, August 22, 1992, 12F.

10. The extensive application of the U.S. Bill of Rights to the states through the vehicle of the Fourteenth Amendment is a modern occurrence. So long as citizens were legally perceived to be citizens of the state first and of the nation second, state guarantees were vital. In recent years, state courts have begun to reassert themselves as protectors of rights, while the federal courts have begun to be less protective in their own decisions.

11. See, for example, David Westphal, "Homeland Security Plan Spurs Liberties Concerns," *Sacramento Bee*, August 9, 2002, posted at http://foi.missouri.edu/terrorandcivillib/homelandsecplan.html; "Numbers," *Time* magazine, December 23, 2002, 21; and "USA Patriot Act," *Wikipedia, the Free Encyclopedia*, posted at http://en.wikipedia.org/wiki/Patriot_act, February 1, 2006.

12. Contrary to popular opinion, a justice of the peace without legal training cannot become a judge on a superior (appeals) court. Qualifications for the superior courts include ten years as a practicing lawyer or a combination of ten years' legal practice and judicial service.

13. A detailed analysis of the 1975 document is available in George Braden's *Citizen's Guide to the Proposed New Constitution* (Houston: Institute of Urban Studies, University of Houston, 1975). The University of Houston served as a research and information center during the revision efforts and published numerous reports beginning in 1973. Scholars from across the state were involved in the Houston research. One, Janice C. May, published a book-length study, *Texas Constitutional Revision Experience in the '70s* (Austin: Sterling Swift, 1975). A summary of the general literature on the revision efforts and of voting behavior can be found in John E. Bebout, "The Meaning of the Vote on the Proposed Texas Constitution, 1975," *Public Affairs Comment* 24 (February 1978): 1–9, published by the Lyndon B. Johnson School of Public Affairs at the University of Texas at Austin.

14. Draft resolution and "Comparison of Current and Proposed Constitutions" provided by the office of Senator John Montford, January 1992.

15. Sam Attlesey, "Texas Constitution Outlasts Plan for Rewrite," *Dallas Morning News*, April 25, 1999, 54A.

16. See, for example, "Member Update: Texas Constitutional Revision," *The Texas Voter* 40 (Winter 2005), insert; and Heber Taylor, "It's Time to Draft a New Texas Constitution," *Galveston County Daily News* (November 9, 2005), available at http://galvestondailynews.com/story.lasso?ewed=2df9eea56de051ec.

3

INTEREST GROUPS

As soon as several of the inhabitants of the United States have taken up an opinion or a feeling they wish to promote in the world, they look around for mutual assistance; and as soon as they have found each other out, they combine. From that moment they are no longer isolated men, but a power seen from afar, whose actions serve for an example, and whose language is listened to.

Alexis de Tocqueville
***Democracy in America*, 1835**

Money doesn't talk, it swears.

Bob Dylan
"It's Alright Ma (I'm Only Bleeding)," 1965

INTRODUCTION

Politics is concerned with the making of public policy, but a great many of its actions have private consequences. When government imposes a tax, or begins to regulate an industry, or writes rules about the behavior of individuals, it makes an impact, not just on the public in general, but on people in particular. Human nature being what it is, those people tend to judge the action not so much on the basis of its value to everyone in general but on the basis of its utility to themselves.

Seeking to obtain more favorable policies, people organize to try to influence government. When they do, they create a problem for democracy. We want our government to take account of the impact of its laws on individuals, but we do not want the special wants of some people to be more important than the common needs of us all.

To the extent that public policy is made or modified at the behest of private interests, democracy is crippled. In Texas, as elsewhere in the United States, special organized interests are always busy trying to influence what government institutions do. As citizens, we have to decide if these groups are merely presenting their point of view to public authorities or if they are corrupting the process of self-government.

The definition of interest groups is the first topic of this chapter. We describe and analyze their activities and move on to look at one of those activities, lobbying, in more detail. We discuss four important groups out of the hundreds that struggle for influence in Texas politics. Finally, the chapter presents an evaluation of the state's interest-group system in the light of democratic theory.

INTEREST GROUPS

Definition

In the broad sense, an interest group is a private organization of individuals who have banded together because of a common cause or interest. The concern here, however, is with **political interest groups**—those that try to influence politicians to make public policy that is consistent with their membership's personal interests or opinion about the public good.

Interest groups can be usefully contrasted with political parties. While the focus of a party is broad, encompassing many different interests, the focus of a group is narrow, comprising just one or a few similar interests. While parties attempt to gain power by running candidates in elections, groups try to affect power by influencing office-holders. Therefore, while parties are forced to appeal to the citizenry in order to marshal support, groups may work entirely behind the scenes. By joining groups, people gain the ability to affect government decisions beyond what they achieve with just their vote.

Who Is Organized?

The two most important things to understand about interest groups are that not all people who share an interest become organized, and that organized citizens are much more powerful than unorganized citizens. Although the famous quotation from de Tocqueville at the beginning of this chapter might lead us to believe that every potential interest spawns an interest group, in fact, some interests are far more likely to be organized than others. Those that are organized are relevant to policy making; those that are not organized are usually irrelevant.

The general rules of interest-group formation are that (1) economic producing groups are more likely to be organized than consuming groups; (2) regardless of the type of group, people with more education and income are more likely to join than people with less education and income; and (3) citizens who join groups out of personal involvement—as opposed to economic stake—tend to feel very strongly about the particular issue that is the group's reason for existence. Consequently, because they are more likely to be organized, producers tend to have more political influence than consumers, the middle and upper classes have more influence than the working classes, and passionate believers have more influence than citizens who are less emotionally involved.

Functions

Interest groups attempt to persuade both the public and individual government officials to take a particular point of view on specific public policies. In trying to be persuasive, they perform five important functions in the political process:

1. They furnish information to office-holders in all branches of government. This activity consists of both communicating their collective opinion on public policy and of supplying policymakers with their version of the facts.
2. They politicize and inform members of their groups, as well as others.
3. They mediate conflict within their groups.
4. They engage in electioneering, especially the contribution of money to candidates, and possibly in other interventions in the governing process, such as filing lawsuits.
5. By disseminating information supporting their own policy stands to citizens, they help to form public opinion.

Interest groups therefore enhance democratic government by supplying information to citizens, contributing to debates about issues, getting people involved in politics, and "shaking up" the established order by influencing institutions. But, because they attempt to skew the process of government toward their own version of appropriate policy, these groups may also be a corrupting influence. A closer look at their activities will show the extent to which they may deflect public policy-making into private channels.

INTEREST-GROUP ACTIVITIES

Electioneering

One of the most common ways that interest groups try to ensure that their efforts at persuasion will be effective is to support candidates for public office. Interest groups that have helped to elect a politician can be confident that they will not be forgotten when that politician takes office.

YOU DECIDE

Should Corporate Political Action Committees Be Banned?

A political action committee (PAC) is an organization that collects voluntary contributions from citizens—generally, those who are affiliated with a particular organization such as a corporation, church, or labor union, or who believe in a particular cause—and distributes them to candidates. Reformers have often called for government to forbid corporations to form PACs.

Pro

⮕ Although "money talks," money is not speech. The First Amendment to the U.S. Constitution should not be interpreted so as to protect the power of money.

⮕ It is bad enough that individuals are able to corrupt the process of government by renting the allegiance of politicians with campaign contributions; it is much worse that corporate interests are able to do so.

⮕ Corporations already possess a great political advantage over ordinary citizens because of their ability to hire lobbyists and buy media advertising; the presence of PACs makes that advantage even more lopsided and unfair.

⮕ The political power of corporations has resulted in public policies that have contributed to the growing inequality of wealth in the United States; in order to permit the reversal of those policies, corporate power must be curtailed.

Con

⮕ The First Amendment protects individual freedom of expression, and citizens should be able to express themselves by contributing money to candidates or organizations.

⮕ A PAC is merely an organization that permits individuals with a shared interest to coordinate their political activity; shared economic interests are just as worthy of representation as religious, ideological, ethnic, or any other kind of interest.

⮕ The supposed political advantage possessed by corporations is a fiction in the mind of so-called reformers. In fact, corporations are over-taxed and over-regulated. They should have more political influence, not less.

⮕ Growing inequality of wealth has been caused by economic trends that are independent of government policies. Besides, differences in material equality reflect differences in merit, and are therefore good, not bad.

Source: Many writings in the field of political science, economics, political philosophy, and journalism.

Usually, the most effective way to help a candidate is to donate money to his or her campaign for public office. Because campaigning demands the purchase of advertising in expensive media, all candidates but the few who are personally rich need to beg wealthy individuals and groups for large amounts of money. Both the politicians and the contributors understand, if only tacitly, that the interest groups expect an exchange: The groups will give the candidates money, and if they win, the candidates give the groups favorable public policy. A politically active interest group that represents a wealthy industry can transfer impressive amounts of money to its favored politicians.

It would be a mistake, however, to believe that just because a group gives money to important politicians it will certainly get what it wants in public policy. Not only do politicians receive money from groups with clashing desires but office-holders may also feel that what a given group wants is too expensive or illegal, would be unpopular with the public, or is simply a bad idea. Interest groups are therefore sometimes surprised and disappointed by the behavior of politicians to whom they have been generous.

A case in point is the Texas Medical Association (TMA), a trade group representing doctors. The TMA contributed many thousands of dollars to mostly Republican candidates in the state during the 1990s.[1] If politics were a simple machine into which individuals and groups poured money and received policy in return, the TMA's largesse would have entitled it to pretty much anything it wanted from Texas government.

The reality was somewhat different. In 2001 the legislature passed a bill, strongly supported by the TMA, requiring Health Maintenance Organizations (HMOs) to pay doctors in a more timely manner and allowing the doctors to file suit if they thought they were being shortchanged by an HMO. Arguing that the law, if enforced, would create more lawsuits, an outcome that he opposed, Governor Rick Perry vetoed the legislation immediately after the close of the session. The veto infuriated the state's doctors. The $395,000 that doctors and hospitals had donated to Perry from 1997 through 2000 had still not ensured his loyalty to their causes. In 2002 the TMA endorsed Perry's Democratic rival, Tony Sanchez, in the gubernatorial race.[2]

The fact that the TMA lost on an important public-policy issue after having invested a small fortune in Texas politicians does not necessarily mean that the public interest won on the issue. (On this point, it is important to note that the TMA is generally not in favor of encouraging medical lawsuits. It staunchly opposes "frivolous" lawsuits filed by patients against doctors.[3]) It might be more accurate to say that one special interest defeated another. Perry had also received $536,000 in campaign contributions from HMOs and insurance companies, which were united in their desire to discourage medical lawsuits.[4] The general public was represented in the fight only in the sense that Governor Perry knew that he would have to answer to the voters during the 2002 election campaign.

There is no point in criticizing the integrity of public officials for being willing to accept large amounts of cash from groups that have their own, rather than the public's, interest at heart. It is the reality of electoral financing, not personal dishonesty, that makes politicians overly sensitive to private, as opposed to public, interests.

At any rate, the TMA soon made up with the Republican leadership. After the 2002 election, the organization replaced the political and lobbying team that had convinced it to back Sanchez, who lost. It then launched a determined campaign to win back the friendship of the state's Republican leadership, contributing $5.3 million to Governor Perry, Lieutenant Governor David Dewhurst, and other lawmakers after the 2002 voting.[5] These contributions evidently had the desired effect. The 2003 legislature passed a new "prompt-pay bill" without the features that had sparked the first Perry veto. When the governor signed it in June, he was flanked in front of the news cameras by the TMA's board of directors. Perry made it clear that he wanted bygones to be bygones. "Whether it's doctors or hospital administrators or any of a host of other individuals who are involved in the delivery of health care in Texas, we are very much open to bringing them back into the tent, so to speak," he said, to everyone's agreement.[6]

And so the Texas Medical Association, having strayed from the majority-party coalition, has bought its way back in. Thus do many interest groups acquire influence in Texas.

Lobbying

To **lobby** means to attempt to influence policymakers face to face. Everyone has the right to try to make an impact on what government does, and it is obvious that a personal talk with a government official has more impact than one anonymous vote. Because of the rules of interest-group formation, however, some groups are much more likely to be able to afford to lobby than others.

Lobbyists.   During the 2005 legislative session there were about 1,500 professional lobbyists registered with the Texas Ethics Commission.[7] Lobbyists vary as much in their experience and competence as the legislators and administrators they are trying to influence. Many are professionals who charge serious money for their persuasive talents. Top flight freelance lobbyists can make more than $1 million a year. Needless to say, it is wealthy special interests that have the resources to hire the best lobbyists. Table 3.1 provides a partial list of the clients and earnings of two of Austin's best-known lobbyists as of 2005.

Not all lobbyists serve special economic interests, and not all amass fortunes. Some "public interest" lobbyists work for their conception of the common good and take home a modest salary for their efforts. But the biases in the interest-group system mean that most of the people doing most of the lobbying are serving narrow, wealthy interests. Table 3.2 displays Texas's rank compared to other states in the number of lobbying entities from various important industries as of the late 1990s. As the table documents, Texas attracts many lobbyists from the energy, insurance, real estate, banking, agriculture, and health care industries.

What Lobbyists Do and How They Do It.   Lobbyists try to see as many legislators as possible every day, buying a lunch, chatting for a few minutes, or just shaking a hand. Most lobbyists are able to get on a first-name basis with each legislator they think might be sympathetic to their goals. The speaker of the House and the lieutenant governor are key figures in the legislature, and lobbyists try, above all else, to ingratiate themselves with these two powerful officials.

TABLE 3.1

Two Texas Lobbyists and Their Clients (partial list)

Lobbyist	Client	Reported earnings (in $ thousands) from client, 2001
Neal Jones	AT&T	25 to 50
	Blue Cross Blue Shield	Less than 10
	General Motors Corporation	25 to 50
	Microsoft	10 to 25
	Pharmaceutical Research and Manufacturers of America	25 to 49
	Wal-Mart	Less than 10
Mignon McGarry	Centerpoint Energy	50 to 100
	Grande Communications	25 to 50
	HCA—Hospital Corporation of America	100 to 150
	Honda North America	25 to 50
	Houghton Mifflin Company	50 to 100
	Pepsi Cola North America	50 to 100
	Texas Association of Obstetricians and Gynecologists	25 to 50
	Yum! Brands, Inc.	50 to 100

SOURCE: Data from the Texas Ethics Commission Web site.

Contributing Money   As discussed, the best way to ensure the sympathetic concern of politicians is to give them money. Few lobbyists are as brazen as East Texas chicken tycoon Lonnie "Bo" Pilgrim, who, during a fight over a new workers' compensation law in 1989, simply handed out $10,000 checks on the floor to senators who spoke on

TABLE 3.2

Texas's Rank in Number of Lobbying Entities by Industry, 1999

Industry	Number of entities employed as lobbyists	Texas's rank
Energy	243	1
Insurance	222	1
Banking	92	2
Real estate	50	2 (tied with 1)
Health care	143	3
Agriculture	73	3
Recreation	20	4 (tied with 1)
Education	66	7
Gambling	20	10
Timber	10	10 (tied with 3)

SOURCE: Diane Renzulli and The Center for Public Integrity, *Capitol Offenders: How Private Interests Govern Our States* (Washington, DC: Public Integrity Books, 2002), 124, 100, 71, 225, 152, 141, 191, 54, 85, 213.

behalf of his favored legislation.[8] But the state capital is thronged at all times, and especially when the legislature is in session, by representatives of interest groups who are eager to use money in a less public manner in the hope that their generosity will be rewarded with favorable laws, rulings, and policies.

The ongoing saga of Texans for a Republican majority and its political action committee, TRMPAC, provides a contemporary example of the intersection and mutual reinforcement of money, private interests, and public power in Texas and elsewhere.[9] By 2001, Republicans were in office in the White House and the U. S. House of Representatives and were soon to be a majority in the U.S. Senate. They controlled the Texas governorship and the state senate, and they had their sights on the state house of representatives. Tom DeLay, U.S. Representative from Sugar Land, and in line to become the majority leader in the House, conceived the idea of creating an organization that would use state and federal Republican Party organizations to bring the money of national corporations to bear on elections to the state house of representatives in Texas. Once Republicans controlled all three branches of the state government, they could then re-draw the district lines for the national House of Representatives, resulting in still more Republicans being elected

Ordinary citizens—those not employed by an interest group—who feel the need to influence legislation have every right to journey to the Capitol in Austin to lobby representatives. During the 2003 legislative session the *Austin American-Statesman* published some rules that amateur lobbyists should remember when trying to make a persuasive argument. During the 2005 session, the *Dallas Morning News* published an article containing similar rules. Here is the combined list:

1. Be persistent, outgoing, and friendly.
2. Be informed about the process of lawmaking and the party and policy position of individual legislators. The Legislature's Web site is a good place to acquire basic facts.
3. Forget the form letters. Many lawmakers refuse to read them.
4. Explain your position and situation as clearly and briefly as possible.
5. Be personal; tell individual stories that help lawmakers understand your perspective.
6. Have available brief, clear, written details.
7. Be flexible; committee hearings often run long or late.
8. Citizens who have a specific new law in mind should approach legislators as much as one year before the start of the next legislative session.

Sources: Dave Harmon, "Texans Mobilize to Fight Cuts in Their Lifelines," *Austin American-Statesman*, March 24, 2003, AB5; Katherine Goodloe, "Capitol Ideas," *Dallas Morning News*, April 10, 2005, E1.

to Congress (see Chapter 6). Presumably, the corporations would then benefit from Republican policies within the state as they had already benefited at the national level.

There was, however, an obstacle to the Republican plan. A law passed in 1903, Title 15, Chapter 251 of the Texas Election Code made it illegal for corporations to contribute money to candidates for public office. The reason for the law is clear. Corporations are concentrations of great wealth. Because elections, especially those of a relatively low level such as those for the state house of representatives, are partly decided on which candidate can afford to buy the most advertising; corporate money, if it is not divided among many candidates in a race but concentrated on one, can be the deciding factor on election day. Because they can easily outspend millions of ordinary citizens, if they are allowed to use their resources, corporations can dominate elections, and government will cease to be of the people, by the people, and for the people. By outlawing corporate campaign contributions in 1903, legislators were attempting to preserve democracy in Texas.

Representative DeLay's plan was an attempt to evade the purpose of the 1903 law. Although not all the details are known, and although the nature of DeLay's control of TRMPAC is under dispute, the general outlines of the plan have been exposed by journalists and Travis County District Attorney Ronnie Earle. In brief, TRMPAC received $2.5 million in corporate contributions from, among others, Sears, AT&T, Bacardi, and several insurance companies. During the 2002 election campaign TRMPAC sent the money, minus some administrative expenses, to the Republican National Committee (RNC) in Washington, then separately forwarded the names of certain Republican candidates for the state house. A short time later, the National Committee contributed the same amount of money to those candidates. TRMPAC and the RNC, in short, engaged in a money-laundering scheme designed to circumvent the state election law. All the Republican candidates favored in this way were victorious, and Republicans became the majority party in the state house. Whether the Republican candidates would not have won without the laundered corporate cash is impossible to say, but it certainly did not hurt them.

After Tom DeLay's indictment for money laundering and conspiracy, some of his political supporters produced a television ad portraying Travis County District Attorney Ronnie Earle as a slobbering attack dog and accusing him of indicting DeLay for partisan ends. In this cartoon, Ben Sargent ridicules the television spot.

SOURCE: Courtesy of Ben Sargent.

Some of the Democrats defeated in the 2002 balloting suspected the outlines of the scheme and filed a civil suit in state court. District Attorney Ronnie Earle launched a three-year criminal investigation. In September 2005 the Travis County Grand Jury indicted DeLay and several of his associates in TRMPAC on conspiracy and money laundering charges. An indictment, of course, is not a conviction. That the purpose of TRMPAC's actions was to evade the law seems clear, but that does not mean that specific individuals were guilty of crimes. On the day of the indictments, the accused launched a public relations campaign, with DeLay accusing Ronnie Earle, a Democrat, of being a "partisan fanatic" who was simply attempting to punish the now Majority Leader for his successful campaigns against candidates of Earle's party. As this book goes to press, the rhetoric is flying freely and can be expected to become more heated as time goes by. But the case will probably be decided in a courthouse by facts and legal argument, rather than in the media by insults and bloviation. (In the spring of 2006 Tom DeLay resigned his seat in the U.S. House, but the legal proceedings continued.)

The charge of partisanship is one that must be addressed, however. You might notice that this example of the shady intersection between private influence and public officials features Republican politicians. The example does not occur here because the authors of this book think that Republicans are less honest than politicians with other party affiliations. Republicans are the most recent offenders to democratic governance because Republicans have recently been the more successful party. As discussed in Chapters 4 and 5, since 1994 Republicans have been consistently successful in Texas elections. When the Democratic Party dominated the state, this textbook contained many examples of Democrats who allowed private influence to dominate public policy. In this respect, the experience of the authors of this book is identical to the experience of District Attorney Earle. When Democrats were in control of the state, Earle prosecuted 12 of them for various crimes against the public (not all of these prosecutions were successful). Since the Republicans have been in control, he has prosecuted three of *them*.[10] The problem lies with those who wish to dominate public policy with private money, not with those who write about it in textbooks or prosecute the offenders.

Not all interest groups represent rich special interests. Public Citizen Texas is a lobbying group that does not represent wealthy private interests and does not try to achieve its objectives through veiled bribery, yet it manages to influence the process of making public policy.[11] Founded in 1984 as a branch of the national an organization of the same name, Public Citizen, has worked to reform state law and practice on consumer safety, pollution, sustainable energy, access to the courts, government ethics, and campaign finance. The organization's rule to not accept contributions from corporations, professional associations, or government agencies has had two consequences. First, it has freedom of action to follow its principles, regardless of whose toes it may step on in the process. Second, it will never be rich. It relies on the dues and contributions of its 5,300 individual members in Texas to keep it running, and on the dedication of its staff.

Despite its relative poverty, Public Citizen has had a series of modest successes over the years. Its influence stems from its skill at marshaling publicity. Whenever journalists need to get a quotation expressing the pro-consumer, pro-honesty-in-government,

Emotional intensity and willingness to organize can sometimes be as important as money in permitting an interest group to have an impact on public policy. This principle is nicely illustrated by the story of Senator Jeff Wentworth (R., San Antonio) and bicyclists during the 2001 legislative session. Wentworth, concerned about traffic safety in rural areas, filed a bill (SB 238) to forbid cyclists from riding in large groups on farm and ranch roads. The law, if passed, would have required all bicyclists on two-lane roads without a shoulder to ride single file and wear a "slow moving vehicle" triangle sign on their backs.

But it turned out that the bicyclists were organized, felt intensely about their hobby, and were more than willing to play political hardball. Members of the Texas Bicycle Coalition (TBC) were extremely displeased with the proposed statute. They argued that it would stamp out charity rides and hinder tourism. They began a statewide effort to convince Wentworth of the error of his ways.

"Oh, I was inundated," Wentworth told journalist Dave McNeely. "I had more e-mails and letters and phone calls on that bill than on all the other bills I'd filed combined. And nearly all the communication was in opposition to the bill." The TBC also staged a demonstration at the capitol building to remind legislators that there were lots of bicyclists, and they were willing to vote on this issue.

Faced with massive opposition, Wentworth chose the prudent course and backed down gracefully. He agreed to a watered-down version of the bill, which would have left it up to county officials to decide if some of their roads were so dangerous that they required special regulations for cyclists. The weaker version of the proposed law, however, was still not acceptable to the TBC, and SB 238 never got out of committee.

Sources: Dave McNeely, "After Agitating Cyclists, Senator Revises Bike Bill," *Austin American-Statesman*, March 29, 2001, B1; and state legislative Web site: www.capitol.state.tx.us/.

anti-special interest point of view, Public Citizen is one of the organizations they call. Upon occasion, such publicity influences the public to pressure government policymakers to take some action that they would otherwise have avoided. Thus, Public Citizen was instrumental in the creation of the Texas Ethics Commission, the passage of a new "lemon law" to protect the buyers of used cars, and the imposition of safety improvements by the South Texas and Comanche Peak nuclear power plants. In 2002 it raised such a clamor over Public Utility Commission Chairman Max Yzaguirre's conflicts of interest (his ties to the crooked energy-trading corporation Enron, which frequently did business before the Commission) that Yzaguirre resigned.

"Most Texans are surprised at how open our government is to input from our citizens," opined Tom Smith, director—and therefore chief lobbyist—for Public Citizen Texas in 2005. "Too few of them take advantage of it."[12] By devoting a great deal of time and energy to lobbying on behalf of ordinary Texans, Smith and the employees of similar public-interest groups hope to make up for the majority's lack of direct influence on state government.

Nevertheless, despite the occasional successes of such "un-rich" lobbying groups as Public Citizen Texas, the crucial role of money in the interest-group system brings up uncomfortable questions about democracy in Texas. Simply to give money to a politician for personal use is bribery and is illegal. Bribery is a danger to democracy because it means that private wealth has been substituted for public discussion in the making of public policy. The disturbing fact is that the line between outright bribery (illegal) and renting the attention of public officials with campaign contributions and entertainment (legal) is a very thin one. Money talks, and those with more of it speak in louder voices, especially in a state characterized by low legislative salaries and no public campaign finance (see Chapter 5). The indictment of the leaders of TRMPAC for stepping far over the line into illegality should not distract us from the truth that a great deal of legal activity in Texas politics consists of special interests purchasing influence with campaign contributions. When policy is made at the behest of a few wealthy interests working behind the scenes, then government is plutocratic, not democratic. It is fair to ask whether Texas is more of a plutocracy than a democracy.

Supplying Information   Thousands of bills are introduced in the Texas legislature every session, and legislators can have no more than a passing knowledge of most of the policy areas involved. Even those legislators who have specialized knowledge need up-to-date, accurate information. Therefore, in Texas as in other states, information is one of the most important lobbying resources.

State agencies have a constant need for information and sometimes no independent means of finding it. They may come to rely on lobbying groups to furnish them with the facts they need. For example, since 1996 the state insurance commissioner has relied upon the Texas Insurance Checking Office (TICO) to gather the data the commission uses to determine auto insurance rates. The Checking Office is a subsidiary of an insurance industry lobbying group. An industry group is therefore supplying the information used to regulate the industry it represents.[13] Consumers might suspect that such data will not show that insurance companies are charging too much for auto insurance.

Regulation of Lobbying.

It would be a violation of the constitutionally protected rights of expression and association for government to prevent individual citizens from organizing to influence the political process. However, government has the authority to regulate the manner in which citizens attempt to exercise their rights. This principle is especially true for the use of money, where the proper freedom to state one's case can easily evolve into the improper attempt to corrupt the system.

Nevertheless, aside from laws of general application regarding such crimes as bribery and conspiracy, Texas makes little attempt to regulate the activities of interest groups except in the area of lobbying. Early attempts at regulation in 1947, 1973, and 1981 were weak and ineffective because no state agencies were empowered to enforce the laws. In 1991, however, the legislature passed a much-publicized "Ethics Bill," which limited the amount of food, gifts, and entertainment lobbyists can furnish legislators and required lobbyists to report the name of each legislator on whom they spend more than $50. Most important, it created an Ethics Commission that could hold hearings on complaints of improper behavior, levy fines, and refer violations to the Travis County district attorney for possible prosecution. Texas seemed at last to have a lobbyist regulatory law with teeth. The 1991 law was not perfect, however. It failed to require legislators to disclose sources of their outside income and also neglected to ban the use of campaign contributions for living expenses. A three-quarters majority is required on the Ethics Commission for some important actions, which handicaps its activities. Finally, although the members of the commission are appointed by the governor, lieutenant governor, speaker of the House, and chief justice of the Texas Supreme Court, those appointees must be chosen from a list of candidates furnished by the legislature.

After passage of the 1991 bill, Speaker Gib Lewis was quoted as saying that he doubted the new provisions would change life at the capitol very much.[14] Subsequent

With only a small amount of exaggeration, Ben Sargent satirizes the crucial role that campaign contributions from wealthy special-interest groups play in determining the actions of the Texas legislature.

SOURCE: Courtesy of Ben Sargent.

events seemed to prove him right. Information about who the lobbyists were, their client lists, and how much they earned from those clients was made available on the Ethics Commission Web site, but legislators still seemed to be unduly influenced by lobbyists. By 2003 pressure was building for a reform of the state's ethics laws. That legislature passed a new bill, which made a variety of changes. Among the amended ethics law's provisions are the following:[15]

1. Candidates for public office, whether they win or not, must disclose cash balances in their campaign accounts and report the employer and occupation of larger donors.
2. Legislators who are lawyers now have to disclose when they are being paid to attempt to delay trials during a legislative session, along with their referral fees. Also, they are forbidden to represent a paying client in front of a state agency.
3. Candidates must file campaign finance reports via the Internet unless they raise or spend fewer than $2,000 a year and do not use a computer to keep their records.
4. Local officials in cities of more than 100,000 in population and school districts with more than 5,000 students must file personal financial statements like those filed by other state officials.

Information is a useful resource in a democracy, and the 2003 Ethics Bill, because it ensures that more information will be available to the public, is a good thing. Furthermore, the provision that forbids legislator–attorneys to practice before state agencies is genuine reform that will make the outright buying of influence more difficult. Nevertheless, the new law does no more than previous "ethics" bills to dilute the impact of private influence on public affairs. As long as legislators' salaries remain below the poverty line, as long as private money dominates public elections, and as long as private information is used to make public policy, the prospects for effective control of lobbying are poor. The TRMPAC scandal illustrates the fact that politicians often devise creative ways to circumvent the laws that are supposed to keep their behavior within ethical boundaries. Without public determination to change the very basis of the political exchange of policy for money, wealth will continue to exercise exorbitant influence over Texas politics.

Persuading the Public

Although most interest-group energy is expended in lobbying government directly, some groups also attempt to influence state policy indirectly by "educating" the public. They buy television commercial time and sponsor independent citizens to write opinion essays on editorial pages of newspapers in order to argue their public policy case to Texans, who, they hope, will then put pressure on their representatives to support the groups' agendas.

The 2005 legislative sessions were good ones for observing the efforts of interest groups to persuade the public on behalf of their private causes. Especially noteworthy was a public-relations battle between phone giants SBC and Verizon Communications on one side and cable companies in alliance with Texas cities on another.[16]

Not so long ago, the telephone and television industries were separate entities. Telephones transmitted private conversations over lines owned by the phone company. Television sets received entertainment that had been broadcast over the airwaves via large transmitters owned by different corporations. Although both industries were partially regulated by government agencies—the Federal Communications Commission in Washington and the Public Utility Commission in Austin—in each case the industry was under the authority of a different set of laws.

With the advent of personal computers in the 1980s, however, the phone business and the television business began to melt into one telecommunications industry. By 2005 most consumers watched television programs that had not been broadcast but had arrived at their homes over coaxial cable, and the cable companies were planning to begin offering telephone services. At the same time, telephone companies, having already merged with computer companies, were planning to get into the video industry, offering phone service and television over the Internet. All these plans, however, were often impeded by communications laws that had been written during a previous era, and all of them brought the two previously distinct industries into conflict.

During the regular and special 2005 legislative sessions two phone titans, SBC and Verizon Communications, attempted to persuade politicians to write a new set of regulations that would help them get into video and thereby compete with cable companies. The law ordered a cable company to negotiate franchise agreements with each city it served. The cities, for their part, exacted concessions from the cable companies, requiring them to carry a variety of public-access channels and pay a fee to the city each year. Since the cable companies enjoyed a virtual monopoly in the provision of clear video programming, they could charge high prices for their services. The arrangement was a win-win situation for both the companies and the municipal governments. Verizon and SBC asked the legislature to exempt their Internet video services from the requirement that they negotiate separate deals with each city. These phone companies lobbied legislators to pass a law allowing them to apply for a single statewide franchise that would enable them to pick and choose the cities, or neighborhoods within cities, where they would offer their new services.

The cable companies cried foul and launched their own lobbying effort in alliance with the Texas Municipal League (whose member cities stood to miss out on a fortune in franchise fees if cable lost this battle) to defeat the phone company bill. The two contending coalitions also conducted a sustained public-relations campaign, each side trying to convince members of the public that their version of telecommunications policy was in the public interest. At first, cable companies attempted to bar the telephone companies' ads attacking them, but soon gave up that fight. The public was treated to an ill-tempered video brawl, with ads accusing the other side of being selfish, mean-spirited, and untruthful, and extolling their own side as being paladins of consumer interests. Meanwhile, various observers and spokespeople wrote op-ed pieces for the newspapers, arguing with their version of relevant arguments and evidence that one choice or the other should be the pick of good citizens in Texas. For a technical issue involving difficult questions of technology, economics, and law, it was a remarkably loud and unavoidable controversy on the state's television screens.

Cable and the cities prevailed in the regular session of the legislature, but in the second special session, the tide turned. Mired in indecision over school finance, legislators managed to pass a telecom bill that handed SBC and Verizon total victory. It is impossible to say whether this outcome was significantly affected by public opinion, was the result of lobbying, or illustrates the triumph of an idea whose time had come.

On September 7, Governor Perry signed the bill into law. That was not the end of the telecom saga, however. The next day, cable firms filed suit in federal court, asking that the state law be tossed out. Not deterred, in October SBC filed an application for a statewide video franchise with the Public Utilities Commission. In January 2006 the cable industry filed another suit in state court attempting to forbid the Public Utility Commission to implement the law. As this book goes to press, the situation is unresolved.

From the standpoint of democratic theory, the efforts of wealthy special interests to create public support through such media campaigns have both reassuring and troubling aspects. On the one hand, by expending their resources on propaganda aimed at ordinary citizens, interest groups greatly expand the amount of information available to the public. In 2005 millions of people were exposed to arguments and information about telecommunication policy through ads and opinion essays who would otherwise have been ignorant that such fights were brewing in the legislature. Because an informed citizenry is a democratically competent citizenry, such campaigns are worthy additions to public debate. On the other hand, the arguments presented in the campaigns completely reflect private, one-sided viewpoints. Whereas the two sides in the telecom debates could choose to speak their positions on television, no one could afford to buy television time to speak for the general public interest. On balance, such campaigns probably do more good than harm, but it is a close call.

Influencing Administrators and Co-Opting Agencies

The executive branch of government is also an interest-group target. In order to implement many of its laws, especially those of a regulatory nature, any legislature often creates administrative agencies or bureaus as part of the executive branch of government (see Chapter 7). In seeking to carry out their administrative function, members of these agencies must interpret laws. Interest groups attempt to influence the interpretation of laws that apply to themselves.

The subject here is the regulatory agencies created to ensure that a particular industry provides honest services at fair prices. Unfortunately, the usual history of these agencies is that, over time, they lose their independent role and become dominated by the interest they were created to control. This transition from guardian of the public interest to defenders of private interests, which has been well documented at the federal level, is called **co-optation**. Co-optation has several causes. First, regulators tend to come from the industry being regulated, and therefore share its values and point of view. Second, it is almost impossible for even the best-intentioned regulators to remain independent from the interest to be regulated because they come to have cordial personal relationships with the people in the industry. Third, while a serious problem may cause an initial public outcry demanding regulation of a private interest—railroads, meat packers, and insurance companies, for instance—once regulatory legislation is passed, the public tends to lose interest and the spotlight of publicity moves elsewhere. From that point on, only the regulated industry is intensely interested in the activities of the government agency. Regulators find that representatives of the industry are constantly in front of them in person, bringing information, self-serving arguments, and the force of personality, while there is no one to speak up for the public.

This co-optation of government regulators in Texas is well illustrated by the history of the state's relationship with the insurance industry. Insurance is a mammoth business that produces more than $3.5 trillion per year in revenue nationwide. Within Texas, the more than 2,200 insurance companies employed 222 lobbying entities during the late 1990s.[17]

The state began to regulate the industry in the late 1800s in order to protect consumers from unscrupulous practices. By the 1980s, however, the board was notorious among consumer representatives for always taking the side of the insurance industry in any dispute with customers. In 1991 the Travis County grand jury issued a report of its investigation into the insurance industry and the board. The grand jury reported that it was "shocked by the size of the problem, frightened by what it portends for our future economic health, and outraged by the ineffective regulation of the state board of insurance. . . The potential exists for a . . . disaster in the insurance industry. . . . We see embezzlement and self-dealing by insurance company insiders and regulators who are asleep at the switch." The report went on to say that "fraud in the insurance industry is widespread and deep and it is covered by falsified documents filed with the state board of insurance."[18]

Partly because of this report, by 1993 the board's practices were so notorious that it had become a political issue. That year the legislature abolished the three-member board, giving its former powers to a single commissioner, transferred some of its power to other state agencies, and renamed the agency the Texas Department of Insurance. Politicians and citizens hoped that because the new commissioner would have clear responsibility for promulgating and enforcing rules, he or she would be more easily held accountable to the public.

The fact that there was one, as opposed to three, people responsible for regulating the insurance industry in the public interest, however, did not change the fact that a wealthy special interest still had all the tools necessary to imprint its private desires upon public affairs. The new institutional structure did nothing to reduce the resources the industry could pour into lobbying; nor did it alter the 16 percent of state legislators with personal financial ties to the industry.[19] Robert Hunter, appointed by Governor Ann Richards as the first insurance commissioner, later reported that when he took the job he had known that the influence of the industry was large. "But until I went and became an insurance commissioner I had no clue as to how big." According to Hunter, several members of the legislature, at least one of whom was an insurance agent, harassed him on a regular basis, demanding that he fire certain employees whose actions had displeased them and threatened to cut his budget if he resisted their direction. Hunter ignored their demands, but he lasted only a year in his job, resigning after Richards' defeat in 1994.[20]

By 2002 the actions of the insurance industry had again made it a political issue.[21] Homeowner premiums had been skyrocketing, and many people had lost their coverage. Moreover, one huge company, Farmers Insurance, was discovered to have engaged in some creative accounting in regard to the documents it filed with the Texas Insurance Commission. While claiming to the state that it had to raise premiums because it was losing money, Farmers submitted other documents to the federal Securities and Exchange Commission asserting that it was extremely profitable.[22]

With citizens in an uproar over their insurance rates, the state's politicians responded. In August 2002, Attorney General John Cornyn filed suit against Farmers, alleging violations of the Texas Insurance Code and the law against deceptive trade practices. Governor Perry participated in the press conference at which Cornyn announced the suit. Shortly thereafter, insurance commissioner Jose Montemayor ordered Farmers to stop a variety of its business practices, although he pulled his punch considerably by giving the company a 90-day grace period, during which it could continue its behavior undisturbed.[23]

The reaction of the insurance industry to this political onslaught was not surprising to people familiar with Texas politics. In anticipation of the attorney general's lawsuit and trouble with the legislature during the 2003 session, in July 2002 five of the state's biggest insurers (excluding Farmers) joined forces to found the Texas Coalition for Affordable Insurance Solutions, an association devoted to applying more influence to the political system. The association quickly hired Public Strategies, Inc., a top Austin public relations and lobbying firm, to represent its interests.[24]

In 2003 the legislature passed insurance-reform bills that required companies to disclose more information and gave the state insurance commissioner the authority to review homeowners' premiums and order reductions where warranted. Supporters of these bills believed that they were fair to both business and consumers. Opponents argued that they did nothing to ensure meaningful rate regulation.[25]

As of 2005, the full import of the various changes in the insurance and tort laws were not easy to evaluate. On the one hand, in April of that year two of the state's largest malpractice insurers announced their intention to cut the rates doctors have to pay for such insurance. On the other hand, during the same month two public-interest groups announced that according to a study they had just completed, home-owners and drivers had been forced to over-pay by $4 billion in 2004.[26]

Whether the insurance reform surge of 2002 and 2003 will have meaningful consequences cannot be confidently predicted. Nevertheless, the episode underscores the point that the history of insurance and politics in Texas is one of cycles. For long periods, companies are successful in co-opting government regulation, and in the regulatory vacuum they induce, they are free to get away with almost anything. After enough abuses accumulate, the public becomes enraged and demands action. At that point there is a spasm of political activity that may, for a time, rein in the behavior of the companies. After the short period of reform, however, the public's attention shifts to other outrages, and the quiet, relentless power of money reasserts itself. In a sense, the relationship of the insurance industry and the political system is a template for the Texas interest-group system as a whole.

Using the Courts

Like the legislative and executive branches, the judicial branch of government also makes policy by interpreting and applying laws. For this reason, interest groups are active in the judicial arena of politics. Groups representing important economic interests make substantial campaign contributions during judicial campaigns, hire lawyers to influence judges with legal arguments, and file suits. Money talks in courtrooms as well as in legislatures and the executive branch.

Nevertheless, the court system can also be an avenue of success for underdog interest groups that have been unsuccessful in pressing their cases either in electoral politics or by lobbying the other two branches of government. An outstanding example is the National Association for the Advancement of Colored People (NAACP). Not only has this organization successfully argued such historically important national cases as *Brown v. Board of Education* (347 U.S. 483, 1954), in which segregated schools were declared unconstitutional, but it has also won vital victories at the state level. In *Nixon v. Herndon* (273 U.S. 536, 1927), the U.S. Supreme Court held that a Texas law excluding African Americans from the Democratic primary was unconstitutional. The Texas legislature attempted to nullify this decision by writing a new law authorizing party leaders to make rulings to the same effect, but this was struck down in *Nixon v. Condon* (286 U.S. 73, 1932). Later, in *Smith v. Allwright* (321 U.S. 649, 1944), the Texas NAACP struck another blow for equal citizenship when the Court held that racial segregation in party primaries on any basis whatsoever is unconstitutional.

In recent decades, with the battle to permit African Americans to vote having been won, the NAACP has tended to de-emphasize civil rights suits and concentrate more on bread-and-butter political issues such as jobs, health insurance, and affirmative action. Nevertheless, the lesson of the organization's early years should not be forgotten: Although dominant interest groups may win most of the time, even the most down-trodden interests can sometimes prevail if they organize and know how to use the court system.

MAJOR INTEREST GROUPS IN TEXAS

Interest groups want publicity for their programs and goals, but they tend to hide their operations. Political scientists have not done extensive research on interest groups in Texas, and even under the best of circumstances the activities of such groups and the precise nature of their influence are difficult to discover. Nevertheless, what follows is an attempt to discuss a few of the dozens of major interest groups in the state. One recent pattern that is clear is that the groups associated with the governing Republicans, such as business and conservative Christians, are much more influential in state policy making than groups associated with the prostrate Democrats, such as organized labor and minority ethnic groups.

The Oil and Gas Industries

As befits their historical status as in the economy of Texas, the oil and gas industries have a close working relationship with state government. In the late 1990s, the industries employed 243 lobbying entities in Austin. Nearly one-third of the legislators had personal financial ties to petroleum.[27] Principal among the organizations that represent petroleum producers are the Texas Oil and Gas Association (TOGA), which represents the industry as a whole but is dominated by the major companies, and the Texas Independent Producers and Royalty Owners (TIPRO), which represents the smaller producers and royalty owners. These groups keep track of the voting of members of the legislature, contribute generously to the campaigns of representatives who are friendly to their interests, and are tireless in providing information to the legislative staff on conditions within the industry. Since oil and gas production is widely distributed within the state, its interest groups have a great deal of influence over a large majority of legislators, whether they are liberal or conservative on other issues.

This influence was demonstrated in the 1999 legislative session. Reacting to a depression in the business caused by a slump in worldwide oil prices, lawmakers passed a law giving small producers a $45 million tax break. Critics pointed out that world copper prices were also depressed, but the legislature did not offer tax relief to the small copper industry in the El Paso area. Copper simply does not have the organizational or financial clout of petroleum in Texas.[28]

By 2005 world demand had sent oil prices above $60 a barrel and gasoline to $3 a gallon. As a result, the Texas oil industry was booming and not in need of special tax breaks from the state legislature. Furthermore, Texas no longer dominated the world of petroleum, and petroleum no longer dominated Texas as it once had. The industry's share of the state's gross domestic product had been falling for decades, as had its share of total employment. Nevertheless, the industry still represented billions of dollars of income and thousands of jobs within Texas. Therefore, although oil and gas were no longer the pre-eminent industries in Texas, TOGA, TIPRO, and their allies continued to be powerful groups in state government. They will continue to be important for many years to come.

Organized Labor

Many Texans think of organized labor as a powerful interest group that has great influence on state policy, but there is little evidence to support this assumption. Historically, the primary explanation for this lack of power is cultural. As discussed in Chapter 1, the conservative political culture that has dominated most of the southern states is antagonistic to labor unions. Texas is no exception, and the public policies the state has produced over the decades have ensured that it would have relatively weak unions. In 2000 only about 505,000, or 5.8 percent of the state's 8.7 million workers, were union members. This figure compared with a national average of 13.5 percent, according to the U.S. Bureau of Labor Statistics.[29] Texas ranked forty-sixth among the states in percentage of its workforce that was unionized (New York had the highest percentage of organized workers).[30]

The Republican takeover of all of Texas's statewide offices in the election of 1994 made the plight of organized labor even worse. The union movement always had a prickly and ambivalent relationship with the conservative Democrats who used to run Texas, but its relationship with Republicans has been, and is, unambivalently hostile. The Republican Party is anti-labor, and labor is anti-Republican. With Republican dominance of the state, the union movement declined into almost total political irrelevance after 1994.

When the Democratic Party attempted to revive its fortunes in 2002, labor moved to assist it. Democratic candidates for important offices addressed the Committee on Political Education of the state American Federation of Labor–Congress of Industrial Organizations (AFL-CIO) at its convention in January, hoping for the organization's endorsement. No Republicans asked to be heard. During the campaign of that year, the AFL-CIO attempted to organize volunteer campaign workers for Democratic candidates and contributed some money. With the party's resounding defeat in 2002, however, labor resumed its wandering in the political wilderness.

Meanwhile, at the national level a group of dissident unions were growing discontented with what they considered to be labor's timidity. In 2005, five large unions withdrew from labor's national umbrella organization, the AFL-CIO, and announced their intention to pursue more militant campaigns to organize unorganized workers, especially in the South. As its first project, the Service Employees International Union chose to try to persuade 8,000 Houston janitors working for ABM, the nation's largest cleaning contractor, to join its membership.[31] As this book goes to press, the outcome of the struggle is unknown. What is known, however, is that the Service Employees will get no help from the Texas state government in their campaign.

The Christian Right

In the late 1970s, a number of national organizations arose calling for a return to "Christian values," as they defined them, in American government and in society. The groups' purposes were to inform religious, politically conservative voters of a candidate's issue positions and to persuade them to participate more actively in local politics. By the 1990s, they were a formidable presence in virtually every level of American politics. These groups have been especially important in the South and thus are well represented in Texas. Together, the conservative religious interest groups are known as the Christian Right.

Although all Christian Right groups do not place the same emphasis on individual issues, they share a cluster of positions on the substance of government. During the 1990s, Kirk Ingels, Austin coordinator of the Christian Coalition, summarized the movement's concerns by saying that "the primary focus" of his group "is to affect public policy so it reflects biblical truth."[32] Members interpret the Bible to be anti-abortion, anti-gay marriage, anti-gun control, anti-taxes, and in favor of constitutional amendments that would mandate a balanced federal budget and permit organized prayers in public schools.

In the 1990s and early 2000s, the groups composing the Christian Right had a profound impact on Texas politics and society. One of the forums in which they are very active is in the arena of local schools. Elections to fill positions on the governing boards of Texas's school districts generally draw fewer than 10 percent of the eligible voters to the polls. A focused, coordinated group can easily elect its favored members. Using their own organization and discipline, Christian Right groups have elected majorities to many of the state's 1,042 school districts. They have also maintained a significant presence, although not a majority, on the state Board of Education.

The most dramatic flexing of the Christian Right's muscles occurred at the state Republican Party conventions of 1994 through 2004. Delegates effectively took over the machinery of the party, writing Christian Right platforms and electing Christian Right party chairs (see Chapter 4).

Texas Republican politicians often make statements that advertise their conservative Christian commitments. The most famous example is probably former Governor, and now President, George W. Bush, who, queried about his favorite political philosopher during the 2000 presidential campaign, answered "Jesus Christ." In a similar vein, Tom DeLay told an interviewer in 1999 that the choices facing American citizens amount to "Will this country accept the world view of humanism, materialism, sexism, naturalism, postmodernism, or any of the other 'isms?' Or will we march forward with a biblical world view, a world view that says God is our creator, that man is a sinner, and that we will save the country by changing the hearts and minds of Americans?"[33] In 2005 Governor Perry signed a law to bar minors from getting an abortion without their parents' consent in front of an audience of "pro-family Christian friends" at Calvary Christian Academy, thus publicizing his allegiance to the conservative Christian agenda.[34]

Despite the domination of Texas by Republicans and the domination of the party by Christian Right perspectives, by 2005 voices were being raised to criticize the alliance and warn of disagreeable consequences if it goes too far. Through the 1990s the Texas Freedom Network tirelessly pointed out that Christian teachings can be, and often have been, interpreted so as to endorse liberal rather than conservative social policy. In the 2000s TFN was joined by Call to Renewal, a national federation of churches and faith-based organizations working to encourage legislatures to adopt more liberal policies toward the poor. One of the founders of Call to Renewal, Jim Wallis, travels the country urging liberal Christians to "take back the faith."[35]

Moreover, some of the policy positions of conservative Christians threaten to damage the state's economy if enacted. When, in 2005, the legislature considered a bill that would have banned research into the medical value of stem-cell research—a cause dear to the hearts of conservative Christians—scientists and scholars warned that such a policy would cause an exodus of scientists and research money from the state.[36]

Even more potentially damaging was the Christian Right's crusade to eliminate the teaching of Darwin's theory of evolution from biology classes and substitute the teaching of "Intelligent Design." Theories of the structure and behavior of living creatures, including humans, that derive from Darwin's original 1859 theory of "natural selection" are endorsed by the overwhelming majority of the world's scientists. Intelligent Design is a variation on the fundamentalist Christian theory of creationism, found in the first chapter of Genesis in the Old Testament, deceptively labeled a scientific theory.[37] Adoption of the Christian Right program on this issue would, in effect, deprive the state's students of their scientific education, thereby crippling the Texas economy in the future. Various studies, including those of Governor Perry's biotech council, have pointed out that Texas lacks much of the human capital—that is, educated people—that it will need to prosper in a scientifically oriented world economy.[38] Yet the state's Republican establishment seems to be encouraging the sort of scientific know-nothingism that is certain to worsen the situation. The 2006 state Republican platform recommended that Intelligent Design be taught as a viable alternative to Darwinism in the public schools, for example.

Thus, the strength of one wing of the Republican coalition—Christian social conservatives—may now be such that it is menacing the interests of the other wing business. Texas Republicans may be approaching a time when the interest-group conflict within their own ranks rivals their conflict with Democrats.

League of United Latin American Citizens (LULAC)

The most venerable of the Hispanic organizations, the League of United Latin American Citizens (LULAC) was formed in Corpus Christi in 1929.[39] Its founding members were very concerned about discrimination against Mexican Americans, especially in public education. In its first three decades, LULAC pursued the goal of equal education as both a private charitable organization and a public crusader. Privately, LULAC formed local self-help organizations to advance Latino education. Its "Little School of the 400" program of the 1950s, for example, which taught Spanish-speaking preschoolers the 400 English words they needed to know in order to survive in first grade in public schools, was so successful that it inspired the national program Head Start. Publicly, the organization persuaded the U.S. Supreme Court to forbid Texas to segregate Mexican Americans in public schools in 1948. Branching out to other issues, in 1953 LULAC won another suit against Texas's practice of excluding Mexican Americans from juries. Then in 1959 it persuaded the state legislature to sponsor its program to teach Latino preschoolers English. Soon the Texas Education Agency was paying up to 80 percent of the program's funding. LULAC may have represented a struggling minority, but it had become part of the state's political establishment; it was a success.

Into the 1970s, LULAC continued to be the standard bearer for Mexican American aspirations for full citizenship in the United States in general and Texas in particular. But in that decade it began to falter. As an organization dispensing millions of dollars in foundation grants, it attracted members who were more interested in advancing themselves than in advancing their ethnic group. Beginning in the mid-1970s, LULAC was rocked by a series of financial scandals. The worst of them occurred in 1994, when the president, José Velez, together with three Taiwanese gangsters, was indicted by a federal grand jury on charges of collecting millions of dollars in a scheme to smuggle Asians and Hispanics into the United States illegally. Not only was the organization troubled by scandal during the 1990s, but it was also racked by internal power struggles. Individuals and various Latino groups fought one another—Mexican Americans versus Puerto Ricans, for example—so that the organization no longer seemed to be a league of *united* Latin American citizens.[40]

The cumulative effect of LULAC's troubles devastated its prestige and membership. Once capable of mobilizing a quarter of a million citizens nationally, by the late 1990s the organization could count on no more than 50,000 active members. At its 1999 national convention in Corpus Christi, there were few people in the audience for its workshops and fewer corporate sponsors. Whereas in 1987 eight national presidential candidates had addressed its delegates, not one showed up in 1999.[41] Younger, better-run organizations such as La Raza and the Mexican American Legal Defense Fund (MALDEF—created by LULAC itself in 1968) seemed to be on the verge of taking over the mantle of this most-respected Hispanic organization.

But LULAC is on its way back. Several honest and competent presidents have put its finances in order, then expanded and reorganized its staff. Just as important, LULAC's leadership has forged a political alliance with the most respected African American organization, the NAACP. In 2002, LULAC's president, Hector Flores, addressed the NAACP's national convention, and Gary Bledsoe, the NAACP's Texas president, addressed the state LULAC convention. The two organizations then hammered out a formal agreement to work together on common issues and goals.[42]

Since 2002 the cooperation between the two groups has not always been smooth. But, aware of their common experience as "communities under siege," in Bledsoe's words, the leadership of the two organizations has worked successfully to suppress the potential conflict between two proud, old organizations that represent two different ethnic constituencies.[43]

The path of the future for LULAC may lie in an expansion of its purposes from advocacy of the interests of Mexican Americans in particular to advocacy of liberal causes in general. There is a danger in this strategy because liberalism has been distinctly unsuccessful in Texas elections for more than a decade. Nevertheless, with an eye to the demographic changes discussed in Chapter 1, LULAC and NAACP leaders are preparing for the day when historical minorities become majorities at the ballot box. Whatever the eventual success of this strategy, LULAC seems to have regained its vigor.

CONCLUSION

Political interest groups present a dilemma to partisans of democratic government. By providing people a channel of input to government other than just their one vote, such groups broaden and intensify citizen participation and are therefore good for democracy. However, by creating a means by which some people are much more influential than others, they often allow private perspectives to dominate public policy-making. This situation is bad for democracy. In Texas, where interest groups are very powerful, the dilemma is acute.

SUMMARY

Interest groups are influential in American and Texas politics because they provide two indispensable resources, money and information. Groups are active in every phase of politics: They engage in electioneering, lobby government officials, co-opt agencies, litigate in the courts, and attempt to persuade the public to support their point of view. Organized groups are frequently effective; unorganized groups generally are not. Private interests thus often dominate public policy.

Although many efforts have been made to regulate lobbying, the results so far have not been encouraging. The Texas political system provides a nearly ideal setting for maximizing interest-group influence. The most powerful groups tend to be those that represent major economic interests. This effect is consistent with the dominant role of the conservative political culture in Texas.

Interest groups are good for democracy in that they enhance debate about public policy and encourage citizens to participate in politics. But they also damage democratic government by substituting private influence for public deliberation in the creation of government policy. In Texas, where interest groups are very powerful, the negative qualities of the interest-group system dominate.

STUDY QUESTIONS

1. What do we mean by the terms *interest group, lobby,* and *lobbyist?* Are interest groups and lobbies the same thing? If you write a letter to your legislator, are you lobbying?
2. What functions do interest groups perform in a democratic society? How do they perform them?
3. What interests tend to be organized? What is the difference in political influence between organized and unorganized groups?
4. How can an interest group attempt to influence public opinion? From the perspective of democratic theory, what is good and what is bad about such efforts?
5. If you were given the job of writing a new state ethics bill that would lessen the impact of private influence over public policy, what would your bill say? Remember that the First Amendment to the U.S. Constitution forbids government to interfere with citizens' rights to freedom of expression and assembly.

SURFING THE WEB

Readers are urged to visit the companion site for this book:

    http://www.thomsonedu.com/politicalscience/kraemer

A great deal of information on lobbyists, their clients, and the amount of money they earn is available on the Web site of the Texas Ethics Commission:

    http://www.ethics.state.tx.us/

The recent activities of the National Association for the Advancement of Colored People (NAACP) are discussed under several headings at its Web site. The court cases mentioned in this chapter, as well as its more recent judicial efforts, can be accessed by clicking the "History" icon.
http://www.texasnaacp.org/

To access other organizations discussed in this chapter:

Texas Independent Producers and Royalty Owners Association
http://www.tipro.org/

Texas Oil and Gas Association
http://www.txoga.org

Texas AFL-CIO
http://www.texasaflcio.org/

Service Employees International Union
http://www.seiu.org/

Texas Christian Coalition
http://www.texascc.org/

Texas Freedom Network
http://www.tfn.org/

Call to Renewal
www.calltorenewal.org/

LULAC
http://www.lulac.org/

Public Citizen Texas
http://www.citizen.org/

NOTES

1. Mary Flood, "Doctors' Orders: Medical Lobby Becomes a Powerhouse in Austin," *Wall Street Journal*, May 1,1999, T1.

2. Dave McNeely, "Doctors Association Riled Up over Business Group's Questionnaire," *Austin American-Statesman*, February 6, 2002, B3; "Survey Suggests More Doctors Prefer Perry," *Austin American-Statesman*, May 14, 2002, B3; Gary Susswein, "Perry's Veto Still a Bitter Pill for Doctors," *Austin American-Statesman*, July 20, 2001, A1; Pete Slover, "Political Checks . . . and Balances," *Dallas Morning News*, January 16, 2003, A1; David Pasztor, "House Gives First Approval to Doctor Discipline," *Austin American-Statesman*, March 19, 2003, B3.

3. Bruce Hight, "Doctors Seek New Remedy to Fight Frivolous Lawsuits Filed by Patients," *Austin American-Statesman*, February 9, 2001, B5.

4. Paul Burka, "No! No! No!" *Texas Monthly*, August 2001, 7; Susswein, "Veto," op. cit.

5. David Pasztor, "Doctors' Lobbying Stirs Concern," *Austin American-Statesman*, September 2, 2003, B1; Texans for Public Justice, "Prop. 12 Proponents Gave $5.3 Million to Perry, Dewhurst, and Lawmakers in 2002," press release, August 29, 2003, 2.

6. R. G. Ratcliffe, "Perry Signs Prompt Pay Legislation," *Houston Chronicle*, June 18, 2003, A17.

7. "Political Intelligence—Conflicted at the Top," *Texas Observer*, April 1, 2005, 4.

8. Paul Burka, "Is the Legislature for Sale?" *Texas Monthly*, February 1991, 118.

9. Information on the TRMPAC scandal comes from the following sources: Andrew Wheat, "Taylor-Made Election Law," *Texas Observer*, March 18, 2005, 13; Jake Bernstein, "TRMPAC in its Own Words," *Texas Observer*, April 1, 2005, 6; Laylin Copelin, "Eight Corporations Added to 2002 Campaign Lawsuit," *Austin American-Statesman*, August 19, 2005, A5; Philip Shenon and Carl Hulse, "DeLay Is Indicted in Texas Case and Forfeits G.O.P. House Post," *New York Times*, September 29, 2005, A1; Anne E. Kornblut, "How a Tested Campaign Tool Led to Conspiracy Charge," *New York Times*, September 29, 2005, A3; Molly Ivins, "DeLay's Pattern: Taking It All a Step Too Far," *Austin American-Statesman*, October 1, 2005, A15; Laylin Copelin, "DeLay Indicted on 2 New Counts," *Austin American-Statesman*, October 4, 2005, A1.

10. Molly Ivins, "DeLay's Pattern: Taking It All a Step Too Far," *Austin American-Statesman*, October 1, 2005, A15.

11. Information about Public Citizen Texas comes from its Web site, listed at the end of this chapter, especially two press releases, "Public Citizen Celebrates 20 Years In Texas" from October 5, 2004, and "Public Citizen Applauds Yzaguirre's Decision to Resign" from January 17, 2002.

12. Smith quoted in Katherine Goodloe, "Capitol Ideas," *Dallas Morning News*, April 10, 2005, E1.

13. James A. Garcia, "Lobbying Group Subsidiary Will Gather Insurance Data," *Austin American-Statesman*, August 27, 1996, B1; information updated by authors on June 3, 2003.

14. Gib Lewis quoted in Laylan Copelin, "New Ethics Bill Sneaks Up on Lawmakers," *Austin American-Statesman*, May 28, 1991, B1.

15. Laylan Copelin, "Ethics Legislation Passes in Overtime," *Austin American-Statesman*, June 2, 2003, B1.

16. Articles in the *Austin American-Statesman* are the source for this discussion of the telecom conflict: "Cable Industry Sues Again over Law," January 28, 2006, F2; Claudia Grisales, "SBC Asks to Provide TV to San Antonio," October 11, 2005, D1; "Cable Firms Sue to Stop Telecom Law," September 9, 2005, C1; "Perry Approves Changes to Telecom Laws," September 8, 2005, C2; Bruce Mehlman and Larry Irving, "On Telecom, Texas Is Set to Bring on Competition," August 31, 2005, A13; Tim Morstad and Gus Cardenas, "Texas Needs to Stand Up to Big Phone Companies," August 18, 2005, A13; Claudia Grisales, "Phone Lobby Spent Big to Outmaneuver Cable Rivals," August 18, 2005, A1; Claudia Grisales, "Phone Companies Gain TV Win," July 18, 2005, B1; Phil King, "On Telecom, Legislature Lost a Chance to Help Consumers," June 30, 2005, A13; Jaime Martinez, "Bill Would Only Widen Digital Divide in Texas," May 17, 2005, A13; Claudia Grisales, "Legislative Battle over Television Looms," May 7, 2005, A1; Claudia Grisales, "Ad War Erupts in Fight over Telecom Reform," April 28, 2005, D1; Gary Chapman, "To Ensure Texas' Future, We Must Rewrite the Rules on Telecom," March 5, 2005, A15.

17. Diane Renzulli and the Center for Public Integrity, *Capitol Offenders: How Private Interests Govern Our States* (Washington, DC: Public Integrity Books, 2002), 95, 100.

18. Elyse Gilmore Yates, "Insure Integrity in the Insurance Industry," *Texas Observer*, February 8, 1991, 11.

19. Renzulli, *Capitol Offenders*, op. cit., 105.

20. Ibid., 97.

21. Bruce, Hight, "Runaway Rates Have Consumers Seeing Red," *Austin American-Statesman*, September 1, 2002, H2; Shonda Novak, "Consumer Groups Call for Regulation of Home Insurers," *Austin American-Statesman*, September 7, 2002, G1.

22. Carlos Guerra, "Insurance Money Trail," *Austin American-Statesman*, August 7, 2002, A11.

23. Ibid.; Shonda Novak, "Insurers Ordered to Retool Pricing," *Austin American-Statesman*, August 14, 2002, A1.

24. Claudia Grisales, "Insurers Join Forces to Lobby Lawmakers," *Austin American-Statesman*, July 27, 2002, A1.

25. Michele Kay, "Insurance Bill Heads to Perry," *Austin American-Statesman*, February 18, 2003, B1; Michele Kay, "Panel OKs Bill to Treat Auto, Homeowners Insurance Alike," *Austin American-Statesman*, March 21, 2003; Christy Hoppe, "Business Lobby Flexes Muscle in Legislature," *Dallas Morning News*, April 14, 2003, A3.

26. Stephen Scheibal, "Malpractice Insurers to Cut Rates," *Austin American-Statesman*, February 17, 2005, B1; Nathalie Gott, "Groups: Consumers Overpaid $4 Billion for Insurance in '04," *Austin American-Statesman*, April 1, 2005, C2.

27. Renzulli, *Capitol Offenders*, op. cit., 124, 115.

28. Molly Ivins, "Compassion Eases the Pain for Oil Bidness," *Austin American-Statesman*, February 20, 1999, A11.

29. Bruce Hight, "Faced with Loss of Legislative Clout, Labor Focuses on State's Top Races," *Austin American-Statesman*, January 14, 2002, A1.

30. www.census.gov/Press_Release/state12.pm.

31. Steven Greenhouse, "Splintered, But Unbowed," *New York Times*, July 30, 2005, B1.

32. Ingels quoted in Chuck Lindell, "Pulpit to Politics Movement Gathers Steam," *Austin American-Statesman*, March 6, 1994, A1.

33. Jim Lobe, "Another Toxic Texan Rises to the Top," Inter Press Service news release, November 16, 2002, 2.

34. W. Gardner Selby, "Abortion Measure Signing to Get Crowd," *Austin American-Statesman*, June 5, 2005, B1; Wayne Slater, "Perry Accused of Playing Politics with Bill-Signing Set at Church," *Dallas Morning News*, June 3, 2005, A1.

35. Wallis quoted in "Political Intelligence—For the Love of God," *Texas Observer*, October 7, 2005, 4.

36. Bill Bishop, "When Policy Defines Identity," *Austin American-Statesman*, May 22, 2005, A1.

37. Michael Ennis, "Dissing Darwin," *Texas Monthly*, April 2005, 64; Robert T. Pennock, ed., *Intelligent Design Creationism and Its Critics: Philosophical, Theological, and Scientific Perspectives*, (Cambridge: MIT Press, 2001); Barbara Forrest and Paul R. Gross, *Creationism's Trojan Horse: The Wedge of Intelligent Design* (Oxford, England: Oxford University Press, 2004).

38. Ennis, "Dissing Darwin," op. cit., 65.

39. This account of the early history of LULAC relies upon Benjamin Marquez, *LULAC: The Evolution of a Mexican-American Political Organization* (Austin: University of Texas, 1993), passim.

40. Lori Rodriguez, "LULAC Turning Puerto Rican," *Houston Chronicle*, July 9, 1994, A25.

41. James E. Garcia, "Latino Politics: Up to LULAC to Reform or Be Left Behind," *Houston Chronicle*, September 25, 1999, OUTLOOK, 1.

42. Lori Rodriguez, "LULAC Leader's Speech at Convention First Ever," *Houston Chronicle*, July 11, 2002, A1; Lori Rodriguez, "LULAC Role Evolves, But Equity Still Focus," *Houston Chronicle*, July 23, 2002, A1; Lori Rodriguez, "Minority Groups 'Fighting as One,'" *Houston Chronicle*, March 1, 2005, B1.

43. Rodriguez, "Fighting as One," op. cit., 1.

4

POLITICAL PARTIES

The political parties created democracy and . . . modern democracy is unthinkable save in terms of the parties. . . . The parties are not therefore merely appendages of modern government; they are in the center of it and play a determinative and creative role in it.

E. E. Schattschneider
Party Government, 1942

A political party is an organization that takes money from the rich and votes from the poor under the pretext of protecting the one from the other.

Anonymous

INTRODUCTION

Both Schattschneider's favorable assessment of **political parties** and the anonymous cynical disparagement of their value are partly true. Parties are the only organizations capable of holding together many fractious interests so that governing is possible. At the same time, in Texas and elsewhere, parties frequently serve democracy badly.

This chapter opens with discussions of ideology and interests, the two bases for much party conflict. It proceeds to a brief history of the state's political parties, a consideration of the major functions of parties, and an outline of party organization in Texas. It then analyzes the "three-faction" system that often makes the state's two-party system confusing and finally gives some attention to the state's occasional third-party efforts. As the discussion proceeds, it will contrast the reality of Texas's party politics with the democratic ideal.

IDEOLOGY: ONE BASIS FOR PARTY CONFLICT

In Texas, as in the other states, party rivalry is often based on differences in ideology. An **ideology** is a system of beliefs and values about the nature of the good life in the good society, about the relationship of government and the economy, about moral values and the way they should be achieved, and about how government is to conduct itself. The two dominant, and contesting, systems of beliefs and values in American and Texan life today are usually referred to as liberalism and conservatism.

Conservatives

The basic principle underlying **conservatism,** at least in economic policy, is *laissez-faire.* Conservatives prefer to allow free markets, not government, to regulate the economy. As noted in Chapter 1, in practice conservative governments often pursue pseudo–*laissez-faire* policies in that they claim to cherish free markets but actually endorse policies that deeply involve government in helping businesses overcome problems in their markets. Nevertheless, at the level of ideology, and certainly at the level of their argument with liberals, conservatives believe that economies run best if governments leave them alone. When contemplating economic problems such as poverty, pollution, unemployment, and health care, conservatives argue that government has caused most of them with over-regulation and that the best way to deal with them is for government to stop meddling and allow the market to work. For example, local land developers do not want a city to tell them how high a sign should be or what kind of landscaping is required to hide ugly buildings or junk cars. Similarly, insurance companies do not want to be regulated by government agencies in terms of the way they treat consumers. Conservatism is consonant with Texas's dominant political culture, at least among Anglos.

Liberals

Liberalism is the contrary ideology. Liberals are suspicious of the workings of unregulated markets and place more faith in the ability of government to direct economic activity. When thinking about economic problems, they are apt to blame "market failure" and suggest government activity as the solution. In regard to local land-use policy, a liberal would want a city government to protect the environment and would work for sign ordinances and landscaping policies. In regard to the insurance industry, liberals favor government regulations to protect consumers from abuses. Also, liberals often want to redistribute wealth and power to help the less fortunate, whereas conservatives want to leave the distribution of wealth and power as it is.

All this is relatively clear. When dealing with issues of personal belief and behavior such as religion, sexual activity, and drug use, however, liberals and conservatives tend to switch sides. Conservatives are generally in favor of more government regulation; liberals are in favor of less. Liberals oppose government-sponsored prayer in school while conservatives favor it; liberals oppose laws regulating sexual behavior while conservatives endorse them, and so on.

Thus, American ideological disputes are confusing because liberals usually favor government activity in the economic sphere but oppose it in the personal sphere, while conservatives usually oppose government activity in the economic sphere but favor it in the personal sphere. This ideological split is the basis for a great deal of rhetorical argument and for intense struggles over public policy (Table 4.1).

As discussed in Chapter 1, Texas has historically been dominated by political conservatism. The distribution of opinions in the population in the present day suggests that this domination does not misrepresent the center of gravity of state public opinion. A survey conducted in 2004 reported that only 14 percent of Texas adults were willing to label themselves liberals, while 40 percent called themselves moderates, and 45 percent claimed the label "conservative." That last number was up seven percentage points in seven years.[1] The meaning of the simple self-reports is not completely clear because in calling themselves conservative, people might be referring to economic issues, social issues, foreign policy issues, or some combination of the three. Moreover, many years of national public opinion research show that a significant percentage of people will label themselves conservative in general but will endorse many specific liberal government programs. Still, the self-reported numbers are sufficiently dramatic to emphasize the weakness of the liberal ideological tradition in the Lone Star State.

INTERESTS: A SECOND BASIS FOR PARTY CONFLICT

An **interest** is something of value or some personal characteristic that people share and that is affected by government activity—their investments, their race, their jobs, and so on. When there is a question of public policy on which the two parties take different positions, people with conflicting interests often line up with the party that favors their interests, whether or not their political ideology is in line with that party's. Moreover, parties often take positions to attract the money and votes of citizens with clashing interests. Thus parties put together **coalitions** of interests in order to attract blocs of voters and campaign contributions. Party positions therefore are almost always much more ambiguous and confusing than they would be if they simply divided according to ideology.

TABLE 4.1

Policy Differences between Liberals and Conservatives

Issue	Conservative position	Liberal position
Economic Issues		
Taxation	As little as possible, and, when necessary, regressive taxes such as sales taxes*	More to cover government spending; progressive preferred*
Government spending	As little as possible, except for military and police	Acceptable to provide social services
Nature of government regulation	More in personal sphere; less in economic	Less in personal sphere; more in economic
Organized labor	Anti-union (because pro-business)	Pro-union (but not necessarily anti-business)
Environment	Favor development over environment	Favor environment over development
Social Issues		
Crime	Support more prisons and longer sentences; oppose gun control	Support social spending to attack root causes; favor gun control
Abortion	"Pro-life"	"Pro-choice"
Affirmative action	Oppose	Support
Government-sponsored prayer in public schools	Favor	Oppose
Foreign Policy Issues		
Human rights as large component of foreign policy	No	Yes
Free trade	More likely to favor	Less likely to favor
Military spending	More	Less
U.S. military intervention abroad	More likely to favor**	Less likely to favor**

*A progressive tax is one that increases proportionately with income or benefit derived, such as a progressive income tax. A regressive tax, such as the sales tax, places proportionately less burden on wealthy taxpayers and more burden on those with lower incomes because any given amount of the tax consumes a larger percentage of a person's income.

**In recent years positions on military intervention have seemed to depend entirely on party affiliation rather than ideology as measured by stances on other issues. For example, liberals tended to support the U.S./NATO bombing war against Serbia in 1999, while conservatives tended to oppose it; yet conservatives tended to support an American invasion of Iraq in 2003, while liberals tended to oppose it.

NOTE: Two words of caution are in order. First, this table presents an extremely brief summary of complex issues, and thus some distortion is inevitable. Second, it would be inaccurate to assume that every liberal agrees with every liberal position or that every conservative agrees with every conservative position. The table summarizes general tendencies only.

For example, Texan Republican Party candidates in recent years have tended to criticize the state's tort laws—the statutes that allow people who believe they have been injured by a business to sue for damages. Republicans have argued that the state makes it too easy to file "frivolous" lawsuits and allows juries to award damages to injured parties that are too large. They have supported "tort reform" by the state legislature. On the other hand, Democrats have tended to side with plaintiffs in lawsuits, arguing that wronged people should have easy access to the courts and should be entitled to large compensation for injuries. They have usually opposed tort reform.

As a result, the sorts of interests who tend to be the target of tort lawsuits, doctors and business owners, for example, have been inclined to contribute money to Republican candidates. The sorts of interests who tend to benefit from such suits, plaintiffs' attorneys, for example, have tended to contribute money to Democrats. This tendency has very little to do with ideology and a great deal to do with who gets what from government.

Not all interests are economic. Mexican Americans and African Americans, for example, have traditionally tended to support the Democratic Party because they have perceived the Republicans as less tolerant of ethnic diversity. Whether an interest arranges people in a politically relevant manner depends on what sorts of questions become issues of public policy.

Interests and ideologies tend to combine in different ways in different people, sometimes contradicting and sometimes reinforcing one another. For example, a Mexican American business executive in Texas would be drawn to the Republicans by her professional interest and drawn to the Democrats by her ethnic interest. She might have had trouble making up her mind about how to vote in the 2006 election. On the other hand, an Anglo real estate developer or an African American labor union president would probably have experienced no such conflict. In each case, the personal ideology of the citizens might either reinforce or clash with one or more of their interests.

The way interests and ideologies blend, conflict, and interact with candidates and parties is one of the things that makes politics complicated and interesting to study.

Table 4.2 summarizes the partisan interest coalitions that have characterized recent Texas politics. It is important to understand that not every person who has an interest agrees with every other person with the same interest, and so citizens who share interests are not unanimous in their partisan attachments. For example, although most of the people in the computer business who contributed large amounts to the parties in the 1990s and 2000s gave to the Republicans, not all did. Similarly, although the great majority of African Americans who voted in those elections supported the Democrats,

TABLE 4.2

Interests Generally Supporting the Two Major Parties

Type of interest	Democrats	Republicans
Economic class	Poor, labor union	Middle, wealthy, management
Professions	Plaintiffs' attorneys, public employees	Physicians, business entrepreneurs
Development vs. environment	Environmentalists	Developers, rural landowners
Industry	Entertainment, lawyers	Oil and gas, computers
Ethnic	African American, Mexican American	Anglo, Asian American
Religion	Catholic, Jewish	Protestant, especially evangelical

thousands did not. The table describes how interests lean in general, not how every person with that interest behaves.

Politics would be fascinating enough if ideologies and interests, once they had arranged themselves into party coalitions, stayed that way. In fact, however, the party battle evolves as history changes the way people live and as party leaders and candidates adopt new strategies to appeal for support. One hundred years ago, the Democratic Party was the conservative party and dominated Texas almost completely. Today, the Republican Party is more conservative and has won every recent statewide election. It is not too much of an exaggeration to say that the history of Texas is written in the story of her two major parties.

TEXAS POLITICAL PARTIES: A BRIEF HISTORY

Texas entered the United States in 1845 as a slave state. Nationally, the Democrats were pro-slavery, while their main opponents, the Whigs, ignored the issue. Moreover, the Democrats had endorsed the admission of Texas to the Union in the 1844 election, while the Whigs had waffled. Thus, most Texans were Democrats.

Party divisions became intense when the Civil War ended in 1865. The Republican administration of Abraham Lincoln had defeated the Confederacy, of which Texas was a member, and freed the slaves. Reconstruction, or northern occupation, settled on all the southern states. White southerners found themselves under the rule of northerners, the military, and African Americans. Rightly or wrongly, they believed themselves to be subject to tyranny by a foreign conqueror. They identified this despotic occupation with the Republican Party. In this emotionally searing experience, the southern politics of the next century were forged. The Democratic Party became the vehicle of southern resistance to northern domination and of white opposition to full citizenship for blacks. As a result, when Reconstruction ended in 1875, Texas, like the other former members of the Confederacy, was a solid one-party Democratic state. It remained a **one-party state** through most of the twentieth century.

Beginning in 1932, the national Democratic Party became dominated by liberals. Southern states such as Texas objected, but it took decades for the national realignment of party ideology to work its way through the South. For many decades, southern politicians and southern voters remained a slowly dissolving conservative faction in the largely liberal national Democratic Party.

It was conservative Republican President Ronald Reagan's landslide re-election in 1984 that finally broke the hold of the Democrats in Texas. Dozens of Republican candidates rode Reagan's coattails to victory in local elections, as did Phil Gramm, the Republican candidate for U.S. Senate. Some local office-holders subsequently lost their re-election bids, but by then Texas could no longer be considered a Democratic monopoly. The 1994 elections saw another Republican surge, with only the state legislature remaining under Democratic control. By 2006, Texas was plainly a Republican-majority state. The governor, lieutenant governor, land commissioner, comptroller, agriculture commissioner, both U.S. senators, a majority of the membership of the state Senate and House of Representatives and of the state's delegation

As party interests and ideologies evolve through history, so do their personnel. Texas passed some sort of a milestone in the late 1990s when both parties became chaired by women for the first time. Republican Susan Weddington was a former businesswoman from San Antonio. Democrat Molly Beth Malcolm was a former teacher and drug counselor from East Texas. In 2003 the Republican Party changed its chairs but retained its female leadership, as Tina Benkiser replaced Weddington. The same year, the Democrats also acquired a new chair, but Charles Soechting was male. Clearly, in the twenty-first century the sex of a politician is of much less importance than it was in earlier times.

to the federal House of Representatives, all nine justices of the Supreme Court and all nine judges of the Court of Criminal Appeals, plus all three railroad commissioners belonged to the GOP ("Grand Old Party," a nickname from the post–Civil War era). Moreover, Texans gave decisive majorities of their major party vote to Republican presidential candidates in 1992, 1996, 2000, and 2004. Table 4.3 illustrates the spectacular growth of Republican office-holders in Texas from 1974 to 2004.

Patterns in Texas's voting history during the last years of the twentieth and the first years of the twenty-first century are illustrated by public opinion research. In a survey taken in late 2004, 51 percent of the state's citizens described themselves as more-or-less regular supporters of Republicans, while only 37 percent were regular supporters of Democrats.[2] Even if the 12 percent of the population who described themselves as independents chose to support Democratic candidates in a given election, those candidates would still not have a majority.

Together the voting and survey data suggest that in the last two decades of the twentieth century Texas went through a political **realignment**—a large percentage of its citizens changed their partisan identification (psychological affiliation resulting in a standing decision to vote for a given party). Until the 1980s, enough Texans had adopted a standing decision to vote for Democrats that the party's candidates could count on winning most of the time. By the twenty-first century, however, enough Texans had changed their psychological affiliations so that Republicans were normally victorious in statewide, although not necessarily in local, elections. Once solidly Democratic, Texas has realigned to be generally Republican.

TABLE 4.3

Growth of Republican Office-Holders in Texas

Year	U.S. Senate	Other Statewide	U.S. House	Texas Senate	Texas House	Other	Total
1974	1	0	2	3	16	53	75
1982	1	0	5	5	36	270	317
1994	2	13	11	14	61	958	1,059
1998	2	27	13	16	72	1,397	1,527
2002	2	27	15	19	88	1,815	1,966
2004	2	27	21	19	87	2,010	2,166

SOURCE: Republican Party of Texas, October, 2005.

FUNCTIONS OF POLITICAL PARTIES

The basic purpose of political parties is to win elections and thus gain the opportunity to exercise control over public policy. While pursuing this goal, they perform one or more functions that make them valuable institutions in a democracy, including the following:

- Involve ordinary people in the political process, especially persuading them to vote and teaching them the formal and informal "rules of the game."
- Recruit political leaders and induce them to restrain their individual ambitions so that the party can achieve its collective purposes.
- Communicate to the leaders the interests of individuals and groups.
- Provide factual information and persuasive argument during public discussion of policy alternatives.
- Structure the nature of political conflict and debate, including screening out the demands of certain people and groups—usually fringe individuals or groups that lack significant public support.
- Moderate differences between and among groups, both within the party and in the larger society.
- Partly overcome the fragmented nature of the political system so that gridlock can be overcome and coherent policy made and implemented.

Political parties in any democracy can be judged according to the extent to which they fulfill these functions well or badly. How do Texas parties measure up?

PARTY ORGANIZATION

All parties are organizations, but they follow many patterns of structure. In general, American parties, compared to those in foreign democracies, are weak. They are not structured so that they can function easily as a cohesive team. Those in Texas are especially weak. As a result, Texas parties do not perform the function of overcoming gridlock and making coherent policy very well. Frequently, they fail to structure conflict so as to make it sensible to most ordinary citizens. A review of state party organization will suggest why this is so.

In Texas, as in most states, parties are divided into a permanent organization and a temporary one (Figure 4.1). The permanent party organization consists of little more than a skeleton force of people who conduct the routine but essential business of the party. The party's primary purpose of winning elections requires far more people and much greater activity. The party comes alive in election years in the form of a **temporary party organization** geared to capturing power.

The Temporary Party Organization

The **temporary party organization** is focused on the spring primary and the fall general elections. It attempts to choose attractive candidates and to mobilize voters to support them. In Texas, party membership is determined by the act of voting; there are no permanent political party rolls. If a citizen votes in the Democratic Party primary, for

FIGURE 4.1

Major Party Organization in Texas

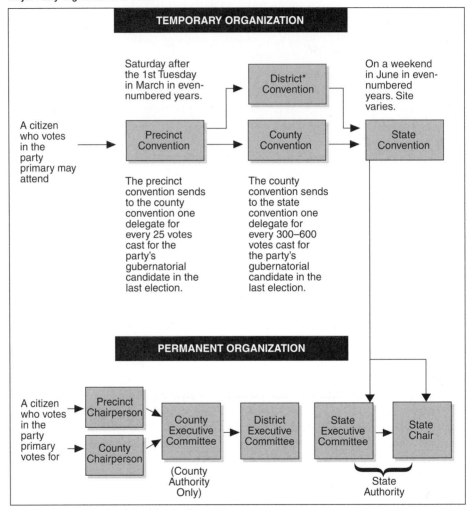

SOURCE: State Democratic and Republican headquarters.

example, his or her registration certificate is stamped, an act that legally prohibits voting in any other party's primary or participating in any other party's conventions.

Precinct and County Conventions.   In the 254 counties of Texas are more than 6,000 precincts, each having from 50 to as many as 3,500 potential voters. Each adult citizen is entitled to have a voice in choosing the precinct chairperson and proposing and voting on resolutions that will establish party policy, but participation in party affairs is low. Normally only a small fraction of those who vote in the primaries, who are themselves only a fraction of the total number of registered voters, who are themselves only a fraction of the voting-age citizens, participates in conventions or other party affairs.

The main function of the precinct convention is to select delegates to the county convention, which is the next echelon of the temporary party organization.[3] And the main function of the county convention is to select delegates to the state convention. Both precinct and county conventions can be short or long, peaceful or filled with conflict, productive of resolutions or not.

The State Convention. Both major parties hold their state conventions over a weekend in June during even-numbered (election) years. The party's state executive committee decides when and where the convention is held. Depending on the year of the election cycle in which it occurs, the June convention performs some or all of the following activities:

1. It certifies to the secretary of state the party nominees for the general election in November.
2. It writes the party platform.
3. It selects the members of the state executive committee.
4. It names the Texas committeeman and committeewoman to the national party committee.
5. It makes the final selection of delegates to the national party convention.
6. During presidential election years it selects a slate of electors to serve in the electoral college in the event that the party's candidates for president and vice president win in Texas.

Party conventions have tended, over the past three decades, to travel in opposite directions—the Democrats from argument to harmony, the Republicans from agreement to acrimony. Until the late 1970s, the liberal and conservative wings of the Democrats often fought viciously over party planks and leadership positions. During the 1980s and 1990s, however, the party came to be dominated more and more at its organizational level by the liberal faction. In conventions the delegates now tend to adopt liberal platforms and save their criticisms for the Republicans.

In contrast, when the Republicans were a small minority, they rarely argued over policy in their conventions. As they grew in state influence, however, Republicans generated greater and greater internal disagreement, especially between social and economic conservatives. The new pattern was set in 1994, when delegates from the Christian Right (see Chapter 3) dominated the convention, electing their favored party chair and writing a platform to their own liking. Among other provisions, the Republicans supported federal and state initiatives to outlaw abortion under all circumstances and recommended that the public schools teach "creation science" in biology classes. The socially conservative platform and the convention's choice of a party chair sparked vigorous opposition from delegates who were economically conservative but more moderate on social issues.

From 1994 to 2006 the Christian Right dominated Republican state conventions, sometimes writing platforms that began with the words, "We believe in you! We believe that you are a sacred being created in the image of God."[4] Again, the religious social conservatives elected their favored people to run the party, and again economic conservatives objected without effect.

Although events in the Democratic and Republican state conventions engender much publicity, their importance should not be exaggerated. Because candidates for public office in Texas are nominated in primaries rather than in caucuses or conventions (see Chapter 5), and because candidates typically raise their own campaign funds independently of the party, the state convention and platform are actually of little importance to what nominees say and do. Candidates typically run to gather support from the large number of potential voters, not the tiny number of party activists who write platforms.

In 1994 the two most important Republican candidates, George W. Bush, running for governor, and Kay Bailey Hutchison, running for U.S. Senate, pointedly ignored the state Republican platform and disassociated themselves from its abortion plank. Bush distributed his own "platform," which disagreed with his party's at several points and strongly differed from it in emphasis. In 1996 Governor Bush publicly disagreed with party chair Tom Pauken on campaign strategy. In 2002 Republican Governor Rick Perry publicly opposed 23 of 46 planks in his party's platform, distanced himself from 16 others, and endorsed only 7.[5]

By 2002 social conservative delegates to the Republican convention were so frustrated with the economic conservative office-holders they termed "RINOs" (for "Republicans In Name Only") that they sponsored Rule 43 as a floor amendment to the platform. This "RINO Rule" would have denied party funds to any candidate who refused to swear to endorse and attempt to implement every party plank if elected. Party chair Susan Weddington, presiding at the convention, managed to squelch the Rule 43 movement, but the uneasy alliance between economic conservatives and social conservatives continued to be a feature of the party in Texas.[6]

In summary, if you want to know what candidates plan to do if elected, you may want to ignore party platforms and pay attention to the positions of the candidates themselves. The platform positions and rhetoric reproduced in Table 4.4 are good indicators of the values and beliefs of the major party activists as groups, but are not reliable guides to the issue positions of candidates as individuals.

The Permanent Party Organization

Precinct Chairpeople.   Citizens who vote in the primary have an opportunity to participate in the selection of precinct and county chairpeople of their party. The precinct chair is the lowest-ranking permanent party official. Elected for a two-year term, the chair is expected to be the party leader at the precinct level, recruiting candidates, arranging for the precinct convention, getting out the vote, and in general beating the drum for the party.

County Executive Committees.   Together the precinct chairs comprise the County Executive Committee, which is charged with two major responsibilities: (1) conduct the party primary elections and (2) conduct the county convention.

TABLE 4.4

2004 Texas State Political Party Platforms

Issue	Republican	Democratic
Church and State	Our Party pledges to exert its influence to restore the original intent of the First Amendment . . . and dispel the myth of the separation of Church and State.	Texas Democrats believe in . . . separation of Church and State to preserve the freedom to pursue our beliefs.
Education	The Party urges the Texas legislature to. . . repeal the "Robin Hood" school funding reallocation system. . . . The Party supports the objective teaching and equal treatment of scientific strengths and weaknesses of all scientific theories, including Intelligent Design. . . .	We should raise teacher pay and protect and enhance a quality state-paid health insurance program for every educational employee. . . . Provide sufficient state funding for all education costs. ["Intelligent Design" not mentioned.]*
Guns	The Party calls upon the Texas legislature and U.S. Congress to repeal any and all laws that infringe upon the right of individual citizens to keep and bear arms.	Not mentioned.
Immigration	The Party believes that security of our borders is an urgent national interest. The Party opposes illegal immigration and all forms of amnesty, or legal status for illegal immigrants. . . .	Not mentioned.
Childcare	The Party opposes any government regulations that will adversely affect the availability, affordability, or the right of parents to choose childcare. [Otherwise not mentioned.]*	Affordable, quality childcare is good for parents, good for children, and vital for the Texas economy. . . . [A list of proposed government policies follows.]*
Abortion	The Party affirms its support for a human life amendment to the Constitution. [Which would effectively outlaw abortion.]*	Texas Democrats trust the women of Texas to make their own decisions about personal matters such as when or whether to bear children.
Labor unions	The Party supports legislation requiring labor unions to obtain the consent of the individual union member before that member's dues can be used for political purposes.	We support . . . the right of all employees, public and private, to organize, collect dues, designate their income voluntarily to organizations and agencies of their choosing, and to negotiate collectively with their employers through representatives of their choice.
Minimum wage	The Party believes the Minimum Wage Law should be repealed.	We support . . . a meaningful increase in the federal minimum wage . . . while enforcing the law Texas Democrats enacted in 2001 to make sure the state minimum wage for farm workers keeps up with increases in the federal minimum wage.

(continued)

TABLE 4.4

2004 Texas State Political Party Platforms (continued)

Issue	Republican	Democratic
Health care	The Party supports market-based, private sector initiatives to improve the portability, quality, and affordability of health care.	Health care is not a privilege reserved for those able to pay for it; it is a right for all people. Access to affordable health insurance should be guaranteed for all Texans. . . . We believe health care coverage should be secured for all children . . ..
Environment	We believe that groundwater is an absolute, vested ownership right of the landowner. . . . We oppose the Endangered Species Act. [Plus many more endorsements of private property rights.]*	We support policies that will clean the air of Texas cities. . . . repeal of provisions in state law which block local ordinances that provide enhanced water quality protection. [Plus many more detailed policy proposals.]*
Homosexuality	Homosexual behavior is contrary to the fundamental, unchanging truths that have been ordained by God. . . . We are opposed to granting of any special legal entitlements . . . to . . . homo-sexuals.	Texas Democrats believe in freedom from government interference in our personal lives. [No specific mention of homosexuality.]*
Homelessness	Not mentioned.	Texas Democrats are committed to ending homelessness by removing barriers and increasing access to services that support progress toward self-sufficiency.

*Information in brackets added by the authors.

SOURCES: Quotations from 2004 state party platforms; Democratic platform supplied by state headquarters; Republican platform obtained from party Web site.

The county convention is presided over by the county chair, the most important official at the local level. Elected for two years to a demanding job, this official is unpaid, although some receive private donations. County chairs are compensated by the state for the expense of conducting their party's primary elections. After the primary election has been held, the County Executive Committee canvasses the vote and certifies the results to the State Executive Committee.

The District Executive Committee.   The district executive committee is the least important permanent party organization. It meets only after the primary to fill vacancies in district offices. Membership varies according to the number of counties and sections of counties that comprise the senatorial district.

The State Executive Committee.   The highest permanent body in the state party is the State Executive Committee, and the highest state party official is the party chair. Both are elected by the state convention. If the party controls the governorship, the chair usually works closely with the governor and is likely to be a friend and political ally. The Republicans in the late 1990s were an exception; there was notable friction and lack of cooperation between party chair Tom Pauken and Governor George W. Bush during and after the 1996 campaign.

In a similar fashion, the chair of the state committee of the party out of power usually has a close relationship with that party's top leaders. By law, the executive committees are responsible for staging the state conventions and for certifying the parties' candidates. They may also perform other functions such as raising funds, distributing information, and assisting with problems at the county level. In recent years, the State Democratic Executive Committee has taken on new importance because of its rule-making authority, and Democratic politicians compete for membership.

The (Un) Importance of Party Organization

American political parties are not "responsible parties"—that is, they neither have centralized control over nominations and financing nor the power to impose the party platform on members. In Texas, parties are especially weak because it is, in fact, the primary election, not the party organization, that is important in determining who is nominated to office. Furthermore, candidates normally rely on their own fundraising and organizing ability more than they rely on their party to help them get elected. As a result, when candidates succeed in capturing an office, they mostly have themselves and the individuals and groups who contributed to their campaign fund to thank for their achievements. They therefore have very little loyalty to the party; they are more likely to feel beholden to some wealthy interest group. Office-holders are often ideologically friendly with others of the same party, but they are not obligated to cooperate with one another. The parties have no discipline over them. The formal and informal party organizations have some ability to fashion a "party attitude" on public policy because they are centers of information flow and personal interaction, but they are incapable of forging a disciplined governing team.

As previously mentioned, in the 1990s and in 2002 important Republican candidates went their own way and pretty much ignored the official state party organizations. In return, that Republican organization showed no love for them. The 1996 state Republican convention at first refused to choose U.S. Senator Kay Bailey Hutchison as a delegate to the party's national presidential nominating convention. She was finally named a delegate only after some intense arm-twisting by Governor Bush. In 1997 state party chair Tom Pauken actually took out ads in newspapers in East Texas urging Republicans to write their legislators, requesting them to "Say No to the Bush Tax Cut!" [7] The Democratic Party has not displayed similar conflicts among party functionaries and elected officials because it has had so few elected officials since 1994. Nevertheless, because Democrats are also nominated in primaries, their party has no more organizational discipline than does its opponent.

The consequence of this lack of organizational cohesion is that Texas parties fail to perform many of the functions that make parties elsewhere useful to democracy. By and large, they cannot recruit political leaders, structure the nature of public debate, or overcome the fragmented nature of the political system by forming officials into disciplined groups. Instead of thinking of parties in Texas as two stable, cohesive teams, therefore, it would be more realistic to imagine them as two (or perhaps, as we

YOU DECIDE

Should Texas Have Responsible Parties?

In 1950 the American Political Science Association sponsored a report entitled *Toward a More Responsible Two-Party System,* in which it stated its organizational position that democracy would work better in the United States if the country's parties were far more disciplined and coherent. In 2002 there was a movement within the Republican Party in Texas to force all candidates to endorse every plank in the party platform, on the theory that democracy in Texas would work better if the Republicans, at least, were disciplined and coherent. Both APSA in 1950 and many Republican activists in 2002 endorsed the idea that disciplined party teams are better for democratic governance than the disorganized, candidate-centered system that prevails both in the nation and in Texas.

Pro	Con
⇨ When candidates from the same party take different positions on issues, it confuses the voters. If candidates were all forced to stand for the same things, citizens would be much more able to understand the choices available to them, which would make for more intelligent voting.	⇨ Election campaigns are often confusing because politics itself is complicated and ambiguous. The solution to confusion is for citizens to better inform themselves, not for parties to impose a false clarity on voting choices.
⇨ Many foreign democracies have disciplined, responsible parties.	⇨ Almost all those foreign democracies have multi-party systems, so the voters have many more choices on election day. There is

shall soon see, three) loose confederations of citizens, interest groups, and office-holders who sometimes cooperate because of occasional ideological agreement and temporarily parallel interests.

TWO PARTIES, THREE FACTIONS

Republicans

Ideologically, the Texas Republican Party tends to be strongly conservative, usually opposing government involvement in the economy but sometimes endorsing such involvement in personal life. Although the party holds two recognizable factions, the

Pro

Probably because politics in those countries makes sense, those countries typically have much higher voter turnout than the United States, and still higher turnout than Texas.

➪ Disciplined parties would prevent wealthy special interests from secretly buying the loyalty of candidates. Once candidates got into office, there would be no betrayals of the public's trust.

➪ Once candidates were forced to endorse a single set of principles in order to run, they would form a cooperating team when in office, and public policy would be both easier to enact and more self-consistent.

Con

no evidence that any of those countries is better governed than the United States, or than Texas.

➪ If wealthy special interests were denied access to candidates, they would simply corrupt parties. The problem is the power of money, not lack of party discipline.

➪ One of the major reasons that candidates vary in their policy positions is that constituencies vary from place to place. Any party that forced all its candidates to say the same thing everywhere would soon discover that most of its candidates lost. Losers do not enact public policy.

Sources: "Toward a More Responsible Two-Party System: A Report of the Committee on Political Parties, American Political Science Association," *American Political Science Review*, vol. 44, September 1950, 15; Austin Ranney, *Curing the Mischiefs of Faction: Party Reform in America* (Berkeley: University of California Press, 1975); Jake Bernstein, "Elephant Wars: The Christian Right Flexes Its Muscle at the Republican Convention," *The Texas Observer*, July 5, 2002, 8–9.

social conservatives (most of whom are members of the Christian Right) and the economic conservatives, it is not appropriate to speak of two opposed groups within the Republican Party. Many Republican office-holders manage to embody both wings of the party as they endorse social conservatism in their *intangible*, symbolic public statements but concentrate on passing *tangible* conservative economic policies while in office.

A good example is governor Rick Perry, who took office in 2000 when governor Bush resigned to run for president, and was elected on his own in 2002. In 2006, looking toward another re-election campaign, he publicly endorsed the teaching of "intelligent design" (a euphemism for Christian creationism) rather than the scientific theory of evolution by natural selection in the state's public-school biology classes.

Since "intelligent design" is a religious doctrine, it would be unconstitutional to teach it in public schools, as courts have held several times.[8] There is consequently very little chance that such a doctrine could be taught in the state's biology classes. Even if such an unlikely event came to pass, the governor would have virtually nothing to do with it because his office does not have the power to set school curriculum for the state. By endorsing the teaching of "intelligent design," therefore, Perry was not making a genuine proposal for a realistic policy option. He was expressing symbolic solidarity with Christian conservatives.

Meanwhile, during his tenure in office, Perry had concentrated on urging the legislature to pass tangible, business-oriented policies such as tort reform, tax relief, and lightening of regulation. He had thus managed to appeal to both halves of his party's coalition, the social conservatives through symbolism and the economic conservatives through policies. As long as Republican politicians such as Perry are able to thus combine both sides of the party in their individual persons, Republicans will not be split into identifiable factions.

Geographic Distribution.   While the Republicans are now greater than Democrats statewide in voter strength, their numbers are unevenly distributed. Republicans tend to be found in cities and the wealthier suburbs, with Dallas and Harris County (Houston) containing about 4 out of every 10 of the state's Republican voters (although a Democrat, Dallas Mayor Ron Kirk, did manage to win this county in his losing race for U.S. Senator in 2002). Other concentrations of support are found in the East and West Texas "oil patches," the German hill country north of San Antonio, and the Panhandle and Llano Estacado. Republicans are also steadily gaining ground in East Texas.

Socio-Economic and Ethnic Distribution.   GOP activists come from a relatively narrow socio-economic, ethnic, and religious base. Most candidates and party activists are Anglo middle- or upper-class businesspeople or professionals. Many activists are evangelical Protestants. Although a sprinkling of African Americans and Latinos can be found among active Republicans, the party has not appealed to significant numbers of minorities since the end of Reconstruction in 1875. In his re-election of 1998, Governor George W. Bush may have received the votes of as many as 49 percent of Mexican Americans, but this number is under dispute. At any rate, the Hispanic support for Bush would seem to have been for his person, not his party. In 2002 Rick Perry garnered only 10 to 35 percent of Hispanic votes, depending on whose survey is consulted.[9] Furthermore, the Republican Party's traditional opposition to policies such as welfare and job-training programs aimed at helping the poor has generally ensured that its activists, if not always its voters, would be fairly wealthy.

Conservative Democrats

Despite the fact that Texas officially has a two-party system, it generally has offered three voting options to its citizens, for the Democrats are traditionally split into two factions. This three-faction system has the advantage of making more choices available to the voters and the disadvantage of making Texas politics more confusing than it might otherwise be.

Conservative Democrats are the representatives of habits of thought and behavior that survive from Texas as it was when it was part of the Old South. This Old South culture is very conservative on social issues, but tends to be conflicted and indecisive on economic issues. Many southerners are normally conservative economically but can be aroused to a fervent belief in the ability of government to protect the little people of society from wealthy individuals and corporations—an attitude that has historically been known as populism. This Populist streak makes the Old South part of Texas hard to predict on economic issues. At the level of the party activists and office-holders, the conservative faction of the Democratic Party is slightly less devoted to laissez-faire than Republicans are but much more so than the liberal faction is. It tends to be conservative on social issues, although conservative Democratic candidates have been known to bend to the left on social issues in order to attempt to persuade minority citizens to vote for them.

The late former U.S. Senator and Secretary of Commerce Lloyd Bentsen and the late Lieutenant Governor Bob Bullock are good examples of conservative Democrats. During the 2002 campaign, three of the Democrats' major candidates, Tony Sanchez (governor), Ron Kirk (U.S. senator), and John Sharp (lieutenant governor) were so conservative that they were virtually undistinguishable from their Republican opponents on economic issues, differing from the GOP candidates primarily on such social issues as affirmative action and abortion.

Geographic Distribution.   The traditional base of the conservative wing of the Democratic Party is the piney woods of East Texas, where the Old South culture is strongest. In the ongoing realignment of Texas voters, however, Republicans have taken over most of the areas that used to be solidly Old South Democratic. In the 2002 election, the Democrats retained majority support in a few areas of East Texas (most important was Jefferson County—Beaumont-Port Arthur-Orange), but East Texas in general went Republican.

Socio-Economic and Ethnic Distribution.   Representing the Old South political culture and the historically dominant wing of the party, conservative Democrats traditionally drew support from all classes in Texas, although much of that support has evaporated as Republicans continue to increase their popularity among the wealthy and the evangelical. Conservative Democrats have also drawn substantial support, historically, from farmers, ranchers, and workers, especially those in rural areas and small cities. Again, this pattern is changing as Republicans become the party of choice.

Liberal Democrats

Liberals usually recommend policies that depend upon a government that is active in economic affairs, especially on behalf of those who have less wealth and power. They tend, however, to oppose government intervention in personal life. The late former Governor Ann Richards, former Agriculture Commissioner (and now radio commentator) Jim Hightower, and former mayor of San Antonio (and also former U.S. Secretary of Housing and Urban Development) Henry Cisneros are good examples of Texas liberal Democrats.

Geographic Distribution.   By 2006 liberal Democrats were most heavily concentrated where Hispanics were numerous—in the counties near the Rio Grande and in South Texas in general, especially the cities of San Antonio and Corpus Christi. Liberals were also fairly strong where labor unions were a factor, especially in far southeast Texas and in the university-and-government enclave of Austin.

Socio-Economic and Ethnic Distribution.   Identifying the socio-economic components of liberal Democratic strength in Texas is a more complex task than in the case of Republicans or conservative Democrats. Liberals form, at best, an uneasy coalition. White middle- and upper-class liberals can support African Americans and Mexican Americans in their quest for equal treatment, but labor unions have been noticeably cool in this area. African Americans and Mexican Americans usually give little support to reform legislation—of campaign spending and lobbying, for example—or efforts to protect the natural environment, which energize Anglo liberals. Many Mexican Americans are reluctant to vote for African American candidates, and vice versa. While it can be said, therefore, that liberal strength comes mostly from labor

Anemia is a disease associated with physical weakness. Here cartoonist Ben Sargent uses anemia as a metaphor for the state Democratic Party's seeming inability to field strong statewide candidates against the dominant Republicans in the 2006 election year.

SOURCE: Courtesy of Ben Sargent.

unions, African Americans, Mexican Americans, and certain educated Anglos, the mix is a volatile one that does not make for stable cooperation.

The Future of the Three-Faction System

The future does not look bright for conservative Democrats in Texas. They are being drained from the right and squeezed from the left. The national party long ago became dominated by a moderate-to-liberal philosophy. Within Texas, Republicans steadily draw away conservative voting support, while liberals continue to dominate the party organization. In 2002 the Democratic Party offered a "dream team"—a slate of conservative candidates for governor, U.S. senator, and lieutenant governor—that differed from its Republican opponents not so much in its ideology as in its diverse ethnicity. This strategy of running a conservative but multicultural team failed badly; each of the three Democrats lost decisively. Yet, as Texas evolves toward a population in which minorities constitute the majority, Democrats are almost certain to continue to nominate many Mexican American and African American candidates. Predictions are always risky, but it is possible to imagine Democratic Party leaders adopting a long-term strategy of running ethnically diverse, albeit liberal, candidates.

It is possible, therefore, to foresee a day in the not-too-distant future when Texas has only a conservative Republican Party and a liberal Democratic Party. If voter turnout rates continue to favor conservative Anglos (see Chapter 5), then this arrangement along the ideological spectrum will ensure that Republicans dominate the state for a long time. If liberal-leaning minorities begin to turn out to vote at higher rates, however, they will alter the party balance decisively. One of the few predictions that can confidently be made about politics is that things will change.

THIRD PARTIES AND INDEPENDENTS IN TEXAS

Texas has had its share of third parties. The Know-Nothing Party made a brief appearance before the Civil War, representing those who objected to Roman Catholics and immigrants. After the Civil War, the Greenback Party, a cheap-money party, made an equally brief appearance. More important was the Populist or People's Party, which represented widespread discontent among farmers and other "little people." The Populists advocated an extensive program of government regulation of big business and social welfare reform. The Populist candidate for president drew 100,000 votes in Texas in 1892—almost 20 percent of the votes cast. The major parties, especially the Democrats under Governor Jim Hogg, adopted some of the Populist positions, and the party ultimately disappeared. As mentioned, however, the Populist spirit has not disappeared from Texas politics.

The Populists were typical of third parties in America. Such parties tend not to achieve permanent status for themselves, but they can be important in influencing the major parties to adopt some of their positions and platforms. Since the Populist era, Texas has seen candidates from the Prohibitionists, Socialists, Socialist-Laborites, Communists, Progressives, Jacksonians, States' Righters, George Wallace's American Independence Party, the Citizens' Party, and the Reform Party.

For a while in the late 1990s and early 2000s, there appeared to be two potentially vigorous third parties in Texas, the Greens and the Libertarians. The Greens occupied the ultra-liberal end of the ideological spectrum, demanding a much more active government to regulate business on behalf of workers and the environment. Libertarians were the consistent anti-government party, opposing any government regulation of the economy (which made them more conservative than the Republicans on economic issues) and equally opposing government regulation of personal life (opposing the war on drugs, for example, which made them more liberal than the Democrats on social issues).

At the turn of the century, both these parties seemed poised to grow into serious competition for the major parties. But both faltered within a few years. The Greens could not even draw enough petition signatures to field one candidate in the 2004 election, and the Libertarians, while achieving ballot space, drew only a tiny response from the voters.

Generally, candidates must be the nominees of some party in order to even think about running for statewide office. After 1859, when Texas revolutionary hero Sam Houston, running on his own ticket, beat Democrat H. R. Runnels for the governorship, there were no significant statewide independent candidates for almost a century and a half. In 2006, however, with the two already tiny third parties fading, citizens disgruntled with the major parties were offered two candidates who were independent of all party backing.

The first 2006 independent, comptroller Carole Keeton Strayhorn, exemplified the dilemma of the "tweeners," the people who are more-or-less in the middle of the ideological spectrum. During the early 1980s, she had been the conservative Democratic mayor of Austin. In 1985 she became a Republican and ran successfully for a series of offices. Always more liberal than most Republicans but more conservative than the typical Democrat, she was as uneasy in her new party as she had been in her former party. As the Republicans consolidated their grip on state government in the early 2000s, she grew increasingly vocal in her criticisms of the policies pursued by her party, especially in regard to education and welfare. In 2006 she announced that she would attempt to obtain the 45,540 signatures (from registered voters who did not vote in either major party's primary) necessary to put her on the November ballot as an independent candidate.

The other 2006 independent was difficult to describe in ordinary political language. A musician, novelist, and humor columnist, Kinky Friedman had had very little to say about politics his entire life when he decided to run for governor in 2005. His campaigning did not do much to dispel the mystery of where he stood on issues, for his "speeches" consisted mainly of comedic one-liners interspersed with clever insults of ruling Republicans. He seemed to appeal mainly to people who were generally disgusted with politics in Texas or to liberals who despaired of voting for a forthright Democratic candidate. He brought a lightness of tone, but no realistic political alternatives, to the campaign of 2006.

It was a commentary on the anemic state of the Democratic Party's health in 2006 that two independent candidates would be better known and better financed than any possible Democratic candidate. Although history has been known to spring surprises, the trend of party politics in the first decade of the twenty-first century threatened to turn Texas into a one-party Republican state.

SUMMARY

Ideology is one of the most important bases for political parties everywhere, but in Texas, where parties have historically been weak, ideology has been more important than party affiliation. The major ideological conflict has been between conservatives and liberals.

Liberals tend to favor government regulation of the economy but oppose it in personal life, while conservatives tend to favor regulation of personal life but oppose it in the economy. These basic differences lead to differences in many areas of public policy, from taxation to abortion. The Texas Republican Party is consistently strongly conservative, but the Democratic Party is split into a conservative and a liberal faction.

The other major basis for political parties is interests, which are based on economic, ethnic, religious, or almost any other characteristic of citizens. Interests combine and conflict with ideologies to make politics complicated and constantly changing.

From 1875 to the 1970s, Texas was a one-party Democratic state. For a generation, however, conservative Anglo citizens have been realigning so that they are now solidly Republican in their voting. Because Anglos constitute the majority in Texas, the state is now almost as solidly Republican as it once was solidly Democratic.

Our political parties are characterized by both temporary and permanent party organizations. Because nominations are made in primaries, however, and because party leaders have no control over candidates or office-holders, party organization is much less important than ideology and interests in explaining the politics of the state. This lack of organizational strength means that Texas's political parties are not "responsible" and hence are incapable of fulfilling some of the functions that they perform in other democracies.

Texas has given birth to a number of third parties, none of which have achieved permanency but several of which have influenced public policy in the state.

STUDY QUESTIONS

1. What are the basic ideological differences between liberals and conservatives? What are the more important policy differences between them?
2. Of these interests, which would be most likely to draw the support of a political party—owners of French Impressionist paintings, people with Lou Gehrig's disease, Irish Americans, heroin addicts, farmers? Why?
3. What are the functions of political parties? How well do Texas parties perform them?
4. Discuss current trends in voter support and party organization in relation to the three factions. Who is growing stronger? Who is getting weaker? Why?
5. Describe briefly the temporary and permanent party organizations in Texas. What political institution renders both of them relatively unimportant in determining the activities of the parties?
6. Are you a Democrat, a Republican, an independent, or a member of another party? Why?

SURFING THE WEB

Visit the companion site for this book:
http://www.thomsonedu.com/politicalscience/kraemer

Each national and state party organization has a Web site full of factual information and propaganda touting its candidates and policy stands:

Texas Republican Party
http://www.texasgop.org/

Texas Democratic Party
http://www.txdemocrats.org/

Texas Libertarian Party
http://www.tx.lp.org/

The Green Party has two factions. The larger and more moderate can be accessed at:
http://www.greens.org/na.html

The smaller and more radical faction of the Green Party can be accessed at:
http://www.gp.org

NOTES

1. We are grateful to Mike Baselice and Daron Shaw for supplying both the 1997 and the 2004 data.

2. We are grateful to Mike Baselice and Daron Shaw for supplying these data.

3. Several of the larger counties—Bexar, Dallas, Harris, and Tarrant, for example—are so populous that they are entitled to more than one state senator. In such counties, each state senatorial district holds its own convention rather than a countywide convention.

4. Sources: 1996 and 1998 state Republican Party platforms, page 1.

5. Ken Herman, "Perry Not Standing on GOP Party Platform," *Austin American-Statesman*, July 12, 2002, 9.

6. Molly Ivins, "Texas Elephants Look to Ostracize the RINOs," *Austin American-Statesman*, June 12, 2002, A17; Jake Bernstein, "Elephant Wars," *Texas Observer*, July 5, 2002, 9.

7. "Political Intelligence," *Texas Observer*, September 26, 1997, 16.

8. Laurie Goodstein, "Issuing Rebuke, Judge Rejects Teaching of Intelligent Design," *New York Times*, December 21, 2005, A1; W. Gardner Selby, "Perry: Add Intelligent Design to Classes," *Austin American-Statesman*, January 6, 2006, A1.

9. Ken Herman, "How Many Hispanics Voted for Bush? Depends Whom You Ask," *Austin American-Statesman*, November 13, 1998, A11; Lori Rodriguez, "Perry's Support Claims Questioned," *Houston Chronicle*, November 7, 2002, A29; Ken Herman, "One Survey Claims 30 Percent of Hispanic Voters Picked Perry," *Austin American-Statesman*, November 13, 2002, B3.

5

VOTERS, CAMPAIGNS, AND ELECTIONS

Suppose they gave an election and nobody came?

Bumper sticker from the 1960s

*Politics has got so expensive that it takes lots of money
to even get beat with.*

Will Rogers
American humorist, 1931

INTRODUCTION

Nothing is more basic to the concept of democratic government than the principle of elected representatives freely chosen by the majority of the people, with every vote counting equally. In an ideal democracy, election campaigns are contests conducted by rival candidates for the people's support. Candidates debate public policy rather than engaging in a competition of personal insult and insinuation. On the official voting day, citizens cast their ballots on the basis of their evaluation of the debate, with almost everyone participating. On the other hand, a bad democracy would be one in which election campaigns deal in trivialities, evasions, and slanders; candidates pay more attention to the wants of special-interest contributors than to the needs of the people; and very few citizens bother to participate on election day.

Is Texas close to or far from the democratic ideal of campaigns and elections? It is the overall purpose of this chapter to provide information that will allow you to begin to answer this question. The first topic comprises the reasons that voting is important to democracy. Then comes an examination of Texas's registration procedures and a discussion of its traditionally low voter turnout. The focus then turns to election campaigns, with special attention to the impact of money on the outcome. A description follows of the various types of public elections in Texas. Having discussed some important principles about Texas elections, the chapter briefly examines them as illustrated by the contests of 1994 through 2006. Finally, there is a comparison of the recent reality of Texas elections with the democratic ideal and an argument that there is much room for improvement.

VOTERS

Why Vote?

As is the case with many important questions, the answer to this one is, "It depends." It depends on whether we view voting from the perspective of the individual voter or of the candidates or of the political system.

From the standpoint of the individual voter, there may seem to be no logic in voting, for public elections are almost never won by the margin of a single vote. The individual voter has very little hope of affecting the outcome of an election. Why, then, do people bother to register and vote? The main reason is that people do not think of voting in completely logical terms. Like other political behavior, voting is governed not only by reason but also by emotion, custom, and habit. Most of us vote primarily because we have been taught that it is our duty as citizens (as, in fact, it is). And even though our single vote is unlikely to affect the outcome of an election, our participation in the governing of the community is important to the self-development of each of us.

From the standpoint of the candidate, voting is extremely important. There is a saying among politicians: "Votes are counted one by one by one." It expresses the insight that although citizens may seem to be part of a mass, it is a mass of individual personalities, each with his or her own motivations, ideology, and hopes for the future. Politicians who forget that each potential supporter is an individual, soon find themselves forcibly retired.

From the standpoint of the political system, elections are crucial. In democratic theory, it is the participation of the citizens that makes government legitimate (that is, morally right and thus entitled to obedience). When citizens neglect or refuse to vote in large numbers, it raises questions about the most fundamental underpinnings of political authority.

Voting also performs other functions in a democratic society. The act of participating in an election decreases alienation and opposition by making people feel that they are part of the system. Further, the electorate does have some effect on public policy by choosing one set of candidates who endorse one set of policies over another. Although one person's vote is very unlikely to swing an election, groups of like-minded citizens who vote the same way can be decisive. Finally, large-scale voting has the added virtue of helping to prevent dishonesty. It is relatively easy to rig an election when only a few people bother to go to the polls. One of the best guarantees of honest government is a large turnout on election day.

So, despite the fact that one vote almost never matters, democracy depends upon each citizen acting as if it does. When people take their vote seriously and act as responsible citizens, the system works. When they refuse to participate and stay home on election day, they abdicate control over the government to the elites and special interests, who are happy to run things. We can partly judge the extent to which a country or state has a decent government by the level of voter turnout among its citizens. How does Texas stack up? This question will be answered shortly. First, however, must take a look at the legal context of the voting act. The most important part of that context is the system of registration.

Registration

Every political system has a voter registration procedure to distinguish qualified voters from those who are ineligible because of immaturity, lack of citizenship, mental incapacity, or other reasons. In most countries of the world, registration is easy; in many countries, the government goes to great lengths to make sure that all citizens are registered before every election.

Like the other former slaveholding states of the old Confederacy, however, for most of its history Texas deliberately limited voting. Through a series of devices, of which the most important were the White primary and the poll tax, Texas prevented voting by almost all African Americans and Mexican Americans, as well as many poor Anglos. Through the 1960s, however, the federal government, especially the courts, invalidated and quashed the whole tricky system of vote suppression in Texas.[1]

By 1971 the state legislature was forced to write an honest law making the ballot box accessible to all citizens. Its major provisions, as amended, are:

1. Initial registration: The voter may register either in person or by mail. A parent, child, or spouse who is registered may register on behalf of the voter.
2. Permanency: The voter remains registered as long as he or she remains qualified. A new voter registration card is issued every two years.
3. Period of registration: Voters may register at any time and may vote in any election, provided that they are registered thirty days prior to the election.

To vote in Texas today, one must meet the following criteria:

1. Be a U.S. citizen 18 years of age by election day.
2. Be a resident of the state and county for thirty days immediately prior to election day.
3. Be a resident of the election precinct on election day.
4. Have registered to vote at least thirty days prior to election day.

The Texas Voter: Government by the People?

Despite the fact that registration has been relatively easy in Texas for more than three decades, voter turnout in the state, while it has been climbing erratically, is still below national levels. Voter turnout means the proportion of eligible citizens who actually cast ballots. Table 5.1 shows that the percentage of Texans voting in both presidential and off-year congressional elections is considerably lower than the percentage voting nationally. An average of 46.4 percent of eligible Texans turned out for presidential balloting in the three decades since the new registration law went into effect, and an average of 27.4 percent turned out for off-year congressional elections. In both the 2004 presidential balloting and the 2002 congressional contest, Texas voter turnout was at least seven percentage points below the level of the country as a whole. In only one election, 2004, did the state's turnout rise as high as 50 percent.

On the one hand, government in Texas is never "by the people." At best, it is by just half the people; often it is by one-quarter of the people or even lesser. On the other hand, the state's voter turnout has been slowly increasing (see Table 5.1). In 2004 at least half of eligible Texans voted for the first time in history. Participation rates in the state thus give both cause for discouragement and cause for optimism in regard to democratic government.

TABLE 5.1

Percentages of Voting-Age Population Voting in National Elections, 1972–2002

	1972	*1976*	*1980*	*1984*	*1988*	*1992*	*1996*	*2000*	*2004*
				PRESIDENTIAL ELECTIONS					
U.S.	55.5	54.3	51.8	53.1	50.2	55.2	50.8	52.2	61.0
Texas	45.4	47.3	44.7	47.2	44.2	49.0	43.0	45.0	52.0

	1974	*1978*	*1982*	*1986*	*1990*	*1994*	*1998*	*2002*
			U.S. HOUSE OF REPRESENTATIVES *(Off-Year Elections)*					
U.S.	36.1	35.1	38.0	36.4	35.0	38.9	37.6	39
Texas	18.4	24.0	26.2	29.1	26.8	35.0	28	32

SOURCES: *Statistical Abstract of the United States,* 101st ed. (Washington, DC: U.S. Dept. of Commerce, Bureau of the Census, 1980), p. 517, 106th ed. (1985), p. 254, 109th ed. (1989), p. 259; Federal Election Commission, Washington, DC; "Political Intelligence," *Texas Observer,* November 27, 1992, 8; "Voter Turnout Higher Than in '98, Survey Says," *Dallas Morning News,* November 7, 2002, A15; Walter Dean Burnham, Department of Government, University of Texas at Austin.

Why Don't Texans Vote?

Compared to the citizens of other democracies, Americans in general are not known for high voter turnouts. But Texans seem to be even less participatory than the residents of many other states. Why? Texas is a rather poor state with a very uneven distribution of its wealth. The poverty rate is important because the poor and less educated, in the absence of strong parties to persuade them to go to the polls on election day, have a tendency to stay home. When the poor don't vote, the overall turnout rate remains low.

The difference between rich and poor citizens is strongly related to differences between turnout rates for ethnic groups. Consider, for example, the self-reported national turnout rates for Hispanics, Anglos, and African Americans in the 2000 and 2004 presidential elections (see Table 5.2):

Other studies confirm that Texas's low voter turnout rate is partly caused by the tendency of its minority citizens to participate at lower rates than Anglo citizens. Thus, those who vote tend to be richer, better educated, and Anglo; those who abstain tend to be poorer, uneducated, and minority.

The variations in voter turnout have major consequences for Texas public policy. In general (and keeping in mind that all generalizations permit exceptions), minority citizens tend to have more liberal opinions than do Anglos. These differences partly result from the fact that minorities are more likely to be poor. When they fail to go to the polls, however, their views become irrelevant. Because the more conservative Anglo citizens vote at higher rates, their preferences are usually the ones that determine which candidates win and therefore which policies are pursued by government. Low minority turnout is one of the major explanations for conservative public policy in Texas. For example, minorities as a whole identify with the Democratic Party in far greater percentages than do Anglos. According to a survey taken in 2002, 29 percent of the state's Anglos identified as Democrats, in addition to 59 percent of Hispanics and 81 percent of African Americans.[2] When minorities don't vote, it hurts Democrats.

But it is not just any Democrats who suffer. The liberal wing of the party needs minority support to win. As Tables 5.3 and 5.4 illustrate, African Americans and Mexican Americans tend to hold views on a variety of important public policy issues that are clearly more liberal than the opinions of Anglos. It seems obvious that if minorities had higher turnout rates, liberal Democrats would win elections much more often. That would mean that government policy in Texas would be more liberal. As it is, the liberals rarely go to the polls; so, state government remains conservative.

TABLE 5.2

Voter Turnout among Major Ethnic Groups, 2000 and 2004 Presidential Elections

Year	Anglo (non-Hispanic White)	Hispanic (any race)	African American
2000	61.8%	45.1%	56.8%
2004	67.2%	47.2%	60.0%

SOURCE: U.S. Census Bureau Web site: www.census.gov/prod. Note that the Census Bureau bases its turnout figures on whether people reported that they had voted, not on direct measures of their participation. It has long been known that people tend to exaggerate the extent of their past participation because voting is a socially desirable activity. Thus, these self-reported figures inevitably contain an upward bias to an unknown extent.

TABLE 5.3

White and African American Public Opinion, 1996–2004

	Percentage agreeing among	
Issue	*Whites*	*African Americans*
Favor government health insurance; 1996	35	53
Support capital punishment (Texas only); 2000	81	44
Feel that racial minorities in this country have equal job opportunities with whites; 2001	53	18
Agree that government should ensure that all citizens have a job; 2004	26	46
Agree that affirmative action should be continued; 2004	12	45

SOURCES: First item from the 1996 National Election Study, reported in William Lasser, *American Politics: The Enduring Constitution*, 2nd Ed. (Boston: Houghton Mifflin, 1999), 184; second item from Christopher Lee, "Majority Think Innocent Have Been Executed," *Dallas Morning News*, June 22, 2000, A1; third item from *The Gallup Poll: Public Opinion 2001* (Wilmington, DE: Scholarly Resources, 2002), 147; fourth and fifth items from 2004 National Election Study, supplied by Professor Daron Shaw of the Government Department of the University of Texas at Austin.

ELECTION CAMPAIGNS

Democracies do not hold elections unannounced. There is a period of time before the voting day in which the candidates attempt to persuade potential voters to support them. This period is the **campaign.** In Texas, would-be office-holders run initially during the primary campaign. Those who win nomination in the primary

TABLE 5.4

Anglo and Mexican American Public Opinion, Early 1990s–2004

	Percentage agreeing among	
Question	*Anglos*	*Mexican Americans*
Government spending should increase on:		
Programs to help blacks; 1990	23.5	53.7
Programs for refugees and legal immigrants; 1990	16.4	41.3
English should be the official language (strongly agree); 1990	45.6	13.7
The basis of job hires and college admissions should be, 1990:		
Government quotas	1.7	19.4
Strictly merit	52.0	29.3
Support death penalty (Texas only); 2000	81	55
Feel that racial minorities in this country have equal job opportunities with Whites; 2001	53	46
Favor aid to Hispanic Americans; 2004	15	44

SOURCES: Rudolfo O. de la Garza, Louis DeSipio, F. Chris Garcia, John Garcia, and Angelo Falcon, *Latino Voices: Mexican, Puerto Rican, and Cuban Perspectives on American Politics* (Boulder, CO: Westview, 1992), 91, 97, 110, copyright (c) 1992 by Westview Press, used by permission of Westview Press; death penalty item from Christopher Lee, "Majority Think Innocent Have Been Executed," *Dallas Morning News*, June 22, 2000, A1; job opportunity item from *The Gallup Poll: Public Opinion 2001* (Wilmington, DE: Scholarly Resources, 2002), 147; final item from the 2004 National Election Study, supplied by Professor Daron Shaw of the Government Department of the University of Texas at Austin.

then campaign to win the general election. Candidates for public office must have two essential resources: people and money.

People

Candidates need both professional and volunteer help. The professionals plan, organize, and manage the campaign; write the speeches; and raise the money. Volunteer workers are the active amateurs who distribute literature, register and canvass voters, and get supporters to the polls on election day. No major election can be won without competent people who are brought together early to plan, organize, and conduct an effective campaign or without a sufficient number of volunteers to make the personal contacts and get out the vote.

The act of volunteering to work on a campaign is not only useful to the candidate; it is of great importance to the volunteers and to the democratic process. People who work on a campaign learn about the stupendous exertions, the difficult decisions, and the painful blunders that make up public life in a free society. They learn tolerance for other points of view, how to argue and evaluate the arguments of other people, and why the media is important. Finally, they learn that when they win, all the faults of the republic are not corrected, and when they lose, civilization does not collapse. They learn, in other words, to be good citizens. In Texas as elsewhere, political campaigns are the most intense means of creating the truly participatory society.

Money

Voluntary participation, the first major resource of campaigns, is thus entirely uncontroversial. Everyone endorses it. But about the second resource, money, there is great controversy. Except in municipal elections, where volunteers are most important, money is the most important campaign resource. Politicians need money to publicize their candidacies, especially via television. The need to buy campaign advertising repeatedly over the course of months in Texas's many media markets makes the cost of running for office in the Lone Star State formidable. For example, Tony Sanchez spent more than $67 million attempting to defeat Rick Perry (62 percent of it for television advertising) and win the governorship in 2002, while Perry spent almost $28 million (73 percent of it for television) to successfully defend his hold on the office. The two major-party candidates for lieutenant governor, David Dewhurst and John Sharp, spent about $12 million between them; the major-party candidates for attorney general, Greg Abbott and Kirk Watson, spent roughly $4.5 million.[3]

This money must come from somewhere. A very few candidates, such as Republican Clayton Williams, who ran for governor in 1990, and Sanchez, are so rich that they are able to finance their own campaigns. The great majority of candidates, however, must get their funding from somewhere other than their own pockets.

The United States is one of the few democracies in the world that does not have **publicly funded campaigns.** In other countries, the government gives tax money to the parties for their campaigning expenses. This practice ensures that the parties, if their candidates are successful, are relatively free of obligation to special interests. In the United States, at every level except the presidency (and there only partially), however, we rely upon **privately funded campaigns.** Candidates and parties must persuade private citizens to part with money, or their campaigns will fail.

YOU DECIDE

Should Texas Require Voters to Have a Photo Identification?

In the 2005 legislative session, Republican representative Mary Denny introduced House Bill 1706, which, if it had passed, would have required citizens to show a photo ID, such as a driver's license, before they could be issued a ballot at a polling booth on election day. The bill passed the House of Representatives over Democratic objections, but was killed by Democratic parliamentary maneuvers in the Senate. Before being defeated, however, it sparked a debate between the parties, both in and out of the legislature.

Pro

▷ Anyone needs a photo identification to rent a videocassette, which demonstrates that such measures are needed to prevent fraud; it is even more important that we prevent fraud in the polling booth.

▷ We cannot allow our democracy to be tarnished by voter fraud, and requiring citizens to prove their identity is a good way to prevent such shenanigans.

▷ Public opinion polls show that at least three-quarters of American citizens favor this law.

▷ This law is an effort by Republicans to prevent the poor, the old, and the uneducated from voting; it is simply a new, more sophisticated poll tax.

Con

▷ A study by Daniel Tokaji of Ohio State University concluded that 6 to 10 percent of Americans do not have a photo ID; this bill would disenfranchise such people in Texas.

▷ There is no evidence that voter fraud, of the kind this bill is supposed to prevent, is a major problem; a much bigger problem for our democracy is voter disenfranchisement.

▷ When citizens lack sufficient information, phony "opinions" can be manufactured by questions that are cleverly worded to produce a desired result; in fact, there is no citizen demand for this law.

▷ This law is simply an effort to make democracy cleaner, and evidently, Democrats do not want clean government.

Sources: Mark Lisheron, "Bill Says You Must Show ID to Vote," *Austin American-Statesman*, April 19, 2005, B1; Tina Benkiser, "Democrats Are Blocking a Bill to Halt Voter Fraud," *Austin American-Statesman*, May 16, 2005, A13; Leticia Van de Putte, "Texans Shouldn't Need Driver's Licenses to Vote," *Austin American-Statesman*, May 18, 2005, A11.

The candidate with the most money does not win every election. In 1990, for example, Clayton Williams out-spent Ann Richards two to one and still lost, and in 2002 Sanchez paid out more than two-and-a-half times Perry's total yet failed to defeat him.[4] But the best-financed candidate does win most of the time. And just because a victorious candidate spent less than the loser does not mean that money was unimportant in the campaign. Ann Richards's expenditure of more than $10 million in 1990, and Perry's expenditure of $28 million in 2002, are large chunks of cash by anyone's accounting. In other words, although money may not be a sufficient resource to ensure political victory, it is still a necessary resource. People who are willing to contribute large amounts of money to campaigns, therefore, are extremely important to candidates.

Where Does the Money Come from?   Most of the money given to candidates comes from wealthy donors who represent some sort of special interest. Individual contributions of $5,000 to $20,000 or more are common in campaigns for major state offices, and people and organizations with wealth or access to wealth are able to rent the gratitude of candidates by helping to fund their campaigns. Ordinary people who have to worry about paying their bills are not able to contribute nearly as much and therefore cannot ensure candidates' attention to their concerns. In this way, private funding of campaigns skews public policy in favor of special interests.

Table 5.5 displays some major contributors to John Cornyn and Ron Kirk during their contest for the U.S. Senate in 2002. Following the election, the people and interests

TABLE 5.5

Major Contributors to John Cornyn and Ron Kirk, U.S. Senate Race, 2002

CORNYN	
Name	*Interest*
Donald Carty	Airlines
Michael Dell	Computers
Ebby Halliday	Real estate
B. J. "Red" McCombs	Auto sales; professional football
Chuck Norris	Motion pictures
Lonnie Pilgrim	Chicken ranching
Richard Rogers	Cosmetics
John Zachry	Construction
KIRK	
Garrett Boone	Container store
Johnnie Cochran	Law
Linda Ellerbee	Television journalism
Donald Fisher	Retail clothing
Herb Kelleher	Airlines
Stanley Pearle	Vision care
Howard Schultz	Coffee retailing

SOURCE: Christy Hoppe, "Ain't It Grand?" *Dallas Morning News*, July 21, 2002, A49.

who supported the winner, Cornyn, had more influence over his decisions about public policy than the people and interests who supported Kirk.

Control of Money in Campaigns.   The power of money in campaigns disturbs partisans of democracy because it seems to create an inequality of citizenship. Everyone has only one vote, but some people are millionaires. Those with more money to contribute seem to be "super-citizens" who can wield influence denied to the rest of us. For this reason, for decades many people have been trying to control the impact of money in both the states and the nation. Their success at both levels is spotty at best.

In Texas several laws have been passed to control the use and disclosure of the money collected by candidates. These laws have been made steadily tougher over the years, but they still allow wealthy individuals to purchase more political influence than is available to their fellow citizens.

The 1903 Terrell Election Law.   This law forbid corporations to contribute money directly to candidates for public office. Representative Alexander Watkins Terrell, the author of the bill, had given a speech in which he had argued that corporations, being free from the individual's personal conscience, would "breed public corruption. . . . When corporations obtain control of government, they use the law as an instrument to perpetuate their power."[5] It was this law, that Representative Tom DeLay and his organization Texans for a Republican majority, were indicted for violating in 2004 (see Chapter 1).

The Texas Campaign Reporting and Disclosure Act of 1973.   As amended, this act outlines procedures for campaign reporting and disclosure. It appears to strengthen the election code in several areas where it had been deficient. The act's major provisions are:

1. Every candidate for political office and every political committee within the state must appoint a campaign treasurer before accepting contributions or making expenditures.
2. Contributions exceeding $500 by out-of-state political committees can be made only if the names of contributors of $100 or more are disclosed.
3. Detailed financial reports are required of candidates and managers of campaign committees. They must include a list of all contributions and expenditures over $50.
4. Violators face both civil action and criminal penalties.

The 1973 law sounds like a genuine attempt to force public disclosure of the financial sponsors of candidates. Its great flaw, however, is that it contained no provision for enforcement. Since laws do not enforce themselves, the public reporting of private contributions was at best a haphazard affair. Moreover, the law failed to impose limits on the amount that individuals or organizations could contribute to campaigns; as long as they reported the amount, they could attempt to purchase as much influence as they could afford.

The 1991 Texas Ethics Law.   In 1991 the legislature passed another ethics bill designed to regulate and moderate the impact of private wealth on public policy in

Cartoonist Ben Sargent reminds us that there is more than one way to corrupt democratic government.

SOURCE: Courtesy of Ben Sargent.

campaigns and at other levels of Texas politics. This law created an Ethics Commission that could hold hearings on public complaints, levy fines, and report severe violations to the Travis County (Austin) district attorney for possible prosecution.

Again, however, the law failed to place limits on campaign contributions. Further, it required a "super majority" of six out of eight commissioners for important actions, a provision that was practically guaranteed to prevent the vigorous investigation of violators. As John Steiner, the Ethics Commission's executive director, stated publicly, "There's very little in the way of real enforcement . . . in most of the laws we administer. It's just an unenforced statute—except that if people don't [obey the law], it gets some bad press."[6] There were attempts to toughen this law during the 1993, 1997, 1999, 2001, and 2005 legislatures, but the efforts failed. (See Chapter 3 for a discussion of the 2003 amendments to this law.)

When the Sunset Commission (SC) began evaluating the TEC in 2002 (see Chapter 7 for a discussion of the SC), the supposed ethics watchdog itself came in for some bad publicity. Journalists reported that the TEC had never issued a subpoena, audited a file, or referred a complaint for criminal prosecution. Further, the Commission could not compel targets of an investigation to respond, and therefore campaign organizations had little incentive to provide complete information. Indeed, the public could not tell if financial disclosure reports were accurate because the TEC did not thoroughly check financial disclosure reports.[7] Journalists, students, and scholars go on consulting the information in the TEC database because it is the only source of campaign contribution information. Its value as an accurate view of the money trail in Texas politics, however, is questionable.

In summary, then, there is very little control over, and very little effort to ensure the public disclosure of, the influence of money in Texas political campaigns. As a consequence, people with money have more influence over politicians than do ordinary citizens. For people who take democratic theory seriously, this situation is probably the most disturbing fact about Texas politics.

Negative Campaigning

Unfortunately, the power of money is not the only thing that bothers observers about Texas—and American—election campaigns. Another disturbing characteristic of contemporary campaigning is the use of personal attacks on candidates by their opponents, generally in television spots. Candidates are accused of everything from drug addiction to mental illness to marital infidelity to financial dishonesty to Satanism. Mainly, they are accused of being liars.

People being imperfect creatures, some of these charges are bound to be true. If anyone's past conduct is scrutinized closely, episodes of untruthfulness, unkindness, or sexual misbehavior can usually be uncovered. Candidates are almost always able to dig up some dirt on one another. Since politicians believe that such attacks are effective, they are placing more and more emphasis on the exposure of their competitors' personal flaws to the exclusion of other strategies. Their television advertising attempts to blow up ordinary human weaknesses into evidence of monstrous immorality, to interpret honest mistakes as proof of demonic evil, and to frighten citizens into believing that their opponents are not just mistaken but hateful.

All over the country, during the campaigns of the 1990s and early 2000s, the television airwaves were full of "attack ads" in which candidates accused one another of being sleazy, untrustworthy individuals, and worse. Journalist Charles Krauthammer's summary of the 1994 campaign could just as easily have been applied to other recent elections: "The basic theme of the 1994 campaign is that everyone running is a liar, a cheat, a crook, or a fraud. . . . Every state in the union will be sending to Congress some brutally excoriated campaign survivor. The 104th Congress is guaranteed to be an assembly of the most vilified persons in every community."[8]

Negative campaigning has a corrosive effect on democracy for four reasons. First, some elections are being decided on the basis of inaccurate or irrelevant charges. Second, discussions of public policy and how to solve national or state problems are shunted aside in everyone's eagerness to throw mud. Third, many good people may decide not to enter political life so that they can avoid being the targets of public attack. Fourth, negative campaigning disheartens citizens, who are thus more apt to stay home on election day. Research by political scientists has concluded that such campaigns may depress voter turnout by as much as 5 percent.[9]

Texas has had its share of negative campaigns, and thus, its share of damage to the democratic ideal. A large part of the gubernatorial race in 1990, during both the Democratic primary and the general election, consisted of accusations of illegal drug use by Ann Richards (who won both races despite the charges). The gubernatorial races in 1994 and 1998 were relatively clean, but some of the other contests were savage. The campaign of 2002, as will be discussed shortly, broke all records for viciousness and distortion. Negative campaigning in Texas seems no worse than it is in most states, but that is bad enough.

PUBLIC ELECTIONS

A public election is the only political activity in which large numbers of Texans—although, as we have seen, rarely a majority—are likely to participate. The state has three types of election: primary, general, and special.[10]

Primary Elections

A primary election is an election held within a party to nominate candidates for the general election or choose delegates to a presidential nominating convention. It is because primaries are so important in Texas that parties are weak. Because they do not control nominations, party "leaders" have no discipline over office-holders and so, in reality, cannot lead.

The Texas Election Code provides that any political party whose candidate for governor received 20 percent or more of the vote in the most recent general election must hold a primary to choose candidates for upcoming elections. Parties whose candidates polled less than 20 percent may either hold a primary or choose their candidates by the less expensive method of a nominating convention. In effect, Republicans and Democrats must hold primary elections, while smaller third parties may select their candidates in conventions.

Under Texas law, a candidate must win the nomination with a majority vote in the primary. If there is no majority winner—as there frequently is not if there are more than two candidates—the two leading vote getters meet thirty days later in a primary runoff election.

There are two types of primary elections:

1. The open primary is one in which any registered voter may participate in a party's primary.
2. The closed primary is one in which only registered members of a party may participate in that party's primary.

Technically, Texas laws provide for a closed primary. In practice, however, voters may participate in any primary so long as they have not already voted in the primary of another party. The only realistic sense in which Texas has a closed primary is that once voters have recorded their party affiliation by voting in one party's primary, they cannot participate in the affairs—the runoff primary or the conventions—of another party during the same year.

General Elections

The purpose of a general election is to choose state and national executives and legislators. They are held in even-numbered years on the Tuesday after the first Monday in November. Beginning in 1974, Texas joined the group of states that elect their governors and other state officials in the off year, the even-numbered year between presidential election years. At the same time, the state adopted a constitutional amendment that extended the terms of office for the governor and other state officials from two to four years.

Unlike primary elections, which are conducted by officials of the political parties, general and special elections are the responsibility of the state. The secretary of state is the principal election officer, although the election organization is decentralized and most of the actual work is performed at the county level. Officially, the county commissioners' court is supposed to appoint election judges, choose the method of voting—paper ballots or some type of voting machine—and pay the bills. In practice, the county clerk conducts absentee balloting and actually performs many of the functions charged to the commissioners' court. Nominees of established parties are placed on the ballot when they win a party primary or are chosen by a party convention. New parties and independent candidates get on the general election ballot by presenting a petition signed by a specified number of qualified voters who have not participated in the primary election of another party. The number of required signatures varies with the office. At the local level, it need not exceed 500; at the state level, it is 1 percent of the votes cast in the last gubernatorial election.

There is no standard election ballot in Texas. Primary ballots vary from party to party, and general election ballots vary from county to county. Sometimes citizens are asked to vote by making small holes in a punch card, sometimes by marking a ballot with a special pen, and more and more often, sometimes by pushing a button on an electronic screen (see box). The ballot lists the offices that are to be filled, beginning with the president (in an appropriate year) and continuing to the lowliest local position. Candidates' political party affiliations are listed beside their names, and candidates of the party that polled the most votes in the most recent gubernatorial election are listed first. Other parties' candidates appear in descending order of that party's polling strength in the prior gubernatorial election. Almost all balloting systems include a method by which the citizen can vote a straight party ticket. A space is provided for write-in candidates. Constitutional amendments, if any, are listed separately, usually near the bottom of the ballot, followed by local referendum questions.

Special Elections

In Texas a number of special elections are held in addition to primary and general elections. They may be called at the state level to fill vacancies in Congress or in the state legislature or to vote on proposed constitutional amendments. At the local level, cities sometimes hold special elections to fill vacancies on the city council. Like their general elections, city special elections are nonpartisan. Party labels do not appear beside the candidates' names, and no party certification is needed to get on the ballot.

Absentee and Early Voting

Texas citizens may vote absentee in any election. With an excuse as to why they will be out of town, they can obtain a ballot and vote by mail. If they wish to vote early, in person, they need no excuse. Voting may be done for a period of two weeks before the election, at the county clerk's office or at a variety of polling places throughout the county. Twenty-five to 40 percent of the voters now typically cast early ballots.

The eSlate

Because there is no standard ballot in Texas, the manner in which voters record their choices varies from place to place and changes with the evolution of technology. In 2002 some counties experimented with the eSlate, a mini-computer that permits citizens to record their partisan choices electronically. By 2004 eSlates were standard voting equipment in Travis, Harris, and Brazos counties.

In theory, voters in the areas where the eSlate was in use could find their preferred candidates on an electronic screen and then record their choices by pressing an "enter" button at the bottom of the screen. The voters' choices would be stored electronically in memory devices in the eSlate. After the polls closed, the units would be delivered to a tabulation center, where the votes would be counted. In theory, this type of cybervoting would be more efficient than previous paper balloting, and less subject to fraud. In practice, the new technology, like the older methods that produced paper ballots, proved to be imperfect. A variety of glitches and mistakes, and perhaps efforts to manufacture results, in the early voting period of 2002 sparked embarrassment, charges of partisan vote-tampering, and threats of lawsuits.

Although paper ballots have never deterred dishonest politicians from attempting to steal elections, the problems with the cyberballots underscored the point that no technology is fool- and fraud-proof. Without actual physical ballots that can be checked and stored, electronic records offer an opportunity for manipulation of the results through hacking and other means available to

cyber criminals. Indeed, a team of researchers at Caltech and MIT that examined voting methods during the 2000 election concluded that the traditional, low-tech paper ballots were *less* likely to be lost or fraudulently miscounted than the new e-ballots.

Although state voting officials, including those in Texas, continued to express confidence in the accuracy of the eSlate system, both computer experts and election experience counseled caution. In the 2004 presidential election, an apparent error by an eSlate in an Ohio county gave George W. Bush 3,893 "extra" votes. In 2005 reports by researchers at Johns Hopkins and Stanford emphasized that the potential for mistakes and fraud was still very much with us.

The solution to ballot fraud will remain the same with eSlate as it has been with previous means of recording votes: eternal vigilance by a suspicious public. There is no technological fix for the problems of democracy.

Sources: Rachel Konrad, "Touch-Screen Vote Machine Gets a Paper Trail," *Austin American-Statesman*, February 6, 2006, J3; John McCarthy, "E-Voting Error Had Given Bush 3,893 Extra Votes," *Austin American-Statesman*, November 6, 2004, A9; Kirk Ladendorf, "Election Machines Get E-Vote of Confidence," *Austin American-Statesman*, November 4, 2004, C1; "Early Voting, Latest Technology," *Austin American- Statesman*, October 19, 2002, A1; Ed Housewright and Victoria Loe Hicks, "County Democrats Say Early Votes Miscounted," *Dallas Morning News*, October 23, 2002, A1; Ed Housewright, "County Tries to Prevent More Ballot Problems," *Dallas Morning News*, October 24, 2002, A23; Ed Housewright, "More Early Voting Problems Surface," *Dallas Morning News*, October 25, 2002, A35; "Votescam in the Electronic Age," *Texas Observer*, December 12, 2002, 12.

ELECTIONS OF 1994 THROUGH 2000

The political realignment toward which Texas had been inching since the 1960s finally arrived in 1994. Republicans successfully defended a U.S. Senate seat, picked up two seats in the U.S. House of Representatives, increased their representation in the Texas legislature, and garnered more than 900 local offices. They won both vulnerable Railroad Commission seats and captured majorities on the state supreme court and the state board of education. George W. Bush defeated incumbent Democrat Ann Richards to become Texas's governor. Until 1984 Texas had been a one-party Democratic state. After 1994 it increasingly looked like a one-party Republican state.

The Republican victory was based on a clear pattern of ethnic and economic class cleavages. Democratic balloting was based on lower-income Anglos, Mexican Americans, and African Americans; while Republicans were supported by the wealthier in general, and wealthier Anglos in particular. Because voter turnout was higher in the areas and among the people in which the Republican candidate was strong, he was the winner.

It was perhaps at the level of the judiciary that the Republican Party made the most spectacular gains in 1994. GOP candidates won every seat they contested on the state court of criminal appeals and supreme court, gaining their first majority on the supreme court since the days of Reconstruction. Republicans captured nineteen local judgeships from the Democrats in Harris County alone. The major long-run impact of the Republican court victories was to replace plaintiff-oriented, pro-lawsuit judges with business-oriented, anti-lawsuit judges.

The fact that the 1994 results inaugurated a lasting pattern rather than a temporary perturbation was illustrated by the results of 1996, 1998, and 2000. Republicans continued to win every statewide electoral contest, as well as all of Texas's electoral votes for president. In 1996 the GOP captured its first majority in the state senate in 120 years. Democrats defended a steadily shrinking majority in the state house of representatives, as well as Texas's 32-member delegation to the national House. Republicans were not triumphant everywhere; local enclaves of Democratic support, such as Austin and the Rio Grande Valley, proved resistant to the dominant pattern. But the state as a whole turned ever more decisively into a Republican stronghold.

ELECTIONS OF 2002 AND 2004

Both the campaign and the results of the 2002 election illustrated important trends and concepts in recent Texas politics. The Democrats began an attempted comeback with several historical forces against them. They had been steadily losing electoral strength since 1984. In the aftermath of the terrorist attacks of September 11, 2001, President Bush had become extremely popular, and he was using his popularity to try to help fellow Republican candidates in their 2002 campaigns. He visited his home state several times, speechmaking and fundraising. The Democrats had no such nationally popular hero to assist them in their campaigns since former President Bill Clinton was profoundly unpopular with a majority of Texans.

At the beginning of the contest, however, Democratic prospects did not look entirely hopeless. Unlike its anemic efforts during the 1998 and 2000 campaigns, the party in 2002 had a strategic plan and the money with which to implement it, or so its leaders thought. If the problem with Democrats was that their natural base of African Americans, Mexican Americans, and Anglo liberals were failing to turn out on election day, then the solution was to nominate candidates who energized the base. The party therefore, with some difficulty in the primaries, managed to nominate an African American, Ron Kirk, as its candidate for U.S. Senate; a Mexican American, Tony Sanchez, as its candidate for governor; and an Anglo, John Sharp, as its candidate for lieutenant governor. The Democratic leadership hoped that Kirk would draw African Americans to the polls, Sanchez would draw Hispanics, and Sharp would draw Anglos, all of whom would vote for the other candidates of the party. Moreover, by persuading multimillionaire Sanchez to be the nominee, party leaders hoped to overcome the lack of funding that had sunk Gary Mauro, the party's nominee for governor in 1998.

Sanchez came through with the funding, contributing more than $60 million to his own campaign, but otherwise the Democratic "Dream Team" flopped. As Table 5.6

TABLE 5.6

Economic and Ethnic Voting in 2002 Gubernatorial Election; Exit Survey Data

Group	% Sanchez (D)	% Perry (R)
Ethnicity		
White, Caucasian	24	70
African American, Black	93	7
Latino, Hispanic	60	35
Annual household income		
$8,000 to 11,999	74	26
$15,000 to 19,999	59	36
$20,000 to 24,999	44	53
$35,000 to 39,999	32	60
$100,000 and above	28	68

SOURCE: Republican Party exit polls conducted immediately after 2002 balloting. We are indebted to Daron Shaw and Mike Baselice for making this information available to us.

illustrates, ethnic and economic voting followed familiar trends, with Democrats capturing large majorities of minority voters and those lower on the income scale, and Republicans commanding the allegiance of Anglos and those with higher incomes. If African American, Hispanic, and Anglo liberals had turned out in massive numbers, they might have created a Democratic victory. In fact, although turnout in some Hispanic and African American districts was up slightly from previous off-year elections, it did not rise nearly enough to offset the overwhelming advantage all Republican candidates enjoyed among Anglo voters.

GOP candidates not only won every statewide office, executive, legislative, and judicial, but captured control of the state House of Representatives for the first time since Reconstruction. Democrats, still clutching a bare 17 to 15 edge in the state's delegation to the U.S. House of Representatives as their only consolation, had reason to wonder if there was anything that could make them a viable party in the near future.

As far as the tenor of the 2002 campaign was concerned, all observers agreed that it was the sleaziest, the most vicious, the least democratically informative contest that anyone could remember. With almost all Texas candidates relatively conservative, there were few issues to disagree about. Democrats accused Republican incumbents of failing to deal with the state's insurance crisis (see Chapter 3), but Republican incumbents' actions against Farmers Insurance during the summer seemed to defuse that issue. Republicans tried to tar their opponents with the label "liberal," but such accusations were not credible, given the public records of Sanchez, Kirk, and Sharp. Instead of a wholesome democratic dialogue over differing views of public policy, citizens were treated to a what one journalist, borrowing a term from football, termed "smash-mouth politics."[11]

The most deplorable contest among a host of negative campaigns was the one between Sanchez and Perry for the governorship. Sanchez's television ads were tough, mean, and personal, but at first they at least dealt with public policy. They blamed Perry for the state's troubled schools, ridiculed him for accepting contributions from energy and insurance interests, and mocked him for being an unelected governor. Toward the end of the contest, however, still behind in the polls, Sanchez made an attack on Perry that was unconnected to any issues before the electorate. Perry's chauffeur had been stopped for a traffic violation by a police officer one day in 2001 as he drove the governor to the capitol building. Not aware that there was a camera and voice recorder on the hood of the police car, Perry had gotten out of the limousine and said to the officer, "Why don't you just let us get on down the road?" Sanchez's campaign got hold of the tapes and played them endlessly in television ads, adding "Rick Perry. Why don't we just let him get on down the road?"

It was unfair and unworthy of a hopeful public servant, but it was not the bottom of the barrel. That was supplied by the Perry campaign. For months, Perry had been running ads informing the electorate that during the 1980s one of Sanchez's banks had been discovered to have been knowingly laundering illegal drug money from Mexico. Although the federal judge who had been in charge of the case was happy to tell anyone that, in fact, he had found that Sanchez had not known about the source of the money, the Perry campaign ignored the truth and kept running the misleading ad.[12]

This was bad enough. But after Sanchez's embarrassing "get on down the road" ad, the Perry campaign retaliated with what was perhaps the most noxious spot in the history of negative advertising. Perry put on camera two former federal Drug Enforcement Administration (DEA) agents, who insinuated that Sanchez had somehow been involved in the slaying of DEA agent Enrique "Kiki" Camarena in 1985. There was neither evidence nor reasoning to support the charge—if Sanchez had not known about the drug laundering, he certainly could not have known of any plans that drug traffickers had to kill an undercover agent—but the Perry campaign played the ad over and over in every media market anyway. Although candidates have accused one another of many reprehensible things over the years, this is probably the first time that one has accused another of being a murderer. The fact that the charge was a fictional one made it all the more indefensible.[13]

The campaign and voting of 2002, therefore, fell very far short of constituting a good democratic election. By and large, candidates failed to inform the electorate by debating issues, contenting themselves with spending their money on misleading personal attacks. For their part, the citizens failed to live up to their responsibilities in a democracy, mainly staying at home on election day.

With few statewide candidates running in 2004, the election that year was more noteworthy for its national than its Texas ramifications. Republican President George W. Bush won his home state handily on the way to a narrow re-election victory over John Kerry. On the heels of reapportionment by the 2003 legislature (see Chapter 6), Republicans finally won a majority in the state's delegation to the U.S. House of Representatives. As far as the future was concerned, the most interesting aspect of the balloting was the surge in voter turnout, as a majority of eligible Texas citizens went to the polls for the first time ever.

ELECTION OF 2006

Since 1994 Texas had generally tracked with the rest of the country in its electoral politics. That is, both the state and the nation moved in a Republican direction. In 2006, however, Texas diverged wildly from the pattern evident in the United States as a whole.

Nationally, 2006 was a "throw the rascals out" election, with citizens furious at the Republican Congress for defending the unpopular war in Iraq and seeming to countenance corrupt governance. Republican President George W. Bush was a particular target of voter ire, as about six in ten respondents in ballot-box exit polls reported that they disapproved of the way he was handling his job. Although Bush himself was not running for anything, independent citizens in particular (those who did not identify with either party) voted against Republican candidates to show their opposition to his foreign policy.[14] The Democrats won both the U.S. House of Representatives and the Senate for the first time in twelve years.

The results in Texas were very different. As they had since 1994, Republican candidates won every statewide office, electing or re-electing candidates to the governorship, lieutenant governorship, railroad commission, attorney general, comptroller, agriculture commissioner, land commissioner, and U.S. Senator, and eight judgeships on the supreme court and court of criminal appeals. They kept their majority among the state's 32-member delegation to the U.S. House of Representatives, although Democrat Nick Lampson did defeat a Republican write-in candidate to capture a seat from the 22nd Congressional district, previously represented by scandal-tarred Tom DeLay. In a single race for one of the seats on the state board of education, Democrat Rick Agosto managed to defeat Republican Tony Cunningham. Otherwise, Republicans continued their domination of the state's political structure.

The most interesting and unusual race was for governor, in which incumbent Rick Perry staved off the campaigns of Democrat Chris Bell, independent Carol Keeton Strayhorn, independent Kinky Friedman, and Libertarian James Werner to win re-election with thirty-nine percent of the vote. Bell, who came in second with thirty percent, won a few counties in areas that have come to be "normally" Democratic—those along the Rio Grande and a handful in central and east Texas. Strayhorn won majorities in a small number of widely-scattered counties while collecting eighteen percent, while Friedman, whose eccentric persona had attracted national attention to his campaign, managed to garner only twelve percent and did not win a single county. Werner received the support of only one percent of the voters. Perry gained support from every area of Texas and won the great majority of the state's counties.

A trend that continued, in both Texas and the nation as a whole, was negative and misleading campaign advertising. One journalist described the national tone of campaign television spots in 2006 as "the sorriest, sleaziest, most disheartening and embarrassing in memory."[15] This may have been a slight exaggeration when applied to Texas, for no candidate stooped so low as to accuse his or her opponent of being a murderer in a TV ad, as Rick Perry had accused Tony Sanchez in 2002. Still, the tone of much television advertising in 2006 was laden with innuendo and contempt for truth, let alone good taste. It was not the worst, but it was bad enough.

There were a few local Democratic wrinkles in the statewide Republican triumph. Austin continued to give its votes to the now-minority party. More surprisingly, Dallas county experienced a strong Democratic surge. Democrats won every countywide office. In the most significant contest, Craig Watkins defeated Toby Shook to become the county's first African American district attorney.[16]

By the 2006 election, Democratic statewide candidates were experiencing great difficulty attracting campaign contributions. Here Ben Sargent portrays the Republican elephant being forced to share campaign money not with the Democratic donkey but with independent candidates Carol Keeton Strayhorn and Kinky Freidman.

SOURCE: Courtesy of Ben Sargent.

CONCLUSION

All in all, a survey of voters, campaigns, and elections in Texas does not present a pretty picture. If the legitimacy of government in a democracy depends upon the participation of the citizens, then the strikingly low voter turnout in state elections raises serious questions about the legitimacy of state government. Moreover, the disparity in turnout between ethnic groups most certainly skews public policy away from the patterns that would prevail if all citizens voted. Looking beyond voting, the great impact of money on political campaigns and elections suggests the possibility, if not the certainty, that wealthy elites control the policy process, rendering irrelevant whatever citizen participation exists. Finally, the dominance of negative campaigning in the 2002 election suggests that Texas's method of picking its public servants lies far from the democratic ideal.

A cynical view of democracy finds much support in Texas electoral politics. There is, however, some cause for optimism. The old barriers to participation that kept people from exercising their citizenship are gone, and in fact voter turnout has been rising slowly and unsteadily in recent years. It is possible that time and education will bring more people to fulfill their potential as citizens. Further, the gubernatorial campaigns of 1990 and 2002 proved that money is not the only thing that counts in Texas politics, which leaves hope for the rise of a more intelligent campaign style.

The system, then, is imperfect but not completely depraved. For anyone trying to make a better state, there are many flaws but some reason to hope that they can be corrected.

SUMMARY

Voting, campaigning, and elections are important to study because in a democracy the legitimacy of the government depends upon the people's participation. Thus, despite the fact that single votes almost never determine the outcome of elections, voting is important to the individual, the candidate, and the political system.

Consistent with its Old South political history, Texas until recently attempted to suppress voting by all but wealthy Anglos. Today voter turnout is still below the national average, which is itself comparatively low. Turnout of black and brown citizens is generally lower than the turnout of whites. This disparity makes public policy more conservative than it would otherwise be.

In campaigns, candidates attempt to persuade voters to support them. In order to do so, they are forced to spend large amounts of money, which means they become dependent on wealthy special interests who contribute to their causes. This dominance of campaigns by money has consequences for public policy. Money is not absolutely decisive in campaigns, however, and candidates who are out-spent by their opponents sometimes win.

There are three kinds of election in Texas. Primary elections are held to choose candidates for general elections. General elections are held to determine who will serve in public office. Special elections are held when they are needed between general elections, often to either fill unexpected governmental vacancies or to ratify constitutional amendments.

A comparison of the reality of Texas electoral politics, especially as illustrated by the 2002 campaign, with the ideal of the democratic polity suggests that Texas falls very far below the ideal, but offers some reasons for hope. In particular, rising voter turnout holds the potential for large changes in Texas politics.

STUDY QUESTIONS

1. In the days when Texas deliberately suppressed voter turnout of everyone but wealthy Anglos, was its government legitimate?
2. What sorts of consequences are the result of differences in turnout by ethnic groups in Texas?
3. What effects does money have on campaigns? Are these good or bad for democratic government?
4. What are the consequences for democratic governance of negative campaigning? Does campaigning in Texas seem to be getting better or worse?
5. In what ways did the general elections of 2002, 2004, and 2006 in Texas conform to the state's historical pattern of voting? In what ways did they depart from the state's historical pattern?

SURFING THE WEB

Visit the companion site for this book:

http://www.thomsonedu.com/politicalscience/kraemer

The central source for information on voters, campaigns, and elections in Texas is the Secretary of State's office:

http://www.sos.state.tx.us

You can access this site and then click on specific icons for the type of information that interests you, such as "2006 General Election," "Voter Information," etc.

Here is one of several Web sites that offers visitors a database of campaign contributions and related information. The idea is to permit citizens to find out who has given money to whom, and with what consequences:

http://www.followthemoney.org

Project Vote Smart offers a site featuring information on candidates and issues, all presented with young citizens in mind:

http://www.youngvoters.org

NOTES

1. "White primary" laws and rules prevented voting in primary elections by anyone who was not Caucasian. Although the 15th Amendment to the U.S. Constitution, passed in 1870, guaranteed the right of all citizens of any race to vote in general elections, it did not apply to primaries. The poll tax law required a citizen to pay a tax months in advance of election day in order to register. Unless registered, citizens were not legally qualified to vote. Poor people, of whom many were minority citizens, were often unable to pay the tax and thus became ineligible to vote. The U.S. Supreme Court invalidated Texas's white primary law in 1944 in *Smith v. Allwright*, 321 U.S. 649. The 24th Amendment to the Constitution, adopted in 1964, forbid the poll tax in federal elections. Under threat of federal action, Texas repealed its state poll tax law in 1966 by amendment of its constitution. The state legislature, however, adopted a severe registration law that was, in effect, a poll tax under another name. A federal court struck down this law in *Beare v. Smith*, 321 F. Supp., 1100 (1971).

2. We are grateful to Mike Baselice and Daron Shaw for supplying these data.

3. Colleen McCain Wilson, "For Sanchez, More Wasn't Better," *Dallas Morning News*, November 7, 2002, A1; Laylan Copelin, "Costs Soar in Race to Be Governor," *Austin American-Statesman*, October 29, 2002, B1; Wayne Slater and Pete Slover, "For Sanchez, Perry, the Well Isn't Dry Yet," *Dallas Morning News*, October 13, 2002, A1; Pete Slover, "Political Checks and Balances," *Dallas Morning News*, January 16, 2003, A1.

4. Wilson, Ibid.; Laylan Copelin and David Elliott, "Williams Outspending Richards 2–1," *Austin American-Statesman*, October 30, 1990, A1.

5. Stephen Scheibal and Bill Bishop, "Finance Law's Past Has Flavor of Texas," *Austin American-Statesman*, September 26, 2004, A1.

6. Quoted in Jeff South and Jerry White, "Computer Network Tracks Politicians' Funds," *Austin American-Statesman*, August 16, 1993, B1.

7. Laylan Copelin, "Ethics Panel's Future Hanging in the Balance," *Austin American-Statesman*, April 24, 2002, A1.

8. Charles Krauthammer, "Pols' TV Ads Make Voters Loathe Them," *Houston Chronicle*, November 31, 1994, A14.

9. Stephen Ansolabehere, Shanto Iyengar, Adam Simon, and Nicholas Valentino, "Does Attack Advertising Demobilize the Electorate?" *American Political Science Review*, vol. 88, no. 4, December 1994, 829–838; Kim Fridkin Kahn and Patrick J. Kenney, "Do Negative Campaigns Mobilize or Suppress Turnout? Clarifying the Relationship between Negativity and Participation," *American Political Science Review*, vol. 93, no. 4, December 1999, 877–889; Stephen D. Ansolabehere, Shanto Iyengar, and Adam Simon, "Replicating Experiments Using Aggregate and Survey Data: The Case of Negative Advertising and Turnout," ibid., 901–p909.

10. We are grateful to Paul Miles of the Texas secretary of state's office for helping us to update this material.

11. Christy Hoppe, "At 'Halftime,' State Candidates Continue Smash-Mouth Politics," *Dallas Morning News*, September 1, 2002, A1.

12. "Judge Says Perry Took Ruling out of Context in Ad," *Austin American-Statesman*, July 31, 2002, B3; Molly Ivins, "The Summer of Our Discontent," *Denton Record-Chronicle*, August 10, 2002, A6.

13. Ken Herman, "Perry Uses DEA Murder in New TV Ad," *Austin American-Statesman*, October 26, 2002, B1.

14. Jeff Zeleny and Megan Thee, "Exit Polling Shows Independents, Citing War, Favored Democrats," *New York Times*, November 8, 2006, A1.

15. Barry Schwartz, "Mr. Bland Goes To Washington," *New York Times*, November 7, 2006, A14.

16. "Watkins: 'A New Day in Dallas County,'" www.WFAA.com, accessed November 8, 2006; Dan Felstein and Chase Davis, "Warning For GOP in Harris County," *Houston Chronicle*, November 9, 2006, A1.

6

THE TEXAS LEGISLATURE

If you can't walk into a room and tell right away who's for you and who's against you, you have no business in politics.

Sam Johnson
President Lyndon Johnson's father

The speaker is the facilitator of making the process work. You're never going to remove his ideas. But it should be a process where everybody can have their say, and the speaker doesn't have an agenda.

James "Pete" Laney
Speaker of the Texas House of Representatives, 1993–2003, quoted in State Legislatures, July/August 2002

INTRODUCTION

Legislative bodies are meant to represent the people and to reflect the differing views of a community, state, and nation. At the same time, they are meant to enact public policy, to provide funds for governmental operations, and to perform a host of other functions on behalf of the people who elected their members. The legislature is particularly important in democratic theory because it institutionalizes the people's choices and translates the people's wants into public policy.

The Texas legislature is still not completely representative of the state as a whole, but, especially from the mid-1980s on, it has increased its diversity along ethnic and gender lines. Because both Hispanics and African Americans have, within living memory, been denied the chance to serve in the legislature by the Anglo majority, greater representation by the members of these two groups is a hopeful sign for Texas democracy. Whether gains by ethnic minorities can be sustained remains to be seen during an era of Republican Party domination in view of the traditional allegiance by these groups to the Democratic Party.

Another problematic area is the dominance of big money in Texas politics. Money always talks in politics, and in early editions of this book we described many instances of the influence of wealthy special interests over Democratic politics. Still, the present Republican majority seems especially susceptible to big money and to the policies it advocates. The school funding crisis described in Chapter 9 represents a classic struggle between the "haves" and the "have-nots."

Texas's biennial legislative sessions are the focal point of the state government. In these every-other-year sessions, legislators must wrestle with important economic and social issues, define public morality and provide methods to enforce it, and attend to strictly political chores, such as redistricting. They are handicapped in these endeavors, however, by a number of structural weaknesses in the legislative system and by a historic lack of public confidence and support.

The Texas legislature, like other legislative bodies, is not very easy to understand because it operates under myriad procedural rules as well as informal norms of behavior for its members. Nevertheless, because the state constitution vests the legislature with considerable power, understanding at least the basics of legislative operation is important.

This chapter examines the organization of the legislature: the constitutional, statutory, and informal aspects of legislative structure; the less formalized internal organization of the two houses; and the support staff. It then looks at the legislature in action, with emphasis on important influences on legislation.

STRUCTURE OF THE LEGISLATURE

Size, Elections, and Terms

With the exception of Nebraska, which has a unicameral (single-house) legislature, the American states have patterned themselves on the **bicameral** model of the U.S. Congress. Article III of the Texas Constitution stipulates that the legislature

The most common cause of a vacancy is resignation. However, membership changes in the 79th Legislature included a death and three call-ups for military service.

is composed of a Senate, with 31 members, and a House of Representatives, with 150 members. Key features of the system for electing legislators include:

1. Selection in the November general election in even-numbered years.
2. Election from single-member districts.
3. Two-year terms for House members and four-year staggered terms for senators.
4. A special election called by the governor to fill a vacancy caused by death, resignation, or expulsion from office.

Newly elected legislators take office in January. Whenever **re-apportionment** to establish districts of approximately equal population size occurs—normally once a decade—senators are elected in the same year. They then draw lots to determine who will serve for two years and who will serve the full four-year term. This situation occurred most recently during the election of 2002.

Sessions

Regular Session.   The constitution provides for regular biennial sessions, beginning on the second Tuesday in January of odd-numbered years. These sessions may run no longer than 140 calendar days. These limitations are a reflection of the emphasis on curbing government that underlay the writing of the state constitution. Six other states (Arkansas, Massachusetts, Montana, Nevada, North Dakota, and Oregon) also have biennial sessions; the remaining states have either annual or effectively continuous sessions.

The short biennial legislative session accentuates all the formal and informal factors that influence legislation in Texas. For example, insufficient time for careful consideration of **bills** heightens the power of the presiding officers, the lobbyists, and the governor. Although there have been a number of changes in the specifics of the legislative sessions over the years,[1] voters have consistently rejected amendments providing for annual sessions. They fear increased governmental power and spending, a reflection of the anti-government attitude implicit in a conservative political culture.

Special Sessions.   The governor can call the legislature into special session. Such a session is limited to a maximum of 30 days. The governor determines the agenda for this session. The legislature cannot call itself into special session to consider legislation, although it did convene itself to consider the impeachment of Governor James E. Ferguson in 1917. If either legislators or the governor wish to add items to the call for a special session, they both must agree to do so. Thirty-one other state legislatures have mechanisms for calling themselves into special session.

The governor may call one special session after another if necessary. However, since the voting public has rejected annual sessions several times, Texas governors usually avoid calling numerous special sessions that might appear to function as annual sessions. The average price tag of about $1.7 million is another discouragement.

Nevertheless, governors sometimes have little choice about calling a special session because too much legislative business—often including the state budget—is unfinished. For example, Governor Bill Clements called two special sessions in 1989 and four in 1990 to deal with school finance and workers' compensation. Six weeks before the regular 1991 session ended, Governor Ann Richards had already called a special summer budget session. An additional budget session was needed in 1991, and public-school finance was the subject of a 1992 session. No special sessions were called from 1993 through 2002. Governor Rick Perry called seven special sessions between June 2003 and April 2006, including three controversial special sessions devoted to congressional redistricting in 2003, and four sessions from 2004 to 2006 to deal with school finance.

Legislative Districts

Single-Member Districts.   Only one senator or representative may be elected from a particular district by the people living in that district. These districts must be roughly equal in population for reasons discussed below under the history of legislative districts. Thus, although some districts are 300 times larger than others in geographical size, based on 2003 official U.S. Bureau of the Census population estimates, each senatorial district should have approximately 712,473 residents, and each House district, approximately 147,244.[2]

Mechanics of Districting.   The legislature is responsible for determining the election district lines for its own members as well as for the Texas members of the U.S. Congress. The number of districts in each legislative chamber is fixed by the constitution so that the task at hand is one of **re-districting,** that is, re-drawing the election districts lines on the map. Achieving equally populated districts does not come easily since the task is a highly political one. The way the lines are drawn will determine which party, and sometimes even which candidate, has the best chance of winning the district.

Because redistricting is so controversial, even to the point of dominating the legislative session in which it occurs, the legislature often fails to get the maps drawn. If the legislature fails to redistrict itself, the Legislative Redistricting Board (LRB) comes into play. The LRB is composed of five *ex officio* state officials; that is, they are members by virtue of holding another office. These five are the lieutenant governor, the speaker of the House, the comptroller of public accounts, the general land commissioner, and the attorney general. Already powerful office-holders, once constituted as the LRB they are responsible for both legislative and congressional redistricting in Texas.

In 2001 the House, which had a slight majority of Democrats, passed a redistricting plan that would have favored a number of Democratic incumbents. The Senate failed to pass a redistricting plan and did not take up the House plan. Consequently, the LRB came into play for only the third time since the procedure was established in 1951. Because only the speaker of the House was a Democrat, the LRB plans for the legislature heavily favored the Republicans.

The plan ended up before a three-judge federal court. Although the court panel consisted of two Democrats and only one Republican, it ended up endorsing its own plan for the Texas House of Representatives and adopted the plan that the LRB had produced for the Senate. The upshot of the redistricting struggle was district maps that clearly favored the Republican Party. Even the Republicans were not happy, though, because some GOP members still had their districts divvied up among other Republicans.[3] However, there was no appeal beyond the three-judge panel. The U.S. Supreme Court, once quick to invalidate legislative districts that seemed to reflect ethnic or racial bias, raised the standard of proof in 1999 to include evidence of intentional, outright racial **gerrymandering** to overturn district lines.[4] That higher standard may make for greater disputes on the way lines are drawn.

The frustrations of redistricting came to a head in May 2003 when powerful U.S. Congressman Tom Delay of Texas convinced Texas House members to introduce a congressional redistricting bill that would give more seats to Republicans. Because the congressional districts had been redistricted in 2001, lines did not have to be redrawn, but the move was a partisan power play. Fifty-one Democrats—known as the Killer Ds by Democrats and the Chicken Ds by Republicans—fled across the Oklahoma border to ensure that the two-thirds quorum necessary to vote on legislation could not be obtained. They killed 223 other bills in the process, survived a tornado, and returned to Austin as soon as the deadline for new legislation had passed. However, Governor Rick Perry indicated the possibility of a special session on redistricting for the summer of 2003. The messy fight sprawled over three special legislative sessions and resulted both in more Republican members of Congress and considerable partisan

Reapportionment is always highly partisan, and Texas Democrats were never more sure of that than after legislative redistricting in 2001 and congressional redistricting in 2003. This Ben Sargent cartoon parodies the many "Survivor"-type reality shows popular on television in the early 2000s.

SOURCE: Courtesy of Ben Sargent.

bitterness. As of 2006 the legality of the Texas Congressional districting process was still under dispute in the U.S. Supreme Court.[5]

History.   Prior to the mid-1960s, legislative districts were a hodgepodge based partly on population, partly on geography, and largely on protecting rural interests. Members of the Senate have always been elected in single-member districts, but those districts reflected land area, not population. Indeed, the Texas Constitution once prohibited a single county, regardless of population, from having more than one senator. House districts were constitutionally based on population, but with limitations that worked against urban counties.[6] In addition, *gerrymandering*—drawing district lines in such a way as to give one faction or one party an advantage—is almost always the norm. One cannot take politics out of a political process!

The federal courts changed the ability of the state to artificially limit representation from urban areas and forced the drawing of legislative districts according to population. In 1962, *Baker v. Carr*[7]—the one-person, one-vote case—made the issue of reapportionment justiciable under the U.S. Constitution in a case involving a legislative districting system that gave one group substantial advantages over another. In 1964, *Wesberry v. Sanders* applied one-person, one-vote to U.S. House districts, and *Reynolds v. Sims,* applied the principle to state legislative districts.[8] The Texas House of Representatives continued to use multimember legislative districts[9] until the courts forced some counties to abandon them in 1975 and others volunteered to do so.

Citizens in urban areas, Republicans, and ethnic minority groups have all been prominent in redistricting suits. As Table 6.1 shows, the predominant ethnic minorities in Texas—African Americans and Hispanics—have made some gains through population-based districting. Ethnic minority groups made up slightly more than 31 percent of the legislature in 2005. However, at that time, the non-Anglo population of the state was slightly more than 50 percent, with Hispanics accounting for more than 35 percent and African Americans for 11 percent.

TABLE 6.1

Ethnicity in the Texas Legislature, 1987–2005

Year	Anglo	Hispanic/Mexican American	African American	Asian American
1987	78.5%*	13.3%	8.3%	0%
1989	77.9	14.4	7.7	0
1991	78.5	13.3	8.3	0
1993	73.5	17.7	8.8	0
1995	72.4	18.8	8.8	0
1997	73.0	18.5	8.4	0
1999	71.8	19.3	8.8	0
2001	71.8	19.3	8.8	0
2003	69.6	21.0	8.8	.6
2005	68.5	21.0	9.4	1.1

*Percentages do not always equal 100 due to rounding. In 2002 the first Asian American was elected to the House; she was joined by a second, a man, after the 2004 elections.

TABLE 6.2

Political Party Membership in the Texas Legislature, 1977–2003, Selected Years of Transition

Year	SENATE (N = 31)		HOUSE (N = 150)		BOTH HOUSES (N = 181)	
	Democrat	Republican	Democrat	Republican	Democrat	Republican
1977	90.3%	9.7%	87.3%	12.7%	87.9%	12.1%
1987	80.6	19.4	62.7	37.3	71.3	28.7
1997	45.2	54.8	54.7	45.3	53.0	47.0
2003	38.7	61.3	41.3	58.7	40.9	59.1

Table 6.2 shows the gains made by Republicans in the modern era, with most of these gains coming in urban areas. After the 2002 elections, Republicans held both houses of the legislature, all the executive offices, and all the major judgeships of the state. Democrats kept a slight edge in Congressional seats until 2005.

In addition to ethnic, party, and urban pressures, legislators have to be concerned with the federal Voting Rights Act of 1965 and have to produce districting plans that the governor will not veto. With all these competing demands, it is no wonder that the legislature usually fails to produce a plan that pleases everyone.

Party and Factional Organization

Historically, Texas was a one-party—Democratic—state (see Chapter 4). In the legislature, unlike the situation in the U.S. Congress and many other state legislatures, political party organization did not exist. As a one-party state, Texas saw factionalism within the Democratic Party replace the party differences that characterized other legislative bodies. Political party affiliation and party organization have grown in importance as Texas became a two-party state, and the emphasis on party has continued as the state moves toward one-party status once again, now as a Republican state.

As Table 6.2 shows, Republican representation in the legislature has grown from minuscule in 1977 to a majority in the Texas Senate by 1997 and in both houses by 2003. Beginning in 1983, party members in the House designated floor leaders. In the 1989 session, House Republicans formed a formal caucus for the first time since Reconstruction, and today they regularly select *party whips*—the persons designated to line up votes on behalf of the official party position. However, in both houses, the presiding officers continue to deal with members on an individual basis, unlike the situation in the U.S. Congress, which is organized strictly along party lines.

The 78th Legislature (2003–2004) was the most blatantly partisan one in the modern era, a point demonstrated both by the congressional redistricting battles and the rude treatment that minority party members—and renegade majority party members—received on the floor of the House. House partisanship continued into the 2005–2006 legislature. Nevertheless, the presiding officers continued to appoint committee chairs from both parties in both the 78th and 79th Legislatures.

In 2005 Speaker Tom Craddick appointed 43 committees, with 33 Republicans as chairs and 10 Democrats. Republicans chaired five of the six permanent subcommittees. In the Senate, Lieutenant Governor David Dewhurst appointed nine Republicans as chairs and six Democrats. Democrats also chaired one of the three permanent sub-committees in the Senate. As the number of Democrats fell in each chamber, so also did the number of minority chairs. Another noticeable difference, even between 2003 and 2005, was that minority party members were no longer being assigned the chairmanship of plum committees.

The liberalism or conservatism of a legislator is often more important than the party label. Liberals versus conservatives and urban versus rural/suburban interests are typical divisions. These differences cut across party lines and are most evident on issues such as taxation, spending, education reform, and social welfare programs. Increasingly, though, liberalism and conservatism reflect the party split.

Compensation

Since 1975 members of the Texas legislature have received a salary of $7,200 each year; this figure was established by constitutional amendment. (Texas is one of only six states that set legislative salaries by constitution.) Legislators also receive a $125 per diem—daily—allowance when the legislature is in regular or special session to assist in paying for lodging, meals, and other expenses as of 2005.When they serve on a state board or council or conduct legislative business between sessions, legislators also are entitled to per diem expenses for up to 12 days a month. In addition, they receive a 35-cent mileage allowance, but the mileage payment is limited to a maximum amount equal to the price of an airline ticket under state-contracted airplane fares. (The mileage allowance is less than an individual can claim on his or her federal income tax.) The presiding officers receive the same compensation but also are entitled to apartments furnished by the state.

As Figure 6.1 shows, as of 2004—the last year for which comparative figures were available—California paid legislators $99,000, almost 14 times what Texas, the second largest state, pays. The Texas legislative stipend is not even half of the federal minimum for a family of three to be above the poverty level! The low level of Texas salaries, which voters have repeatedly refused to change, makes legislators simultaneously more susceptible to lobbying tactics—at $7,200, a free lunch is important—and to diverting their attention to finding ways to earn a decent living. The latter task has become more difficult with the increase in committee work between legislative sessions and in the number of special sessions. It also makes the per diem amount—$125 for the period shown in Figure 6.1—more important.

Under a 1991 state constitutional amendment, the Ethics Commission can convene a citizen advisory board to recommend changes in legislative salary; the proposal must then be submitted to the voters. By 2006, however, no such board had been formed. The Ethics Commission also was empowered to increase the per diem expense money and has done so regularly. The commission itself has been controversial because of the low standards it set for the reporting of contributions to state officials.[10]

The bottom line on legislative compensation is that the salary is very low, especially for a high-population state with a complex legislative agenda. The fringe benefits are rather generous, however. Some Texas legislators have manipulated salary, per diem, and travel reimbursements to bring in more than $75,000 a year. The fundamentally undemocratic aspect of legislative compensation is that citizens have authorized only the $7,200 salary and might be surprised at the total compensation package.

FIGURE 6.1

Legislative Salaries, Per Diem in Ten Largest States, 2004

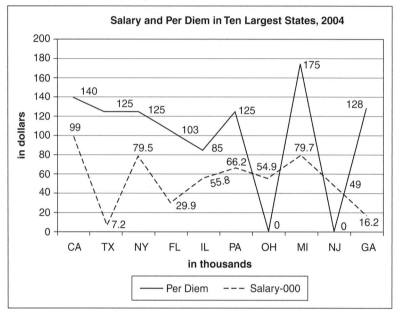

SOURCE: *The Book of the States, 2005 Edition,* vol. 37 (Lexington, KY: Council of State Governments, 2005), 142–143.

Legislators also receive an allowance for operating an office both during the session and in the interim between sessions. These budgets were reduced in the Senate for the 2003 session as a concession to budget deficits but they were increased in the House. Members of the Senate receive $34,000 a month for office expenses unless the senator is also a committee chair with a committee budget to use. Committee chairs in the Senate receive only $31,000 a month. House members receive $11,250. These allowances compare quite favorably with those granted by other states. Additionally, legislators are entitled to retirement benefits if they serve at least twelve years and pay $48 a month. Those benefits are generous because they are pegged to a district judge's salary. A major controversy in 2005 was the legislative decision to raise judges' salaries to $125,000 a year, in effect granting themselves a handsome retirement increase.

MEMBERSHIP CHARACTERISTICS

Formal Qualifications

The formal qualifications necessary to become a member of the Texas legislature are stipulated in Article III of the constitution. They are those commonly required for elected officials: age, residency, U.S. citizenship, and voting status. Members of the Senate must be 26 years of age or older, qualified voters for five years, and residents for one year of the senatorial district from which they are elected. Members of the House must be at least 21 years of age, qualified voters, legal residents of the state for two years, and residents for one year of the district from which they are elected.

Personal Characteristics

The formal qualifications are so broad that a substantial portion of the Texas citizenry is eligible to run for legislative office. However, individuals with certain personal characteristics tend to get elected more readily than individuals who lack these characteristics. These characteristics reflect political, social, and economic realities and traditions and confirm the state's conservative political tradition. That they exist does not mean that they are desirable. Indeed, they indicate that certain groups may be under-represented in the Texas legislature. However, the common personal characteristics also do not necessarily mean that other groups have no spokespersons either among the legislators or the 1,342 lobbyists who registered for the 2005 session. Also, not every legislator has all of these personal characteristics, but an individual elected with none of them would be unusual. In general, Texas legislators are middle-aged white male lawyers or businessmen who are married, have college educations, belong to a number of civic organizations, have considerable personal money as well as access to campaign funds, and have the support of the local media. Historically, they have claimed practice of a mainstream religion. Details of several of these characteristics are shown in Table 6.3.

White, Male.   Race, ethnicity, and gender are all factors in politics. Both ethnic minorities and women are under-represented in the Texas legislature in terms of numbers though not necessarily ideologically. As previously noted, minority membership in the legislature is only about 31 percent, but slowly growing. The first Asian American was elected to the House in 2002; no Native Americans are members of the legislature. Although there are about 100 women for every 97 men in society, slightly less than 20 percent of Texas legislators are women. Of the 58 standing committees in the two Texas legislative chambers in 2005, 13 (22 percent)

TABLE 6.3

Selected Characteristics of Members of the 79th Texas Legislature, 2005–2006

Category	Senate = 31	House = 148–150*
Republicans/Democrats	19/12 (61% to 39%)	86/63 (57% to 42%)
Ethnicity	8 Hispanic, 2 African American (32% minority)	30 Hispanic, 15 African American, 2 Asian American (31% minority)
Women	27 men, 4 women (13% women)	118 men, 31 women (21% women)
Age range	40s–60s	20s–70s
Professions	14 different ones, led by law, fields of business	19 different ones, led by law, business, ranching
Tenure	31 returning (0% turnover)	132 returning, 16 freshmen (11% turnover)

*The House had some instability in 2005–2006 due to a death and military call-ups; part of the time, three more women served in the House as surrogates for their called-up husbands.

SOURCE: Legislative Reference Library at www.lrl.state.tx.us/legis/profile79.html; the official House Web site at www.house.state.tx.us; the Senate Fact Sheet at www.senate.state.tx.us/75r/Senate/Facts.htm; and an e-mail from Representative Garnet Coleman, March 15, 2006.

are headed by women and 9 (16 percent) are chaired by ethnic minorities. Because more African American and Hispanic legislators are Democrats than Republicans, this minority percentage must be put in the context of a session controlled totally by the GOP.[11]

Lawyers and Businesspeople.   Law traditionally has been seen as preparation for politics. In fact, aspiring politicians often attend law school as a means of gaining entry into politics. The result is that attorneys, who make up less than 4 percent of the state's population, hold about one-third of Texas legislative seats. Their numbers have been waning in recent years, reflecting a national trend away from lawyers as legislators. The most frequent business fields are real estate, insurance, investments, and various kinds of consulting. Table 6.4 shows the wide variety of occupations represented in the 78th Legislature in 2005–2006. The Texas legislature, as depicted by occupation, is truly a citizens' legislature.

Fiftyish.   The median age group of members of the Texas House of Representatives is 40 to 49; of the Texas Senate, 50 to 59. Thus, the growing numbers of young adult and elderly citizens do not seem to be proportionately represented, although legislators of any age can speak for the interests of the young and the old. However, given the paltry salary of legislators, most individuals have to wait until they are financially secure to consider running for office.

Other Factors.   Education, marital status, religion, organization, money, and the media are additional factors in legislative elections. Since the late 1970s, virtually all members of the legislature are college educated, and slightly over half hold more than one degree—especially in law or business. The preponderance of legislators are

TABLE 6.4

Occupations and Professions Represented in the 78th Texas Legislature, 2005–2006

Advertising	Engineering	Ministry
Architecture	Farming	Oil and gas
Aviation	Finance and banking	Pharmacy
Business	Firefighting	Public relations
Chiropractic	Food service/hospitality	Ranching/cattle and/or horse
Civics/government/public service	Insurance	breeding
Communications	Investments	Real estate/property management
Computing/information technology	Law	Retired (unspecified)
Construction/development	Manufacturing	Sales and marketing
Consulting	Medicine/health professions	Steel
Education	Military, including retired	Veterinarian

SOURCES: Official House of Representatives biographies, www.house.state.tx.us/members/pdf/biodata.pdf; Senate Fact Sheet, www.senate.state.tx.us/75r/Senate/Facts.htm.

married, although each year more members decline to state whether or not they are married. In 1991 the legislature had its first acknowledged gay man as a member.

Most legislators no longer include religious preference in their biographical information, and it is increasingly difficult to find current information about the religious preferences of Texas citizens. This reality may reflect a greater sensitivity to religious freedom in the state. The most recent information is from the 1990s, when about two-thirds of both houses were Protestant, a little over one-quarter of each house was Roman Catholic, there were a small number of Jews, and several members did not provide information. Those preferences were roughly in keeping with the preferences of the state's residents as a whole, and one can assume that legislators continue to look a great deal like the general public in their religious preferences. The Texas legislature rarely deals with issues that have a basis in religion although someone's religious views may influence thinking about issues such as school vouchers and abortion.

Legislators also tend to be members of the "right" groups. Membership in civic associations, business and professional groups, and social clubs helps to convince voters that the candidate is a solid citizen. Such memberships also provide contacts with potential campaign donors. Campaigning for office can be expensive, although campaign contributions are somewhat unrelated to the actual cost of election since candidates can keep unexpended funds. In 2004, for example, Speaker Tom Craddick raked in $2,778,974 in campaign contributions; at the low end for successful house campaigns were donations of about $25,000. Contributions for Senate candidates showed a narrower range, from $274,028 to $1,340,950 for successful candidates.[12] Actual election costs ranged from less than $10,000 for a safe (noncompetitive) House seat to $1 million or so in a competitive Senate race. Generally, candidates with some personal money are better able to attract financial support than those of ordinary means, in part because they move in monied circles.

Favorable media exposure—news coverage and editorial endorsements by newspapers, magazines, radio, and especially television—is of tremendous importance during a campaign. The media decide who the leading candidates are and then give them the lion's share of free news space. Texas media tend to be conservative and to endorse business-oriented candidates. As Chapter 5 explains, a significant cost of campaigning is the purchase of media advertising.

Experience and Turnover

Seniority has long been of great importance in the committee structure of the U.S. Congress, and Texas voters in many districts are accustomed to re-electing members of the Texas congressional delegation. However, rapid **turnover** of 20 percent to 25 percent has traditionally characterized the Texas legislature, with the result that state legislators have been accused of being inexperienced and amateurish. Nationally, the turnover rate is 16 percent to 19 percent. Even with the major party shift that occurred in 2002, the turnover rate remained in range—22.6 percent in the Senate and 24.7 percent in the House. In 2005, turnover was very low—no new members in the Senate (0 percent) and 16 in the House (less than 11 percent). Moreover, a typical freshman senator is likely to have had prior governmental experience in the

The spring 2006 Republican primaries were unusual because unhappy members of the Parent Teacher Association decided to take on members of Speaker Tom Craddick's legislative team. They achieved some success, getting two winners and three candidates into the run-offs. The biggest victory was University of Texas at Arlington Professor Diane Patrick's defeat of reigning House Public Education Chair Kent Grusendorf.

Source: Dave Mann, "Wrath of the Soccer Moms," *Texas Observer*, March 24, 2006, 6–9, 18–20. This article takes a good look at how grassroots efforts can be successful.

House, and a typical freshman House member may have served on a county commissioners court, city council, or school board.

What causes legislative turnover? Running for higher office, retirement, moving into the more profitable private sector, and reapportionment/redistricting are among the causes. So are tough urban re-election races, changing party alignments, and the accurate voter perception that seniority is not so important in the state legislature as it is in the U.S. Congress. Nevertheless, seniority is important. Not only does it increase the probability that a legislator will be knowledgeable about policy issues, but it also means that the legislator will understand how the system works. In the Senate especially, the more senior members tend to chair committees.

STRUCTURAL CRITICISMS AND SUGGESTED REFORMS

Criticisms

The Texas legislature seems caught in the proverbial vicious circle. Low salaries and short terms force legislators to maintain other sources of income, a necessity that leads to lack of attention to legislative business, especially between sessions. One legislator offered highly visible proof of the insufficiency of legislative salaries when he sought to live on his state salary and thus qualified for the food stamp program! The low salaries cause legislators to be vulnerable to lobbyists' pressures and "help" (see Chapter 3). Also, they contribute to turnover because many legislators have difficulty earning a living between sessions, particularly if there are several sessions and interim committee work to be done.

The electorate, on the other hand, views the legislature as a group whose members work only 140 days every two years and are paid $103 for each workday, or $14,400 for the two-year term, excluding per diem expense money. Voters consistently defeat proposals for both annual legislative sessions and salary increases. Legislators rarely push the issue of salaries, knowing that the public prefers an image of penury. Yet Texans seem to have little difficulty entrusting a *multibillion*-dollar budget to a poorly paid group of legislators whom they view as amateurs at best and scalawags at worst. Furthermore, they seem oblivious to the detrimental effect on legislation of inadequate salaries for both legislators and their staffs and the resulting dependency on special interests or on "gamesmanship" to maximize the per diem payments.

Suggested Reforms

Sessions. The institution of annual legislative sessions has been a major element in all recent efforts at constitutional revision. Annual sessions would allow legislators time to familiarize themselves with complex legislation, permitting them, for example, to bring a little more knowledge to the chaotic guessing game that produces the state's biennial budget. Annual sessions would virtually eliminate the need for costly special sessions when a crisis arises between regular sessions. Annual sessions would provide time for the continual introduction of all those special resolutions—such as declaring chili the official state dish—that have negligible importance for the general public but take up so much valuable legislative time. They would also provide an opportunity for legislative oversight of the state bureaucracy. Coupled with adequate staff support, annual sessions would allow legislators to engage in more long-range planning of public policy.

The legislature also needs to be empowered to call itself into special session. At present, if legislative leaders see the need for a special session and the governor is reluctant to call one, the legislature is helpless. In thirty other states, legislators can initiate a special session either independently or in conjunction with the governor.[13] At a minimum, legislators need more freedom to add to the agenda of special sessions. Even though a session was called for a specific purpose, other significant items could be entered on the agenda and dispensed with, thus lessening the clutter of the next regular session's agenda.

The restrictions on both regular and special legislative sessions result in a high concentration of political power. The presiding officers dictate the flow of business during regular sessions, and the governor dominates special sessions.

Size and Salaries. Some advocates have long recommended that the Texas House reduce its size to 100 members. Other advocates of reform have suggested that since both houses are now elected on the basis of population distribution, one house should be eliminated altogether and a unicameral legislature adopted. But tradition strongly militates against such a change. The physical size of the state poses another risk to reducing the size of the legislature: As population and thus district size continue to grow, citizens will increasingly lose contact with their representatives. A reduction in the number of legislators would be a trade-off between legislative efficiency and representativeness. Although efficiency is important to citizens, so is being represented by someone from a small enough geographic and population area to understand the needs of the people in the district.

More serious are recommendations for salary increases. The $7,200 salary is insufficient to allow legislators to devote their full energies to state business. A salary close to the median salary for the nine other largest states—$58,911—would not, of course, guarantee that legislators would be honest and conscientious and devote all of their working time to the business of the state. However, a decent salary level would ensure that those who wished to could spend most of their time on state business. It might also help to eliminate the retainer fees, consultant fees, and legal fees now paid to many legislators.

Terms of Office.   If Senate members had staggered six-year terms and House members staggered four-year terms, legislators could be assured of having time to develop expertise in both procedures and substantive policy. Moreover, the virtually continuous campaigning by legislators who represent highly competitive urban districts would be reduced greatly, leaving them more time to spend on legislative functions. Less campaigning might also serve to weaken the tie between legislators and the lobbyists who furnish both financial support for campaigning and bill-drafting services.

A new aspect of terms that is emerging in many states is term limitations. Fifteen other states have enacted some type of limit on the number of terms that a legislator can serve.[14] Efforts to amend the Texas Constitution to provide term limits have thus far failed. Term limits are inherently ironic. In an effort to place restrictions on legislators, enthusiasts are robbing future voters of the right to elect an incumbent. Thus, democracy today seeks to eliminate democracy tomorrow.

THE PRESIDING OFFICERS

The presiding officers of any legislative assembly have more power and prestige than ordinary members. In Texas, however, the lieutenant governor and the speaker of the House have such sweeping procedural, organizational, administrative, and planning authority that they truly dominate the legislative scene.

Although most state legislatures have partisan leadership positions analogous to the majority and minority leaders in the U.S. Congress, this is not yet the case in Texas because of the historical one-party tradition and the more recent tendency to have bipartisan leadership even with a resurfacing of a one-party state. The committee chairs hold the secondary positions of power, after the presiding officers. Chairs are appointed by the presiding officers and thus offer no threat to the power of either the speaker or the lieutenant governor.

The Lieutenant Governor

The lieutenant governor is elected independently by the citizenry, serves as president of the Senate but is not a member of it, and does not run on the ticket with the gubernatorial candidate. The lieutenant governor rarely performs executive functions and is chiefly a legislative official. The term of the office is four years.

Twenty-seven other states use the lieutenant governor as the presiding officer of the upper house. But these states (usually) also look to the governor for policy recommendations; their chamber rules are such that the lieutenant governor, far from exercising any real power, is generally in a position similar to that of the vice president of the United States—neither an important executive nor a legislative force. Such is not the case in Texas, where the lieutenant governor is a major force in state politics and the dominant figure during legislative sessions. The lieutenant governor orchestrates the flow of legislation in the upper house.

Republican David Dewhurst, a wealthy businessman and former Central Intelligence Agency (CIA) agent, whose only previous public office was a single term as commissioner of the General Land Office, was elected lieutenant governor in 2002. His was the closest major race in the state, with popular former Comptroller John Sharp, a Democrat, running as his opponent. Both because of a campaign filled with gaffes and his lack of legislative experience, early speculation was that Dewhurst was likely to be an ineffective presiding officer. However, he apparently did his homework before the 2003 session, seeking the advice of experienced senators, organizing the Senate quickly for business, and appointing committee chairs from both parties, a precedent begun thirty years earlier by Lieutenant Governor William P. (Bill) Hobby.

Dewhurst's immediate predecessors were both Republicans. Bill Ratliff, a Senate powerhouse, was selected by his colleagues to act as presiding officer for the 2001 session. Lieutenant Governor Rick Perry, who presided over the 1999 session, had moved up to the governor's mansion in late 2000 following Governor George W. Bush's election to the U.S. presidency. Ratliff chose to return to the Senate rather than run for lieutenant governor. These two short-term presiding officers followed two long-term presiding officers, both Democrats. Bob Bullock ruled the Senate from 1991 until 1999, and Bill Hobby presided over the Senate from 1973 until 1991.

These men displayed a wide range of leadership styles. Hobby was calm and dispassionate; Bullock was often partisan, though such a big supporter of Bush that his Democratic colleagues grew critical; Perry tended to push Republican issues in a partisan fashion; Ratliff was a master of technique. The early evaluations of Dewhurst were that he was a good listener, had assembled an able staff, and was successful in the job. Later evaluations pointed to the friction between Dewhurst and House Speaker Tom Craddick despite Dewhurst's giving in to the governor and speaker on the issue of congressional redistricting, but his remaining penchant for being a "policy wonk" even for good public policy went against the preferences of other Republican power brokers.[15]

Speaker of the House

The speaker of the Texas House of Representatives is an elected member of the House who is formally chosen as speaker by a majority vote of the House membership at the opening of the legislative session. The results of the election are rarely a surprise; by the time the session opens, everyone knows who the speaker will be. Candidates for speaker begin maneuvering for support long before the previous session has ended. And during the interim between sessions, they not only campaign for election to the House in their home districts but also try to secure from fellow House members written pledges of support in the race for speaker. If an incumbent speaker is seeking re-election, usually no other candidates run, although Democrat Senfronia Thompson challenged Tom Craddick in 2006.

It is important for legislators to know whether the speaker is seeking re-election because they must decide whether to back the incumbent or take a chance on supporting a challenger. The decision is crucial: The speaker can reward supporters by giving them key committee assignments—perhaps even the opportunity to chair a committee—and by helping them campaign for re-election to the legislature. A House member who throws support in the wrong direction risks legislative oblivion.

Until 1951 speakers traditionally served for one term; from 1951 to 1975 they served either one or two. The House seems to have abandoned the limited-term tradition, however. Billy Clayton served four terms as speaker (1975–1983). Both Gib Lewis (1983–1993) and James E. (Pete) Laney (1993–2003) served five terms.

When a majority of Republicans was elected to the House in 2002 for the first time since Reconstruction, Tom Craddick, a long-time Midland legislator, quickly secured the necessary votes to become speaker in 2003. Controversy surrounded him instantly because his staff was filled with insurance industry lobbyists at a time when insurance reform was likely to be a significant item in the forthcoming legislative session—he seemed to be going against the admonition in the chapter-opening quotation of not having his own agenda. It is not unusual for legislative leaders or state executives to appoint prominent lobbyists to their staffs; mainly former legislators, the lobbyists tend to be very wise in the ways of state politics. In Craddick's case, though, it is was the tie to the insurance lobby as well as allegations that he had shown favoritism in the previous legislative session toward interests represented by his daughter, a lobbyist. Craddick added fuel to the proverbial fire because he also did away with seniority appointments on the all-important budget-writing committee, loosened controls over House committee spending, and was slow in making committee appointments. Democrats were concerned that the minority voice would be stifled and alleged that Speaker Craddick had loaded important committees with ultra-conservative ideologues. Craddick's approach was widely criticized as the 2003 session progressed.[16]

Craddick's more partisan approach was bound to draw complaints because Democrats were in the minority for the first time in 130 years. Perhaps a major factor was simply the contrast in the Craddick style than that of his predecessor, Laney, whose approach was lower key. However, Craddick's subsequent behavior as leader made it clear that his approach was, as a popular expression states, "my way or the highway." The media, political analysts, and other observers, including Republicans concerned about the public schools, grew increasingly critical of the speaker's stranglehold on the House and his relentless defense of his positions.[17] In the modern era speaker styles have run the gamut from that of reform (Price Daniel, Jr., and Laney) to partisanship and even ethics violations (Lewis). In the case of Craddick, the style is raw use of power.

Pro Tempore Positions

Pro tempore ("for the time being") positions are largely honorific in Texas. At the beginning of the session, the Senate elects one member to serve as president pro tempore to preside when the lieutenant governor is absent or the lieutenant governor's office becomes vacant pending the selection of a replacement. At the end of the session, another individual is elected to serve as president pro tempore during the legislative interim; this person is usually one of the senior members. House rules also provide for the speaker to appoint someone to preside over the House temporarily or to appoint a speaker pro tempore to serve permanently. Whether to select anyone at all and who the individual will be are options left to the speaker.

The state struggled with public-school funding and other major issues from 2003 on, but the legislature focused on a questionable congressional redistricting instead of on pressing needs. This Ben Sargent cartoon sums up legislative and executive leadership during the period as an empty gas tank.

SOURCE: Courtesy of Ben Sargent.

Presiding Officers' Powers of the Chair

Procedural Powers

1. Appoint one-half or more of the members of substantive committees and all members of procedural and conference committees (both houses require only that some members have experience, and, under Speaker Craddick, House Appropriations has no seniority requirement).
2. Appoint the chairs and vice chairs of all committees.
3. Determine the jurisdiction of committees through the referral of bills.
4. Interpret procedural rules when conflict arises.
5. Schedule legislation for floor action (especially important in the Senate, which lacks a complex calendar system).

6. Recognize members who wish to speak, or not recognize them and thus prevent them from speaking.

Institutional Powers

1. Appoint the members of the Legislative Budget Board and serve as the chair and vice chair.
2. Appoint the members of the Texas Legislative Council and serve as chair and vice chair.
3. Appoint the members of the Legislative Audit Committee and serve as chair and vice chair.

POWERS OF THE PRESIDING OFFICERS

By constitutional mandate, the presiding officer in the Senate is the lieutenant governor, and the presiding officer in the House of Representatives is the speaker of the House. The powers the holders of these two positions enjoy are derived from the rules of the legislative body over which they preside and are of two basic sorts. The first has to do with the organization of the legislature and legislative procedure. In varying degrees, all presiding officers exercise this power of the chair. The second sort of power is institutional, and it has to do with the maintenance of the legislature as an organ of government. A reform-oriented House or Senate can limit the powers of the presiding officers, and in fact did so in 1973 when some committee slots were reserved for seniority appointments. However, tradition and the realities of politics militate against any real overthrow of the powerful legislative leadership and allow changes in the rules by leaders seeking to consolidate power, as was the case by Speaker Craddick in 2003. So does the legislative amateurism that results from short sessions, low pay, and turnover in membership. Powerful leaders are a convenience, albeit sometimes a tiresome or costly one. The significance of some specific procedural and institutional powers of the lieutenant governor and speaker of the House is discussed in the following sections.

Procedural Powers

Legislative committees have life-or-death power over bills. Legislators' appointments to major committees, especially as chair or vice chair, largely determine their influence in the legislature as a whole. Presiding officers can thus use their power of appointment to reward friends and supporters with key positions on important committees and to punish opponents with insignificant positions on minor committees.

Committee Membership.   In both houses, the majority of the members of all substantive standing committees are appointed by the presiding officer while a minority gain their seats by seniority. The speaker also appoints all members of procedural committees dealing with the internal business of the House as well as all Appropriations Committee members. When Pete Laney became speaker in 1993, he loosened the committee system by eliminating the budget and oversight chair (which Gib Lewis had added to each committee to increase his appointment power) and by eliminating five standing committees. In doing so, he reduced his own power. Tom Craddick took a different approach as speaker beginning in 2003 by eliminating all seniority appointments to the Appropriations Committee and staffing it with carefully chosen budget liaisons from 27 other committees. In 2005 he eliminated some seniority positions from other committees. In the Senate, the lieutenant governor, as president of the Senate, has long played an especially influential role in deciding committee membership because Senate rules have never stipulated that a majority of appointments must be based on prior service. The presiding officers appoint all committee chairs and vice chairs. The governor may make appointments to special interim study committees that function between legislative sessions, but the legislature has the power to approve or disapprove the appointments.

Representatives of special interests, as well as legislators, are frequently involved in the bargaining that eventually determines who will fill committee slots. Interest groups want friends on committees who have influence in their areas of interest, so they lobby the presiding officers in an effort to secure appointments favorable to them.

Conference Committees.   A bill seldom passes both houses in identical form. Each time one fails to do so, a conference committee must be appointed to resolve the differences. Before 1973 conference committees could, and frequently did, produce virtually new bills. Since 1973 they have been limited to ironing out differences. This limitation is not followed closely, however, and it may be changed at any time because it must be re-adopted each session.

Five members from each house are appointed to conference committees by the respective presiding officer. Each house has one vote on the conference committee report—in other words, three members of each house's team of five must agree on the conference version of the bill—before the bill can be reported back to the House and Senate. The conference report must be accepted or rejected, without change, by each house. Thus conference committee members are key figures in the legislative process. Most conference reports, or versions of the bill, are accepted because of the press of time.

Appointees to conference committees usually share the viewpoints of the presiding officers on what should be done with the bill in question. Representatives of special interests often become involved in conference committee deliberations in an attempt to arrange trade-offs or bargains with the presiding officers, making one concession in exchange for another. Sometimes, however, the main proponents of the two versions of the bill work out a compromise and the committee never meets.

Committee Chairs.   The standing committees control legislation, and their chairs, who specify the committee agenda as well as subcommittee jurisdiction and assignments, control the committees and their budgets. Lobbyists for special interest groups also work hard to influence the selection of chairs and vice chairs of committees. Their hope is that the chair will be someone who has been friendly in the past to interests represented by the lobbyists. The dynamics of lobby influence on the legislature are described in Chapter 3. The reward and punishment aspect of committee appointments is especially evident in the appointment of chairs, for it is through them that the presiding officers control legislation. Seniority is relatively unimportant in determining committee chairs.

Obviously, political enemies of the lieutenant governor or the speaker are not likely to chair standing committees. For example, Lieutenant Governor Bullock appointed only Democrats as committee chairs for the 1991 session in a futile effort to block growing Republican strength. In 2003 Speaker Craddick named a number of less-experienced House members to positions as chairs and vice chairs saying that he wanted "fresh minds."

Referral.   Which committee has jurisdiction over what type of legislative proposal is ill-defined by the Texas legislature because of the growth in the number of committees. In 2001 the House had 38 committees; in 2005, 43—the number continues to creep up. The Senate had 13 committees in 2001 and grew to fifteen for 2003 and 2005.

The Senate numbers go up and down with different sessions. In both chambers, the presiding officers enjoy more discretion in referring bills to committees than do their counterparts in the U.S. Congress, where committee jurisdictions are relatively clear. The greater the degree of ambiguity, the more power the presiding officer has to refer a bill to a committee that will act favorably or negatively on it, depending on the wishes of the presiding officer. The presiding officer of the Senate may be over-ruled by the members, who can force a change in referral.

Some factors that the presiding officers consider when assigning bills to committees are (1) the position of their own financial supporters and political backers on the bill; (2) the effect of the bill on other legislation, especially with regard to funding; (3) their own ideological commitment to the bill; (4) the record of support or nonsupport of the bill's backers, both legislators and special interests; and (5) the bargaining in which the bill's backers are willing to engage, including promises of desired support of or opposition to other bills on which the presiding officers have strong positions and a willingness to modify the bill itself.

Scheduling and the Calendar.   In all legislative bodies, bills are assigned a time for debate. This scheduling—placing bills on a legislative calendar—determines the order in which bills are debated and voted on. In the U.S. Congress, the majority leader controls the two Senate calendars; the Rules Committee of the House assigns bills to one of five calendars. In Texas the presiding officers heavily influence to which calendar, and where on that calendar, a bill will be assigned. The Texas House uses four calendars; additionally, the House uses seven categories to group bills and resolutions in these calendars. The Senate has one official calendar plus the intent calendar, explained later.

Ways to Block a Bill

The Filibuster

Former Senator Bill Meier, who talked for 43 hours straight in 1977, holds the Texas and world records for filibustering. More recently, in 1993, Senator Gonzalo Barrientos stopped just short of 18 hours in an unsuccessful effort to protect Barton Creek and its popular swimming hole in his Austin district.

The Technicality

One of the most bizarre events in the history of the Texas legislature occurred in 1997, when conservative Representative Arlene Wohlgemuth, angry at the blockage of a bill requiring parental notification before girls under 18 could get an abortion, raised a point of order about the calendar for May 26. The effect was to kill 52 bills that were scheduled for debate because the point of order concerned the calendar itself. Her fellow legislators referred to the incident as the "Memorial Day Massacre" and were irate that months of work, including the delicate negotiations between the House and Senate members to achieve compromise bills, apparently had been for naught. After tempers cooled, legislators began to find ways to resurrect some of the bills by tacking them onto other bills that had not been on the calendar for Memorial Day and by using resolutions.

Pocketing

The presiding officers can also block bills by pocketing them; that is, they can decline to send a bill to the floor for debate even though a committee has given it a favorable report. Often a presiding officer pockets a bill because it virtually duplicates one already in the legislative pipeline or to keep an unimportant bill from cluttering up the agenda near the end of the session when major legislation is pending.

Scheduling is more important in Texas than in some other states or in Congress because of the short biennial legislative session. A bill that is placed far down on the schedule may not come to the floor before the session reaches its 140-day mandatory adjournment. In addition, the calendars are called in an order, and some calendars do not allow debate. For example, it is highly advantageous to have a bill placed on the Local, Consent, and Resolutions Calendar in the House, which is used for uncontested legislation. The timing of debate may well determine the outcome of the vote.

Legislative strategies include trying to delay the call of a bill until negative votes can be lined up or, on the other hand, trying to rush a bill through before opposition can materialize. A bill can be slowed down by tacking on frivolous amendments. Another factor to be considered in Senate scheduling is the possibility of a **filibuster**, which is an effort by someone who does not have enough votes to defeat a bill to "talk it to death." A simple majority vote is necessary to stop debate. In the closing days of the session, when much important legislation must still be considered, a filibuster can be very effective. In addition, senators can **tag** a bill. Tagging marks a bill and requires a delay of at least 48 hours before the proposed legislation can be heard in committee. Like the filibuster, such an action in the waning days of the session is usually sure death for a bill.

Although their power is great, the presiding officers do not have absolute control of the calendars. Bills can be—and usually are—taken off the single Senate calendar out of order by a two-thirds vote, although in many cases it is the lieutenant governor who wields the influence to arrange the change. For a member who wants to propose consideration of a bill out of order, the consent of the lieutenant governor, who can choose to recognize that member or not, is essential. Indeed, when Bill Hobby was lieutenant governor, he formalized this procedure of asking for a bill to be taken up out of order by establishing an *intent* calendar. In the House, the Calendars Committee and the Local and Consent Calendars Committee actually control the placement of bills on the calendars, making the speaker's power indirect. However, the speaker appoints committees, their chairs, and their vice chairs.

Recognition.   One prerogative of the presiding officer of any assembly is to recognize individuals who wish to speak. In legislative bodies, with the occasional exception of presiding officers who are simply arbitrary, the recognition power is traditionally invoked in a fair and judicious manner.

In Texas the lieutenant governor actually has more formal recognition power than does the speaker. A quirk in Senate procedure stipulates that a bill must receive a two-thirds vote before floor consideration can actually begin. This procedure, rather than the calendar, has the effect of determining if and when a bill will be considered. The bill's sponsor must be recognized by the lieutenant governor before the bill can be moved for consideration. The sponsor also needs the presiding officer's support to garner the necessary

The two-thirds rule is rarely violated, and the minority counts on it as a means of bottling up an undesirable bill. An exception was made by Lieutenant Governor David Dewhurst in 2003 to force the congressional redistricting bill onto the floor.

The lieutenant governor/president of the Senate votes only in case of a tie; the speaker is a voting member of the House. One of the most extraordinary uses of speaker power occurred in 1967 when Speaker Ben Barnes voted to make a tie, then voted again to break the tie on a bill he favored. He thus cast two votes on the same bill.

two-thirds vote; a lieutenant governor who opposes a piece of legislation can often influence 11 senators to block consideration of the bill. The consequence of this concentration of power is that the presiding officer almost single-handedly controls legislation in the Senate.

Procedures.   At the beginning of each regular session of the Texas legislature, each house adopts the rules of procedure that will govern that session's legislative process. Although procedures can change considerably, many rules are carried over from one session to another or are only slightly modified. Numerous precedents determine how those rules that are carried over will be applied. Of course, all parliamentary rules are subject to interpretation by the chair.

Procedural interpretation, recognition of those wishing to speak, determination of the timetable for debate, referral of bills, and the appointment of committees and their chairs combine to make the presiding officers powerful indeed. Although none of these powers is unusual for a club president, they take on great significance when we realize that they are used to determine the outcome of policy struggles within a major state. Moreover, the average legislator, who must contend not only with the tremendous influence of the presiding officers but also with other aspects of the Texas legislative system—short terms, short sessions, poor pay, marginal staff support—has no desire to try to wrest control from the presiding officers, even if such a move were politically feasible. House members, especially, are always seeking staff assistance because their office budgets are less than those of senators. Students often volunteer and regularly become very responsible members of a representative's staff. Some become paid staffers.

Institutional Powers

The presiding officers also appoint the members of three important arms of the legislature: the Legislative Budget Board, the Legislative Council, and the Legislative Audit Committee. Each of these bodies exists to serve the legislature as a whole, providing policy guidelines at the board level and technical assistance at the staff level.

The fact that legislators' office budgets do not allow them to employ many professional (as opposed to clerical) staff members makes these arms of the legislature even more important. Members of the legislature have three basic sources of assistance and information: the three agencies described here, state bureaucrats, and lobbyists.

Even major legislative committees have limited budgets for professional staff. Not only do the presiding officers control these three policy-setting and policy-recommending bodies but, for all three, the president of the Senate and the speaker of the House serve as co-chairs. The powers of the three agencies, especially the Legislative Budget Board, were beefed up in 2003 by legislative action.

The Legislative Budget Board.   At the national level, in most states, and even in most cities, the chief executive bears the responsibility for preparing the budget. In Texas, the governor and the legislature each prepare a budget, and state agencies must submit their financial requests to both. The legislative budget is prepared by the Legislative Budget Board (LBB), which is a 10-member joint Senate–House committee that operates continually, whether or not the legislature is in session. In addition to the presiding officers, there are four members from each house, including automatically the chairs of committees responsible for appropriations and finance. Because of the importance of these "money" committees, their chairs sometimes develop power bases within the legislature that are independent of the presiding officers.

A professional staff assists the board in making its budget recommendations and then often helps defend those recommendations during the session. The state appropriations act closely follows the LBB recommendations. Additionally, the staff assists the legislature in its watchdog functions, overseeing state agency expenditures, including, since 2003, the Texas Performance Review described in Chapter 7 and Chapter 10.

The Legislative Council.   The 14-member Legislative Council includes the presiding officers and 6 members of each house who are appointed by their respective presiding officer. The council oversees the work of the director and professional staff. During the session, the Legislative Council provides bill-drafting services for legislators; between sessions, it investigates the operations of state agencies, conducts studies on problems subject to legislative consideration, and drafts recommendations for action in the next session. In short, it is the legislature's research office.

The Legislative Audit Committee.   In addition to the presiding officers, the other four members of the Legislative Audit Committee are the chairs of the taxing committees, the House Appropriations Committee, and one additional senator.[18] The state auditor, appointed by the committee for a two-year term subject to two-thirds confirmation by the Senate, heads the professional staff. This committee oversees a very important function of all legislative bodies, the postaudit of expenditures of state agencies—to ensure their legality—by the auditor and his staff.

The auditor's staff also checks the quality of services and duplication in services and programs provided by state agencies, although the auditor's authority to issue management directives was severely curtailed in 1988. The work of the professional staff is highly detailed, involving a review of the records of financial transactions. In fact, the larger state agencies have an auditor or team of auditors assigned to them virtually year round.

LIMITS ON PRESIDING OFFICERS

It may seem that the presiding officers are nearly unrestrained in their exercise of power. However, several factors, both personal and political, prevent absolutism on the part of the speaker of the House and the lieutenant governor.

YOU DECIDE

Should Seniority Determine Committee Chairs in Texas?

Seniority is extremely important in the Congress of the United States. The seniority rule for determining congressional committee chairs is that the chairmanship goes to the member of the majority party with the longest continuous service on that one committee in that one house of Congress. Senators or U.S. Representatives in their party caucuses can bypass this rule but seldom do. In Texas a committee chair need not belong to the majority party, and the presiding officers determine all the chairs and vice chairs regardless of seniority.

Pro	Con
Texas should select legislative committee chairs by a predominantly majority party–seniority procedure because:	Texas should not use the majority party–seniority procedure favored by the U.S. Congress because:
⇨ The speaker of the House and the lieutenant governor would not be so all-powerful.	⇨ The short legislative session cries out for tight control by the presiding officers.
⇨ The party that the voters prefer would dominate the policy process.	⇨ The majority party did not get all of the votes, and the Texas system allows both parties to have some voice in public policy.
⇨ The chair would always be someone knowledgeable about the committee and its work.	⇨ The most senior person is not the only legislator in the House or Senate who knows procedure or understands the work of the committee.
⇨ The chair would fully understand the legislative process.	⇨ Hard work and a willingness to learn are more important than time spent in office.

Personality and Ambition

Although there is always the danger that presiding officers may become arbitrary or vindictive and thus abuse their office, generally speaking they are so powerful that they do not need to search for ways to gain influence other than persuasion, compromise, and accommodation. Arbitrariness is a function of personality, not of the office. Moreover, a presiding officer who is interested in higher governmental office or a lucrative executive position in the business world will not foolishly alienate special interests.

Legislators

State senators and representatives have their own power bases, without which they probably would not have been elected. Long-time members not only have supporters across the state, including influential special interest groups, but they also have the advantage that seniority brings in the legislature itself, especially if they have served as the chair of a major committee for more than one session. For example, Senator Bill Ratliff, already a seasoned committee chair as the head of the powerful Education Committee, became even more powerful when he was tapped to chair the Finance Committee in 1997 and 1999. After serving as the Senate presiding officer in 2001, he became chair of the powerful State Affairs Committee in 2003, then declined to run for re-election in 2004.

Although it may appear that the membership always seems to follow the lead of the presiding officers, in many cases the members hold the same ideological positions to begin with. The leadership usually is conservative, and so are most legislators. In other instances, members will go along with the leadership in hopes of being able to act independently later on matters of importance to themselves or their districts.

Finally, the powers of the presiding officers are largely granted by House and Senate rules. A totally arbitrary leader whose abuse of the system became intolerable could be stripped of power, as Speaker "Uncle Joe" Cannon was when the U.S. House revolted against him in 1910 because of his abuse of power.

Lobbies and State Administrators

Over the past 50 years, as the number of governmental agencies and bureaucrats at all levels has increased, alliances have developed between private and public interests. A presiding officer faced with such an alliance is seldom able to overcome it. Indeed, these coalitions and the presiding officers often share political viewpoints, making confrontation unlikely.

The public is seldom considered by these alliances, especially when the more powerful special interests of the state (such as oil and gas, insurance, banking, and real estate) are involved. An example of bureaucracy/private-interest alliances is that of the Texas Education Agency and the Texas State Teachers Association. When the legislative committees with jurisdiction over, say, roads or education, join these alliances, the confederation is a very powerful one.

The Governor

Constitutionally, the governor is a weak chief administrator, and hence the alliance of state bureaucrats is with the lobbyists and not with the chief executive. But the governor is by no means a weak chief legislator. The governor's veto power is almost absolute because the legislature often adjourns before the governor has had to act on a bill. A governor who wants a particular piece of legislation enacted can threaten the legislature with a special session if the legislation seems to be in jeopardy. Because special sessions are costly to state legislators in terms of both time and money, such a threat can be a powerful tool for the governor. The governor must be prepared to make good on such a threat, as, for example, Bill Clements did when he called a special session on tort reform—that is, changes in the basis of civil lawsuits—in 1987 after failing to get action from the 1987 Legislature. Another one of the governor's strengths lies in the strong ties a conservative (usually the political orientation of a Texas governor) has to the same interest groups as the legislators have. Such ties often make it possible to call on these interest groups to support a gubernatorial position in conflict with the legislature.

The Electorate and the Constituents

Legislative bodies were created to be the people's voice in government. In reality, however, the citizens are usually unable to exert as much influence over the leadership and members of the Texas legislature as state officials and private interests do. One reason for this situation is the power of campaign contributions; another is the lack of concern on the part of most citizens about what goes on in Austin. Public interest perks up in the face of governmental scandal, but the ordinary day-to-day legislative events do not interest most Texans, who have neither the education nor the time to become specialists in the details of governing. Public apathy and the lack of understanding of the legislature's work contribute mightily to the resistance to change that is so often manifested when efforts at constitutional reforms are made. Nevertheless, legislators are well aware that such issues as education reform and income tax create public interest, and they live in dread of having to consider such provocative matters.

HOW A BILL BECOMES A LAW IN TEXAS

The Texas Constitution specifies that a bill be used to introduce a law or a change in a law. Bills that pass successfully through both houses become acts and are sent to the governor for signature or veto. In addition to bills, there are three types of resolution in each house:

1. *Simple resolutions* are used in each house to take care of housekeeping matters, details of business, and trivia.
2. *Concurrent resolutions* are similar to simple resolutions but require the action of both houses. They are used for adjournment, for example.
3. *Joint resolutions* are of major interest to the public because they are the means of introducing proposed constitutional amendments.

Each bill or resolution is identified by an abbreviation that indicates the house of origin, the nature of the legislation, and a number. For example, S.B. 1 is Senate Bill 1; S.J.R. indicates a joint resolution that originated in the Senate. Bills may originate in either house or in both simultaneously, with the exception of revenue bills, which must originate in the House. In the regular session of the 78th Legislature in 2005, a total of 9,338 bills and resolutions of all types were introduced. Of these, 4,961 were passed, including nine proposed constitutional amendments. Many of these items were resolutions, however. The number of actual bills considered was 5,484, with 1,389 passing.

The governor vetoed 19 bills. Each special session results in about 100 to 200 other bills being introduced, with many of them being variations on the same theme. During a redistricting year, the number of pieces of legislative is somewhat smaller.

Because the smaller membership of the Senate enables it to operate with less formality than the House, we will use the Senate to trace the path of a bill through the legislative process. In both houses, knowing "who's for you and who's against you," as the chapter-opening quotation says, is important.

The major differences in the procedures of the two houses are:

1. The House has almost three times as many committees as the Senate; therefore, the speaker has a greater choice in determining where to refer a bill.
2. The calendars are different (as explained earlier in this chapter).
3. Debate is unlimited in the Senate, whereas House debate is usually limited to 10 minutes per member and 20 minutes for the bill's sponsor.

To be enacted into law, a bill must survive four legislative steps and a fifth step in the governor's office (Figure 6.2).[19] As a legislator attempts to get his bill passed, the opening quotation from Sam Johnson is particularly apt: Success depends on knowing who one's friends are.

Step 1: Introduction and Referral

Every bill must be introduced by a member of the legislature, who is considered its sponsor. The bill may either be filed with the clerk if the legislature is not in session or be introduced by a member on the floor. If a bill has several sponsors, so much the better—its chances of survival will be greatly enhanced. Introducing the bill constitutes the first reading. The lieutenant governor—in the House, the speaker—then refers the bill to a committee. If the bill is to survive, it must be assigned to a friendly committee.

Step 2: Committee Action

Standing committees are really miniature legislatures, where the nitty-gritty of legislation takes place. Legislators are so busy—particularly in Texas, with its short, infrequent sessions—that they seldom have time to study bills in detail and so must rely heavily on the committee reports. A bill's sponsor, well aware of the committee's role, will do everything possible to ensure that the committee's report is favorable. It is particularly important to avoid having the bill pigeonholed—put at the bottom of the committee's agenda, with or without discussion, never to be seen again—or totally rewritten, either by the committee or, if the bill is referred to a subcommittee, by the subcommittee. If the bill can escape being pigeonholed, its sponsor will have a chance to bargain with the committee in an effort to avoid too many changes in the bill.

The committee may report the bill favorably, unfavorably, or not at all. An unfavorable report or none at all kills the bill. Unless there is a strong minority report, however, there is little reason for the committee to report a bill unfavorably; it is easier to pigeonhole it and avoid floor action completely.

FIGURE 6.2

How a Bill Becomes a Law in Texas

This figure traces the passage of a bill that originated in the Senate. Steps 1–3 for the Senate and House would be reversed if the bill originated in the House. This example presumes the need for a conference committee.

SENATE

Step 1. Bill is introduced, numbered, given first reading, referred to committee.

Step 2. Committee holds hearings, deliberates, and either pigeonholes the bill, reports it unfavorably, or reports it favorably. Favorable report may include amendments or be a substitute bill. Committee report is printed and distributed to Senate.

Step 3. Senate has second reading, holds debate, amends bill, possibly has a filibuster. Senate then has third reading, debate, amendments only by two-thirds vote. Passed bill is sent to House.

HOUSE

Step 1. House has first reading, and bill is referred to committee.

Step 2. Committee action is the same as in Senate.

Step 3. Floor action is similar to Senate except that no filibuster is possible and scheduling the bill for debate is more complex. Amended bill is returned to Senate.

SENATE AND HOUSE

Step 4. Conference committee irons out differences in House and Senate versions of the bill. Both houses vote on conference compromise bill. Clean copy of the conference bill is prepared. Bill is enrolled and certified in both houses, and sent to the governor.

GOVERNOR

Step 5. Governor may sign the act, let it become a law without his or her signature, or veto it.

left to administrative agencies. Nevertheless, in the short 140-day session, legislators must acquaint themselves with the proposals, try to push their own legislative programs, attend to a heavy burden of casework (tending to constituent problems and requests), spend countless hours in committee work, meet with hometown and interest-group representatives, and hear the professional views of state administrators who implement programs. All the while, they must avoid going into debt because their salaries are inadequate and their personal businesses or professions may slide when the legislature is in session.

Lenient lobbying laws—such as no grace period between leaving the legislature and becoming a lobbyist—lack of public support for adequate information services for legislators, and the need for continual campaigning make the average legislator easy prey for special interest groups. Indeed, on many issues the interests of a legislator's district and of special interest groups overlap and are difficult to distinguish.

Legislators' frustrations are especially evident when the biennial budget is considered. Appropriations are the real battleground of legislative sessions. There always are more programs seeking support than there is money to support them. Power struggles over money continue because each individual who promotes a program—be it for highways, public schools, higher education, law enforcement, utilities rates, environmental protection, lending rates, or welfare administration—believes in either its moral rightness or its economic justification. The winners of these struggles are determined not only by the power and effectiveness of the groups themselves but also by the political preferences of the legislators. Furthermore, the winners largely determine public policy for the state; few government programs can operate without substantial amounts of money.

Lack of public understanding and support is another handicap for legislators. The public often criticizes politicians for being unprincipled and always willing to compromise. But the role of compromise in democracy, and especially in legislative bodies, is undervalued by the citizens. Caught in all the cross-pressures of the legislative system, members rarely have the opportunity to adhere rigidly to their principles. Those who watch closely what happens in the legislature are not the electorate back home but campaign supporters, lobbyists, and influential citizens. Members must satisfy these people as well as bargain with their colleagues if they are to have any chance of getting their own proposals through the legislature or, in fact, being reelected for another term.

Legislators may have to vote for new highways that they view as superfluous to get votes for issues that are important to them and their home districts. They may have to vote in favor of loan-sharking to gain support for tighter regulation of nursing homes. They may have to give up a home-district highway patrol office to obtain funds for needy children. Just as legislators who hope to be successful must quickly learn the procedural rules, they must also learn the art of legislative compromise and horse-trading.

An additional difficulty legislators face is adjustment to the shifting trends within the legislature. Long dominated by rural Democratic conservatives, in recent years the legislature has become more urban/suburban and more Republican. When urban issues are at stake, temporary bipartisan alliances among big-city legislators are frequently formed. Compounding the problem of party and geographic transition is the

Step 3: Floor Action

Once a bill is reported out of committee, it must be scheduled for debate. The calendar is rarely followed in the Senate, so the sponsor moves to suspend the regular calendar order and consider the bill out of sequence. Before taking this action, the sponsor generally obtains an assurance from the presiding officer that she or he will be recognized and thus given an opportunity to make the motion. When the bill receives the necessary two-thirds vote on the motion, it can proceed to a second reading and floor debate. If the second reading has not occurred by the time the legislature is within 72 hours of adjournment, the bill dies. Senators have unlimited privilege of debate; they may speak as long as they wish about a bill on the floor. Sometimes senators use this privilege to filibuster. If a bill is fortunate enough not to become entangled in a filibuster, debate proceeds. During the course of debate, there may be proposed amendments, amendments to amendments, motions to table (that is, lay the bill aside), or even motions to send the bill back to committee. However, if a bill has succeeded in reaching the floor for discussion, it is usually passed in one form or another by a simple majority vote. A third reading of the bill precedes the voting.

One peculiarity of Texas legislative sessions is the constitutional provision for a "split session" of 120 days: The first 30 days are supposed to be devoted to the introduction of bills and resolutions, emergency matters, and confirmation of recess appointments by the governor; the next 30 days to committee hearings; and the final 60 days to floor action on bills and resolutions. However, the session can last up to 140 days, and this provision does not prescribe specific activities for the final 20 days of the session. Moreover, the legislature may bypass the split session provision by taking advantage of another constitutional provision that allows each house to determine its own schedule by a four-fifths vote, or the governor can declare an emergency. In practice, both houses require a four-fifths vote for the introduction of bills after the first 60 days or for voting on a bill during the first 60 days. A governor usually uses the emergency power sparingly—for example, when state government must take care of a crisis and cannot wait for a bill to take effect months later.

In the House: Steps 1 through 3 Repeated

If it was not introduced in both houses simultaneously, a bill passed in the Senate must proceed to the House. There, under its original designation (for example, S.B. 341), it must repeat the same three steps as in the Senate, with the exceptions noted earlier. A bill has little chance of passing if a representative does not shepherd it through. This situation also is true in reverse, when a bill passes the House and then is sent to the Senate. Speaker Pete Laney introduced a number of reforms in 1993 to expedite legislative process and to try to ensure that members had time to think about the actions they were about to take. Speaker Tom Craddick was not obligated to continue all these rules, but a six-hour rule in the waning days of a session does exist; that is, members must have the list of bills to be considered at least six hours in advance. The following discussion assumes that the bill being followed has passed the House, but one amendment was added that was not part of the Senate's version.

Step 4: Conference Committee

Because the Senate and House versions of the bill probably differ, it must go to a conference committee, which consists of ten members, five appointed from each house by the presiding officers. If the House and Senate versions of the bill have substantial differences, the conference committee may attach several amendments or rewrite portions of the bill. The report of the conference committee must be voted on as it stands; neither house can amend it. It must be accepted, rejected, or sent back to the conference committee. If it fails at this time—or, indeed, at any other stage—it is automatically dead. No bill can be introduced twice during one legislative session. If the bill passes both houses, it is sent to the governor.

Step 5: The Governor

The governor has 10 days, excluding Sundays, to dispose of acts. If the legislature adjourns, the 10-day period is extended to 20 days. The governor has three options for dealing with an act. The first is to sign it, thus making it law.

The second is to allow the bill to become law without signing it (a rare procedure). If the governor does not sign it, a bill becomes law in 10 days if the legislature is in session and in 20 days if it is not. By choosing this rather weak course of action, the governor signifies both opposition to the bill and an unwillingness to risk a veto that could be over-ridden by a two-thirds vote of both houses or that would incur the disfavor of special interest groups supporting the bill.

Third, the governor may veto the bill. A veto is a formal action requiring the governor to send a message to the legislature indicating disapproval of the bill. Although it is possible for the legislature to over-ride a veto by a two-thirds vote, the governor often receives legislation so late in the session that the act of vetoing or signing it can be deferred until the session has ended. A veto then is absolute, since it must be over-ridden during the same legislative session in which the act was passed and the legislature cannot call itself into special session. Because recent legislative sessions have been faced with one crisis after another and too little time to deal with issues, the governor's powers have been strengthened through the use of the veto and threats of a veto.

If the governor chooses to veto, the veto applies to the entire bill, except in the case of appropriations bills. On appropriations bills, the governor has the power of item veto; that is, specific items in the bill may be vetoed. This is a powerful gubernatorial tool for limiting state spending, one that the U.S. president had briefly but no longer possesses. For example, Governor Clements, in his first term, vetoed all the special appropriations for universities that underwrote such activities as student scholarships and research institutes.

The two most recent governors offer a vivid contrast in the use of the veto power.

Governor Bush allowed several important bills to become law without his signature, disdaining the veto. Governor Perry vetoed a record-setting 82 bills in 2001, including many bills that were popular with his political party.

If a newly passed bill contains an emergency clause, it becomes effective as law immediately (or at whatever time is specified in the bill). If it does not, it becomes

Public Policy, Legislative Style: A 2005 Sampler

The legislature convened in January 2005 with one huge issue facing it—the funding of public education. Also in question was whether or not Republicans could actually govern now that they were the dominant party; in the past, the Republicans mainly blocked undesirable Democratic legislation but did not have to solve problems. By mid-April 2006, the legislature was meeting in special session for the seventh time, with public education still being the critical agenda item. Although legislators had time to engage in a brutal, but questionable, battle over redistricting for three special sessions, they failed to deal with school finance. As of mid-May 2006, the 78th Legislature passed the following:

- A $139 billion biennial budget that was 19 percent greater than that of the previous biennium
- School finance reform (2006 special session)
- Congressional redistricting
- Stabilization of the teacher retirement system
- Overhaul of the workers' compensation system
- Facilitation of telephone companies entering the cable business (special session)
- Hunting rights on private land even if the land is annexed to a municipality that prohibits the use of firearms

- Designations of Navasota as the blues capital of the state; Dublin as the Irish capital; Madisonville as the mushroom capital; and Buda as the outdoor capital; along with *pan de campo* as the official bread; the cast-iron Dutch oven as the official cooking implement; and Blue Lacy as the official dog
- Proposed constitutional ban on gay marriages (passe by the electorate)

The legislature failed to resolve the following:

- Legalization and taxation of video gambling
- Clarification of the death penalty in the case of mentally retarded defendants
- Requirement of recorded legislators' votes

Sources: Terrence Stutz, "We Couldn't Deliver," *Dallas Morning News*, May 31, 2005, 1A, 10A–11A; Mike Trimble editorial, "It's Official: We're Governed by Idiots," *Denton Record-Chronicle*, May 2005, 18A; *Texas Observer*, June 24, 2005, especially pp. 6–19; "Legislative Leaderboard," *Dallas Morning News*, June 19, 2005, 2P; Paul Burka and Patricia Kilday Hart, with Courtney White, "Th Best and the Worst Legislators of 2005," *Texas Monthly*, July 200 107–119; "Symbolic Achievements," *Texas Highways*, December 2005, 49.

effective 90 days after the session ends. Again, there are special circumstances for appropriations bills, which always become effective on September 1.

LEGISLATIVE HANDICAPS

The public often thinks that the legislature accomplishes very little. In fact, given the limitations under which it must labor, it is amazing that the legislature accomplishes as much as it does, as Lancy's chapter-opening quotation notes. The forces influencing legislation are complex and varied—interest groups, the powers of the presiding officers, constitutional limitations, political parties, the role of committees, short and infrequent sessions, inadequate salaries, and the prerogatives of individual members.

Each legislator must face about 9,000 bills and resolutions every time the legislature convenes in regular session, except that legislators traditionally file about 10 percent to 15 percent fewer bills when the agenda includes redistricting. Some of the bills and resolutions are substantively important; but many are trivial matters that could be

fact that the two houses have not changed in the same way.

The Senate has been Republican since 1997. While the Republicans held a 19 to 12 edge in the Senate in 2003 and 2005, operating in a nonpartisan mode was still necessary because, by Senate rules, 11 senators can block any legislation.

Even with a Democratic majority in the House of Representatives, the alliance of conservative Democrats and Republicans gave the House a distinctly conservative flavor beginning in the mid-1980s. The Texas House of Representatives seemed to draw some strength from the reforms of

Whose Bill Is It, Anyhow?

In response to a question posed by one of the authors, an Austin lawyer–lobbyist, a 20-year veteran with the Texas legislature, thought a moment. He then replied, "Here at the legislature, if you ask the question, 'Whose bill is it?' what you mean is, which lobby wrote it. If you want to know which legislator is sponsoring the bill, you ask, 'Who's carrying the bill?' That'll give you some idea of how influential lobbyists are."

Speaker Laney, who brought a higher sense of ethics as well as fairer procedures to the lower chamber for the 1993–2002 decade. However, liberal–conservative skirmishes were plentiful, and knowledgeable political observers correctly predicted a further turn toward the more conservative Republicans in 2003.

SUGGESTED PROCEDURAL REFORMS

We suggested ways to improve the formal structure of the legislature earlier in this chapter. Improvements in legislative organization and procedures also are needed, especially in the areas of committees and ties to lobbyists.

Committees

The 21 House committees of 1973 were a more workable number than the 43 of 2005–2006, but 14 or 15 would be better. With 14 or 15 committees, less ambiguity about committee jurisdiction would occur. The Senate must also be alert to avoid expansion of its committee system, given the increase from nine in 1985 to fifteen in 2003, with three permanent subcommittees. The 31 senators are stretched rather thin in allocating their time among that many committees. It often seems that each new major state problem results in the creation of a new committee—and another committee chair to use for political leverage. In addition, both houses could make more use of joint committees instead of submitting every issue to separate study and hearings; a joint budget committee is particularly needed. Fewer committee meetings would give legislators more time to familiarize themselves with the issues and the content of specific bills. Fewer committees might also increase the chances for adoption of uniform committee rules throughout the two houses. Additional and more independent committee staff also are needed. Fewer committees would make paying for adequate numbers of staff members more feasible and might help to eliminate the practice of committee chairs mixing their office staff with staff hired by the committee, thereby allowing committee staff to focus solely on committee business.

The Lobby

Until legislators are willing to declare their independence from lobbyists and state administrators, the legislature cannot be independent of all but the public's interests. Such a change would depend on many factors: citizen attitudes; public willingness to allow adequate legislative sessions, pay, and staff support for legislators; public financing of election campaigns; and a commitment on the part of legislators to give up the social and economic advantages of strong ties to the lobby. The likelihood of total independence from the lobby is not high: All legislative groups have some ties to special interests. At a minimum, however, Texas needs to abandon such blatant practices as allowing lawyer–legislators to accept retainer fees from corporations that subsequently send lobbyists to Austin to influence these same legislators. A starting point in reform was Speaker Laney's rule prohibiting members of his staff from accepting a job as a lobbyist for one year after leaving the speaker's office.

CONCLUSION

In its conservatism the Texas legislature reflects the political preferences of the majority of voting Texans. Moreover, unlike the U.S. Congress, where fragmentation of power makes coherent public policy virtually impossible, the powerful presiding officers in Texas make coherent public policy highly likely. Thus, for all its problems, the Texas legislature can be highly representative of the distribution of opinion among citizens who participate on election day. Since the Texas legislature is centralized, it is capable of translating public preferences into policy, at least when the governor and presiding officers can reach agreement. Because so few Texans vote, however, the legislative body often translates the preferences of the richer and better-educated minority into policy. Although liberals then criticize the content of public policy, they cannot deny that the policy is rational from the standpoint of most Texas voters. However, after years of being successful at criticism and naysaying, the Republicans have had an obvious problem as the majority party in the twenty-first century: an inability to produce effective public policy and a tendency toward stalemate. Thus far, they have proved to be better at representation than at governance.

SUMMARY

In many ways, the Texas legislature is typical of state lawmaking bodies: in its large size (181 members), its domination by Anglo males, its somewhat limited professional staff, its relatively short terms of office for its members (two years in the House and four in the Senate), and its reliance on legislative committees as the workhorses of the legislative process. Nevertheless, the following features of the Texas legislature are atypical, especially compared with the legislatures of other large urban states:

1. The legislature is restricted to one regular session of 140 days every two years.
2. Legislators are paid only $7,200 a year, although they receive generous per diem payment for expenses.

3. The presiding officers—the speaker of the House and the lieutenant governor in the Senate—are pre-eminent in the legislative process. If either presiding officer is inclined to be arbitrary, democracy suffers.

4. The shifting memberships of the large number of committees—15 in the Senate and 43 in the House in 2005—make it difficult for legislators to develop expertise in specific areas of legislation. This problem is worse if high turnover is added to the mix.

5. Special interest groups have an extraordinary influence on both the election and the performance of legislators. This dominance raises the issue of when and how constituents' voices are heard.

6. The short legislative session allows a conference committee to play a major role in shaping legislation and also gives the governor a chance to veto legislation with no opportunity for the legislature to over-ride the veto. These procedures raise questions about citizen input and majority rule.

Texas legislators face the biennial task of developing sound public policy for a major state without jeopardizing the support of the presiding officers or of the special interest groups that are crucial to their re-election. Moreover, they operate in a highly constrained environment with both structural handicaps and lack of public confidence. They succeed better than one might expect, given the many handicaps they face. Nevertheless, changes in legislative organization and procedure would improve legislative efficiency and independence. Recommendations for reform include the following:

1. Annual sessions
2. Higher salaries, in the $59,000 range
3. Four-year terms for House members and six-year terms for senators
4. Reduction in the number of legislative committees
5. Restrictions on the influence of the lobby coupled with more staff support

Were these reforms to be implemented, the Texas legislature might be better prepared to govern the second-largest state in the nation.

STUDY QUESTIONS

1. What does "one person, one vote" mean? What have been its implications for Texas? Do you think this concept is responsible for the increases in ethnic minority representation in the legislature? Why or why not?

2. What are the characteristics of the average Texas state legislator? Is it significant that the legislature is in fact likely to under-represent important groups in the state's population? Why? What role do you think legislative pay plays in under-representation of some groups?

3. What are the problems caused by a biennial legislative session?

4. In what ways are the presiding officers of the Texas legislature extremely powerful? Why do you think this situation exists? What are the implications for democratic government?

5. You are a member of the Texas Senate and you are opposed to a bill that has been introduced. What strategies to defeat the bill are available to you at various stages in the legislative process?

SURFING THE WEB

Visit the companion site for this book:
http://www.thomsonedu.com/politicalscience/kraemer

An overview of Texas Legislative procedures:
http://www.capitol.state.tx.us/capitol/legproc/summary.htm

A membership roster of the Texas House of Representatives, 79th Legislature:
http://www.capitol.state.tx.us/tlo/house/house.htm#committees

(then click on "Committees" under "Texas House")

A list of House committees, 79th Legislature:
http://www.house.state.tx.us/committees/welcome.htm

A membership profile of the Texas Senate, 78th Legislature:
http://www.senate.state.tx.us/75r/Senate/Facts.htm

A list of Senate committees, 78th Legislature:
http://www.capitol.state.tx.us/tlo/senate/senate.htm#committees

(then click on "Committees" under "Texas House")

NOTES

1. For example, at one time the legislature could spend an unlimited number of days in session, but the per diem (daily) expense coverage ended after 120 days.

2. The Texas population was officially estimated at 22,086,674 in the 2003 follow-up to the 2000 census. Dividing that figure by 31 for senatorial seats and 150 for representatives results in these numbers. Obviously, citizens move in and out of districts; so, the numbers are not exact, and they change as the population increases. For that matter, the census itself is not entirely accurate due to undercounts of persons who are missed by the census takers; the estimated number of persons not counted in Texas was almost 400,000.

3. A good account of the Republican feuding can be found in Patricia Kilday Hart, "Party Poopers II," *Texas Monthly,* December 2001, 60, 62, 64.

4. *Hunt v. Cromartie,* 526 U.S. 541 (1999).

5. See Tim Storey, "Supreme Court Tackles Texas," *State Legislatures,* April 2006, 22–24.

6. A county was entitled to a maximum of seven representatives unless its population exceeded 700,000; then one additional representative could be elected for each additional 100,000 in population.

7. 369 U.S. 186 (1962).

8. 376 U.S. 1 (1964) and 377 U.S. 533 (1964).

9. A multimember district is one in which two or more representatives are elected by all of the people in that district. All the representatives represent all the people of the district. Multimember districts tend to reduce considerably the ability of ethnic minorities to win election, and the citizens tend not to be sure which representative is truly theirs.

10. Andrew Wheat, "The Public Right to 'No,'" *Texas Observer,* April 7, 2006, 13, 20.

11. For a scholarly analysis of voting behavior and group cohesion in the legislature, see Arturo Vega, "Gender and Ethnicity Effects on the Legislative Behavior and Substantive Representation of the Texas Legislature," *Texas Journal of Political Studies* 19 (Spring/ Summer 1997): 1–13.

12. See www.followthemoney.org.

13. *The Book of the States, 2005 Edition,* vol. 37 (Lexington, KY: Council of State Governments, 2005), 126-129.

14. Ibid., 111.

15. See Terrence Stutz, "Dewhurst Working to Prove He's Ready," *Dallas Morning News,* January 20, 2003, 1A, 9A; Paul Burka, "Uncivil Union," *Texas Monthly,* June 2005, 8, 10, 12; and Paul Burka, "First, Dew No Harm," *Texas Monthly,* February 2006, 15, 18.

16. See, for example, Pete Slover, "Craddick Sets Panel Lineups," *Dallas Morning News,* January 31, 2003, 31A, 34A; and Paul Burka, "So Far, So Bad," *Texas Monthly,* May 2003, 6, 10, 12.

17. See, for example, "Christy Hoppe, "Whose Political Style Will Win in Austin?" *Dallas Morning News,* May 20, 2005, 1A, 8A; Paul Burka, "Ruthless People," *Texas Monthly,* December 2003, 14, 16, 18; Jake Bernstein and Dave Mann, "Rate of Exchange," *Texas Observer,* March 12, 2004, 4–7, 18–19; and S. C. Gwynne, "How Did Tom Craddick Become the Most Powerful Speaker Ever—and the Most Powerful Texan Today? Let Us Count the Ways," *Texas Monthly,* February 2005, 100–103, 186–191.

18. As is true in Congress, the taxing committees of the Texas legislature are known as Finance in the Senate and Ways and Means in the House.

19. See also http://www.capitol.state.tx.us/capitol/legproc/diagram.htm.

7

THE GOVERNOR AND STATE ADMINISTRATION

Why does anyone want to be governor of Texas? The governorship is like the super-super gift in the Neiman-Marcus Christmas catalog—something for the man who has everything and absolutely unique!

Anonymous political scientist

We all know the special interests speak with a loud voice, but it is the quiet voice of the common interests that we must listen to.

Governor Rick Perry,
quoted in *The Dallas Morning News*

INTRODUCTION

Democratic theory pays much more attention to the legislature than to the executive. Nevertheless, because chief executives and administrative agencies are important components of government, they too should be measured against the democratic ideal. In Texas, the legislature has been the dominant branch of state government through most of the state's history. Indeed, Texas is often cited for the weaknesses associated with the governor's office. However, a Texas governor with ideas and boldness can capture the support of the public and greatly enhance the limited constitutional and statutory powers of the office. Leadership, bargaining skills, and persuasive ability rather than the formal powers of the governorship are the keys to gubernatorial success. The most obvious recent example is George W. Bush, who parlayed the Texas governorship into the presidency of the United States.

This chapter is divided into two distinct parts. The first part looks at various aspects of the governorship. It examines the basic structure of the governor's office, the formal qualifications for the office, the personal characteristics of those who are typically elected to it, the roles that the governor plays, and the limitations on those roles. The second part examines the remainder of the executive branch, looking at the rise of big government in the state, the structure of state administration, and bureaucratic power.

PART I: THE GOVERNOR

Basic Structure of the Governor's Office

Election, Term of Office, and Tenure. In Texas the governor is chosen in a statewide election held during the even-numbered years in which there is no presidential election. The candidates are selected in party primaries held earlier in the year (see Chapter 5). The thinking behind holding the gubernatorial election in the "off year" is that national issues will not overshadow state issues. However, election contests for the Texas governor's office often focus on personalities, not issues, so that the importance of the off year is lost, and its main effect is that fewer people vote because they do not have the presidential election as a drawing card. In fact, voter turnout reached a modern low of 16 percent of registered voters during the 1994 primaries. The lieutenant governor is selected in the same manner but runs independently of the governor.

In 1974, when a 1972 constitutional amendment went into effect, the governor's term of office was extended from two to four years. There is no constitutional limit on the number of terms a governor may serve in Texas. Until World War II, Texas governors were routinely elected for two terms. During and after the war, three terms prevailed. Modern governors serving four-year terms have had difficulty being re-elected; the long-term likelihood is that governors will serve no more than two terms. Competition for the office and the difficult and controversial problems governors face both suggest that a third full term will be unlikely.

Impeachment and Succession. In Texas a governor may be removed from office only through an impeachment proceeding. Impeachment is similar to a grand jury indictment; that is, it is a formal accusation. The state constitution is silent on what impeachable offenses are.[1] By implication and by the precedents set in the impeachment of Governor James E. Ferguson in 1917, however, the grounds are malfeasance, misfeasance, and nonfeasance in office—in other words, official misconduct, incompetence, or failure to perform.[2]

The impeachment procedure in Texas is similar to that at the national level. The House of Representatives, by a majority vote of those present, must first impeach the executive. Once the formal accusation is made, the Senate acts as a trial court; a two-thirds vote of the senators present is necessary to convict. Penalties for conviction are removal from office and disqualification from holding future governmental offices in the state. If there are criminal charges, they must be brought in a regular court of law.

Succession refers to providing for a new governor or an acting governor if the duly elected state chief executive cannot serve for any reason. If a governor is removed from office by impeachment and conviction, dies in office or before taking office, or resigns, the constitution provides that the lieutenant governor shall become governor. A 1999 constitutional amendment further stipulated that should the governor become disabled, the lieutenant governor would carry out the duties of the office; should the governor die or otherwise be unable to return, the lieutenant governor would become governor for the rest of the term of the governor who had vacated the office. If the lieutenant governor is unable to serve, the president pro tempore of the Senate would carry out the duties. Once the lieutenant governor becomes governor, the lieutenant governor's position is vacant. The vacancy would be filled within 30 days by the election of a member of the Senate to serve until the next general election. The amendment clarified some issues previously addressed by statute.

The last time a governor was impeached was in 1917, and the last time one died in office was in 1949. Running into trouble with the voters is thus more common than being removed from office or dying. In 2006 the governor's race was a free-for-all. Incumbent Rick Perry had three opponents in the Republican primary—Larry Kilgore, Star Locke, and Rhett Smith. Four Democrats—Felix Alvarado, Chris Bell, Bob Gammage, and Rashad Jafer—vied for their party's nomination. James Werner ran as a Libertarian candidate. By far, the greatest interest was created by the six independent candidates, whose ranks included not only Larry Camp, Marcus Cherry, William Jean, and Mike Redlich, but also two well-known and colorful figures, Kinky Friedman, a writer and musician, and Carole Keeton Strayhorn, the Republican comptroller of public accounts, who had sparred with Perry for years.

Compensation. A 1954 amendment allows the legislature to determine the salary of the governor and other elected executives. The legislature provided generous increments for many years, raising the governor's salary from $12,000 in 1954 to $99,122 in 1992–1993. Then the state budget allowed no raises for state employees for five years. The salary was raised to $115,345 for fiscal year 2001 (FY 01), and the salary of other elected executives was increased to $92,217. These salaries remained the same through FY 07. The lieutenant governor is paid as a legislator—$7,200 a year—although he receives a salary supplementation for acting as governor whenever the governor leaves the state.

Once second only to New York, the Texas governor's salary had slipped to twenty-third by the end of 2004.[3] In that year, the New York governor was paid $179,000, and the California governor was paid $175,000.

The governor also receives numerous fringe benefits. The constitution provides an official mansion, and other benefits include a travel and operating budget, a car, the use of state-owned aircraft, bodyguards furnished by the Texas Department of Public Safety, and offices and professional staff, including an executive assistant. These benefits compare favorably with those of other governors.

Staff. Like other chief executives, the governor alone is unable to perform all the functional and ceremonial tasks assigned to the governor's office. Assistance in fulfilling these obligations comes from a personal staff and from the professional staffs of the divisions that make up the Office of the Governor. Certain staff members are assigned to act as legislative liaisons—in effect, to lobby for the governor's programs—and often it is through them that the governor makes known an impending threat to veto a particular piece of legislation. Other staff members are involved in recommending candidates for the hundreds of appointments the governor must make to state boards, commissions, and executive agencies. The governor's aides also prepare the executive budget, coordinate the various departments and activities of the governor's office, and schedule appointments and activities.

The number and characteristics of gubernatorial staff members vary considerably from one governor to the next, depending on his or her political philosophy and the types of staff members hired. Ann Richards (1991–1995), for example, had a gender- and ethnic-diversified staff

Show Me the Money

Although well paid, particularly in comparison to legislators with their $7,200 salaries, the Texas governor is by no means the best-paid executive on the state payroll. Top-dollar honors belong to the larger universities in the state—University of Texas (UT) at Austin, Texas A&M University, the University of Houston/Main Campus, the University of North Texas, and Texas Tech University, all of which are the hub institutions of systems. The chancellors of the university systems and the presidents of the largest institutions receive base salaries of several hundred thousand dollars. Beyond that, they get all sorts of perquisites, such as houses and cars, that substantially increase their compensation. In addition, some large institutions pay bonuses for successful fund-raising, and some chancellors receive supplemental pay from individual institutions in the system—particularly medical schools. Dollars raised from local funds are used to supplement rather modest state-appropriated salaries. These large salaries often are matters of contention when university appropriations are discussed—and, for that matter, among faculty when the president gets a raise but faculty members do not. In 2006, for example, when David Smith resigned as chancellor of the Texas Tech University System, the university still paid him $716,000 as salary and $371,000 in deferred compensation. However, even these salaries pale when compared to those of the football coaches at UT-Austin and Texas A&M. Following the Longhorns' national championship in 2006, Coach Mack Brown's salary was raised from just under $2.2 million to $2.5 million. Even in high schools, big 5-A school coaches earn in excess of $100,000, far more than the principal or teachers. If salaries are a measure of priorities, then Texans must value football first; education, second; and general government, third.

Sources: "Paid to Quit: Smith's $1.1 Million Deal," KCBD-TV, February 23, 2006; "Texas' Brown Getting Hefty Pay Raise," http://sports.espn.go.com/ncf/news/story?id=2310990, January 29, 2006.

of almost 400. George Bush (1995–2000) reduced the staff to about 137 people. Rick Perry, who originally became governor in 2000 after Bush's resignation to run for U.S. president, has had staffs of varying size, ranging from 198 to 266 in 2004. Only

Florida has had a larger governor's staff.[4] New York, New Jersey, and Louisiana are the other states that have 100 or more staff members in the governor's office.

The comparison among Richards, Bush, and Perry is somewhat deceiving, since the payroll changed very little from one administration to the next. Richards followed a traditional populist approach of creating many jobs for "the people," although they did not pay well. Bush and, to an extent, Perry followed a traditional businesslike approach of appointing fewer people but at much higher salaries. Moreover, there is a long tradition of the governor's office serving as the spawning place for new state programs or temporary housing programs that got into trouble as independent agencies—for example, Perry's moving Economic Development and Tourism back to his office. As a result, the number of divisions— and thus the number of staff members—vary over time as the programs are formed, then move out into separate units.

Qualifications for Governor

Formal Qualifications.   Like the qualifications for members of the legislature, the formal qualifications for governor are so broad that several million Texans could legally run for the office.

Article IV of the Texas Constitution stipulates that the governor must be at least 30 years old, be a citizen of the United States, and have been a resident of Texas for the five years immediately preceding the election.

Personal Characteristics.   Formally qualifying for the governorship and actually having a chance at being considered seriously as a candidate are two very different matters. The social, political, and economic realities of the state dictate that personal characteristics, not stated in law, help to determine the victors in gubernatorial elections. Some of these personal characteristics are based on accomplishments, or at least a positive involvement, on the part of the gubernatorial aspirant. Others are innate traits that are beyond the control of the individual.

These characteristics are similar to but even more stringent than those for members of the legislature. In short, unless something unusual occurs in the campaign, tradition dictates that the successful candidate for governor will be a white Anglo-Saxon Protestant (WASP) male who is politically conservative, involved in civic affairs, and a millionaire. More than likely, but less inevitably, this individual will have held some type of office, usually attorney general or lieutenant governor, although being a professional politician is sometimes a liability among voters with a penchant for electing "good ol' boys." The most atypical governor in more than a half-century was Ann Richards, 1991–1995, who was the state's second female chief executive.[5]

Texas is one of five states that have had two or more women as governor; Arizona has had three while Connecticut, Kansas, and Washington have each had two.

Source: *The Book of the States 2005*, vol. 37 (Lexington, KY: Council of State Governments, 2005), 471–472.

TABLE 7.1

Roles of the Governor

Constitutional and Statutory Roles	*Informal and Symbolic Roles*
Chief Executive	Chief of Party
Chief Legislator	Leader of the People
Commander in Chief/Top Cop	
Chief of State	
Chief Intergovernmental Diplomat	

Roles of the Governor and Limits on Those Roles

The governor must play at least seven roles. Five are formal; that is, they are prescribed by the constitution and supplementing statutes. Two are informal and symbolic; that is, they derive from the Texas political setting (Table 7.1). Governors of all states play similar roles, as does the nation's president, who also has added responsibilities in the areas of diplomacy and economics.

The personality of the governor and the political and economic circumstances that prevail during a governor's administration largely determine which roles are emphasized. As the first opening quotation in this chapter indicates, the governorship is a unique office, and its distinctive qualities are further highlighted by the varied approaches taken by different governors.[6]

Recent governors serve as examples. The governor acknowledged to be most atypical, Ann Richards (1991–1995), was grounded in Travis County politics and got high marks for the quality and diversity of her appointments, for forcing changes in the controversial boards governing some state agencies—especially the State Insurance Board and the Board of Pardons and Paroles—and for exerting executive control over other agencies, such as the Texas Department of Commerce. Richards insisted on high standards of ethics, though some of her staff members stumbled later on. She also worked hard at economic diversification.

However, Richards's approach to legislative relations was partisan and heavy handed, and, while she was appreciated for her sense of humor, she sometimes had difficulty persuading legislators on policy issues. Her 1994 bid for re-election was inept, and she also faced the national Republican sweep. Richards lost decisively to George W. Bush even while enjoying high popularity ratings.

Bush, son of a former president,[7] operated very differently from Richards. The George W. Bush approach to legislators was nonpartisan, low key, and consensus building (in contrast to his style as president). Bush saw himself as a deal maker. He campaigned on four issues—reform of the juvenile justice system, setting limits on civil lawsuits (tort reform), more flexible and better public education, and restrictions on welfare. These issues were common throughout the country in 1994. Once elected, Bush stuck with those issues and pushed each through the 1995 Legislature. While he was successful in part by further expanding public school flexibility in the 1997 legislative session, his push for major changes in the Texas tax system was rebuffed. He had to settle for a proposed constitutional amendment to increase the tax exemptions for homesteads.

Speculation was keen already during the 75th Legislature in 1997 that George W. Bush was trying to create a platform from which to launch a presidential bid in the year 2000. By the time the 76th Legislature met in January 1999, no doubt existed about the governor's political plans. The *Wall Street Journal*, whose political philosophy is closely aligned to that of Bush's "compassionate conservatism," summarized the year by noting the total dominance of the capitol complex by a governor who was out of state campaigning much of the time. The *Journal* staff particularly noted the Bush "'Yellow Rose Garden' strategy of having potential presidential supporters and advisers, along with world leaders, come to Austin" as overshadowing "anything that was happening across the street at the state Capitol."[8]

Lieutenant Governor Rick Perry moved into the governor's office when Bush was elected president. He had the disadvantage of not having been elected to the top spot but the advantage of a rather easy 2001 legislative session as his first. The session was undistinguished until it adjourned. Then Perry vetoed 82 bills, some of which had bipartisan support and some of which were critical to his own party. As the title of an article in *Texas Monthly* magazine noted, he seemed to want to be known as "No! No! No!"[9] The magazine went on to rank him as "furniture" in its biennial assessment of the legislative session, meaning that he occupied space without affording leadership.

Perry began the 2003 session as the first Republican governor since Reconstruction to have his party as the majority in both houses of the legislature, but the new Republican majority was faced with an almost $10 billion budget deficit, and Perry was still trying to live down the extraordinarily negative campaign in the governor's race against Democrat Tony Sanchez. While Perry's "no" approach was in evidence by his making clear he wanted no new taxes, he publicly disavowed his party's right wing, which wanted to dismantle health and human services programs to meet budget demands—the need to hear the quiet common voice mentioned in the second chapter-opening quotation. He particularly warned the legislature not to put Texas into the position of being the only state without a children's health insurance program. Still, in mid-session, Perry's popularity ratings were less than 50 percent,[10] and print journalists statewide criticized his lack of leadership.

The criticism increased during the 2005 session when once again the legislature failed to solve the school finance problem (see Chapters 8 and 10). Moreover, Perry displaced a distinctly partisan streak by calling three special sessions to force redrawing congressional district lines that would favor Republican candidates but did little to address school funding.

Formal Roles and Limitations

The Texas Constitution was written at a time when concentrated power in the hands of a single state official was viewed with great apprehension. E. J. Davis, the last Republican governor until 1979, held office from 1870 to 1874 in an administration characterized by corruption and repression. Consequently, when the 1876 Texas Constitution was drafted, the framers reacted against the Davis administration by creating a constitutionally weak governor's office (see Chapter 2).

Today the governor must still cope with a highly fragmented executive branch that includes five other elected executives, two elected boards, and a complex system of

In the early 2000s, neither the governor nor the legislative leadership seemed able to provide adequate leadership to move the state out of the quagmire of inadequate school finance policy.

SOURCE: Courtesy of Ben Sargent.

powerful policy-making boards and commissions. Recent governors have sought greater institutional power with modest success, and Rick Perry made substantial progress toward modernization of the Texas governor's office with a series of bills passed by the 78th Legislature in 2003. These bills resulted in control of the economic development office, health and human services, and the chairmanship of many state boards.[11] He also succeeded in reducing the power of the state comptroller, a potential rival. He continued to seek greater power for the governor's office into 2006 in such areas as border policing and wiretapping. Prior to the 2003 changes, the Texas governor's office ranked slightly below average among all states in institutional power; the increase in power in Texas paralleled modest increases across the country.[12]

Chief Executive.   News stories frequently describe the governor as the "chief executive," referring to gubernatorial control over the state **bureaucracy** and the governor's **appointment and removal**, budgeting, planning, supervisory, and clemency powers. Although this is one of the governor's most time-consuming roles, it also is one of the weakest, as the following discussion illustrates.

Appointment.   Texas is said to have a long ballot because a large number of state officials are elected by the people rather than appointed by the governor. The list of officials elected on a statewide basis includes the lieutenant governor, whose major role is legislative; the attorney general; the comptroller of public accounts; the commissioner of the General Land Office; and the agriculture commissioner. In addition, members of the Texas Railroad Commission and the State Board of Education are elected. Since they are elected independently, they feel no obligation to the governor, and since they may want the governor's job, they may even wish to make the incumbent look bad.

The most visible executive appointments made by the governor are those of secretary of state, commissioner of education, commissioner of insurance, commissioner of health and human services, and executive director of the Economic Development and Tourism Division. The governor also appoints the director of the Office of State–Federal Relations and the adjutant general, who heads the state militia. The governor fills any vacancy that occurs in one of the major elected executive positions, such as railroad commissioner. In such an event, the governor appoints someone to fill the vacancy until the next election. The governor also appoints all or some of the members of about two dozen advisory councils and committees that coordinate the work of two or more state agencies.

The governor has a major effect on state policy through appointments to more than 100 policy-making, multimember boards and commissions. Examples include the University of Texas System board of regents and the Public Utility Commission. The members of these boards are appointed by the governor, usually for a six-year term, but with the following limitations:

1. The terms of board and commission members are overlapping and staggered to prevent the governor from appointing a majority of the members until late in the first term of office.
2. The statutes establishing the various boards and commissions are highly prescriptive and often specify a certain geographic representation and occupational or other background characteristics of the members.[13]
3. Appointments to some boards and commissions must be made from lists supplied by members of professional organizations and associations.[14]

One other important use of the appointment power is filling vacancies in the judiciary. Although Texas has an elected judiciary, every legislature creates some new courts, and vacancies occur in other courts. The governor makes appointments to these benches until the next election. Indeed, more than half of the district court judges in the state are first appointed and subsequently stand for election.

The governor must obtain a two-thirds confirmation vote from the Senate for appointments; the president needs only a simple majority from the U.S. Senate. And, as in national politics, there is a practice of "senatorial courtesy" whereby the Senate will usually honor the objection of a senator from the same district as the nominee for appointment by refusing to approve confirmation.

Texas's short biennial legislative session, however, permits the governor to make many interim appointments when the legislature is not in session. This practice gives these appointees a free ride for periods as long as 19 months. These recess appointments must be presented to the Senate within the first 10 days of the next session, whether regular or called.

Another aid to the governor is incumbency. If a governor is re-elected, he or she will be able to appoint all members of these boards and commissions by early in the second term. The governor will then have considerable influence over policy development.

Removal.   The governor has only limited removal power in Texas. The governor can remove political appointees whom he or she has appointed, with the consent of the Senate, a power in effect only since a 1980 constitutional amendment. The governor also can remove personal staff members and a few executive directors, such as the one in the Department of Housing and Community Affairs. However, the governor cannot remove members of boards and commissions appointed by the preceding governor or executives elected by the people. This lack of removal power deprives the governor of significant control over the bureaucrats who make and administer policy on a day-to-day basis. As a result, the governor has difficulty implementing policies through the state bureaucracy.

The three general methods for removing state office-holders are:

1. *Impeachment*, which involves a formal accusation—the impeachment—by a House majority and requires a two-thirds vote for conviction by the Senate.
2. *Address*, a procedure whereby the legislature requests the governor to remove a district or appellate judge from office (a two-thirds vote of both houses is required).
3. *Quo warranto* proceedings, a legal procedure whereby an official may be removed by a court.

Budgeting.   By law, the governor must submit a biennial budget message to the legislature within five days after that body convenes in regular session. This budget is prepared by the governor's Office of Budget, Planning, and Policy. The Legislative Budget Board (LBB), however, also prepares a budget for the legislature to consider, and traditionally the legislature is guided more by the legislative budget than by the governor's. The executive budget indicates to the legislature the governor's priorities and signals items likely to be vetoed. With the exception of the item veto, the Texas governor lacks the strong formal budgetary powers not only of the president but also of many other state executives (see Chapter 10). However, beginning in 2003, the legislature voluntarily shared power with the governor in the area of budget planning.

Planning.   Both modern management and the requirements of many federal grants-in-aid emphasize substate regional planning, and the governor directs planning efforts for the state through the Office of Budget, Planning, and Policy. When combined with budgeting, the governor's planning power allows a stronger hand in the development of new programs and policy alternatives. Though still without adequate controls over state programs, the governor has had a greater voice in suggesting future programs over the past two decades, mainly because many federal statutes designated the governor as having approval power for federal grants.

Especially in his first term, Bill Clements approached his job from the planning perspective, including the development of the Texas State Government Effectiveness Program to make state agency management more efficient and by the creation of the

Texas 2000 Commission to look at issues that will become increasingly more pressing in this century. During the Richard's administration, Comptroller John Sharp—in part at the request of the governor to allow a more rational appropriations act for fiscal years 1992–1993—developed an elaborate system for monitoring the performance of state agencies; in turn, state agencies had to engage in a massive strategic planning effort. The Texas Performance Review has continued as a vital part of state government though it is now under legislative control.

Supervising.   The state constitution charges the governor with the responsibility of seeing that the laws of the state are "faithfully executed" but provides few tools for fulfilling this function. The governor's greatest supervisory and directive powers occur in the role of commander in chief (described later). Governors can request reports from state agencies, remove their own appointees, and use political influence to force hiring reductions or other economies. But lack of appointment power over the professional staffs of state agencies and lack of removal power over a predecessor's appointees do limit the governor's ability to ensure that the state bureaucracy does its job.

The governor thus must fall back on informal tactics to exercise any control over the administration. In this respect, the governor's staff is of supreme importance; if staff members can establish good rapport with state agencies, they may extend the governor's influence to areas where he or she does not have formal authority. They are aided in this task by two factors of which agency personnel are well aware: the governor's leadership of the party and veto powers (both discussed later).

Clemency.   The governor's power with regard to acts of clemency (mercy) is restricted to one 30-day reprieve for an individual sentenced to death. In cases of treason against the state (a rare crime), the governor may grant pardons, reprieves, and commutations of sentences with legislative consent. The governor also may remit fines or bond forfeitures and restore driver's licenses and hunting privileges. In addition, the governor has the discretionary right to revoke a parole or conditional pardon. Beyond these limited acts, the state's chief executive officer must make recommendations to the Board of Pardons and Paroles, which is part of the Department of Criminal Justice. Although empowered to refuse an act of clemency recommended by the board, the governor cannot act without its recommendation in such matters as full and conditional pardons, commutations, reprieves, and emergency reprieves.

Chief Legislator.
Although the legislature tends to dominate Texas politics, the governor is a strong chief legislator who relies on three formal powers in carrying out this role: message power, session power, and veto power.

Message Power.   The governor may give messages to the legislature at any time, but the constitution requires a gubernatorial message when legislative sessions open and when a governor retires. By statute, the governor must also deliver a biennial budget message. Other messages the governor may choose to send or deliver in person are often "emergency" messages when the legislature is in session; these messages are a formal means of expressing policy preferences. They also attract the attention of the media and set the agenda for state government. Coupled with able staff work, message power can be an effective and persuasive tool. Rick Perry used the message power considerably during the 2003 session. In addition to the State of the State address and the budget message, he focused on homeowners, automobile, and malpractice insurance rates and later on redistricting.

Session Power.   As discussed in Chapter 6, the legislature is constitutionally forbidden to call itself into special session; only the governor may do this. Called sessions are limited to a maximum duration of 30 days, but a governor who wants to force consideration of an issue can call one special session after another. The governor also sets the agenda for these sessions, although the legislature, once called, may consider other matters on a limited basis, such as impeachment or approval of executive appointments. As the complexity of state government has grown, legislators sometimes have been unable to complete their work in the short, biennial regular sessions. When they fail to complete enough of the agenda, they know they can expect a special session.

Special sessions offer a way around the restricted biennial legislative session of 140 days. The eight governors before Bush called a total of 34 special sessions. Bill Clements called six; Ann Richards called only two. Bush called none, a reflection in part of his ability to get along with the legislative leadership and in part of the budget surplus. Rick Perry called seven special sessions in the 2003–2006 time period.

Veto Power.   The governor's strongest legislative power is the veto. Every bill that passes both houses of the legislature in regular and special sessions is sent to the governor, who has the option of signing it, letting it become law without signing it, or vetoing it.[15]

If the legislature is still in session, the governor has 10 days—Sundays excluded—in which to act. If the bill is sent to the governor in the last 10 days of a session, or after the legislature has adjourned, the governor has 20 days—including Sundays—in which to act. If the governor vetoes a bill while the legislature is still in session, that body may over-ride the veto by a two-thirds vote of both houses.

Because of the short legislative session, important bills are often sent to the governor so late that the legislature has adjourned before the governor needed to act on them. In such instances, the veto power is absolute. The legislature cannot over-ride if it is not in session, and consideration of a bill cannot be carried over into the next session. Short biennial sessions thus make the governor's threat of a veto an extremely powerful political tool.

The governor has one other check over appropriations bills, the **item veto**.[16] This device permits the governor to delete individual items from a bill without having to veto it in its entirety. The item veto may be used only to strike a particular line of funding, however; it cannot be used to reduce or increase an appropriation.

The item veto illustrates a reality of gubernatorial power in Texas. The governor's power over legislation is largely negative—the governor finds it easier to say no than to get his or her own legislative agenda adopted.

Commander in Chief and Top Cop.   The state of Texas does not independently engage in warfare with other nations and thus would seem to have no need for a commander in chief. However, the governor does have the power to declare martial law; that is, to suspend civil government temporarily and replace it with government

Governor Rick Perry vetoed a record 82 bills passed by the legislature in 2001, including several that were important to his own Republican Party. By the end of 2005, he had vetoed another 69.

SOURCE: Courtesy of Ben Sargent.

by the state militia and/or law enforcement agencies. Although seldom used, this power was invoked to quell an oil field riot in East Texas in the 1930s and to gain control of an explosive racial situation in North Texas in the 1940s. Additionally, the governor is commander in chief of the military forces of the state (Army and Air National Guard) except when they have been called into service by the national government. The head of these forces, the adjutant general, is one of the governor's important appointees. The governor also has the power to assume command of the Texas Rangers and the Department of Public Safety to maintain law and order. These powers become important during disasters such as a flood or tornado, when danger may exist from the aftermath of the storm or from unscrupulous individuals such as looters. They were invoked in 2005 to help ensure an orderly evacuation of people from the Gulf Coast as Hurricane Rita threatened.

In routine matters, the governor is almost wholly dependent on local law enforcement and prosecuting agencies to see that the laws of the state are faithfully executed. When there is evidence of

A governor may use the commander-in-chief role in conjunction with leader-of-the-people to garner goodwill. In 2005 Governor Rick Perry traveled to Iraq to visit Texas National Guard members who had been called into active duty.

wrongdoing, the state's chief executive often brings the informal powers of the governor's office to bear on the problem, appealing to the media to focus public attention on errant agencies and office-holders.

Chief of State.   Pomp and circumstance are a part of being the top elected official of the state. Just as presidents use their ceremonial role to augment their other roles, so do governors. Whether cutting a ribbon to open a new highway, leading a parade, or serving as host for a visiting dignitary, the governor's performance as chief of state yields visibility and the appearance of leadership, which facilitate the more important executive and legislative roles of the office. In the modern era, the governor is often the chief television personality of the state and sets the policy agenda through publicity. Ann Richards, for example, was a national television celebrity, sometimes more popular outside the state than inside. More and more, Texas governors are using the ceremonial role of chief of state, sometimes coupled with the role of chief intergovernmental diplomat, to become actively involved in economic negotiations such as attracting new plant locations. Efforts are directed toward both foreign and domestic investments and finding new markets for Texas goods. In such negotiations, the governor uses the power and prestige of the office to become the state's salesperson. Mark White and Bill Clements both made significant use of this role to attract new businesses to the state. Ann Richards strongly pushed for U.S. Senate approval of the North American Free Trade Agreement (NAFTA) because of the likelihood of expanded Texas–Mexico trade. One historic function of the chief of state is tossing out the first ball at the opening baseball game; in the case of George W. Bush, he was one of the owners of the Texas Rangers until the beginning of 1998. In 2005–2006 Rick Perry used this role to call attention to the problem of illegal immigration along the Texas–Mexico border.

Chief Intergovernmental Diplomat.   The Texas Constitution provides that the governor, or someone designated by the governor, is the state's representative in all dealings with other states and with the national government. This role of intergovernmental representative has increased in importance for three reasons. First, federal statutes now designate the governor as the official who has the planning and grant-approval authority for the state. This fact has given the governor's budgeting, planning, and supervising powers much more clout in recent years, and federal budget philosophy (see Chapter 10) further enhances the governor's role.

Second, some state problems, such as water and energy development, often require the cooperation of several states. For example, in 1981–1982, Governor Clements and five other governors tried to plan solutions for the water problems of the High Plains area. Additionally, although the U.S. Constitution precludes a governor from conducting diplomatic relations with other nations, Texas's location as a border state gives rise to social and economic exchanges with the governors of Mexican border states on matters such as immigration and energy, especially with growing NAFTA commerce. Rick Perry, following the national tragedy of the September 11, 2001 attack on the World Trade Center in New York, often played this role as leader of the state's homeland security effort, which was part of the national internal security program.

Governor George W. Bush used his commander-in-chief powers in an unusual way in late 1999 and 2000. In his bid for the Republican nomination for president, Bush traveled across the United States. During these campaign tours, he was protected by the Texas Department of Public Safety, which always protects the governor. Thus, a few state troopers and Texas Rangers got to see much of the country for a change. The protection was paid for by the Bush campaign.

Third, acquiring federal funds is always important, since they relieve the pressure on state and local government revenue sources. Often, the governor works in concert with other governors to secure favorable national legislation, including both funding and limits on unfunded federal mandates. The governor tends to be an active member of the National Governors Association and an active participant in the National Governors Conference. He is also active in political party groups. The Texas governor takes his place among these proactive governors.

A more traditional use of the governor's intergovernmental role is mandated by Article IV of the U.S. Constitution, which provides for the rendition (surrender) of fugitives from justice who flee across state lines. The Texas governor, like other governors, signs the rendition papers and transmits them to the appropriate law enforcement officials. Law officers are then in charge of picking up the fugitives and returning them to the appropriate state.

Informal Roles and Limitations

In addition to the five "hats" described here, there are at least two others that the governor must wear. They have no basis in law, but they are nevertheless important to the job. The degree of success with which the governor handles these informal roles can greatly affect the execution of the formal ones.

Chief of Party.   As the symbolic head of the Democratic or Republican Party in the state, the governor is a key figure at state party conventions and usually is the leader of the party's delegation to national conventions. A governor may, however, have to compete with a U.S. senator from his party. Governors are able to use their influence with the party's State Executive Committee and at party conventions to gain a subsidiary influence over candidates seeking other state offices. An active, skilled governor can thus create a powerful relationship with state legislators and bureaucrats that the more formal roles of the office do not permit. The governor also wins some political influence by campaigning for other party candidates who are seeking state or national offices.

Governor Bill Clements, the first modern Republican governor of Texas, used the party role extensively to extend Republican influence through his appointment power. He appointed enough Democrats to maintain the goodwill of the majority leadership. Governor Ann Richards also made key executive and judicial appointments from among her Democratic Party colleagues. While generally supporting the party position on redistricting, she also showed some willingness to deal with the Republicans in exchange for GOP support for legislation that she and the Democrats wanted, such as a state lottery.

Governor George W. Bush in 1995 operated on a nonpartisan basis and secured the support of both members and leaders of the Democrat-majority legislature for his legislative program. He also made his own Republican Party angry by cooperating with the Democrats and by having a moderate position on a number of issues. For example, Governor Bush and Speaker of the House Pete Laney worked especially well together, and Bush told the state party bigwigs to back off from trying to defeat Laney in his 1996 re-election bid. In 1997 he fared somewhat less well with the legislature, even though the Senate had become Republican, in part because of resistance to his tax plan by conservative members of the GOP. In 1999 his obvious ambition to be president of the United States resulted not only in Republican Party loyalty but also in considerable Democratic support for someone who could potentially influence national policy in the state's favor.

Rick Perry's role as party leader is less clear. He has to contend with the U.S. president and two U.S. senators as well as the leaders of both houses of the state legislature for primacy in the state party. He has faced budget shortfalls, a failed school finance policy, and congressional redistricting, among other issues. While he helped to solidify Republican dominance in the state—for example, by calling three special sessions in 2003 on redistricting—and by refusing to consider school funding without tax cuts, he was not given high marks for ideas or leadership, hence, the 13 other candidates for governor in 2006.

Leader of the People.   Most Texans, unaware of the limitations on formal gubernatorial powers, look to the chief executive of the state for leadership in solving the state's problems and to serve as their principal spokesperson on major issues. A skilled governor can turn this role to substantial advantage when bargaining with other key figures in the policy-making process such as the presiding officers, legislators, and top bureaucrats in the state's administration. For example, through the media the governor can rally public support for programs and policies. Indeed, in an era of instant media coverage, a governor can use the press to considerable advantage by creating "photo ops" and arranging for goodwill appearances.

Choosing to accept invitations to speak is another way a governor can gain public exposure and thus support for programs and plans, including the budget. Public appearances usually serve as occasions for emphasizing gubernatorial accomplishments. They also allow a governor to show concern for ordinary citizens with extraordinary problems, as when the governor visits tornado or flood sites. In keeping with the traditionalistic tenor of the state, some governors use this role to show that they are "active conservatives."

Coupled with the strong legislative role, this informal role is critical to a governor's success. Leadership has been depicted as consisting of two parts: the ability to "transact"—that is, to make things happen—and the ability to "transform"—that is, to decide what things should happen.[17] The successful Texas governor is one who can both make things happen and decide what policies ought to happen.

A populist approach is consistent with the values of democracy. So is a more conservative approach that addresses issues that the public reiterates with each opinion poll. Thus, although having different positions—except that both wanted to improve public education—and using different styles, Ann Richards and

George W. Bush both demonstrated leadership. Rick Perry's leadership has been the most problematic. He seems to create a problem for himself each time he acts decisively. For example, at the same time that he disavowed the influence of powerful lobbyists, he appointed one as his chief of staff. And, while he called for the common interests to be heard, his legislative agenda provided few clues as to how to solve the state's many problems. Even when earning praise for an orderly hurricane evacuation in 2005, he was criticized for not giving adequate thought to traffic routes and gasoline supplies.

PART II: THE EXECUTIVE BRANCH

State agencies must prove [their] worth or they will disappear.

Fiscal Notes

The governor is the nominal head of the executive branch of Texas government, but, as the second part of this chapter points out, the executive branch is a complicated structure. The governor, in fact, has limited control over much of it.

State Administrative Agencies

Although we must concede that a state bureaucracy is needed to carry out government policy, we might be happier if the Texas administration were easier to understand. Even for the experienced observer, state administration in Texas is confusing; for the novice, it is perplexing indeed. There are three essential characteristics of the state administration that cause this confusion:

1. There is no single, uniform organizational pattern.
2. There are numerous exceptions to the traditional bureaucratic characteristic of hierarchy.
3. The number of state agencies depends on one's method of counting.

There are at least five types of top policy-makers, in state agencies: (1) elected executives; (2) appointed executives; (3) an elected commission and an elected board; (4) ex officio boards and commissions; and (5) appointed boards and commissions (Table 7.2). Agencies headed by an elected or appointed executive follow traditional hierarchical principles in that a single individual clearly is "the boss" and thus is ultimately responsible for the operation of a particular department or office. But the agencies that are headed by a multimember board or commission have three or six or even nineteen bosses, whatever number constitutes the membership of the board. Although there is also a hierarchical organization in these agencies, it begins with the professional staff of the agency, the level below the policy-setting board.

Another complication is that one office, board, or commission may be responsible for the general policies of a number of separate agencies. For example, the Board of Regents of the University of Texas is the policy-making board for the entire University of Texas system, which includes 15 campuses that are separately funded.

TABLE 7.2

Types of Administrative Agencies in Texas

Agencies Headed by Elected Executives

    Office of the Attorney General

    Department of Agriculture

    Office of the Comptroller of Public Accounts

    General Land Office

Agencies Headed by Appointed Executives

    Examples: Office of the Secretary of State, Texas Department of Insurance

Multimember Boards and Commissions

    Elected Board and Commission: State Board of Education, Texas Railroad Commission

    Example of Ex Officio Board: Bond Review Board

    Examples of Appointed Boards and Commissions: Public Utilities Commission, Texas Higher Education

        Coordinating Board

As of fiscal year 2006–2007, at least 231 agencies, institutions, and independent programs are funded by general appropriations. This list is not all-inclusive, however, because not all agencies are budgeted, especially ex officio ones and regulatory commissions that derive their revenues from fines and fees. A rough count of just the policy-making boards, commissions, departments, and offices—excluding the courts and related agencies, the legislature and its staff agencies, and the offices of elected executives—yields about 100 agencies.[18] Community/junior colleges are excluded from this number because they have locally appointed boards; as are the multiple campuses of health and mental health agencies. Legislators worked to reduce the number slightly in 2003 by reorganizing health and human services agencies. Thus, one can see why the number of state agencies is usually expressed in approximate terms. In the space allotted here, there is no way to name, much less describe, all of the state agencies, but a few of the most important are described briefly in the following pages.

Agencies with Elected Executives. Five state officials, in addition to the governor, are elected on partisan ballots for four-year terms. They are, in theory at least, directly accountable to the citizenry for their performance and their integrity in office. One of these, the lieutenant governor, presides over the Texas Senate and does not head an executive office. The lieutenant governor performs as an executive only when the governor is away from the state or upon succession to the governorship. The other four elected officials are department heads. The incumbents noted are those in office as of spring 2006.

Attorney General. Along with the governor, the lieutenant governor, and the speaker of the House, the attorney general is one of the most powerful officers in Texas government. Although candidates for the position often run on an anti-crime platform, the work of the office is primarily civil. As the attorney for the state, the attorney general and his or her staff represent the state and its agencies in court when the state is a party to a case. The Office of the Attorney General is also responsible for such varied legal matters as consumer protection, anti-trust litigation, workers' compensation insurance, organized-crime control, environmental protection, and enforcing the payment of child support.

The attorney general's greatest power, however, is that of issuing opinions on questions concerning the constitutionality or legality of existing or proposed legislation and administrative actions. These opinions are not legally binding, but they are rarely challenged in court, and thus effectively they have the same importance as a ruling by the state's supreme court (see Chapter 8). Because the attorney general's opinions often make the headlines, and because the attorney general works with all of the state agencies, the office is second only to the governor's office in the public recognition it receives. Because the position is regarded as one of the steppingstones to the governor's office, attorneys generals often encourage publicity about themselves, their agency, and their support groups with an eye to possible future election campaigns. Republican Greg Abbott, a former Texas supreme court justice, was first elected in 2002, stressing his philosophy of judicial restraint.

Comptroller of Public Accounts.   The comptroller (pronounced "con-TROL-ler") is responsible for the administration of the state tax system and for performing pre-audits of expenditures by state agencies. In addition, as a part of the budget process, the comptroller certifies to the legislature the approximate biennial income for the state. Under the Texas Constitution, the legislature is precluded from appropriating more funds than are anticipated in state revenues for any biennial period. Texas, like most other states, must have a balanced budget. Since 1996, following the phase-out of the treasurer's office, the comptroller is also the state's banker. As such, the comptroller is the custodian of all public monies and of the securities that the state invests in or holds in trust. The office also issues the excise tax stamps used to indicate the collection of taxes on the sale of alcoholic beverages and cigarettes in the state. In short, the comptroller takes in the state's revenues, safeguards them, and invests them. This merger of the two offices made the comptroller's position even more powerful than it already was.

Republican Carol Keeton Strayhorn, a former mayor of Austin and Texas Railroad Commission member, was elected as the first woman comptroller in 1998 and was re-elected in 2002. Calling herself "one tough grandma," she continued the rigorous examination of state agencies, known as the Texas Performance Review, established by her predecessor, John Sharp. She also led the process to make state government accessible through the Internet. Both of the latter two powers were removed from the comptroller's office in 2003 in retaliation for Strayhorn's sharp criticism of the governor and other fellow Republicans. She ran for governor as an independent in 2006.

Commissioner of the General Land Office.   Only Texas and Alaska entered the Union with large amounts of public lands, and only they have land offices. About 22.5 million Texas acres, including the submerged lands extending from the coastline to the (marine) three-league limit, are administered by the commissioner of the General Land Office, whose land management responsibilities include:

1. Supervise the leasing of all state-owned lands for such purposes as oil and gas production, mineral development, and grazing (over 14,000 leases).

2. Administer the veterans' land program, by which veterans may buy land with loans that are backed by state bonds.
3. Maintain the environmental quality of public lands and waters, especially coastal lands.

Republican Jerry Patterson was first elected as commissioner in 2002. He, like all land commissioners, must try to balance environmental interests with land and mineral interests. Patterson is a former state senator.

Commissioner of Agriculture.   Farming and ranching are still important industries in the state, even though only about 1 percent of the population is engaged in agriculture. The Department of Agriculture, like its national counterpart, is responsible both for the regulation and promotion (through research and education) of the agribusiness industry and for consumer protection, although these functions may sometimes be in conflict. Departmental activities are diverse—for example, enforcing weights and measures standards, licensing egg handlers, determining the relative safety of pesticides, and locating export markets for Texas agricultural products. Pesticides illustrate the conflicting nature of the roles assigned to this office. Limiting pesticides to those that are safe for workers, consumers, and the environment may be detrimental to the profits of farmers. Election to this office is specified by statute rather than by the state constitution. Republican Susan Combs, a fourth-generation rancher, was first elected in 1998 and re-elected in 2002. When Carol Strayhorn opted to run for governor in 2006, Combs ran for comptroller.

Agencies with Appointed Executives.   One example of an agency headed by an appointed executive is the Office of the Secretary of State. The state constitution stipulates that the governor shall appoint the secretary of state, whose functions include safeguarding the great seal of the state of Texas and affixing it to the governor's signature on proclamations, commissions, and certificates. In addition to this somewhat ceremonial duty, the secretary's duties include certifying elections (verifying the validity of the returns), maintaining records on campaign expenditures, keeping the list of lobbyists who register with the state, administering the Uniform Commercial Code, issuing corporate charters, and publishing the Texas Register—the official record of administrative decisions, rules, regulations, and announcements of hearings and pending actions. Governor Rick Perry appointed Roger Williams, an automobile dealer and prominent Texas Christian University supporter, to the office in 2005. The secretary of state's office, though appointive, can sometimes be a springboard to elective office. Three recent elected office-holders—Lieutenant Governor Bob Bullock, Governor Mark White, and Mayor Ron Kirk of Dallas—were once secretary of state.

Boards and Commissions.   Multimember boards or commissions head most state administrative agencies and make overall policy for them. These boards appoint chief administrators to handle the agencies' day-to-day responsibilities, including the budget, personnel, and the administration of state laws and those federal laws that are carried out through state governments. Two have elected members. The others have appointed or ex officio members.

Elected Boards and Commissions.   As we have mentioned, the Texas Railroad Commission (TRC) is one of the most influential agencies in the state, and the three persons who are its members are powerful indeed. The commission has tremendous political clout in the state because of its regulation of all mining and extractive industries, including oil, gas, coal, and uranium. Its control of intrastate surface transportation—railroads, buses, moving vans, and trucks—is of growing importance because of the importance of trucking rates to economic development. The commission even has national influence because of its authority over the national pipeline system through hookups to producing wells in Texas. Its members are chosen in statewide elections for staggered six-year terms. In 1994 the TRC became all-Republican for the first time.

The State Board of Education was created as an elected body. As part of the public school reforms of 1984, it was made an appointive board. In 1987 the voters overwhelmingly approved returning it to elective status. Fifteen members are chosen by the voters from districts across the state. A majority of the board's members are conservative Republicans with strong socio-religious viewpoints. This fact has introduced a concern because the long-standing controversy about the board's selection of textbooks for public schools has resurfaced; the selection process has often centered on disagreements about social and/or religious viewpoints such as creationism.

Ex Officio Boards and Commissions.   There are many boards in the state administration whose members are all ex officio; that is, they are members because of another office they hold in the administration. When these boards were created, two purposes were served by ex officio memberships: The members usually were already in Austin (no small matter in pre-freeway days), and they were assumed to have some expertise in the subject at hand. An example is the Bond Review Board, which includes the governor, lieutenant governor, comptroller, and speaker of the House and ensures that debt financing is used prudently by the state.

Appointed Boards and Commissions.   Most of the state's laws are administered by boards and commissions whose members are appointed rather than elected and by the administrators the boards then appoint. The members of many boards are appointed by the governor, but some other boards have a combination of gubernatorial appointees and appointees of other state officials and/or ex officio members. They vary in size and, as a rule, have general policy authority for their agencies. Members serve six-year overlapping terms, without pay.

There are three broad categories of appointed boards and commissions: (1) health, welfare, and rehabilitation; (2) education; and (3) general executive and administrative departments. Examples from each category are (1) the Health and Human Services Council; (2) the Texas Higher Education Coordinating Board; and (3) the Parks and Wildlife Department and the Public Utility Commission, respectively.

Appointed Boards and Citizens.
The Case of the Public Utility Commission. How do the 100 or so policy-making boards affect the ordinary citizen? One example is the Public Utility Commission of Texas (PUC), which fosters competition and promotes a utility *infrastructure* (the basic physical structure for delivery of public utilities such as pipelines, cables, and transformers). The PUC has been very busy since the legislature deregulated the electric

industry in 1999, both overseeing procedures for deregulation and trying to ensure the availability of adequate and reliable electric power. A second focus is overseeing the telecommunications industry. Any Texas citizen can contact the PUC's Office of Customer Protection to complain about unreliable electric or telecommunication service or seeming misdeeds on the part of providers of those utilities. For example, if a Texas college student has been "slammed" (had her telephone service switched without authorization from one carrier to the next), has been "crammed" (had unauthorized charges on his telephone bill), or is unable to resolve a dispute with the manager of an apartment complex due to the submetering of electric service, the PUC represents a possible solution to the problem.

The Case of the College Governing Board. Public community colleges, private universities, and public universities all have a board of trustees or board of regents. These board members set policy for the college and appoint the president. At a typical board of regents meeting, the board members (1) renewed the president's contract; (2) approved a resolution increasing the amount of fees for most courses; (3) granted tenure to 20 faculty members; and (4) approved the hiring of a new dean of business. Each of these actions affected students—directly in the case of the fee increases and indirectly in the case of the three types of personnel actions. Beginning in late 2005 each college board includes a nonvoting student member.

The Case of the Parks and Wildlife Board. If you are an outdoors person who likes to camp, fish, or hunt, then the annual decisions of the Parks and Wildlife Board on what fees will be levied for these activities will be of interest. Texas traditionally has had very low parks and wildlife fees compared with other states. If that annual fishing license suddenly costs $100 instead of $28, you might have second thoughts about this form of recreation. Anglers are also affected by this board's decisions concerning what type of fish to release into the lakes of the state.

State Administration: What Is It?

This chapter looks briefly at the types of state agencies that exist in Texas. Now, it will turn to the topic of bureaucracy. As often as not, bureaucracy becomes a dirty word when used to refer to the organization of government.

Few of us need an introduction to the concept of bureaucracy because public administration is a part of daily life. Traffic police, public school principals, highway workers, clerks in state and federal offices—they are all bureaucrats who apply and enforce public policies. Together, these bureaucrats make up the state administration. But what, really, is bureaucracy, and why does there seem to be so much of it?

Bureaucracy is a way of organizing people and activities in both government and business. The three characteristics we most associate with it are *hierarchy*, levels of power in an organization with maximum authority at the top; *specialization*, with everyone fitting into a niche and becoming an expert by performing particular tasks repeatedly; and *formal rules and regulations*, the notorious "red tape."[19]

When the United States was basically an agricultural nation, there was no need for either big government or big business. As people left farms and small towns and migrated to big cities to find work, the resulting urbanization of the nation created a host of problems: transportation, unemployment, sanitation, education, and so on.

FIGURE 7.1

State and Local Government Employment in Texas, 1980–2005

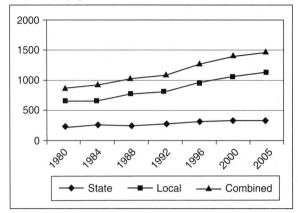

SOURCE: *Texas Almanac*, 1982–1983, 1986–1987, 1990–1991, 1994–1995, 1998–1999, 2002–2003, and 2006–2007 editions (Dallas: A.H. Belo/*Dallas Morning News*, 1981, 1986, 1989, 1993, 1997, 2001, 2006), 410, 597, 502, 467, 548, 548, 576, respectively.

Federal, state, and local governments tried to solve these problems by providing services, and these services required numerous employees and organizations. For example, the federal Interstate Commerce Commission was created to tackle excessive railroad rates, while the Texas Employment Commission—now called the Texas Workforce Commission—was created to place workers into jobs. Later, agencies such as the Texas Department of Human Services (now split into two other agencies) and various county welfare agencies were created to deal with hard-core poverty. The result of these needs for more government has been the sprawling, powerful administrative state we know today.

As Figure 7.1 indicates, in recent years the number of state and local employees has grown, but so also has the state's population. Even when bad economic times required hiring freezes, such as in 1987–1988 and in 2001–2003, government seemed to maintain its size though it was also required to be more productive—to provide more services for the same dollars. In fact, when the private economy is poor, government often has to hire workers to deal with the increased workload in such areas as unemployment and public health. This situation was particularly apparent at the national level during the Great Depression of the 1930s. In addition, the population of the state has been growing rapidly, thereby creating a demand for more government services.

Bureaucracy: Survival Techniques

In the push and scramble of overlapping jurisdictions and overlapping authorities, agency personnel in Texas must fight for funds if they want their agency, and their jobs, to continue. Because the administrators operate in the political arena, they use political tactics to achieve their goals, just as state legislators and the governor do. Administrators must develop their own sources of political power if they want policies favorable to them enacted into law. In doing so, they rely occasionally on public goodwill but more often on elected officials, interest groups, and their own expertise.[20]

Sources of Bureaucratic Power.   Bureaucrats and bureaucratic agencies gain power and influence through highly varied sources. These sources include **clientele groups**, legislators, the governor, and their own expertise and information.

Clientele Groups.   The cornerstone of an agency's political clout is its relationship with its clientele group or groups—that is, the interest group(s) that benefit from the agency's programs. This relationship is mutually beneficial. Agency and clientele have similar goals, are interested in the same programs, and work together in a number of ways, including sharing personnel, information, and lobbying strategies. The greater the economic power of the interest groups, the stronger are the political ties between them and "their" agencies—so strong, in fact, that "regulation" often becomes promotion of the clientele group's interests. When this situation occurs, the agency is known as a "captive" agency; agency personnel and decision processes have been co-opted by the clientele group. When powerful legislators are added to the network in support of clientele-endorsed programs and budgets, an "iron triangle" of power occurs.

Among the better-known clientele/agency relationships are the relationships of the oil, gas, and transportation industries with the Texas Railroad Commission, the banking industry with the Texas Department of Banking, and the Texas State Teachers Association with the Texas Education Agency. By and large, the interest groups are seeking to use the agencies as protection against their competitors.

The Legislature.   Relationships with legislators are of two types: direct and indirect. First, agencies directly attempt to influence legislation and their budgets by furnishing information in writing and through testimony to legislative committees. In addition, agency executives work hard to get to know the speaker of the House, the lieutenant governor, and the members of the Legislative Budget Board and the Legislative Council, all of whom operate year-round, even when committee chairs and other legislators have gone home. Second, agencies use their clientele groups to try to influence legislation, budgets, and the selection of legislative leaders. During budget shortfalls, a number of state agencies—including higher education—became adept at finding powerful groups such as chambers of commerce and specially formed support groups to try to ward off agency budget cuts.

The Chief Executive.   As noted earlier in this chapter, the governor's power over state agencies is weak, but bureaucrats nonetheless want gubernatorial support. A governor who is a skillful chief legislator can help an agency get its budget increased or add a new program. The chief executive also can act as a referee when an agency does not have the support of its clientele group and can give an agency visibility when it might otherwise languish in obscurity. The governor's legislative and party roles can be used to influence neutral legislators to look favorably on an agency, and the governor can greatly affect an agency's success or failure through appointments to the policy board or commission that oversees it. To state administrators, the chief executive is more powerful than the formal roles of the gubernatorial office would suggest. This power was demonstrated in 1991 when Governor Richards forced the reorganization of the Texas Department of Commerce, ending its practice of expensive foreign "economic development" trips. Four years later Governor Bush helped the insurance industry by pushing for limitations on lawsuits but demanded reasonable rate behavior in return.

Expertise and Information. Expert information is a political commodity peculiar to bureaucrats, who enjoy a unique position in state government through their control of the technical information that the governor and legislators must have in order to develop statewide policies. Bureaucracies have a particularly strong advantage in Texas because the legislative committee system is inconsistent in producing legislative expertise. For the legislator who does not want to use the agency's information, the only alternative source is often the agency's clientele group. For example, if the legislature is trying to determine whether the state is producing enough physicians, the Board of Medical Examiners, the Department of State Health Services, and the Texas Medical Association are all ready to furnish the information.

Bureaucratic Involvement in the Policy-Making Process.
Bureaucrats become involved both when public policy is developed and when it is executed. Their involvement is not so obvious as that of the governor and the legislature.

Execution of the Laws. The primary task of state bureaucrats is to execute the laws of Texas. In carrying out this task, however, they have considerable **administrative discretion;** that is, they are relatively free to use their judgment as to just how the laws will be carried out. Regulatory boards illustrate most clearly the power of administrative agencies. When the Public Utility Commission determines the transmission cost of service—the cost of moving electricity from a generating plant to the retail distributor—it is making (administrative) rules that, like legislative statutes, have the force of law; it is, therefore, performing a quasi-legislative function. And when the Alcoholic Beverage Commission decides who will be issued a license to sell beer, wine, and distilled spirits, it is performing a quasi-judicial function by determining whether a person has the right to go into business.

Often a statute passed by the legislature creates a general framework for implementing a program of regulation or service, but state agencies have considerable discretion in interpreting statutes. Consequently, the policy-making boards, commissions, and authorities are very important in determining what government actually does. Especially in a state like Texas, which lacks a cabinet system and an integrated executive branch, the average citizen is affected daily by what these boards do, but that citizen may have little understanding of how the boards work or how to approach them. Compounding the problem is the fact that the chair is basically an equal member of the board, so that no single, readily identifiable person is in charge.

This board/commission structure makes it more difficult for citizens to participate. Moreover, these boards usually appoint an executive director, or college president, to carry out their policies, and that executive officer has considerable influence over board policies. For example, a college student may wish to protest the abolition of a popular major. Whose decision was it? The college's board of regents? The Texas Higher Education Coordinating Board's? Were the students consulted before the decision was made?

However, administrative discretion can be a positive factor in effective government. A common example is the decision of a Department of Public Safety law enforcement officer to allow one suspect to go free in the hope that he will lead criminal intelligence agents to a more important suspect.

Influencing Legislation. Bureaucrats directly influence the content and meaning of statutes that are passed by the legislature, and they do so in three principal ways: by drafting bills, by furnishing information to legislators, and by lobbying. During its short session, the Texas legislature is under great pressure to draft, consider, and dispose of needed legislation. State bureaucrats are eager to aid the lawmakers, and two ways in which they do so are mutually beneficial: furnishing specialized information to legislative committees and drafting bills that individual legislators may then present as their own. Legislators thus gain needed assistance, and administrators are able to protect their agencies by helping to write their own budgets and developing their own programs.

Bureaucrats also influence legislation by lobbying legislators for or against proposed bills under the guise of furnishing information. Agencies usually work closely with their clientele group or groups in this endeavor. The governor is also lobbied not only for support of legislation favored by agencies and their clients but also for appointments to agencies that are acceptable to them and their clients. If successful, both these lobbying activities can greatly influence both the decisions of legislators and the policies set by boards and commissions. Moreover, the Texas Public Employees Association, especially strong among the state's classified employees, is an active lobby at budget time on matters of salary and fringe benefits.

Harnessing the Administrative State

As part of the state's system of checks and balances, the governor has a veto over legislative acts and the legislature can impeach a governor or refuse to confirm gubernatorial appointments. As well as controlling various offices and agencies that report directly to them, all three traditional branches of government—executive, legislative, and judicial—have means of holding the bureaucracy, sometimes called the "fourth branch" of government, in check. Democratic theory posits that government should be elected by the people, but most administrators are not. The governor and other elected executives have legitimacy. State administrators must derive as much legitimacy (popular acceptance) as they can from these elected officials.

During the 1980s, the issue of bureaucratic accountability to the people through their elected representatives became increasingly important at both the state and national levels because of tight budgets and public desire to maximize each tax dollar, as well as a strong, conservative anti-government trend. The importance of accountability was dramatically brought home in 1991 when the governor and the legislature agreed that no budget would be forthcoming for the 1992–1993 biennium until all state functions were audited to determine whether money was being wasted. This effort, led by Comptroller John Sharp, received attention nationwide and was a model for a similar effort—the National Performance Review chaired by Vice President Al Gore—by the Clinton administration. Citizen demand for accountability and government response to it illustrate that both citizens and elective officials play a role in harnessing the administrative state.

How Much Accountability to the Chief Executive? It would seem logical to make the bureaucracy accountable to the governor, the chief executive and nominal head of the state administration. But the governor's powers were intentionally limited to avoid centralizing governmental power in any one office. For example:

1. Appointment powers are restricted and removal powers are limited.
2. There is no true executive budget in spite of recent gains in gubernatorial influence.
3. The executive is fragmented: Four departments, a major commission, and a major board are headed by elected officials, and many separate agencies deal with related functional areas—more than 19 policy-making boards, not including community college district boards, are involved in the area of education alone.

Even if there were a complete reorganization of the executive branch, including the creation of consolidated departments headed by officials who constituted a governor's cabinet such as thirty-nine other states have, the sheer size and diversity of the bureaucracy, coupled with other demands on the governor's time and staff, would make executive control loose and indirect. Just as it is difficult to hold a president responsible for the actions of a Social Security clerk in Laramie, Wyoming, so also would it be difficult to hold a governor responsible for the actions of a college professor in Canyon or a welfare caseworker in El Paso.

Nevertheless, stronger supervisory control would allow the governor to exercise greater influence over major policy decisions. With a consolidated executive branch, unencumbered by elected administrators, and with managerial control over the state budget, the chief executive would have more hope of implementing policy. The advantage of a strong chief executive as the head of a more truly hierarchical structure of administration would be that overall responsibility would be vested in a highly visible elected official who could not so easily be dominated by special interests.

How Much Accountability to the Legislature?   Legislative bodies exert many controls over administrative agencies. In Texas, with a dominant legislative branch, these controls can take on considerable importance.

Legislative Oversight.   Legislatures traditionally have been guardians of the public interests, with powers to oversee administrative agencies. These powers include budgetary control, the postaudit of agency expenditures to ensure their legality, programmatic control through the statutes, investigation of alleged wrongdoing, and impeachment of officials. Although traditional *legislative oversight* is somewhat effective in Texas, several factors militate against its total success. One is the tripartite relationship among legislators, bureaucrats, and special interest groups. Legislators may be reluctant to ruffle the feathers of groups that supply them with campaign contributions by pressing their oversight vigorously. These groups, in turn, often have strong connections to the bureaucracy. Another is the high turnover of legislative committee personnel. A third is the lack of ongoing supervision because legislators are on the job only part time as a result of Texas's short biennial legislative sessions. Much of the burden of oversight falls on the Legislative Budget Board, the Legislative Council, and the Legislative Audit Committee, although none of these has sufficient staff or time to do a thorough job, and none is well known to the general public.

A substitute for direct legislative oversight is legislation that micromanages an agency or set of agencies and requires some other agency to be the control force. A specific example is the highly specific legislation passed in the 1997 session that dictates the core curriculum, the admission standards, and the maximum number of credit hours at publicly assisted colleges and universities. The Texas Higher Education Coordinating Board was put in charge of enforcing these statutes.

Sunset Act.   With the passage of the Sunset Act by the 65th Legislature in 1977, Texas established a procedure for reviewing periodically the existence of all statutory boards, commissions, and departments—except colleges and universities. As the quotation opening this part of the chapter indicates, a poor review can result in the disappearance of the agency. More than 200 agencies and advisory committees are included, and new ones are added as they are created. These reviews are conducted by a twelve-member Sunset Advisory Commission made up of five senators and five representatives appointed by their respective presiding officers, who also appoint two citizen members. The commission chair and vice chair alternate between the Senate and the House appointees and are designated by the lieutenant governor and the speaker.

The commission can determine the list of agencies to be reviewed before the beginning of each regular legislative session so long as all agencies are evaluated within a 12-year period. The agencies must submit self-evaluation reports, and the commission coordinates its information gathering with other agencies that monitor state agencies on a regular basis, such as the Legislative Budget Board, legislative committees, and the offices of the state auditor, governor, and comptroller. After the Sunset review, the legislature must explicitly vote to continue an agency, and it may also reorganize the agency or force it to modify its administrative rules and procedures.

At the end of the 2005 legislative session,[21] the Sunset process had resulted in the following:

- Public membership on state boards and more public participation
- Stronger prohibitions against conflicts of interest
- Improved enforcement processes
- Elimination of overlap and duplication
- Abolition of 32 agencies
- Abolition of 20 additional agencies, with functions transferred to other agencies
- Merger of 12 agencies
- Approximately $766 million in savings and increased revenues to the state since inception of the sunset process

The Sunset Commission's 2007 agenda includes 24 agencies. Among the most prominent are the Texas Education Agency, the Veterans' Land Board, the Texas Department of Criminal Justice, and the Board of Pardons and Paroles.

How Much Accountability to the Public?   Our government is based on the premise that it will be accountable to the people it governs. If accountability cannot be achieved directly by having all citizens of a political division meet to vote directly on laws and policies, theoretically it can be achieved through representatives who meet in government and report to their citizen-constituents.

Elective Accountability.   Given the vast bureaucracy and the difficulty encountered by voters who try to make intelligent decisions regarding the multitude of names on the long ballot in Texas, the elective process has become an unsatisfactory method of ensuring responsible administrative action. Long ballots tend to lead to confusion, not accountability, and once in office, incumbents can usually count on being re-elected simply because the voters recognize their names. In view of these problems, Texas citizens need some way to check on the activities of particular administrators (and their agencies) on whom public attention, for whatever reason, is focused. Until the passage of the three acts described next, there was no ready way to gain the necessary information.

Open Records and Meetings.   Under the Texas Open Records Act, originally passed in 1973, the public, including the media, has access to a wide variety of official records and to most public meetings of state and local agencies. Sometimes called "sunshine" legislation because it forces agencies to shed light on their deliberations and procedures, this act is seen as a way to prevent or expose bureaucratic ineptitude, corruption, and unnecessary secrecy. An agency that denies access to information that is listed as an open record in the statute may have to defend its actions to the attorney general and even in court.

   The 1987 Open Meetings Act strengthened public access to information by requiring governmental bodies to certify that discussions held in executive sessions were legal or to tape-record closed meetings. Closed meetings are permitted when sensitive issues such as real estate transactions or personnel actions are under consideration, but the agency must post an agenda in advance and submit it to the secretary of state, indicating what items will be discussed in closed session. Since 1981 the legislature has also required state agencies to write rules and regulations in understandable language. In recent years, the Texas Open Records Act has been frequently amended to permit exceptions. For example, many search committees looking for city managers, executive directors of agencies, and college presidents were being foiled by premature disclosure of the names of individuals they were considering and sought some protection from the act.

   In 1999 the legislature strengthened open meetings provisions by placing firm restrictions on staff briefings that could be made before governing bodies at the state and local level. Two new types of exceptions emerged from the 76th Legislature—economic development and utilities deregulation—but these were seen as protections on behalf of the public when a government was in a competitive situation.[22] That is, while Texas government became even more open following the 1999 session, governments were allowed to have closed meetings when competitive issues were the topic of discussion.

YOU DECIDE

Does the Texas Governor Need More Power?

The powers of the Texas governor used to be ranked almost at the bottom of gubernatorial powers in the fifty American states. More recently, the Texas governor's institutional powers—those established by constitution and statute—rank just about in the middle and have been growing. Indeed, the powers of the governor of California are considered less than those of the Texas governor, although the New York governor has greater power.

Pro

Texas should, by statute or constitutional amendment, increase the power of the governor because:

⇨ Bureaucrats have far too much discretion to act when there is no clear executive authority.

⇨ The public is confused by the number of elected officials in Texas (the long ballot).

⇨ Democracy is better served when a single, highly visible, powerful individual can be held accountable by the public.

⇨ A governor needs to be able to control all boards and commissions soon after election in order to implement policies he or she favors.

⇨ A more powerful governor would mean that the legislature's power could be lessened.

⇨ Texas needs its governor to have meaningful budget authority.

Con

Texas should not, by statute or constitutional amendment, increase the power of the governor because:

⇨ The personal power of the governor—based on margin of electoral victory and personal persuasion—is already great.

⇨ The veto power is virtually absolute.

⇨ Dispersion of power is a good way to keep one person from gaining too much control.

⇨ The governor's clout is obvious when one considers the salary, the size of the staff, and the lack of effort over the years to remove the governor from office.

⇨ Democracy is served better when the legislature is the more powerful institution because the people are closer to their elected representatives than to the governor.

⇨ Increasing the governor's power may create a more partisan political environment.

The 2005 legislature further strengthened the open meetings law by requiring that all members of public boards—elected or appointed, state and local—receive training in the proper conduct of closed meetings. It also beefed up the conflict-of-interest statute.

Whistle-Blower Protection.   The 1983 Legislature passed an act affording job security to state employees who spot illegal or unethical conduct in their agency and report it to appropriate officials. The national government established the precedent for "whistle-blower" legislation in 1978. The term *whistle-blower* comes from the fact that employees who report illegal acts are "blowing the whistle" on someone. The implementation of this act has not been promising, however. One spectacular case in which a whistle-blower was fired from the Department of Human Services took five years to resolve.

SUMMARY

Although fairly well paid and endowed with a four-year term, the governor of Texas is still constitutionally somewhat weak as a state officer, and the successful approval and implementation of the governor's budgetary and programmatic policies depend more on the incumbent's adroitness in developing leadership and political skills than on his or her formal powers. Although certain gubernatorial roles are strong, such as legislative, regional planning, and law enforcement powers, the governor is noticeably weak as a chief executive. The executive role is limited by:

1. Five other elected executives and two elected policy boards.
2. Fragmentation resulting from the fact that the state bureaucracy is controlled by multimember boards and commissions.
3. Restrictions on appointments and removals of state officials.
4. The dual budget system.

Since the governor's ability to control the bureaucracy is limited, we must look to other devices to control big government in Texas. Three recent measures—the Open Records Act, the Open Meetings Act, and the Whistle-Blower Act—have made strides in the direction of giving Texas citizens a responsible bureaucracy. These statutes are augmented by such traditional controls as the legislative audit and the legislature's power to investigate bureaucratic activities. Legislative control has also been bolstered by the Sunset Act.

Nevertheless, the fragmented nature of state administration allows bureaucrats considerable leeway to apply their own priorities in carrying out legislative mandates. The most obvious suggestions for reform would require consolidating agencies with similar functions in a single department headed by a single executive who reports to the governor. The result would be a cabinet system similar to those used by the national government and many other states. The new departments might include the following:

• Public and Higher Education
• Health and Human Services
• Natural Resources

- Highways and Public Transportation
- Public Safety and Criminal Justice
- Commerce and Economic Development
- Administrative Services
- Professional and Occupational Licensing

Chapters 10 and 11 cover the state budget and major policy issues in Texas. Together they provide a picture of state elected officials and state administration in action.

STUDY QUESTIONS

1. Would you like to be governor of Texas? Why or why not? Do you have the formal qualifications to be governor? How closely do you resemble the informal profile that describes a typical governor?
2. Why do you think many analysts regard chief legislator as the governor's most significant role?
3. What are the five types of policy-makers in Texas administrative agencies? What do each of the elected executives and the two elected commissions do?
4. What are the sources of bureaucratic power? How are bureaucrats involved in the policy process?
5. What devices are available to both elected officials and the public to keep the bureaucracy in check?

SURFING THE WEB

Visit the companion site for this book:
> http://www.thomsonedu.com/politicalscience/kraemer

The home page of the Texas governor:
> http://www.governor.state.tx.us

Information on the various divisions of the governor's office:
> http://www.governor.state.tx.us/divisions

The fast way to locate all state agencies and their home pages:
> http://www2.tsl.state.tx.us/trail/agencies.jsp

A thorough look at the Sunset process:
> http://www.sunset.state.tx.us

NOTES

1. The Texas Constitution does spell out the grounds for removing judges, however. Other officials subject to impeachment include the lieutenant governor, the attorney general, the commissioner of the General Land Office, the comptroller, and appellate court judges. The grounds stipulated for impeachment of judges include partiality, oppression, official misconduct, incompetence, negligence, and failure to conduct the business of the court. See Fred Gantt, Jr., *The Chief Executive in Texas* (Austin: University of Texas Press, 1964), 123.

2. Ferguson was impeached and convicted for mishandling public funds, conduct brought to light because funds for the University of Texas were involved.

3. *The Book of the States 2005,* vol. 37 (Lexington, KY: Council of State Governments, 2005), 218–219.

4. Patrick Fisher and David Nice, "Staffing the Governor's Office: A Comparative Analysis," *The Book of the States 2005,* 203–207.

5. The only other female governor in Texas was Miriam A. (Ma) Ferguson, who served two non-consecutive terms, 1925–1927 and 1933–1935; her husband had been impeached while governor and convicted in 1917.

6. Thad L. Beyle, "Being Governor," *The State of the States* (Washington, DC: CQ Press, 1996), 77–107, discusses how governors might be evaluated, including the index developed by the National Governors Association.

7. Texas claims the current president, George W. Bush, and three former U.S. presidents: Dwight Eisenhower, who was born in the state; Lyndon Johnson, who was a lifelong resident; and George Bush, who moved to Texas during an oil boom when he was a businessman, not a politician.

8. "The Big Winners and Losers of 1999: The Governor Had a Banner Year, While Local Education Lost Out," *Wall Street Journal,* December 29, 1999, T1.

9. Paul Burka, "No! No! No!" *Texas Monthly,* August 2001, 7–10.

10. Wayne Slater, "Support for Perry Up a Bit from Last Fall," *Dallas Morning News,* March 24, 2002, 19A.

11. See the following bills passed in 2003: H.B. 2292, regular session; H.B. 7, third called session; and S.B. 2, third called session. S.B. 2, Article 7, third called session, 78th Legislature, exempts river authorities, junior college districts, agencies headed by one or more statewide elected officials, agencies with a majority of board members not requiring Senate confirmation, and agencies reporting to one or more elected officials. Purely local boards are also exempted.

12. Thad Beyle, "The Governors," *Politics in the American States: A Comparative Analysis,* 8th ed. Virginia Gray and Russell L. Hanson (Washington, DC: CQ Press, 2004, 212–213); and Thad Beyle, "Being Governor," *The State of the States* (Washington, DC: CQ Press, 2006), 61.

13. For example, three members (half of the total) of the Commission on Alcoholism and Drug Abuse must be recovering substance abusers.

14. This practice is most common with the licensing and examining boards in various health care fields.

15. Unlike the president, the governor does not have a "pocket veto." The governor must send a veto message to block a bill; laying it aside without a signature results in the bill's becoming law, even if the legislature adjourns.

16. Congress granted the U.S. president the item veto in 1996; Bill Clinton used the power 82 times before the Supreme Court nullified it in 1998.

17. James McGregor Burns, *Leadership* (New York: Harper and Row, 1978), 42–45.

18. The numbers in this paragraph are based on an actual count of entries from a list in *Fiscal Size Up: Texas State Services, 2006–2007 Biennium* (Austin: Legislative Budget Board, December 2005).

19. Max Weber is considered the classic expert on bureaucracy. See "Bureaucracy," in *From Max Weber: Essays in Sociology,* translated, edited, and with an introduction by H. H. Garth and C. Wright Mills (New York: Oxford University Press, 1946), 196–244.

20. A classic study of bureaucratic power at the national level is Francis Rourke, *Bureaucracy, Politics, and Public Policy,* 4th ed. (Boston: Little, Brown, 1986). Rourke's framework is adopted here.

21. Sunset Advisory Commission, *Guide to the Sunset Process,* January 2006, available at http://www.sunset.state.tx.us/guide.pdf, and Sunset Advisory Commission, *Sunset Process Report Card,* revised February 2003, available at www.sunset.state.tx.us/78.htm.

22. See Alan J. Bojorquez, "New Open Government Legislation," *Texas Town & City* (October 1999), 11–14.

8

THE JUDICIARY AND THE SYSTEM OF JUSTICE

Nothing can contribute so much to [the judges'] firmness and independence as permanency in office.

Alexander Hamilton
Federalist #78, 1787

The law, in its majestic impartiality, forbids the rich as well as the poor to sleep under bridges, to beg in the streets, and to steal bread.

Anatole France (Jacques Thibault)
French Nobel Prize–winning writer, Le Lys Rouge, 1894

INTRODUCTION

The judiciary—the system of courts, judges, lawyers, and other actors in the institutions of justice—presents several serious problems for democratic theory. Judges are the arbiters of conflicts within society and the interpreters of the rules by which we govern ourselves. Many people think that judges should be able to hold themselves above the dirty struggles of the political process. As a consequence, there have always been those who followed Alexander Hamilton in arguing that judges should be as independent as possible from the democratic necessities of elections, interest groups, and money. On the other hand, many others have pointed out, over the years, that democracy requires that important decision makers be accountable to the public and therefore made to stand for election. Troubling questions for any political system include: Are judges part of the political process? If they are, how can they come to office in a manner that ensures that they will be fair and impartial but still accountable to the public?

In Texas, the traditional answer has been to come down firmly on the side of democracy and to make judges answerable to the people. It turns out, however, that when judges are treated like other politicians they become vulnerable to the suspicion that they are allowing private interests to corrupt their views on public affairs.

Furthermore, the importance of money in the judicial system has another disquieting aspect: It creates doubts as to whether the courts are fulfilling the democratic ideal that they provide equal justice to all. If access to legal representation is expensive, and if the outcome of trials depends on adequate representation, then do poor people have a fair chance in a courtroom? Because of these suspicions and doubts, the Texas judiciary is a troubled democratic institution.

This chapter first examines the political nature of judges, then follows with a summary of the important features of the judicial branch of government in Texas. The focus then shifts to a consideration of the players in the state system of justice. The remainder of the chapter is devoted to some of the vexing problems facing the state judiciary and an overview of some of the outputs of the system—the substance of justice.

POLITICIANS IN BLACK ROBES

As a tradition of their profession, most judges in Texas and elsewhere have attempted to live up to Hamilton's recipe for judicial power by pretending to be aloof from the political process. Judges wear black robes, are addressed as "Your Honor" in the courtroom, write opinions in a specialized language that is beyond the understanding of most citizens, and in general try to speak and act in a way that indicates that they are not part of the messy business of governing.

This performance is not entirely insincere. Over the centuries great jurists in England and the United States have developed—and are developing—neutral, impersonal criteria to use in making decisions. The ideal is that a judge is like a surgeon operating on a patient or a scientist examining evidence to support or contradict a hypothesis: impartial and incorruptible, above passion and prejudice. The ideal judge rules on evidence and procedure purely on the basis of fairness and established principles. Common observation suggests that this ideal has some basis in reality and that judges are less moved by partisanship and outside influence than are legislators or governors.

But the notion that what judges do is not political is a well-polished myth. Whenever judges apply a statute, and especially when they interpret a constitution, they make choices among competing rules, individuals, and groups. When a judge makes a decision, somebody wins and somebody loses. Those somebodies can be not only individuals but very large groups of people, who win or lose a great deal and care intensely about the outcome of the decision.

As a consequence, the coalitions of interests that tend to oppose each other in political parties also tend to adopt differing philosophies of judicial interpretation. Republican judges, in perfectly good faith, usually interpret words so as to favor the interests displayed in Table 4.2 in Chapter 4. Democratic judges, also in good faith, generally interpret words so as to favor a conflicting set of interests. In other words, judges make laws, and the constitution, in the process of interpretation. As a result, Texas judges, and especially members of the Supreme Court and Court of Criminal Appeals, are crucial components of the state's political system.

Texas Judge W. A. Morrison, a former justice of the Court of Criminal Appeals, made no bones about his personal contribution to the state's system of laws in 1964. "I have engrafted into the law of this great state my own personal philosophy," he stated. He explained that during his first day on the bench as a young man, the other two judges could not agree on more than a dozen cases, and so Morrison cast the deciding vote in every one. He attributed his having "engrafted" his personal philosophy into the state's law to a greater degree than most judges to the fact that he came to the bench young and remained longer than most.[1]

Another Texas jurist, District Judge John Dietz, clearly acknowledged the political aspect of his job in 2002:

> I redistribute wealth. I decide whether someone can keep theirs or (must) give it to someone else.[2]

The fact that in Texas judges are elected makes the political nature of their work even more obvious. As one state jurist proclaimed in the early 1970s:

> This job is more politics than law; there's no two ways about it. Hell, you can have all kinds of dandy ideas, but if you don't get yourself elected, you can sell your ideas on a corner somewhere. Politics isn't a dirty word in my mouth.[3]

Although judges from the rival political parties frequently split in judicial philosophy, in their analysis of individual cases they can also disagree intensely with others of the same party. A case in point is a verbal brawl that erupted in the Texas Supreme Court in 2000 over the proper interpretation of a law requiring a doctor to notify the parents of a girl under the age of 18 before performing an abortion on her.[4] All nine of the justices were Republicans, but the case reveals the depth of disagreement on important judicial principles that can exist between nominal allies.

In 1999 the legislature had passed the "parental notification" bill, and Governor George W. Bush signed it. Mindful of federal courts' history of voiding state anti-abortion laws, however, the legislature had put in a "judicial bypass" clause, allowing an underage girl to get an abortion without informing her parents if she could convince a state judge that she met certain criteria. Among the criteria were that she was mature and well informed. In early 2000 a pregnant teenager ("Jane Doe" in court discussions) had asked a judge to give her a judicial bypass and was turned down. She appealed, and the problem quickly landed on the docket of the state's highest civil court.

The case brought up important questions of interpretation. What did "mature" and "informed" mean when applied to a teenager? Had the legislature intended to make judicial bypass a relatively easy and common process or something difficult and rare? By a 6 to 3 vote, in March 2000 the court ruled that the legislature had intended the criteria to be relatively easy to meet and, over-ruling the lower appeals court, granted permission to "Jane Doe" to have an abortion.

Although all nine justices were members of the same party, the partisan unanimity masked an ideological divide. The three dissenters exploded in outrage. "The plain fact is that the statute was enacted to protect parents' right to involve themselves in their children's decisions and to encourage that involvement as well as to discourage teenage pregnancy and abortion," fumed Justice Nathan Hecht. "The court not only ignores these purposes, it has done what it can to defeat them." The majority's "utter disregard" for legislative intent was "an insult to those legislators personally, to the office they hold, and to the separation of powers between the two branches of government." No less annoyed, Justice Priscilla Owen charged that the majority had "manufactured reasons to justify its action," and "acted irresponsibly." (This vote and statement contributed to Democratic opposition in the U.S. Senate to Owen's appointment as a federal judge; see Chapter 1.) Justice Greg Abbott accused the majority of practicing "interpretive hand-wringing."

In response, several members of the majority criticized Hecht's "explosive rhetoric," accusing him of having "succumbed to passion." To interpret the law as the dissenters urged, argued Justice Al Gonzales, would be to misunderstand the new law and "would be an unconscionable act of judicial activism."

In this one episode, the true nature of the judiciary stood revealed. Fair-minded or not, judges bring as many preconceptions and differences of outlook to their work as do legislators or executives. They have ideological commitments. They have no Olympian detachment from the issues they decide. They are politicians in black robes.

THE PLAYERS IN THE SYSTEM OF JUSTICE

The judiciary is part of an entire system that attempts to interpret and apply society's laws. A brief summary of the parts of this system, and some of its subject matter, follows.

The Attorney General

Over the years the attorney general (AG) has developed an unusual and highly significant power, the authority to issue **advisory opinions.** The constitution establishes the attorney general as Texas's chief legal officer and as legal adviser to the governor and other state officials. The legislature later expanded the scope of the AG's advisory activity. Out of this expansion has arisen the now firmly established practice that the legislature, agencies of the executive branch, and local governments seek advice on the constitutionality of proposals, rules, procedures, and statutes. In 2005 Greg Abbott handed down 101 "Attorney General's Opinions" dealing with the constitutionality of proposed government laws or actions and one decision interpreting the Open Records Act. His office supplied various state and local governments with 11,765 Open Records Letter Rulings, answering their requests for advice on whether to release specific information.[5]

Rather than filing a court action that is expensive and time consuming, Texas officials who go to the attorney general obtain a ruling on disputed constitutional issues in a relatively brief period of time and at almost no expense. The Texas judiciary and virtually everyone else in the state have come to accept these rulings, although sometimes with a good deal of grumbling.

The most publicized attorney general's ruling of recent years, and perhaps in history, dealt with the divisive subject of affirmative action. For some years prior to 1996, the University of Texas Law School had been favoring African American and Latino applicants in its admissions process—that is, minority applicants were judged by a lower set of standards than were Anglo applicants. An Anglo woman, Cheryl Hopwood, had been turned down for admission to the law school despite the fact that her qualifications (grades and Law School Aptitude Test scores) were higher than those of some minority applicants who had been admitted. Hopwood sued in federal court. In 1996 the fifth circuit federal appeals court ruled in Hopwood's favor, deciding that such "reverse discrimination" against Anglos was unconstitutional.[6]

The federal Fifth Circuit Court's decision was significant as it stood because it applied to the state's premier law school. Nevertheless, its scope did not extend to other schools.

On February 5, 1997, however, Attorney General Dan Morales dismayed Texas's university community by issuing Letter Opinion 97-001, in which he decreed that the federal court's ruling had outlawed race as a consideration in any admissions process or financial aid decision at any public school. Affirmative action was therefore forbidden in all Texas public colleges.[7]

In 1999 Morales's successor as attorney general, John Cornyn, issued another opinion that called Morales's ruling too broad and rescinded it. Cornyn stopped short of actually claiming that Morales's reasoning was wrong, merely stating that colleges should wait and see how an appeal of the Hopwood decision to the U.S. Supreme Court turned out.[8] Although the Supreme Court declined to hear Texas's appeal, in 2003 it in effect reversed the Hopwood decision when it upheld the affirmative action program at the University of Michigan. After several years, therefore, Texas universities were again free to consider race in their admissions policies.[9]

Litigation continued to swirl around the issue of affirmative action, and both the state and the nation as a whole expected more legal controversy. Nevertheless, the important point here is that in one of the most important and intensely conflict-ridden issues in Texas, policy has been set neither by the state legislature nor the governor but by the attorney general. Such is the power of this institution in state government.

Lawyers

As it is in the rest of the country, the legal profession is a growth industry in Texas. In 2004 the state was home to 74,446 attorneys and was adding them at the rate of about 400 each year. The legal profession differs substantially in socio-economic and other characteristics from the population in general. Most lawyers are white males[10] who come from relatively wealthy families. In 2004, 30 percent of Texas lawyers were women, 4 percent were African American, and 7 percent were Hispanic. As is the case in many other areas of American life, however, the pool of attorneys is presently being broadened to become more diverse in its ethnic and gender background.

The State Bar of Texas

All lawyers who practice within the state are required to maintain membership in the State Bar and pay annual dues. The State Bar occupies a unique position: It is an agency of government, a professional organization, and an influential interest group active in state politics.

Judges

As Figure 8.1 illustrates, the Texas judicial system is complicated. It has two tracks, one for civil and juvenile and one for criminal litigations, and several levels—original jurisdiction, intermediate appeals, and a top appeals court for each track, the Texas **Supreme Court,** and the **Court of Criminal Appeals.** The jurisdictions of courts at the lower levels are not completely clear, and so judges often find themselves with over-lapping and competing authority. The intricate, ambiguous nature of judicial author-ity has sparked periodic calls for reform. In the most recent attempt to simplify the jobs of judges, the Texas Research League wrote in 1991 that "The Texas judiciary is in disarray, with the courts in varying parts of the state going their own way at their own pace. . . . Texas does not have a court system in the real sense of the word."[11]

Despite such appeals, judges continue to make decisions within a complex and fragmented system. The following sections present a brief description of the activi-ties of that system of 2,669 courts and 3,221 judges from its lowest to its highest levels (Figure 8.1).[12]

Municipal Courts.   City courts are authorized by the state constitution and by state laws to handle minor criminal matters involving a fine of $500 with no possi-bility of imprisonment (class C misdemeanors), where they have concurrent juris-diction with justice of the peace courts. They also have **exclusive jurisdiction** over municipal ordinances and can impose fines of up to $2,500. Municipal courts have no civil jurisdiction and deal mainly with violations of traffic laws. They generally do not keep records of trials. In fiscal 2005 there were 1,378 municipal court judges, who disposed of 7,659,420 cases.

Most municipal judges are appointed by the governing body of the city, although in a few cities they are chosen in nonpartisan elections. Terms of office are usually two years. Their salaries are paid entirely by the city and are highly variable.

Justice Courts.   Until recently these were known as "justice of the peace" courts, and their judges are still known as justices of the peace (JPs). They are **original trial courts** with both **civil** and **criminal jurisdiction.** Such courts deal with misdemeanor criminal cases when the potential punishment is only a fine. They have exclusive

FIGURE 8.1

Court Structure of Texas

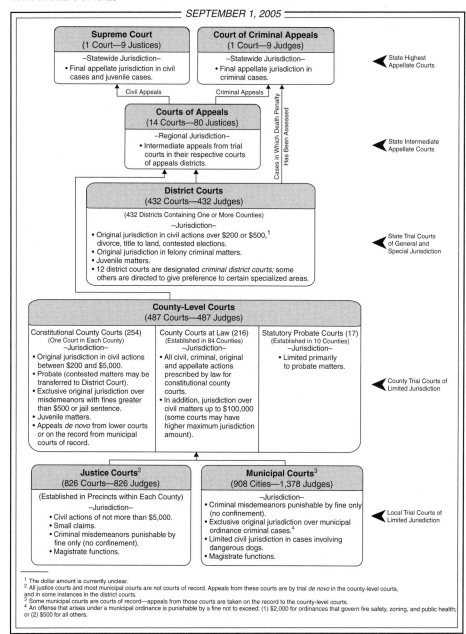

SOURCE: *Annual Statistical Report for the Texas Judiciary Fiscal Year 2005* (Austin, Office of Court Administration, December 2005), 3.

jurisdiction over civil cases where the amount in controversy is $200 or less and concurrent jurisdiction with both county and district courts when the amount in controversy is $5,000 or less. The JPs also act as judges of small claims courts and as notaries public and, like other Texas judges, are authorized to perform marriages. In all but the largest counties they may function as coroners, and in this role they may be required to certify cause of death, despite the fact that few if any JPs have medical training.

Justices of the peace are elected by the voters of the precinct and, like other county officials, serve for four years. Salaries range from practically nothing to more than $60,000 per year, depending on the size of the precinct, the volume of activity, and the generosity of the county commissioners. Texas's 826 justice courts disposed of 2,670,633 criminal cases and 271,348 civil cases in the fiscal year ending August 31, 2005.

County Courts. The Texas Constitution requires each county to have a court of record, that is, a court where a complete transcript is made of each case. Judges of these 254 "constitutional" courts need not be lawyers but only "well-informed in the law of the state." They are elected for four-year terms, and their salaries are paid by the counties and are highly variable. County court judges in urban areas can be paid more than $100,000 per year. At the other end of the scale, judges in rural counties can bring home closer to $10,000. Vacancies are filled by appointments made by the county commissioners court.

Not all constitutional county courts exercise judicial functions. In large counties, the constitutional county judge may devote full time to the administration of county government. When county courts do exercise judicial functions, they have both original and **appellate jurisdiction** in civil and criminal cases. Their **original jurisdiction** extends to all criminal misdemeanors where the fine allowed exceeds $500 or a jail term may be imposed. County courts also hear appeals in criminal cases from justice and municipal courts. In civil matters, constitutional county courts have concurrent jurisdiction with JP courts when the amount in controversy is between $200 and $5,000.

The volume of cases in approximately 30 of the state's larger counties has moved the legislature to establish a number of specialized county courts at law, with jurisdiction that varies according to the statute under which they were created. Some exercise jurisdiction in only one area—civil, criminal, probate, or appellate matters—while others are in effect extra, generalist county courts. Judges for these 233 county courts at law and probate courts must be attorneys. They are paid the same amount as the judges in the constitutional county courts.

Appellate jurisdiction from the decisions of county courts rests with the courts of appeals. County courts disposed of 146,939 civil, 613,226 criminal, and 7,717 juvenile cases in fiscal year 2005.

State Trial Courts: The District Courts. In Texas, district trial courts are the principal trial courts. There were 432 of these busy courts as of 2005. Each has a numerical designation—for example, the 353rd District Court—and each court has one judge. Most district courts have both criminal and civil jurisdiction, but in the metropolitan areas such courts often specialize in criminal, civil, or family law cases.

District court judges must be attorneys who are licensed to practice in the state and who have at least four years' experience as lawyers or judges prior to being elected to the district court bench. The 79th Legislature raised their basic state salary to $125,000 as of December 1, 2005,[13] and this sum is supplemented by additional compensation in most counties. Terms are for four years, with all midterm vacancies being filled by gubernatorial appointment.

Cases handled by district court judges are varied. The district courts usually have jurisdiction over felony criminal trials, divorce cases, suits over titles to land, election contests, and civil suits in which the amount in controversy is at least $200. They share some of their civil jurisdiction with county courts, depending on the relevant state statute and the amount of money at issue. District court cases are appealed to a court of appeals, except for death-penalty criminal cases, where appeal is made directly to the Court of Criminal Appeals. In fiscal year 2005 district courts disposed of 545,614 civil, 256,998 criminal, and 38,058 juvenile cases.

An additional complication to the allocation of jurisdiction is that at least one court in each county must be designated as the juvenile court to handle Texans younger than 17-years-old who are accused of crimes. These courts can be district courts, county courts at law, or constitutional county courts.

Intermediate State Appellate Courts: The Courts of Appeals.   The courts of appeals have intermediate civil and criminal appellate jurisdiction. Unlike the lower courts, appellate courts—the courts of appeals, the Court of Criminal Appeals, and the Supreme Court—are multi-judge courts that operate without juries. Appellate courts consider only the written records of lower-court proceedings and the arguments of counsel representing the parties involved.

Texas's 14 courts of appeals, each of which is responsible for a geographical district, have from 3 to 14 justices per court, for a total of 80 judges statewide. In each court the justices may hear cases *en banc* (together) or in panels of three. All decisions are by majority vote. Justices are elected for staggered six-year terms and must have the same qualifications as justices of the state's supreme court: Each must be at least 35 years of age and have 10 years' legal experience either as a practicing attorney or as a practicing attorney and judge of a court of record. Associate justices receive an annual salary of $137,350, and the chief justice, elected as such, receives $140,000. Within each district, counties are authorized to supplement the basic salary up to $7,000, or $7,500 for the chief judge.

Jurisdiction of the courts of appeals consists of civil cases appealed from district courts, county courts, and county courts at law and of criminal cases, except for capital murder, appealed from the lower courts. They both review the decisions of lower-court judges and evaluate the constitutionality of the statute or ordinance on which the conviction is based. Decisions of the courts of appeals are usually final, but some may be reviewed by the Court of Criminal Appeals or the Texas Supreme Court. The courts of appeals disposed of 5,117 civil and 7,040 criminal cases in fiscal year 2005.

Highest State Appellate Courts.   Texas and Oklahoma are the only states to have split their highest appellate jurisdiction between two courts: a supreme court that hears only civil cases and a Court of Criminal Appeals for criminal cases. Each has responsibility not only for reviewing the decisions made by lower-court trial judges but also for interpreting and applying the state constitution. It is this last power of constitutional interpretation that makes these courts of vital political importance.

The Court of Criminal Appeals.   This is the state's final appeals court in criminal matters, although in rare instances its decisions may be appealed to the U.S. Supreme Court. It considers writs of error, filed by losing attorneys who contend that their trial judge made a mistake in applying Texas law and who wish to have the verdict overturned, and writs of *habeas corpus,* in which attorneys claim that a certain person has been unlawfully detained and should be released. In fiscal year 2005 this court disposed of 7,550 cases, in the process writing 474 opinions. Among these cases, it heard 36 appeals of the death penalty, of which it affirmed 34, overturned one, and ordered a DNA test for one.

Qualifications for judges of the Court of Criminal Appeals and the justices of the Supreme Court are the same as those for justices of the courts of appeals. The nine judges of the Court of Criminal Appeals are elected on a statewide basis for six-year staggered terms, and the presiding judge runs as such. Vacancies are filled by gubernatorial appointment. Cases are normally heard by a three-judge panel. The salary is $150,000 per year, with the presiding judge receiving $152,500.

The Supreme Court.   Like its counterpart at the national level, the Texas Supreme Court is the most prestigious court in the system. Unlike its national counterpart, it hears only appeals from civil and juvenile cases. It has no authority over criminal cases.

Qualifications for Supreme Court justices are the same as those for the judges of the courts of appeals and Court of Criminal Appeals. There are nine justices on the bench, including a chief justice who campaigns for election as such. All are elected for six-year staggered terms, with three justices elected every two years. Salaries are the same as those for the Court of Criminal Appeals.

The Supreme Court's original jurisdiction is limited, and most cases that it hears are on appeal from the lower courts of appeals. Its caseload is somewhat lighter than the caseloads of other state courts; it disposed of only 136 cases in fiscal year 2005, writing as many opinions in the process. Nevertheless, when the court grants a "petition for review" of a lower court's decision, the chances are good that it will overturn that court's ruling. It reversed the decision of the intermediate appellate court in 63 percent of the cases in which it granted such a petition in 2005.

The Supreme Court also performs other important functions. It is empowered to issue writs of mandamus—orders to corporations or persons, including judges and state officials other than the governor, to perform certain acts. It conducts proceedings for the involuntary removal of judges and makes administrative rules for all civil courts in the state. In cooperation with the Texas Equal Access to Justice Foundation, it administers funds for the program that provides legal services to the indigent.

In addition, the Supreme Court plays a unique role for the legal profession in Texas. It holds the power of approval for new schools of law; it appoints the Board of Law Examiners, which prepares the bar examination; it determines who has passed the examination; and it certifies the successful applicants as being entitled to practice law in Texas. And, as will be discussed shortly, it formulates a set of guidelines for proper behavior by judicial candidates within the state.

Grand Juries

Grand juries meet in the county seat of each county and are convened as needed. Grand jurors are chosen from a list prepared by a panel of jury commissioners—three to five persons appointed by the district judge. From this list, the judge selects 12 persons who sit for a term, usually of three months' duration. Grand jurors consider the material submitted by prosecutors to determine whether sufficient evidence exists to issue a formal indictment. Normally, the cases considered are alleged felonies—serious crimes. Occasionally persons are indicted for misdemeanors—minor crimes—as was Speaker of the House of Representative Gib Lewis in December 1990. In Texas grand juries are frequently used to investigate such problems as drug trafficking within the community, increasing crime rates, and alleged misconduct by public officials. As mentioned in Chapter 1, in 2005 a Travis County grand jury indicted U.S. House majority leader Tom DeLay and two of his political associates on charges of violating Texas's campaign finance laws.

Trial Juries

Trial juries make actual decisions about truth and falsehood, guilt and innocence. Under Texas law, defendants in civil cases and anyone charged with a crime may demand a jury trial. Although this right is frequently waived, thousands of such trials take place within the state every year. Lower-court juries consist of six people, and district court juries have twelve members. The call to duty on a trial jury is determined through the use of a jury wheel, a list generated from the county voter registration, driver's license, and state identification card lists.

Although it is the duty of every citizen to help run the state judicial system by serving on juries, the government recognizes that time is money, and that therefore it is appropriate to pay jurors for their participation. Nevertheless, until 2005 jurors were reimbursed at the rate of only $6 a day, an amount that could often not even compensate them for the price of their lunches. A 2003 study on jury participation rates reported that only 19 percent of those summoned to jury duty in Dallas and Houston actually showed up, and argued that the low pay was a major reason for the cities' inability to motivate those called to serve.

Spurred by the report, and urged to action by some of the state's prominent judges and attorneys, the 2005 state legislature upped jurors' pay for the first time since 1954. As of January 1, 2006, jurors will still receive $6 for the first day of work but are paid $40 for each subsequent day.

Source: Steve Quinn, "Texas Jurors Getting $34-a-day Raise," *Denton Record-Chronicle*, December 30, 2005, A2.

Police

The state maintains an extensive organization primarily for the enforcement of criminal law. In addition to the judiciary and various planning and policy-making bodies, Texas has more than 67,000 law enforcement officers staffing state and local police agencies. Principal among these is the Texas Department of Public Safety (DPS). The DPS, with headquarters in Austin, employed 3,496 commissioned officers in 2006.[14] It is one of only eight state police agencies across the nation empowered to conduct criminal investigations.

The other law enforcement officers are employees of the 254 county sheriff's departments and more than 1,000 local police departments. Coordination and cooperation among these police agencies is sometimes haphazard and sometimes effective.

ISSUES FACING THE TEXAS JUDICIARY

The job of a judge is an ambiguous one in a democratic society. Many people believe, with Alexander Hamilton, that judges serve society best if they are independent, that is, if they are at least partly insulated from outside pressures. The best way to insulate judges is to appoint them for life. Yet democratic theory requires that all public officials be accountable to the public, which would seem to demand that they all be subject to frequent review through regularly scheduled elections. Although some scholars have tried to argue that judges should be both independent and accountable, the two concepts are inherently contradictory.[15]

In practice, various levels of government have tried to compromise the two desirable-but-incompatible goals in different ways. At the federal level, for example, judges are appointed by the president and serve for life, whereas in many states, including Texas, their jobs must be ratified periodically by the voters in partisan elections. Other states use a variety of means to try to compromise the two principles. Some have nonpartisan elections, some require the legislature to select judges, some delegate the task to the governor, and so on. Whatever compromise is chosen, it is never satisfying to everyone. National politicians frequently argue that federal judges must be made more accountable, while in Texas there are always some prominent people arguing that state judges should be made more independent.

There is no easy answer to the dilemma of accountability versus independence; citizens must make up their own minds. Here are two of the ways the argument has surfaced in Texas.

Is Justice for Sale?

The fact that Texas judges are elected has created the perception that they can be corrupted by campaign contributions. Because judges have to run for office like other politicians, they also have to raise money like others. When lawyers who practice in the courtrooms of judges or others with a direct interest in the outcome of legal cases give them campaign contributions, it raises the uncomfortable suspicion that those judges' court rulings might be affected by the money.

James Andrew Wynne, Jr., is a judge in the North Carolina Court of Appeals. The North Carolina judicial system is similar to the one in Texas, with partisan elections for almost all levels. In 2002 Judge Wynne used a vivid metaphor to summarize the uneasiness of those who suspect that justice may be for sale in such judicial systems. Suppose, he mused, that major-league baseball umpires had to run for office, and the players were allowed to contribute money to their campaigns: "Under that scenario, how can anyone have the confidence in the strike calls of an umpire if you know the pitcher contributed $10,000 to select that umpire to call the game?"[16] It is a fair question. Wealthy private interests may taint the administration of justice just as they deform the public policy made by other institutions. (Perhaps Judge Wynne's argument had some effect. Before the 2004 election, North Carolina instituted partial public financing of state judicial campaigns.)[17]

The possible corruption of justice is not just a theoretical problem. In the 1990s, Texas and Alabama had the most expensive judicial races in the country.[18] Some individual law firms contributed more than $100,000 to a single judicial candidate.[19] In the 2000s, free-spending judicial races spread to many other states, and the Texas experience became typical. In the 2004 campaigns, West Virginia and Illinois seemed to feature the most expensive races, with one campaign in the latter state costing the two major candidates 9 million.[20] But Texas judicial races continued to require large amounts of cash. In 2003, for example, Texans for Public Justice (TPJ) analyzed the campaign finances of 87 winning candidates for the intermediate courts of appeals. TPJ concluded that attorneys contributed 72 percent of the funding for those successful races.[21] It is difficult to imagine that judges would be able to forget the source of their campaign resources when arbitrating the cases of attorneys who have supported them.

Responding to the public perception that justice might be for sale, in 1995 the legislature passed the Judicial Campaign Fairness Act (JCFA). This legislation limited individual contributions to statewide judicial candidates to $5,000 each election and prohibited law firms from contributing more than $30,000 to individual Supreme Court candidates. Judicial candidates were also forbidden to accept more than $300,000 from all political action committees.

As Ben Sargent points out with satirical exaggeration, Texas's system of financing judicial campaigns can lead to the suspicion that justice is for sale.

SOURCE: Courtesy of Ben Sargent.

Although the clear intent of the JCFA was to stop the contamination of the Texas judiciary by money, events almost immediately proved it to be ineffective. In 1996 Justice James A. Baker of the Supreme Court allowed an attorney with a case pending before him to participate in his fundraising efforts.[22] When journalists reported this obvious conflict of interest, the bad publicity forced Baker to withdraw from the case. His withdrawal solved the immediate concern about one questionable case, but it did not address the basic problem. As long as attorneys are allowed to raise campaign funds for judges, there will be public doubts about the impartiality of the judiciary. The JCFA, while it was well intentioned, does not address this fundamental problem.

In 2000 two consumer-advocacy groups filed suit in federal court, arguing that when Texas allows judges to solicit campaign contributions from lawyers who might appear in their courts, the state violates its citizens' constitutional rights to fair trials. They lost the case, with U.S. District Judge James Nowlin writing, "The issue of limiting campaign contributions and/or potential contributions are questions for the citizens of Texas and their state representatives, not a federal court."[23] Given this decision, if the Texas system of financing judicial elections is to be changed, the impetus must come from inside the state.

In 1988 the New York State Commission on Government Integrity made a thorough survey of methods of selecting state and local judges. It concluded that (1) there is "no persuasive evidence correlating systems of judicial selection with the quality and integrity of judges" and (2) an appointive system does not "necessarily produce more qualified judges nor fewer corrupt ones."

In 2001 political scientist Melinda Gann Hall published a systematic evaluation of the consequences of supreme court selection processes in the fifty states. Her conclusion was that state high court judges who are appointed are not, as a group, more independent from the political process than are judges who are elected in partisan races. In short, there is no proof that the way Texas chooses its judges is an unusually bad way, or that some other way would be better.

Sources: Frank D. O'Connor, "New York Should Continue to Elect Its Judges," *New York Times*, June 11, 1988, 14; Melinda Gann Hall, "State Supreme Courts in American Democracy: Probing the Myths of Judicial Reform," *American Political Science Review*, vol. 95, no. 3 (June, 2001), 326.

Partisan Elections?

Texas is one of ten states that chooses most of its judges in partisan elections. The consequence of the state's system is that judges are like other politicians in that, although they do not campaign all the time, they must always be thinking about the next election. Like other politicians, they are aware that what they do or say today may affect their chances for re-election tomorrow. Unlike other politicians, however, judges are supposed to be fair and impartial when trying cases and pay no attention to the possible partisan consequences of their decisions.

This task is too difficult for imperfect humans. With the next election always just over the horizon, partisanship comes to permeate a courthouse, and the struggle for advantage may taint the quest for impartial decisions. After her defeat in the 1994 Republican landslide, Democratic District Judge Eileen O'Neill wrote a sad analysis of the impact of Texas's judicial electoral processes on its justice system:

As the campaign season approaches at the courthouse, lines get drawn. Sitting judges join in the search for contenders for open, and sometimes occupied, benches. Judges become guarded in their comments to colleagues and suspicious of their staffs. . . . By November, most everyone belongs to a side, willingly or otherwise, with some perceived stake in the outcome.[24]

While some reformers are trying to make Texas judges less like other politicians, on June 22, 2002, the U.S. Supreme Court issued a ruling that makes them more like politicians. Until that date, state judicial candidates were required to follow Canon 5(1) of the Texas Code of Judicial Conduct, which stated, "A judge or judicial candidate shall not make statements that indicate an opinion on any issue that may be subject to judicial interpretation by the office which is being sought or held. . . ." In other words, judicial candidates were forbidden to discuss the issues they might be required to decide.

In *Republican Party v. Minnesota*, however, the Court struck down a state restriction almost identical to the one in Texas. Writing for the 5 to 4 majority, Justice Antonin Scalia enunciated the principle that "We have never allowed the government to prohibit candidates from communicating relevant information to voters during an election."

Two months later, the Texas Supreme Court issued a new code, which still prevents candidates from promising to decide a specific case in a specific manner but permits them to indicate a general attitude on a question that might come before their court. The result of this change will certainly be that judicial candidates will campaign on issues more than ever before. In the 2002 and 2004 campaigns, Texas judicial candidates managed to avoid being backed into corners in regard to their specific views on specific issues. But it would not be foolish to anticipate a future campaign in which candidates for the Supreme Court or Court of Criminal Appeals might debate each other on television and thereby be forced to make promises about how they would decide on certain high-profile issues.

Sources: Christy Hoppe, "Ruling Likely to Change Texas Judicial Elections," *Dallas Morning News*, June 28, 2002, A20; "Texas Judges Can Now Opine Publicly," *Austin American-Statesman*, August 23, 2002, B7; *Judicial Selection in Texas: Nothing's Perfect* (Austin: League of Women Voters, 2002), 3.

It would be placing too much faith in human self-restraint to expect justice to be blind under such circumstances.

People who want to change the way Texas chooses its judges argue that circumstances such as the one sketched by Judge O'Neill are unavoidable in a selection system that rests upon partisan elections. But others are less eager to throw out the democratic baby with the partisan bath water. All systems have flaws, and the democratic appeal of partisan elections is strong. As David Willis, an adjunct professor of law at the University of Houston, wrote in a defense of Texas's system:

> Judicial candidates, like everyone, have philosophical preferences. Choosing a partisan label suggests a whole cluster of attitudes toward the role of government in addressing social challenges. It is an inexact science, but why deprive us of this crucial information about a candidate?[25]

Scholarly research supports Professor Willis's point. Studies show that the most important factor in allowing citizens to predict how judges will decide cases is their political party. Republican judges tend to favor business and people with power and wealth; Democrats tend to favor labor unions, the poor, and social underdogs in general. In other words, Texas has the perfect system for allowing its citizens to elect judges who share their ideologies.[26] Moreover, as the box detailing research on the consequences of different types of judicial selection explains, there is no good evidence that a different system of choosing judges would produce a more honest system than the one Texas has now. An appointive or nonpartisan system might not create a better judiciary, and would be less democratic.

Equal Justice?

Judicial selection is not the only serious problem facing the Texas system of justice. The state has for some time been in the center of another argument over the way it affords legal representation to poor people accused of crimes.

The Texas criminal justice system does not affect all citizens equally. It imposes severe burdens on the poor and particularly on members of ethnic minorities— the same groups who are at a disadvantage in other areas of politics. Legal fees are expensive —in 2006 the standard lawyer's fee was more than $200 per hour—and the system is so complex that accused people cannot defend themselves without extensive and expensive legal help. The result is that the prisons, and death row, are full of poor people. Wealthier defendants can afford to hire attorneys, and in any case they are often offered plea bargains that allow them to stay out of prison. Until recently, however, Texas lacked a system of public defenders to provide free legal assistance to alleged criminals who were too poor to pay a lawyer, except in the case of defendants who had been convicted of capital murder and sentenced to death. Judges, using county rather than state funds, appointed private attorneys to represent indigent defendants. Frequently these attorneys were inexperienced or already busy with paying private clients.

Journalist Debbie Nathan spent time observing the way county-appointed attorneys interacted with their indigent clients. Her summary had to be troubling to citizens who think that the poor, too, should be entitled to competent legal counsel when they are accused of a crime:

> What I witnessed was low-grade pandemonium. Attorneys rushed into court, grabbed a file or two, and sat down for a quick read; this was their first and often most lengthy exposure to their new client's case. Confused-looking defendants, mostly Hispanic or African American, met their counsel amid a hubbub of other defendants, defendants' spouses, and defendants' squalling babies.[27]

Reformers argued that, if justice was to be done, Texas should have a system of public defenders equal in number and experience to the public prosecutors. Without such procedures, the system inevitably discriminated against poor defendants, who tended to be minority citizens. For example, in 1993 the Texas Bar Foundation sponsored a study by the Spangenberg Group of Massachusetts of the state's system of appointing attorneys for indigents accused of murder. The Spangenberg Group's conclusions about Texas justice were consistent and unambiguous:

> In almost every county, the rate of compensation provided to court-appointed attorneys in capital cases is absurdly low . . . the quality of representation in these cases is uneven and . . . in some cases, the performance of counsel is extremely poor.[28]

If such deficient legal representation was common for citizens accused of murder, which is a high-profile crime, then the representation afforded people accused of lesser crimes must have been even worse. It stood to reason that defendants who received

The democratic ideal of equal justice for all citizens faces a severe test when poor people are accused of crimes. If they cannot pay a private attorney and the state refuses to provide them with competent counsel, they stand little chance of receiving an adequate defense.

SOURCE: Courtesy of Ben Sargent.

inferior public legal representation would be convicted more often, and be given harsher sentences, than defendants who could afford to hire private attorneys. Indeed, a study in the early 1990s concluded that a white person convicted of assault had a 30 percent chance of drawing a prison sentence, while a Hispanic with a similar record had a 66 percent chance and an African American a 76 percent chance.[29]

In short, the ironic motto suggested by the Ben Sargent cartoon, "All the justice you can afford," was a challenge to the legitimacy of the Texas judicial system. The state was far from achieving the democratic ideal that everyone is equal before the law.

Responding to such persistent and intense criticism of the way the state's legal system treated the poor, the 2001 legislature moved to make it more equitable. The Texas Fair Defense Act, sponsored by Senator Rodney Ellis of Houston, was designed to standardize and better fund indigent defense. Although the law left counties, not the state, with the primary responsibility for providing lawyers for poor defendants, it required prompt appointment of counsel, mandated quick attorney–client contact, ordered the counties to create a standard of qualification for attorneys, charged them with setting a fee schedule for defense attorneys, and imposed other requirements. Just as important, it appropriated $19.7 million in state funds each year to supplement the $90 million the counties typically spend on indigent defense.

In 2003 the Texas Defender Service and the Equal Justice Center cooperated to study how the Fair Defense Act was being implemented. Their conclusions were disturbing to advocates of equal justice for all. Studying the 33 counties that had accounted for 87 percent of those sent to death row since 1976, they reported that only Lubbock and Brazoria Counties were fully complying with the law. The 31 others were failing in their obligation to provide adequate counsel to indigent defendants for various reasons, including insufficient compensation for attorneys, low standards, and unsatisfactory or complete lack of standards for defense lawyers. The actual facts are somewhat ambiguous because in a follow-up report by National Public Radio, some county officials claimed that they were in fact complying with the law but had merely failed to report their activities to authorities in Austin.[30] The best that can be said now is that troubling questions remain about the adequacy of the defense that the state provided its accused indigent citizens.

THE SUBSTANCE OF JUSTICE

The subject thus far has been an examination of problems and issues in regard to the functioning of the state's judicial system. It is time to turn to some of the outputs of that system—civil liberties, civil rights, and criminal justice.

Civil Liberties and Civil Rights

Civil liberties are the basic freedoms that are essential to the survival of a democratic society—the rights to speak, write, worship, and assemble freely. The term *civil rights* refers to the rights of all citizens to fair and equal treatment under the law, including the rights of people accused of or convicted of crimes to be treated humanely. Civil rights also include electoral rights—the right to run for office and vote in honest elections. Both the United States and Texas constitutions contain **bills of rights** that guarantee our basic freedoms, including those of speech, the press, and religion. But constitutions have to be interpreted, and there are always disagreements about exactly what sorts of activities are protected.

In regard to "freedom of speech," for example, does it include the right to plan to overthrow the government? Spout racist propaganda on a local cable television access program? Wear a T-shirt lettered with obscenities to high school? Publicly burn an American flag? Write in a blog that the President of the United States should be impeached? Such questions generate disagreement among public-spirited citizens. When the disagreements lead to people being put in jail, courts are called upon to decide what a bill of rights means.

To take another example, virtually everyone believes in freedom of religion. But what, exactly, does that freedom mean? In 1999 authorities permitted a high school student to pray over a public address system prior to a football game in Santa Fe (Texas, not New Mexico). Was that prayer constitutional because it allowed her to exercise her right to freedom of religion, or was it unconstitutional because it enabled her to impose her beliefs on others through official school technology? A recent Fifth U.S. Circuit Court of Appeals ruling had appeared to forbid such prayers, but a federal judge in Houston sided with the student. In 2000 the U.S. Supreme Court decided the specific case against the student and the school district, but the controversy will never die.[31]

Civil liberties refers to those actions that government cannot take. Civil rights refers to those actions that government must take to ensure equal citizenship for everyone.

Historically, cultural traditions in the Old South were not particularly hospitable to civil rights and liberties. As reflections of this culture, until recently Texas courts did not much concern themselves with protecting any rights except property rights. In particular, for much of the twentieth century, Texas judges did not intervene when the Anglo majority violated the civil rights of African Americans and Mexican Americans by preventing them from voting, denying them equality before the law, offering them a grossly inferior education, and so on. These blights on democracy were overturned by federal rather than state courts.

One particularly famous example of federal intervention in Texas politics to protect the rights of a helpless minority dealt with the subject of treatment of convicted criminals by the prison system. Federal Judge William Wayne Justice ruled in 1980, on a lawsuit that had been filed by inmate David Ruiz in 1972, that Texas's overcrowded prison system made it impossible to avoid subjecting prisoners to "cruel and unusual punishment," thus violating the Eighth Amendment to the U.S. Constitution. On the date Ruiz filed his suit, the state prison system housed 15,700 inmates. Justice, who is aptly named, virtually took over the prison system, ordering new facilities built and new rules enacted. For more than two decades, under Justice's guidance, the prison system was greatly expanded and improved. In 2002 with the state prison population at about 145,000, Justice finally ended federal supervision.[32]

Texas has come a long way since the days when the federal courts had to force the state to give its minority citizens the most basic democratic rights. It is now too late for state judges to act as the champions of society's less fortunate in regard to basic civil rights and liberties; that battle has been won. Nevertheless, there are still controversies that pit the "haves" against the "have-nots," and the state judiciary has not missed the battle. In particular, state courts have been deeply involved in the struggle over the financing of Texas's schools.

Education: A Basic Right?

In 1987 Texas District Judge Harley Clark shocked the Texas political establishment by ruling in the case of *Edgewood v. Kirby* that the state's system of financing its public schools violated its own constitution and laws. Clark's ruling referred to Article VII, Section 1, which requires the "Legislature of the state to establish . . . an efficient system of public free schools," and part of Article 1, which asserts that "All free men . . . have equal rights." Additionally, the Texas Education Code in Section 16.001 states that "public education is a state responsibility," that "a thorough and efficient system be provided," and that "each student enrolled in the public school system shall have access to programs and services that are appropriate to his or her needs and that are substantially equal to those available to any similar student, notwithstanding varying local economic factors." The state's educational system, however, did not begin to offer equal services to every child. During the 1985–1986 school year, when the Edgewood case was being prepared, the wealthiest school district in Texas had $14 million in taxable property per student and the poorest district had $20,000. The Whiteface Independent School District (I. S. D.) in the Texas Panhandle taxed its property owners at $0.30 per $100 of value and spent $9,646 per student. The Morton I. S. D. just north of Whiteface taxed its property owners at $0.96 per $100 evaluation, but because of the lesser value of its property was able to spend only $3,959 per student.

Gross disparities such as these made a mockery of the constitutional and statutory requirements, as well as the demands of democratic theory for equal educational funding. An estimated one million out of the state's three million school children were receiving inadequate instruction because their local districts could not afford to educate them. Democracy requires only equality of opportunity, not equality of result. But inequality of education must inevitably translate into inequality of opportunity. The courts were following the dictates of democratic theory in attempting to force the rest of the political system to educate all Texas children equally. (It is worth noting that since 1971, 19 state supreme courts have likewise held that their state's school funding system unconstitutionally discriminates against poor districts.)[33]

The appropriate remedy was to transfer some revenue from wealthy to poorer districts. But, given the distribution of power in Texas, and especially the way it is represented in the legislature, this strategy was nearly impossible. As explained in Chapters 4 and 5, because of the lack of voting participation by the state's poorer citizens, its wealthier citizens are over-represented in the legislature. Despite the fact that a badly educated citizenry was a drag on the state's economy and therefore a problem for everyone, taxpayers in wealthier districts resisted giving up their money to educate the children of the poor in some other district. Their representatives refused to vote for some sort of revenue redistribution, regardless of what the court had said.

In October 1989 the Texas Supreme Court unanimously upheld Clark's ruling that the system was unconstitutional and told the legislature to fix it. There followed four years of stalling, blustering, and complaining by the House and Senate. Several times the courts threw out laws that made cosmetic changes in the state's school system without addressing the central problems of unequal funding.

Finally, in 1993 the legislature passed a law that would take about $450 million property-tax dollars from 98 high-wealth districts and distribute them to poor districts. (The media instantly dubbed this the "Robin Hood Law," after the twelfth-century English bandit who allegedly robbed from the rich and gave to the poor.) In January 1995 the Texas Supreme Court upheld the new law by a bare 5 to 4 majority.

The 1995 decision was not the end of the issue. Wealthy citizens continued to complain about the Robin Hood law and to file lawsuits against it. Beginning in 2001 several school districts challenged the plan on the grounds that it violated the state constitution. In order to fulfill their obligations both to their own and to other districts' children, they argued, that they were forced to peg their property-tax rates at the constitutional ceiling of $1.50 per $100 of assessed evaluation. Therefore, by in effect forcing all districts to tax at the same top rate, the Robin Hood law violated the constitution's ban on a statewide property tax. The slow movement toward a state supreme court decision in this case through 2005 undoubtedly encouraged legislatures to adopt a wait-and-see attitude and thus not do anything to upset the tax applecart (see Chapters 6 and 10).

In November 2005, the state supreme court declared the Robin Hood law unconstitutional on the narrow grounds that it forced school districts into a statewide property tax. The court did not address the larger issue of whether redistribution of wealth between rich and poor districts was itself constitutional. The justices gave the legislature until June 1, 2006, to reform the system.[34] Governor Perry called a special session of the legislature for the spring of that year.

Although the entire Texas political establishment was under the gun during the May 2006 special session, its task was greatly eased by the state's $10.5 billion surplus. With so much extra money to spread around, the governor, the lieutenant governor, and the speaker of the House were able to give something to both rich and poor school districts (for the financial details, see Chapter 10). Essentially, they increased the amount of money the state would give to poor districts—the state's share of funding public education went up from 38 percent to about 50 percent—while cutting property taxes for wealthier citizens and reducing the amount that wealthy districts had to share. The whole, agreeable scheme depended on the continued generation of a surplus by a roaring state economy. As long as the economic boom lasted, everyone would be willing to live with the results.[35]

Nevertheless, nearly two decades of litigation and political struggle have made one thing clear. The state judiciary, at least in this one area, has become the champion of the underdog. There never would have been a Robin Hood law in 1993 or a special legislative session in 2006 if the courts had not held the feet of the legislature and the governor to the fire. Texas courts missed the boat on civil rights and civil liberties, but they are ahead of the curve in educational equity. In this one area, Texas judges have somehow risen above the burdens of history and are attempting to force the people of Texas to live up to their democratic ideals.

Criminal Law

Even if the Texas court system were perfectly organized, even if all the dilemmas about judicial selection were to be resolved, and even if Texans arrived at a solution to the problem of equal justice for rich and poor, the state's courts would still be facing major difficulties dealing with crime. There are simply too many accused criminals being arrested for any system to handle. In 2004 Texas police made 1,128,131 arrests, including 938 for murder, 23,261 for aggravated assault, and 112,677 for drug possession.[36]

Despite the fact that the crime rate has declined since the early 1990s, the remaining high levels of street crime, leading to a large number of arrests, have swamped the courts, making Texas's 3,221 judges, the most of any state, still not enough. Members of the public, justifiably outraged over the fact that "you can't walk the streets at night in safety," demand that officials "lock 'em up and throw away the key." But the truth is that the system is not able to handle all of today's accused criminals, let alone tomorrow's.

Given this impossible situation, judges do what they can to keep the system functioning by accepting **plea bargains.** A defendant pleads guilty to a lesser charge—say, manslaughter instead of murder—and receives a lesser penalty (less time in prison or a probated sentence), and a trial is avoided. In fiscal year 2005 more than 98 percent of criminal cases were thus resolved without a trial.[37] Because a plea bargain often puts the criminal back on the streets quickly, it does almost nothing to make society safer. Ordinary citizens are often appalled at the swiftness with which violent criminals are recycled into their neighborhoods, but the courts have found no other way to handle the problem of a crushing caseload.

Unfortunately, the iniquity of putting guilty people back on the street is sometimes matched by the opposite injustice: convicting the innocent. The chronic overcrowding of the court system, added to the problems of equal treatment for the poor, creates an inefficiency in the administration of justice that can have tragic consequences. Quite simply, Texas courts make mistakes. Sometimes innocent people are convicted of crimes.

That Texas juries have convicted, and Texas judges have sentenced, people to prison and worse for crimes they did not commit, is not a merely theoretical speculation. During the 1990s, advances in the science of DNA testing enabled chemists to re-evaluate the evidence used to convict defendants of a variety of crimes. When they examined old evidence, they sometimes came to the conclusion that certain prisoners could not possibly have committed the crimes for which they were sitting in prison. (Sometimes, to be sure, the new tests confirmed the guilt of the convict.) In the United States as a whole, at least 100 people have been released from prison after DNA tests proved them innocent.[38] A number of these have been in Texas. For example, in 2001 Governor Perry pardoned Calvin Edward Washington, who had been convicted in 1986 of rape and murder. DNA evidence established that Washington had been in prison for 15 years for a crime he did not commit.[39] Similarly, in 2004 Perry pardoned Josiah Sutton, who had served 4½ years of a 26 year sentence, after DNA tests cleared him of a 1998 rape.[40]

The unarguable fact that Texas courts have convicted innocent defendants is doubly troubling because the state employs **capital punishment**—the death penalty. From 1976, when the U.S. Supreme Court re-instituted the ultimate punishment after a four-year hiatus, to the end of 2005, the state executed 352 men and 3 women. This number represents more than one-third of the total executions carried out in the United States during those years. In 2005 Texas executed 19 prisoners and sentenced 15 more to die by lethal injection.[41] Although there is no evidence to prove it, the state's experience with DNA evidence and convicted felons in prison strongly suggests that some of those executed criminals were actually innocent. It is not a comforting thought for citizens who would like to believe that their system of justice lives up to its name.

Public opinion polls consistently show that a large majority of Texans support capital punishment for murderers, although the total proportion with such views varies somewhat according to the wording of the question.[42] Nevertheless, the status of the death penalty is a very lively issue in Texas (see You Decide box), and makes for a constant controversy underlying all other questions of justice in the state.

YOU DECIDE

Is Capital Punishment Justified?

Texas is one of thirty-eight states that executes criminals convicted of murder. Since the U.S. Supreme Court reinstated capital punishment in 1976, more than 1,000 convicted killers have been put to death, and more than one-third of that number have been in Texas. Large majorities in the United States as a whole and Texas in particular support the concept of capital punishment, but there is a vocal minority that strongly opposes the practice. The arguments for and against capital punishment are both moral and practical.

Pro	Con
⇨ Executions are expensive because they are delayed by frivolous appeals. Eliminate those appeals and the cost will fall.	⇨ It costs more than $2 million to execute a criminal, about three times the cost of imprisoning someone for 40 years.
⇨ Not executing people costs lives also. Convicts escape and kill, and they kill while in prison. No executed person has ever committed murder again. New scientific techniques, such as DNA testing, make the system less mistake-prone.	⇨ No matter how careful the judicial system, some innocent people are bound to be executed.

SUMMARY

Although judges attempt to present themselves as above politics, their function of interpreting laws and constitutions is a highly political one. Because they are part of the political system, the way judges use their power can be analyzed within a larger discussion of democratic theory.

The Texas system of justice includes many players besides judges. Because of his power to issue opinions interpreting the constitution, the attorney general is particularly important, but the police, lawyers, and the members of grand and trial juries all have their part to play.

A variety of difficult democratic problems confront the judiciary. Because Texas judges are elected, they must accept private contributions in order to be able to campaign. When those contributions come from lawyers and others with business before their courts, it raises the suspicion that money may impair a judge's

Pro

➪ The death penalty does not deter criminal behavior.

➪ Two wrongs do not make a right.

➪ Killing is always wrong, whether done by an individual or by the state.

➪ The system of capital punishment is racially biased.

Con

➪ Social science studies are inconclusive as to whether capital punishment deters crime. Besides, a main purpose of capital punishment is retribution, not deterrence.

➪ Forcing a murderer to pay with his life is not wrong; it is justice.

➪ The majority of Americans believe that killing is sometimes justified, as in defense of the country or to punish murderers.

➪ Statistical studies show that African American murderers are no more likely to be executed than White murderers.

Sources: Hugo Adam Bedau (ed.), *The Death Penalty in America: Current Controversies* (New York: Oxford University, 1997), passim; Audrey Duff, "The Deadly D.A.," *Texas Monthly,* February 1994, 38; Jim Mattox, "Texas' Death Penalty Dilemma," *Dallas Morning News*, August 25, 1993, A23; Thomas Sowell, "The Trade-Offs of the Death Penalty," *Austin American-Statesman*, June 15, 2001, A15.

impartiality. During the 1990s the legislature attempted to regulate judicial campaign contributions in order to restore public confidence, but the state's experience since the law went into effect suggests that the reform is not having its intended effect.

Another controversy facing the Texas judiciary concerns the fact that judges must run for office in partisan elections. While this practice does tend to increase the democratic legitimacy of the judiciary, it also raises questions about their impartiality and ability to make decisions fairly. A third problem for the judiciary is that the high cost of legal representation tends to make justice available only to those who can afford it. Although the state has made recent attempts to improve its system of representation for poor defendants, it has a rocky road ahead to achieve the democratic ideal of equal justice.

The output of the Texas judicial system has improved in some ways in recent years. Whereas Texas judges were traditionally slow to protect the civil rights of ethnic minorities, since the 1980s they have courageously taken on the rest of the political establishment, including especially the legislature, in ordering a more equitable distribution of school revenues. The state's criminal justice system has improved somewhat, but it still makes mistakes and convicts innocent people, leading some critics to question its reliance on capital punishment.

STUDY QUESTIONS

1. What reasons would some people give for believing that judges are politicians? What reasons would others give for believing that judges are not politicians? With whom would you agree?
2. What is the attorney general's advisory opinion? How did it evolve? Why is it important?
3. What reasons are given for supporting the state's system of selecting judges? What criticisms are made of that system? Do you support the present system or would you rather see a different one adopted?
4. What are civil rights and liberties? Why are they important? Why is it necessary to have courts protect them?
5. Do you support capital punishment for convicted murderers? Why or why not?
6. In what ways has the Texas system of justice improved in the last few decades? In what ways has it deteriorated or remained unsatisfactory?

SURFING THE WEB

Visit the companion site for this book:
   http://www.thomsonedu.com/politicalscience/kraemer/

Much information on the organization of the Texas judiciary, as well as far more than anyone could hope to assimilate on the courts, is available from the state's Office of Court Administration:
   http://www.courts.state.tx.us/

Information on recent court cases is available from the TexLaw online service:
   http://www.texlaw.com/

Information on the activities of the Texas Bar Association is available at:
   http://www.texasbar.com

For a critical look at the influence of campaign contributions in judicial races, log on to the Texans for Public Justice Web site:
   http://www.tpj.org/

Statistics about the past and future application of the death penalty in Texas is available from the Texas Department of Criminal Justice Web site:
   http://www.tdcj.state.tx.us/ (Click the "General Information" icon at the top of the display, then click "Death Row Information" from the list of options.)

   To find more information supporting the death penalty, log on to the Web site of the organization Pro-Death Penalty.com:
   http://www.prodeathpenalty.com.

To find more information opposing the death penalty, log on to the Web site of the organization National Coalition to Abolish the Death Penalty:
   http://www.ncadp.org.

NOTES

1. "Gin 'Barbed' Cases Make Morrison Fun," University of Texas *Daily Texan,* February 19, 1964, 1.

2. Dietz quoted in Arnold Garcia, Jr., "Do You Know Who Your Judges Are? Maybe You Should Find Out," *Austin American-Statesman,* September 14, 2002, A11.

3. Quoted in Donald Dale Jackson, *Judges* (New York: Atheneum, 1974), 98.

4. Most of the information in this discussion comes from Bruce Hight, "Justices Bickering over Abortion Law," *Austin American-Statesman,* June 23, 2000, B1; the court case is *Re: Jane Doe,* number 00-0024, June 22, 2000.

5. Texas Attorney General's Office Web site: http://www.oag.state.tx.us/ searched on February 12, 2006.

6. *Hopwood v. State of Texas,* 78, E.3d 932 [5th Cir. 1996].

7. Attorney General's Letter Opinion 97-001, February 5, 1997.

8. Attorney General's Letter Opinion JC-107, September 3, 1999; and Juan B. Elizondo, Jr., "Cornyn Rescinds Hopwood Opinion," *Austin American-Statesman,* October 12, 1999, A1.

9. *Grutter v. Bollinger et al.* (539 U.S. 2003); *Gratz et al. v. Bollinger et al.* (539 U.S. 2003).

10. State Bar of Texas Web site: http://www.texasbar.com, consulted on February 12, 2006.

11. *Texas Courts: A Study by the Texas Research League,* Report 2: "The Texas Judiciary: A Proposal for Structural-Functional Reform" (Austin: Texas Research League, 1991), xi.

12. *Annual Statistical Report for the Texas Judiciary, Fiscal Year 2005* (Austin: Office of Court Administration, December 2005), 3–15, 21–30, and passim; salary data updated by Sandra Mabbett of the Office of Court Administration on February 17, 2006.

13. W. Gardner Selby, "State's Judges Get Their Raises," *Austin American-Statesman,* September 9, 2005, B3.

14. Texas Department of Public Safety Office of Public Information, February 13, 2006.

15. Bruce Fein and Burt Neuborne, "Why Should We Care about Independent and Accountable Judges?" *Journal of the American Judicature Society,* vol. 84, no. 2, September/October, 2000.

16. Wynne quoted in Michele Mittelstadt, "Political Money Eroding Trust in Judicial System," *Dallas Morning News,* February 22, 2002, A6.

17. David B. Rottman and Roy A. Schotland, "2004 Judicial Elections," in *The Book of the States,* vol. 37 (Lexington, KY: Council of State Governments, 2005), 30–38.

18. Laura Castaneda, "D.C. Worst, Utah Best on Litigious List," *Dallas Morning News,* January 3, 1994, D1.

19. Lloyd Doggett, "Judicial Campaign Fairness Act Essential," *Austin American-Statesman,* May 26, 1993, A17.

20. Rottman and Schotland, op. cit., 305.

21. Texans for Public Justice, *Lowering the Bar,* available on the TPJ Web site, listed under Surfing the Web in this chapter.

22. Mike Ward, "High Court Justice Leaves Case Involving Campaign Solicitor," *Austin American-Statesman,* April 13, 1996, B6.

23. Connie Mabin, "Suit Fails to Change Judicial Elections," *Austin American-Statesman,* September 28, 2000, B1.

24. Judge Eileen F. O'Neill, "Judicial Lottery Snake-Eyes for Texas," *Houston Chronicle*, November 20, 1994, C1.

25. David J. Willis, "Separate Myth, Fact on Texas Judicial System," *Houston Chronicle*, February 5, 1995, C1.

26. Henry R. Glick, "Courts: Politics and the Judicial Process," in Virginia Gray and Russell L. Hanson (eds.), *Politics in the American States: A Comparative Analysis*, 8th ed. (Washington, DC: Congressional Quarterly, 2004), 249.

27. Debbie Nathan, "Wheel of Misfortune," *Texas Observer*, October 1, 1999, 22.

28. The Spangenberg Group, *A Study of Representation in Capital Murder Cases in Texas* (Austin: State Bar of Texas, Committee on Legal Representation for Those on Death Row, 1993), 157, 163.

29. Jeff South, "Inequality Found in Sentencing," *Austin American-Statesman*, September 4, 1993, A1.

30. David Pasztor, "Death Penalty Law Not Being Followed, Study Finds," *Austin American-Statesman*, October 29, 2003, B1; National Public Radio report, October 29, 2003.

31. Paul Mulshine, "Whose Religion?" *Austin American-Statesman*, April 4, 2000, A1; David Jackson, "High Court Rejects Pre-Game Prayer," *Dallas Morning News*, June 30, 2000, A1.

32. Ed Timms, "30-Year Texas Prison Battle Ends," *Dallas Morning News*, June 9, 2002, A1.

33. Kenneth K. Wong, "The Politics of Education," in Grey and Hanson (eds.), *Politics in the American States*, op. cit., 368.

34. Jason Embry, "School Tax System Unconstitutional," *Austin American-Statesman*, November 23, 2005, A1; Maeve Reston, "Taxpayers' Lawsuit Challenges State's School-Finance System," *Austin American-Statesman*, April 6, 2001, B5; Alberta Phillips, "School Finance Gives Robin Hood Bad Name," *Austin American-Statesman*, April 27, 2001, A15.

35. Jason Embry and Corrie MacLaggan, "It's Finished: All of School Finance Plan Goes to Perry," *Austin American-Statesman*, May 16, 2006, A1; Christy Hoppe, "School 'Fix' Plan: Is It Sufficient?" *Dallas Morning News*, May 13, 2006, A1.

36. *Crime in Texas: 2004* (Austin: Texas Department of Public Safety, 2005), 83–89.

37. *Annual Statistical Report for the Texas Judiciary 2005*, op. cit., 33.

38. Leonard Pitts, "100 Death-Penalty Mistakes and We're Still Counting," *Austin American-Statesman*, April 16, 2002, A11.

39. "Perry Pardons Man Who Was Cleared by DNA Test," *Austin American-Statesman*, October 11, 2001, B3.

40. Kristen Hays, "Perry Pardons Man Wrongfully Convicted of Rape," *Austin American-Statesman*, April 15, 2004, B2.

41. Michael Graczyk, "Texas Executed 19 in '05, Fewer Than in '04," *Austin American-Statesman*, December 18, 2005, A1.

42. Hart-Hanks Texas Poll, Fall 1994; David Sedeno, "In Search of Alternatives," *Dallas Morning News*, March 16, 2003, A43.

9

LOCAL GOVERNMENT

The new city manager is (1) invisible, (2) anonymous, (3) nonpolitical, and (4) none of the above. Increasingly, modern city managers are brokers, and they do that brokering out in the open.

Alan Ehrenhalt
1990, *Deputy Editor, Governing: The Magazine of States and Localities*

State-versus-local tension is getting worse. Locals fear state budgets will be balanced at their expense. They may be right.

Alan Greenblatt
***Governing: The Magazine of States and Localities*, 2002**

INTRODUCTION

In 1875 when the Texas Constitution was being written, only 8 percent of the state's population lived in urban areas. By the 2000 federal census, Texas was 83 percent urban based on the proportion of the population living in places with a population of 2,500 or more. The U.S. Bureau of the Census and the Texas State Data Center forecast that Texas will have 66 percent more people in 2025 than it had in 2000, although the current rate of population growth indicates that the projection is underestimated. Much of this population growth will be among people who have specific problems—Hispanics and the elderly in particular—and most of it will be in urban areas. Much of the state's history and many of its problems are linked to urbanization and population growth.

Once one of the most rural states, Texas is now one of the most urban. Most of the change has taken place since 1950, when the development of such industries as petrochemicals and defense began luring rural residents into cities. Like many American cities, Texas cities are virtually unplanned. Growth patterns are determined largely by developers, who give little thought to the long-range effects of their projects on the total community. Only in the past quarter-century has community planning come to be taken seriously. In Texas and elsewhere, the nation's domestic problems—racial strife, unemployment, inflation, storm damage, delinquency, crime, substance abuse, inadequate health care, pollution, inadequate transportation, taxation, and the shortage of energy—seem to be focused in the cities. But before we examine city government and its problems, we will step back in time and look at the first unit of local government: the county.

Local government is an especially rich field for exploring whether the tests of democratic government outlined in Chapter 1 have been passed. Americans have long viewed local government as the government closest and most responsive to them. In looking at the organization, politics, and finance of Texas's local governments, we also look closely at whether citizens really are most involved at the local level.

COUNTIES: ONE SIZE FITS ALL?

Historical and Legal Background

The county is the oldest form of local government in America, and in rural Texas it is still the most important. Today there are 3,043 counties in the forty-seven states that have this form of government. Texas has the largest number of counties—254—in the nation. In Texas, as in other states, the county is a creation of state government.[1] Since citizens could not be expected to travel to the capital to conduct whatever business they had with the state, counties were designed to serve as units of state government that would be geographically accessible to citizens. Until city police departments assumed much of this role, the sheriff and the sheriff's deputies were the primary agents for the enforcement of state law. County courts still handle much of the judicial business of the state (see Chapter 8), and they remain integral to the state judicial system.

Many state records, such as titles, deeds, and court records, are kept by the county; many state taxes are collected by the county; and counties handle state elections. Counties also distribute many of the federal funds that pass through the state government en route to individuals, such as welfare recipients. Thus, most dealings that citizens have with the state are handled through the county. Yet, strangely, state government exercises virtually no supervisory authority over county governments. They are left to enforce the state's laws and administer the state's programs pretty much as they choose.

County officials are elected by the people of the county and have substantial discretion in a number of areas. For example, they can appoint some other county officials and set the tax rate. The result is a peculiar situation in which the county is a creation of state government, administering state laws and programs—with some discretion on the part of its officers—while county officials are elected by the people of the county and are in no real way accountable to the state government for the performance of their duties. Not surprisingly, county officials view themselves not as agents of the state but rather as local officials. One result is that enforcement of state law varies considerably from county to county. In other states, too, counties are considered units of local government although they typically have significant responsibilities in such policy areas as public welfare.

Counties have often found themselves saddled with unnecessary offices, such as treasurer, school superintendent, and surveyor. In November 1993 Texas voters were asked not only to eliminate the county surveyor office in McLennan and Jackson Counties but also to eliminate the need for a statewide vote in all counties wishing to abolish this office. The vote was more than 6 to 1 in favor of eliminating the office. In 2002 voters in a statewide referendum overwhelmingly supported allowing counties to declare the office of constable vacant if no one had filled the office in seven years. Both of these votes reflect the problem that arises from the "one-size-fits-all" structure of Texas county government.

Organization and Operation of County Government

The Constitution of 1876, which established the state government, also set out the organization and operation of county government. The same concerns apply to both governments, and there are close parallels in their organization and operation. For example, the decentralized executive found at the state level is reproduced at the county level in the county commissioners[2] court and semi-independent county agencies.

Structure. Since the county is the creation of the state and has no home-rule authority, the organization and structure of county government are uniform throughout Texas. Tiny Loving County, with a declining population of 52, and enormous Harris County, with a growing population of more than 3.6 million, have substantially the same governmental structure—a structure that, unfortunately, is a burden to both. As Figure 9.1 illustrates, the basic structure consists of a county judge and four commissioners.

Apportionment. When county commissioners drew precinct lines, they used to draw them on some basis other than population. Unlike gerrymandering, where the object is to perpetuate the position of the dominant party or faction, county precinct apportionment was for the purpose of re-electing on an equal geographic basis.

FIGURE 9.1

Organization of County Government in Texas

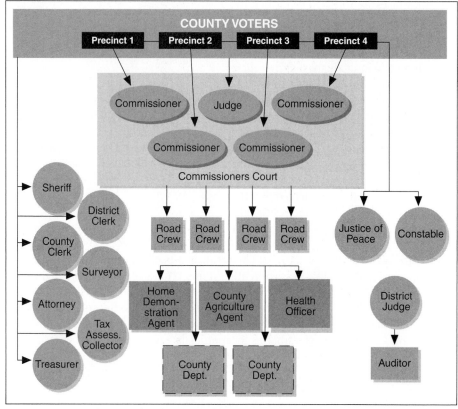

SOURCE: George D. Braden, *Citizens' Guide to the Texas Constitution,* prepared for the Texas Advisory Commission on Intergovernmental Relations by the Institute of Urban Studies, University of Houston (Austin, 1972), 51. Used by permission.

Roads, a major county function, were often more important than people. Not only were roads the life line for the state's rural population, which was once in the majority, but also contracts for roadwork represented the best opportunity for individual commissioners to wheel and deal. As a result, county commissioners often created precincts with great disparities in population.

In 1968 one precinct in Midland County, composed of the city of Midland, contained 97 percent of the people in the county; the remaining 3 percent were distributed among the other three precincts. The U.S. Supreme Court, in a case against Midland County, ruled that all counties had to abide by the one-person, one-vote rule that had been applied earlier to the U.S. House of Representatives and to state legislatures (*Avery v. Midland County,* 88 S.Ct. 1114, 1968). The ruling resulted in some commissioners courts voluntarily redistricting on the basis of population; in other counties, judges ordered population-based redistricting. County apportionment has resurfaced as an issue in recent years in disputes over adequate opportunities for ethnic minorities to contend for county offices in counties with substantial political party competition and in urban counties with fast-growing suburbs.

Commissioners Court.   *Commissioners court* is a misnomer. This "court" is not a judicial body but an executive (policy-administering) and legislative (policy-making) body for the county. Each of the four commissioners is elected from a district called a precinct. All county elections are partisan; that is, candidates run as Democrats, Republicans, or minor-party candidates.

Although the county commissioners act as the administrative arm of the state for public welfare and public health functions, they can do a great deal more. The commissioners can institute a variety of programs, including major undertakings such as county hospitals, libraries, and various welfare programs. They also build and maintain jails. Counties are active in economic development activity. To support these activities, the commissioners control the county budget by both setting the tax rate and appropriating money. The commissioners are also responsible for apportioning all election districts in the county.

Individually, each commissioner is responsible for his or her own precinct, including the establishment of road- and bridge-building programs, which represent a major expenditure of county funds. Only 10 percent of Texas counties have a consolidated road-and-bridge department. Commissioners like this function because their constituents can see directly what they are doing and because controlling transportation in outlying areas gives them a great deal of political clout.

Other County Officials.   The *county judge* is selected in an **at-large election**; at large means jurisdiction-wide. The position does not require legal credentials other than "being well-informed in the law." The county judge performs many functions. As a member of the commissioners court, the judge presides over and participates fully in that body's decision making. As a member of the county election board, the county judge receives the election returns from the election judges throughout the county, presents the returns to the commissioners court for canvassing, and then forwards the final results to the secretary of state. In any county with a population of less than 225,000, the county judge also serves in the administrative capacity as county budget officer. County judges also have the authority to fill vacancies that occur on commissioners courts. They are notaries public, can perform marriages, and can issue beer, wine, and liquor licenses in "wet" counties. Many citizens see the county judge as a representative of the people and ask her or him to intervene with other elected officials and county bureaucrats. Many county judges have strong county-wide power bases and are influential politicians.

The county judge also presides over the county court, although the position does not require legal credentials other than being well-informed in the law. County judges devote time to such matters as probate of wills, settlement of estates, appointment of guardians, and in many counties, hearing lawsuits and minor criminal cases. However, in larger counties the county commission usually relieves the judge of courtroom responsibilities by creating one or more county courts-at-law (see Chapter 8 for a discussion of the Texas judiciary).

The two major nonjudicial legal officers of the county are the *county sheriff* and the *county attorney*; both are elected at large. The sheriff has jurisdiction throughout the county but often makes informal agreements involving a division of labor with the police of the municipalities in the county. Particularly where large cities are involved, the sheriff's office usually confines itself to police work in the area of the county outside the city limits but is a frequent participant in multi-jurisdictional task forces to address special needs such as drug trafficking. The county sheriff has comprehensive control of departmental operations and appoints all deputies, jailers, and administrative personnel. Depending on the size of the county, the sheriff's department may have a substantial annual budget.

As the head of the county's legal department, the county attorney provides legal counsel to the county and represents it in legal proceedings. The attorney also prosecutes misdemeanors in the justice of the peace and county courts.

Another important elective office in the county is that of *county clerk*, who is elected at large. The county clerk is recorder of all legal documents, such as deeds, contracts, and mortgages; issues all marriage licenses; and is the clerk of both the county court and the commissioners court. Many of the responsibilities for the conduct of elections are performed by the county clerk (see Chapter 5).

The *assessor–collector of taxes* collects the *ad valorem* (general property) tax for the county, collects fees for license plates and certificates of title for motor vehicles, and serves as the registrar of voters. In counties of 10,000 or more in population, a separate assessor–collector is elected at large; in smaller counties, the sheriff serves as assessor–collector. Although the assessor–collector's responsibilities have been lightened by a uniform tax appraisal district's conducting the assessment, in many counties the void has been filled by the county acting as the collection agent for other taxing units such as municipalities and school districts.

Other legal officers of the county are the *justices of the peace* (JPs) and the *constables*. Most but not all counties have at least one justice of the peace and one constable for each of the four precincts. Larger counties may have as many as eight JP districts. The justice of the peace is at the bottom of the judicial ladder, having jurisdiction over only minor criminal and civil suits. The constable has the duty of executing judgments, serving subpoenas, and performing other duties for the justice of the peace court. Like the commissioners, the constables and JPs are elected for four years on a partisan basis by district.

The county has a number of other officers, some of whom perform important functions. In counties with a population of more than 35,000, state law requires that an *auditor* be appointed by the district judge having jurisdiction in the county for the purpose of overseeing the financial activities of the county and assuring that they are performed in accordance with the law. A *county health officer* to direct the public health program is also required by state law, and in most counties, a *county agricultural agent* and a *home demonstration agent* are appointed by the commissioners court for the purpose of assisting (primarily) rural people with agriculture and homemaking. Both of the latter officers are appointed in conjunction with Texas A&M University, which administers the agriculture and home demonstration cooperative programs.

An Evaluation of County Government

When industrial firms experience problems, they call in teams of management consultants who make a searching examination and a critical evaluation of the firm's operation. If a management consulting firm could be engaged to make a thorough examination of county government in Texas, its report would very likely include the following topics.

Structure and Partisanship.   The county in Texas is a nineteenth-century political organization struggling to cope with a twenty-first-century society, a fact that
causes counties to be viewed as "horse-drawn buggies." In many states, counties have
the same flexibility as cities to choose a form of government that is appropriate for
the size and complexity of that particular jurisdiction. In Texas all county governments are structured the same way, and the emphasis is on *party politics* because all
officials are elected on a partisan basis. The positive aspect of partisanship is that the
average voter can understand more clearly what a candidate's approximate political
position is when the candidate bears the label "Republican" or "Democrat" than when
the candidate has no identifying tag. One negative aspect is a heavy reliance on a
spoils system—that is, on the appointment of deputy sheriffs, assistant clerks, and
road workers on a political basis.

Nationally, although most counties operate with a commission, urban counties
serving the majority of the nation's citizens operate with a county manager or
appointed administrator. Texas, of course, offers no such flexibility for the larger
counties; however, many of the county judges in larger counties have appointed an
administrator to help them oversee county matters. Although the current structure is
uniform and simple, it also makes it difficult to produce decisions for the benefit of
all or most county residents because of the emphasis on precincts. In turn, the
precinct focus makes it difficult to enjoy economies of scale such as purchasing all
road-paving materials for the county at one time. Thus, one may conclude that one
size does not fit all very well.

The partisanship and restrictive structure can lead to governance problems.
Commissioners often squabble over petty matters. Citizens have difficulty deciding
whom to blame if they are dissatisfied with county government since the commissioners serve as a collective board of directors for the county. For example, a troublesome sheriff—a not uncommon phenomenon—may be re-elected by the voters, who
blame the county commissioners for the sheriff 's performance. Similarly, the voters
may focus on the county judge, who has one vote on the commissioners court just
like the other members, when other members of the court should be the object of
attention. Such confusion can happen in any government, but the large number of
elected officials—mirroring the state pattern—compounds the problem.

A plus for counties is that they are less bureaucratic than other governments, so
the average citizen can deal more easily with a county office. One reason for this ease
of access may be that, unlike the state government, county government does not have
a clear-cut separation into legislative and executive branches and functions. The
merger of executive and legislative functions, which is called a unitary system, also is
found in some city and special district governments. It can sometimes produce a
rapid response to a citizen problem or request.

One county judge assessed county government by noting that many county officials are highly responsive to public demands when they must face competitive elections. In fact, he argued, counties are the last true bastions of "grassroots politics,"
whereby government is close to all the people in the county. Although the court sets
much of the policy and the tone for the conduct of county operations, it lacks the
authority to give explicit orders to subordinate officials. Nevertheless, this county
judge pointed out that by controlling the budget the commissioners court can often

dictate the behavior of other elected officials. Additionally, counties have the lowest tax rates of all the governments in Texas.[3] Another county judge put it this way: "We do meat-and-potatoes government . . . not flashy, press-release government, but good government."[4]

Thus, the evaluation of county organization and politics is mixed. The public often shows little interest in county government. Voter turnout is low, and even the media tend to ignore county government and focus instead on big city, state, and national political events. The county is a horse-drawn buggy in structure. It is often highly democratic, especially when it advocates the interests of groups ignored by other governments, since the commissioners must secure support for re-election. However, the willingness of commissioners and other elected officials to attend to the needs of individuals and to deal with details can easily lead to corruption.

Management Practices.   With the exception of a few of the larger counties, county government in Texas is one of the last bastions of the *spoils system*, under which persons are appointed to government jobs on the basis of whom they supported in the last election and how much money they contributed. While a spoils system helps to ensure the involvement of ordinary citizens in government, it also leads to the appointment of unqualified people, especially in jobs that require specialized training. A spoils system can also lead to a high turnover rate if the county tends to usher new elected officials into office on a regular basis.

From a management standpoint, a merit system—a *civil service* or *merit system* of recruitment, evaluation, promotion, and termination is one based on qualifications— and a pay scale that can attract and hold competent personnel would improve governmental performance. This system would be fair, both to employees, because they would be properly paid for their labors, and to taxpayers, because they would get a return on their dollars. Only a handful of Texas counties have made significant strides toward developing professional personnel practices such as competitive hiring, merit raises, and grievance processes.

Two other features of county government illustrate its tendency toward inefficient management: decentralized purchasing and the road-and-bridge system. *Decentralized purchasing* means that each commissioner and each department makes its own purchases. Quantity discounts, which might be obtained if there were a centralized purchasing agent, are unavailable on small-lot purchases. Also, the possibility for graft and corruption is great. To be sure they will get county business, sellers may find themselves obliged—or at least feel that they are—to do a variety of favors for individual officials in county government. This situation is not unknown in the other governmental units but becomes more widespread in highly decentralized organizations.

Unless a Texas county belongs to the elite 10 percent that have a unit system for county-wide administration of the *roads and bridges*, individual commissioners may plan and execute their own programs of highway and bridge construction and maintenance at the precinct level. The obvious result is poor planning and coordination, as well as duplication of expensive heavy equipment. These inefficiencies are important because counties, like other local governments, must cope with taxpayer resistance to providing more funding for government. Thus, efficient performance is a must.

Lack of Ordinance Power.   Texas counties have no general power to pass ordinances—that is, laws pertaining to the county. They do have the authority to protect the health and welfare of citizens, and through that power they can regulate the operation of a sanitary landfill and mandate inoculations in the midst of an epidemic. They can regulate subdivision development in unincorporated areas, sometimes sharing power with municipalities and, for flood control, with the federal government. However, the lack of general ordinance power means that, for example, they cannot zone land to ensure appropriate and similar usage in a given area, and they have trouble guarding against rutted roads and polluted water sources when land developers or gas drillers start to work.[5]

Texas counties have no authority to pass ordinances that, for example, could regulate land use in rural areas.

SOURCE: Courtesy of Ben Sargent.

In rural areas, the lack of county ordinance power manifests itself in many ways. Fireworks stands inevitably are erected a few feet outside a city's jurisdiction; contractors frequently take more liberties with sound construction principles in rural areas; and controversial establishments such as topless bars, noisy gun ranges, and polluting cement plants find homes in unincorporated county areas.

Recommendations.   Having reviewed Texas county government, the mythical management consultants probably would recommend greater flexibility in this form of government, particularly in heavily populated areas, to encourage more professional management of personnel, services, purchasing, and all other aspects of county government. They would urge counties to take advantage of economies of scale by centralizing purchasing and adopting a unit system of road and bridge construction and maintenance. They probably would not yet explore any of the forms of city–county cooperation that exist in such areas as San Francisco, Honolulu, and Nashville, since counties in Texas are not yet ready to function as cities. The exceptions are El Paso County, where the county and city have explored consolidation, and Bexar County (San Antonio), where the county judge has advocated merger. The largest Austin newspaper has also urged some consideration of "government modernization" on the Travis County commissioners. Such changes would require a constitutional amendment.

Prospects for Reform.   Given these obvious disadvantages, what are the prospects for changing county government in Texas? County commissioners, judges, sheriffs, and other county officers, acting individually and through such interest groups as TACO (Texas Association of County Officials), are potent political figures who can and do exercise substantial influence over their state legislators. Unfortunately for the taxpayers, most county officials have shown little willingness to accept changes in the structure and function of county government. The exceptions are usually county commissioners in more heavily populated counties who have taken a number of steps to professionalize government, including the appointment of personnel and budget experts. They are outnumbered 10 to 1 by commissioners in less populous areas. Thus, substantially more citizen participation will be necessary if change is to occur. If city residents, who tend to ignore county politics, were to play a much more active role, reform might be possible because of the sheer numbers they represent when approaching legislators.

CITIES: MANAGED ENVIRONMENTS

State legislatures traditionally have been less than sympathetic to the problems of the cities, partly because of rural bias and partly because they wished to avoid being caught in the quagmires of city politics. Therefore, the states (including Texas) established general laws for the organization of city governments, to which municipalities were required to conform. But these general laws were too inflexible to meet the growing problems of the cities, and around the turn of the century there was a movement toward municipal **home rule**. The home rule laws permitted the cities, within limits, to organize as they saw fit.[6]

The home rule amendment to the Texas Constitution was adopted in 1912. It provides that a city whose population is more than 5,000 be allowed—within certain procedural and financial limitations—to write its own constitution in the form of a city charter, which would be effective when approved by a majority vote of the citizens. Home rule cities may choose any organizational form or policies as long as they do not conflict with the state constitution or the state laws.

Two legal aspects of city government in Texas that are growing in importance are *extraterritorial jurisdiction* (ETJ) and *annexation*. The option of ETJ gives cities limited control over unincorporated territory contiguous to their boundaries; that is, cities get some control over what kind of development occurs just outside the city limits. The zone ranges from a one-half-mile in distance for cities under 1,500 in population to 5 miles for those over 25,000. Within these zones, municipalities can require developers and others to conform to city regulations regarding construction, sanitation, utilities, and similar matters.

Annexation power allows cities to bring adjacent unincorporated areas in the ETJ into the municipal boundaries. Doing so helps prevent suburban developments from incorporating and blocking a larger city's otherwise natural development. It also allows a city to expand its tax base. In the 1950s and 1960s, municipalities could make great land grabs without any commitment to providing services, but over the years annexation powers have been curbed. The legislature in 1999 tightened requirements considerably with the passage of SB89, placing greater restrictions on cities about notifying individuals in the area to be annexed. The 1999 law set off an explosion of annexations, particularly in the Dallas–Fort Worth area, prior to the notification provision's going into effect. Since 2002, the cities must immediately provide fire, police, and emergency services to the annexed area and must improve such infrastructure as roads, water supply, and sewer systems within two-and-one-half years. Prior to 1999, the annexation statute required notification by public announcement, not by apprising individual residents, and it required provision of services but over a four-and-one-half-year period.

Much of the economic and residential growth around the larger cities in the state has been in "edge" cities—those on the edge of the metropolitan center. Thus, municipalities are likely to rely on ETJ and annexation even more in the future in an effort to control growth and development.[7]

Organization of City Government

Traditionally, municipalities were organized into one of three types of government: *mayor–council, commission, and council–manager*. Within those categories, mayor–council governments were often designated as "strong" or "weak" depending on how much power the mayor had. The commission form is rarely used, but, increasingly, municipalities have developed hybrid forms of government that combine features of the other two standard forms. Thus, it is often difficult to place individual cities into one of the traditional categories.[8] Nevertheless, it is still easiest to understand forms of city government by reviewing the basic categories, while understanding that various combinations are common.

As of 2005, Texas had 1,210 municipalities. Of these 375 are home-rule cities with the capacity to determine their own form of organization, and 835 are *general-law* cities. General-law cities are either ineligible for home rule because they have populations under 5,000 or are slightly larger cities that have not yet adopted a home-rule charter. General-law cities can organize under any of the three basic forms of government:

 Houston has long been known as the only major American city without zoning ordinances that dictate what can be built where—homes, offices, and factories. In the past, city leaders have used such terms as "communist plot" and "socialized real estate" to describe zoning. Voters have explicitly and repeatedly rejected it, most recently in 1993. As a result, a church, office tower, and home can be found adjacent to one another. Recently, however, Houston officials have recognized that an unplanned city is a chaotic city and have moved to bring some discipline to new development. In order to channel and regulate construction without actually resorting to zoning, the city has begun to rely on carefully crafted deed restrictions.*

*See, for example, "'Anything Goes' Houstonians May Go the Limit: To Zoning," *New York Times*, October 27, 1993, 1; Patrick Barta, "To Limit Growth, Houston Turns to Deed Restrictions," *Wall Street Journal*, May 12, 1999, T1, T3.

aldermanic (a variant of the mayor–council type), council–manager, or commission. However, state law limits the size of the council, specifies other municipal officials, spells out the power of the mayor, and places other restrictions on matters that home-rule cities can decide for themselves. Because of their small size, most of the general-law cities have chosen the aldermanic model, although the municipal clerk often acts as chief administrative officer for the city.

Home-rule cities have overwhelmingly opted for the council–manager plan of government. Of the 313 cities for which information was available,[9] 282 (90 percent) used the council–manager form, another 15 had created a hybrid mayor–administrator form, and only 16 operated under the mayor–council plan. None uses a straight commission form, although some city councils call themselves "commissions." Among general-law cities, only 47 (5 percent) were recognized council–manager or mayor–administrator cities.[10]

The Council–Manager Form. Dallas and San Antonio are two of the largest cities in the country—along with Phoenix, Arizona—using this organizational model (Figure 9.2) but smaller cities such as Beeville, Gainesville, and Yoakum also operate with this form of government. Under the **council–manager form**, a city council of five to fifteen members, elected at large or by districts, appoints a city manager who is responsible for the hiring and firing of department heads and for the preparation of the budget. A mayor is elected at large or by the council; the mayor is a member of the council and presides over it but otherwise has only the same powers as any other council member.

Proponents of council–manager government, including many political scientists, traditionally have argued that this form of government allows at least some separation of politics and administration. They believe the council makes public policy and, once a policy is set, the manager is charged with administering it. In reality, however, politics and administration cannot be separated; the city manager must make recommendations to the council on such highly political matters as tax and utility rates and zoning,[11] as the brokering role cited by Alan Ehrenhalt in the opening quotation indicates. Nevertheless, some citizens claim to perceive a distinction in this type of government between politics and policy-making on one hand and administration on the other, and many are convinced that it is the most efficient form of city government.

For all its efficiency and professionalism, council–manager government does have some problems. First, council members are part-time and their tenure is often short; thus, they may rely heavily on the manager for policy guidance. Because the manager

FIGURE 9.2

Council-Manager Form

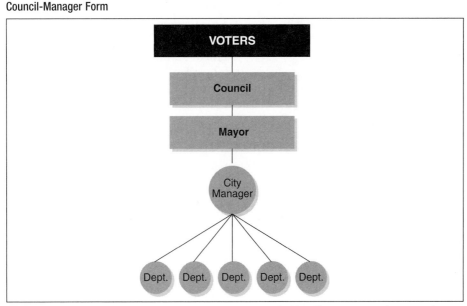

SOURCE: Adapted from *Forms of City Government* (Austin: Institute of Public Affairs, University of Texas, 1959), 23. Used by permission.

is not directly responsible to the voters, this practice makes it more difficult for the average citizen to influence city hall, and many citizens react negatively to reading in the local newspaper about the city manager's policy recommendations, even though the council must approve them. Second, the comparison is frequently drawn between council–manager government and the business corporation because both involve policy-making "boards" and professional managers. When coupled with the emphasis on efficiency, this image of a professionally trained "business manager" also tends to promote the values of the business community. The result is that festering political problems, especially those involving ethnic minorities and the poor, may not be addressed in a timely manner. However, the increasing number of council–manager cities with district elections and mayors directly elected by the people has tended to mute this problem somewhat, as representation on city councils has become more diversified. Also, city managers are now trained to be sensitive to all citizens.

The Mayor–Council Form.   In the mayor–council form of municipal government, council members are elected at large or by geographic districts, and the mayor is elected at large. The mayor–council form has two variants: the weak mayor–council form and the strong mayor–council form. In the *weak mayor–council form*, other executives such as the city attorney and treasurer are elected also; in the *strong mayor–council form*, the mayor has the power to appoint and remove other city executives.

In the strong mayor–council form, the mayor also prepares the budget, subject to council approval. In both mayor–council forms, the mayor can veto acts of the city council, but typically fewer council votes are needed to over-ride the mayor's veto in a

On Becoming a City Manager

How does one become a city manager? A city manager usually has a Master's degree in public administration, public policy, or public affairs. The most common route is an internship in a city while still in school, followed by a series of increasingly responsible general management positions: administrative assistant, assistant to the city manager, assistant city manager, then city manager. Alternatively, an individual may begin in a key staff area (for example, as a budget analyst, then budget director, then director of finance) or in a major operating department (for example, as an administrative assistant in the public works department), then as an assistant director, then director. Usually the individual holds these positions in a series of cities.

weak mayor–council city than in a strong mayor–council city. An individual city charter may combine elements of both strong and weak mayor–council government—for example, giving the mayor budget control while also allowing for other elected positions. Figure 9.3 illustrates the strong mayor–council form.

The words *strong* and *weak* are used in reference to a mayor's powers in the same way that the word *weak* is applied to the Texas governorship. The terms have to do with the amount of formal power given the chief executive by the city charter. An individual mayor, by dint of personality, political savvy, and leadership skills, can heavily influence local politics regardless of restrictions in the city charter.

The strong mayor form is most common among the nation's largest cities, while the weak mayor form prevails in smaller communities. In Texas, among the state's largest cities, only Houston operates with mayor–council government. The other large cities have council–manager government. Small cities with the mayor–council form include Hitchcock and Robstown.

FIGURE 9.3

Strong Mayor–Council Form

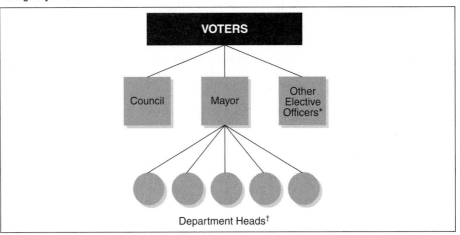

Department Heads†

*In a number of strong mayor–council cities, the chief of police and some other department heads are elected, although that is not the case in Texas.

†Common departments are fire, police, streets and sanitation, utilities, parks and recreation.

SOURCE: *Forms of City Government* (Austin: Institute of Public Affairs, University of Texas, 1959), 10. Used by permission.

Many political scientists favor the strong mayor–council form of government because it seems most likely to provide the kind of leadership needed to cope with the growing problems of major urban areas and because it focuses on an elected, not an appointed, official. One reason for this belief is that the mayor and council members, especially in larger cities, are full-time paid officials who can devote their time to the development of public policy and oversight of governmental services. Thus, policy proposals come directly from elected officials. If these officials represent a broad public interest, as opposed to narrow interest groups, democracy is well served.

The Mayor–Administrator Form.   The *mayor–administrator form* of municipal government, also called the *chief administrative officer* (CAO) and the *mayor–manager form*, is growing in popularity nationwide. This plan has generated interest because it combines the overt political leadership of a mayor–council plan with the professional management skills identified with council–manager government. It also recognizes the amount of time that governing takes in a large city and encourages salaries for elected officials. Typically, it arises when the mayor realizes a need for managerial assistance. In this form, the city manager reports only to the mayor, not to the council as a whole, and focuses on fiscal/administrative policy implementation. The mayor provides broad policy leadership in addressing major problems such as crime and economic development. In Texas, some smaller cities such as Argyle and Mathis use a city administrator plan, but often the smaller communities use the hybrid only until a charter election can be held to adopt council–manager government. Elsewhere, mayor–manager government is often practiced in consolidated city–county governments such as Lexington-Fayette County, Kentucky, and some cities such as San Ramon, California.

A variant of mayor–manager government is arising in larger municipalities. In Texas and across the country, large cities using the council–manager plan have seen disputes develop among the mayor, council members, and managers as assertive mayors work to carve out a larger role for themselves. The growing interest of big-city mayors in controlling both the political and the administrative aspects of city government is illustrated by events in Dallas. First, in 1992–1993 Mayor Steve Bartlett, a former U.S. Congressman, and City Manager Jan Hart struggled for control, with Hart ultimately leaving in 1993 to enter the private sector. In 1997 Mayor Ron Kirk struggled more with the Dallas city council, which resisted his bid for greater power, than he did with City Manager John Ware, but his intent was the same as Bartlett's; to gain control of the city's executive establishment. In 2002 a charter review commission initiated by Dallas Mayor Laura Miller began studying stronger formal powers for the mayor and the possibility of eliminating the city manager position. Two elections on the issue of a strong mayor–manager form for Dallas were held in 2005; both resulted in retention of the traditional council–manager form. More cooperative mayor–manager relationships *can* exist in large cities, as for example, is the case in Fort Worth.

The Commission Form.   Under the *commission form* of organization, elected commissioners collectively compose the policy-making board and function, as individuals, as administrators of various departments such as public safety, streets and transportation, finance, and so on. They are usually elected at large. Although initially widely copied, the commission system has more recently lost favor because many

YOU DECIDE

Should Large Cities Abandon Council–Manager Government in Favor of a Strong Mayor–Council Form?

It is not uncommon across the country for cities to switch from council–manager government to mayor–council or mayor–manager (mayor–administrator) government once they near or exceed one-half-million people in size. In Texas, Dallas has struggled bitterly with the issue of possible change, while El Paso moved from mayor–council to council–manager government. What do you think the very large cities (e.g., Austin, San Antonio, and Fort Worth) should do?

Pro

Any large city should adopt a new municipal charter calling for a strong mayor–council form because:

⇨ It needs a strong chief executive as leader, someone elected to provide political and policy direction for the city.

Con

A large city that has council–manager government should keep its present governmental form because:

⇨ A strong mayor would just divide the community because mayors must spend more time tending their electoral bases to ensure that their friends win and their enemies lose rather than focusing on making city government work efficiently and effectively for all citizens.

think that individual commissioners tend to become advocates for their own departments rather than public-interest advocates who act on behalf of the entire city. Also, the city commission form is subject to many of the same problems as the county commission, including corruption and unclear lines of responsibility. Although some cities still call their city councils "commissions," Texas home-rule cities have abandoned this form of government, which was invented in Galveston to cope with the cleanup and rebuilding made necessary by the great hurricane of 1900. Some general-law cities still have a commission government.

Which Form Is Preferable?   The only clear answer is that council–manager government seems to work best in middle-sized cities (from 25,000 to 250,000 or so in population). These cities are largely suburban and prefer this form's emphasis on business-like efficiency and the distance it maintains from party politics and from state and national political issues. Smaller cities that can afford a city manager also

Pro

⇨ The mayor and the manager disagree publicly too much.

⇨ The city has district council elections. Only the mayor can represent the whole city. Austin has at-large elections.

⇨ City managers tend to favor business interests.

⇨ It is too easy for the city manager and the rest of the bureaucracy to perform poorly without anyone knowing.

⇨ More citizens would vote if the mayor's race mattered more.

⇨ The city could address its out-and-out political problems better.

Con

⇨ The mayor can provide leadership even in a city manager form of government.

⇨ The city manager is bound by a national code of ethics that requires him or her to stay out of politics and focus on making sure things run well.

⇨ The mayor and individual council members would be more likely to jockey for political position in a different form of government.

⇨ Day-to-day operations are so complicated in a big city that a professional manager needs to be in charge of them.

⇨ A strong mayor is more likely to "break the bank" in giving away political favors.

⇨ Large cities with mayor–council or mayor–manager government still have major political problems.

often do well with that form, but most use a mayor–council form. The really large cities often fare best with either a mayor–council form or a mayor–manager form, since they need the political focus provided by the elected mayor.[12]

City Politics

The discussion of forms of city government and their characteristics provides a substantial amount of factual information about the operation of the city, but it says little about how city government really works. Who gets the rewards, and who is deprived? Which individuals and groups benefit most from city government, and which groups bear the burdens? The electoral system used by Texas cities is an indication of how the rewards and deprivations are distributed. Although the party identification of candidates is well known in cities like Beaumont and El Paso, all Texas cities hold **nonpartisan elections**. In most Texas cities, municipal elections are held during the spring in a further attempt to separate city government from party politics. In this electoral setting, private interest groups such as local real estate associations or home owners may sponsor a slate of candidates for municipal office, just as a political party would, under the guise of a civic organization that purportedly has no goals except efficient and responsive government. Such a claim is misleading, however. These groups do have goals and are highly effective in achieving them. In some cities, a charter association or good government league exists; these organizations inevitably reflect the interests of conservative business elements in the community. In other cities, environmentalists or neighborhood advocates or anti-tax groups may launch well-organized single-issue campaigns. In addition, a number of more or less ad hoc groups usually appear at election time to sponsor one or more candidates; and in all Texas cities, independent candidates also come forth with their own campaigns to seek public office.

Closely associated with nonpartisan elections is the system of electing candidates for the city council *at large*. All voters select all the members of the council and vote for as many candidates as there are positions on the council. In another practice widely followed in Texas cities, the **place system**, the seats on the council are designated as Place 1, Place 2, and so on. In this type of election, candidates who file for a particular place only run against other candidates who also file for that place.

Voting is still city-wide. The at-large, by-place system predominates in smaller cities, although one of the state's largest cities, Austin, also uses it. Increasingly, however, Texas cities whose population is 50,000 or more are amending their charters to provide for a district system, wherein candidates are required to live in a particular geographic area within the city and run against only those candidates who also live in the district. Voters choose only among candidates within their district, although the mayor is usually elected at large. In some cities, the council is composed of some members elected by district and some elected at large. Often the change to **district elections** occurs as the result of a successful court suit based on discrimination against minorities, who find it difficult to win election in a city-wide race. Running in districts costs less money and has the advantage of allowing minority candidates to concentrate their campaigning in neighborhoods with large numbers of individuals who share the candidate's ethnic background. Frequently, additional council seats are created when a city switches to district elections.

Advocates of at-large and by-place elections argue that the council focuses on city-wide concerns and that having district elections results in a fragmented council whose members tend to focus only on the problems of their electoral district. They also think that district elections are incompatible with council–manager government, which predominates in the state's home-rule cities, because they make local elections "too political." Advocates of district elections think that the council is more representative when members are elected by wards or districts because minorities, spokespersons for citizens groups, and individuals without personal wealth have a better opportunity to be elected and will be more inclined to address "local district" problems. They believe that government is political by nature, and so all political viewpoints should be represented.

Questions about the organization of elections and the nature of representation are at the heart of the democratic process. One measure of a city's democratic morality is the extent to which all significant ethnic, religious, economic, and geographic groups are fairly represented. Thus, democratic theorists sometimes recommend district elections over at-large elections except in small municipalities, where candidates are likely to be known by most voters.[13]

Controversy also exists over whether elections should be nonpartisan. As discussed in Chapter 5, nonpartisan elections rob the voters of the most important symbol that they have for making electoral choices: the party label. Without knowing whether a candidate is a Democrat, a Republican, or a member of some other party, how does the voter decide how to vote? In answering this question, critics of nonpartisan elections say that voters depend on personalities and extraneous matters. For example, television personali-

Changes in Texas politics are most evident in the major cities, where leaders and interest groups reflect newer interests and where the sacrosanct principle of nonpartisanship is sometimes violated. Austin, San Antonio, Houston, Dallas, El Paso, Fort Worth, and Galveston have had women mayors, as have more than 200 smaller communities. El Paso and San Antonio have elected Mexican American men as mayors, and Houston and Dallas have elected African American males.

Austin, Houston, and Dallas have become the homes of large groups of politically active homosexuals. In all three cities, politicians of many ideological persuasions seek the support of the Gay and Lesbian Political Caucus.

In the big cities, the importance of neighborhood representation and ethnic representation has intensified to such an extent that it is difficult to gain a workable consensus for establishing public policy. Instead, individual council members sometimes advocate the needs of their districts to the exclusion of concerns about the city as a whole.

ties and athletes frequently win elections simply because they are better known than their opponents are. These critics also think that nonpartisan elections rob the community of organized and effective criticism of the government in power. Since most candidates win as individuals rather than as members of an organized political party with common goals and policies, their criticism is sporadic and ineffectual, and meaningful policy alternatives seldom are stated. Chapter 4 points out that Texas political parties are not well organized. The blame for weak party organizations is often placed on nonpartisan local elections because the parties have no strong grassroots input. A fourth criticism is that nonpartisan elections encourage the development of civic organizations that are, in essence, local political parties whose purposes and policy goals are not always clear to the voters.

Advocates of nonpartisan elections obviously disagree. They think that the absence of a party label allows local elections to focus on local issues, not on national issues about which the municipal government can do little or nothing. They note that television personalities, athletes, and actors are also elected under party banners. Moreover, they point to the fact that local civic groups clarify, not confuse, local issues. Home owners, taxpayers, and consumers have become political forces that stand in contrast to the traditional business-oriented civic associations. As a result, participation is enhanced, although resolving political disagreements has become more difficult.

At-large elections, nonpartisan voting, and holding elections in the spring apparently do contribute to low voter turnout. A municipal election with as many as 25 percent of the eligible voters participating is unusual. Many local elections are decided on the basis of the preference of only 5 percent or 10 percent of the eligible voters. Moreover, in all elections, the older, affluent Anglos vote more frequently than do the young, the poor, and the ethnic minorities. The structure of municipal elections in Texas, particularly when those elections are at-large, tends to perpetuate the dominant position of the white middle-class business community. Thus, when we measure municipal government against the criteria for a democratic government, we find some problems of representation, especially among the less affluent and among ethnic minorities.

SPECIAL DISTRICTS: OUR HIDDEN GOVERNMENTS

Perhaps the best way to introduce the topic of special districts is to look at the changes in Texas local government shown in Table 9.1. The number of counties has been stable for almost a century; the number of school districts has steadily declined as districts consolidate to gain greater economy and efficiency. The number of municipalities has increased largely because unincorporated suburbs on the edges of central cities have become incorporated cities. The big increase is non-school special districts, which doubled in number in a 30-year period; their growth has finally slowed.

What Is a Special District?

A special district is a unit of local government created to perform limited functions. Its authority is narrow rather than broad, as in the case of the city or the county. Any further definition is almost impossible; special districts vary enormously in size, organization, function, and importance. A few early special districts were created by the constitution, but Texas statutes now stipulate that the legislature itself can create special districts, that counties and municipalities can create some types of special districts (especially for utilities, other basic services, and economic development), and that even state agencies can create some special districts (usually involving natural resources).

TABLE 9.1

Number of Units of Local Government in Texas, 1972–2002

Type of government	1972	1982	1992	2002	% change 1992–2002
Counties	254	254	254	254	0
Municipalities	1,000	1,121	1,171	1,196	+2.1
School districts	1,157	1,125	1,101	1,090	−1
Other special districts	1,215	1,692	2,266	2,245	−1
TOTAL	3,626	4,192	4,792	4,785	−0.1

NOTE: One of the school districts is classified as dependent on another local government, most likely a county.

SOURCE: U.S. Department of Commerce, Bureau of the Census, *2002 Census of Governments*, vol. 1, no. 1, Government Organizations (Washington, DC: December 2002), Tables 1, 3, and 5.

Texas has more than two dozen types of special districts. About one-fourth of these are housing and community-development districts, while another one-fourth are concerned with problems of water—control and improvement, drainage, navigation, supply, and sanitation. Yet another 254 are state-mandated tax appraisal districts. Other types of frequently encountered special districts are airport, soil conservation, municipal utilities, hospital, fire prevention, weed control, and community college. Independent school districts are discussed separately.

Every county has a tax appraisal district that is responsible for assessing property and providing up-to-date tax rolls to each taxing jurisdiction—county, municipalities, school districts, and other special districts. This system began in 1982 to eliminate the confusion caused by different taxing jurisdictions setting different values on property.

No single state or county agency is responsible for supervising the activities or auditing the financial records of all these special districts. Such supervision depends on the type of district involved. For example, community college districts are supervised by the Texas Higher Education Coordinating Board and the Texas Education Agency as well as by a local board. Average citizens, however, have a hard time keeping track of the many special districts surrounding them. This lack of uniformity and resulting confusion are caused in part by the various ways in which special districts have been created.

Why Special Districts?

The growth of special districts appears to have been slowed by consolidation and, perhaps, saturation, in recent years. Yet, Texas still has more special-purpose governments than any states other than Illinois (3,145) and California (2,830). Why do we have so many special districts? First, *our established governments—the cities and counties—are inadequate to solve many of the increasingly diverse problems of government.* The problem of flood control can seldom be solved within a single city or county, for example, and it frequently transcends state boundaries. Too, special districts are part of the price we pay for governmental institutions such as counties that were fashioned more than a century ago and are not always capable of addressing complex modern problems such as water supply. The Harris County Flood Control District has existed since 1937, for example, to fight the frequent floods in the Houston area because the county alone could not solve the problem.

Second, part of the attraction of special districts is that *they are easy to organize and operate.* Political leaders of cities and counties frequently promote a special district as a solution to what might otherwise become "their problem," and the legislature is willing to go along. Creating a hospital district, for example, means that the city and the county do not have to raise their taxes to cover the costs of operating a public hospital. Hunt Memorial Hospital District (Greenville and Commerce areas) is illustrative.

Third, in a few instances, *special districts have been created primarily for private gain,* usually to benefit land speculators and real-estate developers by increasing the value of their holdings. Once enabling legislation has been obtained from the state, it

The Denton County Development Districts No. 6 and 7 illustrate the problem with special districts. These districts built and operate Lantana, a large upscale housing development. The commissioners were elected by three voters who also created the districts in the one election held in 2000. Commissioners meet on a weekday in Dallas, posting meeting notices on a tree along a busy street that is partially obscured by shrubbery. They have authorized $137 million in bonds; they are paid $150 per meeting; and none of the three lives in Lantana.

Source: Peggy Heinkel-Wolfe, "Tree Stumped," *Denton Record-Chronicle*, February 19, 2006, 1A, 10A.

requires only a handful of votes in the sparsely settled, newly created district to authorize a bond issue for the development of water, sewer, and other utilities. Municipal utility districts (MUDs) are a good example of the consequences of a lack of effective state regulation of special districts. They often result in extremely high utility rates and utility-related taxes for those who live in them. Economic development districts created by counties have the ability to collect taxes that are used mainly for private benefit. Examples include a district in Bexar County created to establish a golf-course resort, one in Smith County that allowed a builder and his employees to constitute the board governing a district created to fund a truck stop, and a Hays County water control and improvement district that benefited only one California-based homebuilder.[14] Denton County became so profligate in creating special taxing districts to help the developers of luxury housing additions that the attorney general in 2001 announced new rules for approving bond elections affecting such districts.

Fourth, *special districts offer great flexibility to government organizations* and have the added attraction of rarely conflicting with existing units. A two-city airport such as Dallas–Fort Worth International is the result of a flexible airport authority.

Fifth, with highly technical problems such as flood control or water supply, *the special district offers the opportunity to "get it out of politics."* In other words, it is possible to take a business-like approach and bring in technical specialists to attack the problem. The Wise County Water Control and Improvement District 1 is an example. Such districts really are not apolitical but they do allow the focus to remain on the task at hand.

Assessment of Special Districts

Special districts other than school and appraisal districts are *profoundly undemocratic.* They are indeed "hidden governments," with far less visibility than city or county governments. It is not an exaggeration to say that every reader of this book is under the jurisdiction of at least one special district. Yet it will be a very rare reader who knows what those districts are, how much they cost in taxes, who the commissioners or other officials of the districts are, whether these officials are elected or—as is more frequently the case—appointed, and what policies they follow. Special district government is largely unseen and frequently unresponsive to the people. Thus, when we apply the test of democratic morality, we find that special districts fail to meet the standards of participation and public input.

Because most special districts are small in size and scope, they are not economical. Their financial status is often shaky, so that the interest rates taxpayers must pay on bond issues used to finance many types of special district projects are exceptionally high. Economies such as large-scale purchasing are impossible.

Finally, one very serious consequence of the proliferation of special districts is that *they greatly complicate the problems of government, particularly in urban areas.* With many separate governments, the likelihood is greater that haphazard development, confusion, and inefficiency will occur. No single government has comprehensive authority, and coordination among so many smaller governments becomes extremely difficult. Texans have been reluctant to experiment with a comprehensive urban government. Their individualism demands retention of the many local units, although metropolitan areas such as Miami and Nashville have succeeded with comprehensive government.

Lawmakers in the 78th Legislature in 2003 quickly disagreed over special taxing districts. Senator Ron Wilson (a Houston Democrat) introduced legislation to make it even easier to create such districts. Long-time foe of the districts, Senator Jane Nelson (a Denton County Republican) immediately revealed the proposal to the public saying, "It just means we're going to have to be more careful, more vigilant, for a longer time."

Source: Pete Slover, "Taxing Districts May Be on Fast Track," *Dallas Morning News*, January 17, 2003, 16A.

Instead, Texans rely on one of the 24 *regional planning councils*, also known as councils of governments (COGs), to provide coordination in metropolitan areas. These voluntary organizations of local government provide such functions as regional land use and economic planning, police training, and fact-finding studies on problems such as transportation.

Given the inadequacies of comprehensive planning and periodic revenue shortfalls at the local level, special districts will surely continue to exist. Under current conditions, they are too easy to create and operate as short-range solutions to governmental problems. Continued creation of special districts without adequate planning and supervision will result not in a solution but rather in a worsening of the problems of local and particularly urban government.

School Districts

School districts are an exception to much of the foregoing discussion of special districts for several reasons. First, school board members are publicly elected, most commonly in an at-large, by-place system. Second, their decisions are usually well publicized, with the local newspapers and broadcast media paying careful attention to education decisions. Third, considerable public interest in and knowledge about school district politics exist. Indeed, although county or city public hearings sometimes fail to attract a crowd, as soon as a school board agenda includes a topic such as a property tax increase, determining attendance districts—basically, who gets bused and who does not—or sex education, the public turns out for the debate. Fourth, the number of school districts has been steadily declining for 50 years. Finally, although the local boards have a substantial amount of control over such matters as individual

Large urban school districts have had the same struggles over district versus at-large elections that cities have had.

At-large proponents argue that "children," not "politics," should prevail. District proponents argue for "representation." In Dallas, the board is elected by district and has been sharply divided. Bill Rojas, a new superintendent hired in the fall of 1999, had already tangled with several board members before Thanksgiving and was dismissed in July 2000. Mike Moses, a former state education commissioner and Texas Tech professor, replaced him and was able to work effectively with the board until he stepped down in 2005 and was replaced by Michael Hinojosa, whose tenure began with a crusade for fiscal responsibility.

In the Panhandle, one district has tried an alternative election method. Amarillo has used an experimental voting procedure to try to find a compromise between district and at-large elections.

school management, location of schools, and personnel, the state is the ultimate authority for basic school policies and shares in the funding of public schools.

LOCAL GOVERNMENT FINANCE

County Finance

The financing of local government varies a great deal depending on the type of government. Counties depend heavily on local property taxes and on inter-governmental transfers, chiefly welfare money that is passed down from the national government to the Texas Health and Human Services Commission to the counties. They also receive state money to maintain rural farm-to-market roads and state highways. The inter-governmental money is beyond the control of the local government. The other significant source of county money is the property tax. The commissioners court is required to meet annually to set the property tax rate, which may not exceed the prescribed 80 cents per $100 valuation except in special circumstances authorized by the legislature. Counties also get miscellaneous income from local charges collected from hospitals, toll roads, and recreation facilities and from fines, special assessments, and interest earned. Selected counties also have been authorized to collect a sales tax.

A typical Texas county spends the largest share of its budget on health and welfare programs. Not only are counties the "pass-through" agencies for implementing welfare programs but they are also responsible for indigent health care. Another cost that has risen over the past decade is that of jails, as counties struggle to meet court-imposed minimum jail standards. County law enforcement costs depend on how much unincorporated land there is in the county. For example, in Dallas County, little unincorporated land exists, thereby minimizing the sheriff's enforcement range. In Harris County, much of the county is unincorporated and dependent on the sheriff's office.

Of course, individual Texas counties vary greatly in both revenue and expenditures, depending on whether they are rural or urban, rich or poor, large or small. They also vary according to the services demanded by the residents.

City Finance

The most important sources of municipal funding are the property tax, sales tax, borrowing through bonds, and user fees, especially for utilities such as water, solid waste pickup, wastewater, and electricity. Other sources include intergovernmental transfers, miscellaneous fees and fines such as liquor licenses and traffic fines collected by the municipal court.

Municipalities spend their money on diverse services. The largest areas of expenditure are utilities (laying all those water lines costs a lot of money!); police and fire protection; parks, recreation, and environmental compliance; and streets. Interest on debt is significant in many municipal budgets.

School and Other Special District Finance

School districts depend on two revenue sources—property taxes and state assistance. In Texas, however, state aid pays less than half the cost of public education, thereby putting considerable pressure on the property tax. Chapter 8 discusses the legal issues surrounding public school finance in Texas, including efforts to distribute some dollars from rich to poor districts. The two largest differences in spending in richer versus poorer districts is in facilities (posh buildings, full computerization versus bare bones) and enrichment activities (choir trips to Europe versus a poor-quality field for athletics and bands).

Other special districts have a variety of funding sources depending on their purpose, and their expenditures vary just as widely. One really cannot generalize about them. For example, a transit authority will depend on fees and grants and will spend its money on equipment and people to operate it. A junior college district will depend on property taxes, state aid, and student funds and will spend its money on programs and to some extent buildings. A water district will depend on fees and will spend its money on infrastructure to a large extent.

Both cities and counties face resistance from taxpayers over increased property taxes, a vexing issue because general-purpose governments have been able to maintain or sometimes even lower the property tax, but special districts, especially school districts, have continued to increase the rate. All local governments face federal and state policy changes that result in shifting local priorities. The quotation at the beginning of the chapter that "locals fear state budgets will be balanced at their expense" refers to all Texas local governments, but especially counties, cities, and school districts. The federal budget moved back to deficit status in 2002, and national priorities were focused on international matters, not domestic problems. State budgets across the country faced shortfalls in the early 2000s. Already strapped local governments had reason to fret.

As a result of political-fiscal pressures, local governments have become creative in identifying new revenue sources, such as impact fees charged to developers for putting in infrastructure (streets, utilities) in new subdivisions or athletic fees charged to students who want to participate in sports. Public–private cooperation has stretched local dollars for everything from park construction to Fourth of July celebrations. Sometimes, however, local governments have had to curtail services such as allowing lawn clippings to be hauled to the landfill or providing fine arts programs in the high school.

LOCAL GOVERNMENT: PROSPECTS FOR THE FUTURE

There is little doubt that the trends toward urbanization and suburbanization will continue, with the result that metropolitan problems will become more acute than they are today. The problem of rapid growth and dealing with a sprawl that often cuts across county lines is most evident in the Austin–San Marcos, San Antonio,

Houston, Dallas, and Fort Worth–Arlington metropolitan areas. The problems of growth are compounded when one considers that Houston–Galveston and Dallas–Fort Worth are considered consolidated metropolitan statistical areas (where two metro areas run together). What are the prospects for local governments in Texas under these circumstances?

There are several developments worth noting. As urban problems and local finance problems become more acute, national and state governments are being forced to pay more attention to them. One major consideration in the 1999 legislative struggle over utility deregulation was the recognition that the legislature would have to find a way for both cities and private companies to retire their debt on power plants. This recognition came about in part because the legislature is becoming more "citified."

Another significant development occurred in August 1978, when the voters of Houston and six of its suburbs approved the creation of a Metropolitan Transit Authority with taxing power and authority to establish transit systems as alternatives to Houston's increasingly congested freeways. By 2004 Houston had opened its light-rail system. Other Texas metropolitan areas have followed suit, and even medium-sized cities are developing *transit systems*. It has long been obvious that the practice of virtually every person's using a personal motor vehicle is incompatible with increasing urbanization. Smog, congestion, and rush-hour gridlock do not make for a high quality of life. Because Texas cities will surely continue growing, mass transit systems must be established if urban transportation is to avoid sinking into hopeless gridlock.

Another development is that of *strategic planning*, a type of planning that focuses on identifying a mission and pursuing it in an opportunistic manner, that is, taking advantage of any favorable situation that comes along. At the same time, strategic planning requires the community to understand the consequences of its actions. For example, a community that strives to attract high-technology companies might aggressively recruit electronics plants, either ignoring or finding a way to cope with some of their environmental problems.

A fourth area of concern for the future is *interlocal cooperation*. The COGs are one example of how local governments—counties, cities, and special districts—are working together to solve their common problems. Cooperative ventures such as city–county ambulance service, city–school playgrounds and libraries, and multiple-city purchasing are other examples. In recent years, these public cooperative arrangements have been augmented by agreements with private organizations such as business development associations and nonprofit service agencies. The most recent examples of cooperation are the ad hoc regional organizations that have sprung up to deal with terrorism, such as the Dallas–Fort Worth Homeland Security Alliance. Indeed, local interorganizational agreements are the most dynamic element of modern intergovernmental relations and can help to overcome some of the negative effects of the growing number of governments.

A fifth area of concern is *ordinance-making power for counties*. The lack of ordinance-making power is becoming a serious problem in various areas, including safety, environmental, and aesthetic standards, as well as other matters. For example, an issue of growing concern is the lack of control over adult bookstores and massage parlors that set up shop just outside a municipality, where control of them becomes a problem for the county. Indeed, counties asked for legislative relief in 1989 on this specific issue but did not get it. Counties want and need ordinance-making power but have thus far been denied it, primarily because of the opposition of the real-estate developers who can, for example, create developments in unincorporated areas that do not have to meet rigorous city building codes.

A sixth major problem that will continue to plague local governments is *funding*. With a deteriorating economy, the financial strains have worsened. Also, unlike costs in many enterprises, local government costs are not subject to economies of scale. In manufacturing, for example, producing more cars or soap bars results in lowered unit costs (the cost of one car or one soap bar). This principle does not hold true for picking up more bags of garbage or cleaning more streets or teaching more children. Burgeoning populations that move farther and farther away from the central city make delivery of services more costly.

Texas cities in 2005 and early 2006 were severely impacted by Hurricanes Katrina and Rita. The former resulted in tens of thousands of persons, especially New Orleaneans, fleeing Katrina in favor of Houston, Dallas, and many other Texas cities. The latter caused major damage to the Texas Gulf Coast, especially in the Golden Triangle (Beaumont–Port Arthur–Orange and surrounding towns). Houston hosted more evacuees than any other city. Because of its successful response to the crisis, the city was named "Texan of the Year" for 2005 by the *Dallas Morning News*.

SUMMARY

Local governments are the governments that are most likely to have a daily impact on the citizen, and much of this effect is critical to the quality of life. Will our children get a good public education, or should we save to send them to private school? Is our neighborhood safe, or will we have to live behind triple-locked doors with a guard dog for a companion? Will we enjoy a reasonably efficient and economical transportation system, or will we have to fight dangerous and congested freeway traffic two or three hours a day to get to and from our jobs?

The answers to these and a hundred other critical questions are given by the units of local government. And Texas counties, cities, special districts, and COGs seem ill prepared to provide optimum solutions. County governments are anachronisms—holdovers from an earlier, nonindustrial, nonurban period of American political history. City governments are better organized

How to Get Involved in Local Government

Local government is the logical starting point for exercising your democratic rights and participating in government. Here are a few suggestions for getting involved:

- Go to the party precinct conventions held immediately after the primary elections (see Chapter 5).
- Attend a public hearing and speak out.
- Organize a petition drive on a matter of importance to you—saving the trees along a planned freeway route, for example.
- Attend a neighborhood meeting.
- Attend a meeting of the city council, county commission, or school board.
- Talk to the city clerk or the county clerk to find out how to volunteer for an advisory committee or citizen task force.
- Volunteer to work for a local candidate during an election.

and have more comprehensive powers, yet they too are handicapped by a variety of factors, including the rapid increase in urban population, the proliferation of independent special districts, and the limited and frequently reluctant cooperation of state and national government. The COGs, as voluntary organizations, provide only very limited solutions to problems arising from the need for organized, coordinated planning. All local governments will face serious revenue problems for the foreseeable future.

Texas, like most states, will undoubtedly continue to become more and more urbanized. Consequently, problems such as congestion, poor housing, inadequate schools, and crime will grow. It is imperative that local governments both represent the diversity of the state and govern effectively. Democracy is about both participating and getting things done.

STUDY QUESTIONS

1. What is a home-rule city? What forms of government are used in home-rule cities? Why do you think most home-rule cities have council–manager government?

2. Pretend you are consultant to a city of 250,000 people. Your advice is sought on how to structure municipal elections. How would you advise this city about the timing of city elections and whether to have nonpartisan candidates and at-large elections? Why?

3. Why does Texas have so many special districts, and what are some of the problems associated with them?

4. Which type of local government do you think is truly at the "grassroots"; that is, which type most nearly represents all the citizens and works hardest to solve human problems?

5. Attend a meeting of your city council, school board, or county commission. Then describe for your fellow students what you learned by attending the meeting. As an alternative, identify an issue of local importance and trace the resolution of that issue through the local newspaper for the semester.

SURFING THE WEB

Visit the companion site for this book:

http://www.thomsonedu.com/politicalscience/kraemer

Instead of "name," type in the name of a Texas city of your choice. This URL often will work if the city has not created a different Web site.

http://www.ci.name.tx.us

Instead of "co," type in the name of a Texas county of your choice. This URL often will work if the county has not created a different Web site.

http://www.co.name.tx.us

Visit the home page of the Texas Department of Housing and Community Affairs (roughly the equivalent of the U.S. Department of Housing and Urban Development):

http://www.tdhca.state.tx.us

Check out the Texas Municipal League site for legislation affecting local governments:

http://www.tml.org

Explore the laws affecting local government by viewing the Texas Local Government Code:

http://www.capitol.state.tx.us/statutes/lg.toc.htm

NOTES

1. Our discussion of county government in Texas relies in part on Robert E. Norwood, *Texas County Government: Let the People Choose* (Austin: Texas Research League, 1970). Norwood's monograph is the most extensive work available on the subject. A second edition, co-authored with Sabrina Strawn, was published in 1984.

2. Although one often sees commissioners court written as "commissioners'" (with an apostrophe), Chapter 81 of the *Texas Local Government Code* is explicit about the lack of an apostrophe.

3. Bell County Judge John Garth, in a conversation with one of the authors on February 21, 1991.

4. Travis County Judge Bill Aleshire in "Elected County Officials—Unlike City—Actually Run Government," *Austin American-Statesman*, September 16, 1996, A15.

5. See, for example, Robert Elder, Jr. and Brad Reagan, "Rural Counties Try to Stay One Step Ahead of Growth," *Wall Street Journal*, July 12, 2000, T1, T3.

6. Provisions covering how both home-rule and general-law municipalities can organize are found in Chapters 9 and 21 through 26 of the *Texas Local Government Code.* An extensive look at the concept of home-rule both in Texas and nationally can be found in Dale Krane, ed., *Home Rule in America* (Washington, DC: Congressional Quarterly Press, 2000).

7. See Robert H. Wilson, "Understanding Urban Texas," *Discovery: Research and Scholarship at the University of Texas at Austin*, 15, no. 2, March 1999, 34–37.

8. See Victor S. DeSantis and Tari Renner, "City Government Structures: An Attempt at Clarification," *State and Local Government Review* 14, Spring 2002, 95–104; *Model City Charter*, 8th ed. (Washington, DC: National Civic League, 2003).

9. *Texas Almanac, 2006–2007* (Dallas: *Dallas Morning News*, 2006), 451–464, by count.

10. Additional information on forms of government came from http://www.icma.org in the section entitled "Who's Who: Recognized Local Governments." This section is accessible only to members of the International City/County Management Association and provides a list of cities that meet the criteria to be considered as either a council–manager government or a government with a professional general administrator.

11. A thorough look at modern council–manager government can be found in John Nalbandian and George Frederickson, eds., *The Future of Local Government Administration: The Hansell Symposium* (Washington, DC: International City/County Management Association, 2002); in the monthly issues of *PM: Public Management*, published by ICMA; the work of James H. Svara (see, for example, "Conflict and Cooperation in Elected-Administrative Relations in Large Council–Manager Cities," *State and Local Government Review*, 31, Fall 1999, 173–189; Charldean Newell, ed., *The Effective Local Government Manager*, 3rd ed. (Washington, DC: International City/County Management Association, 2004).

12. See, for example, Robert B. Boynton, "City Councils: Their Role in the Legislative System," *The Municipal Year Book, 1976* (Washington, DC: International City Management Association, 1976), 67–77; Tari Renner and Victor S. DeSantis, "Contemporary Patterns in Municipal Government Structures," *The Municipal Year Book, 1993* (Washington, DC: International City/County Management Association, 1993), 57–68; Daniel R. Morgan and Robert E. England, *Managing Urban America*, 4th ed. (Chatham, NJ: Chatham House, 1996), 58–80.

13. John Nalbandian discusses local representation in "Tenets of Contemporary Professionalism in Local Government," in George W. Frederickson, ed., *Ideal and Practice in Council–Manager Government*, 2nd ed. (Washington, DC: International City/County Management Association, 1995) 157–171.

14. Reese Dunklin and Brooks Egerton, "'Designer Districts' Benefit Developers," *Dallas Morning News*, July 3, 2001, 1A, 12A.

10

THE STATE ECONOMY AND THE FINANCING OF STATE GOVERNMENT

It almost goes without saying that the demands on state government grow whether or not the revenue that funds them increases. . . . Lawmakers are going to have to give serious, thoughtful, and credible consideration to the tough issues Texas is going to face in the next legislative session.

Senator Bill Ratliff
Speaking as Lieutenant Governor, 2002

I will be proud to sign this plan that will reward teachers and reform our schools, provide a record property tax cut that will make home ownership more affordable, reduce the net tax burden on Texans by nearly $7 billion, and improve our tax system so it is fairer because it is broader.

Governor Rick Perry
Following the 2006 Special Session

INTRODUCTION

The ability of any government to generate the revenues needed to provide the programs and services that citizens want is directly tied to the economy. Are most people working? Are wages good? Are profits high? Is money available for loans to finance business expansion and home ownership? This chapter begins by sketching the boom-and-bust economy of the state and the effects that economic volatility has on budget making. Texas emerged from the economic troubles that began in 1983 when oil prices plummeted, wreaking havoc on the Texas economy and on state finance. The state then enjoyed sizable surpluses in the three legislative sessions from 1997 to 2001, making it possible to address a number of program needs. By the time the 2003 Legislative session began, Texas, along with the rest of the nation, was in deep economic doldrums. Like most other states, Texas faced a major deficit—just under $10 billion—but, unlike the national government, the state cannot just go into debt and continue providing state services. By 2005–2006, the economic picture had improved, as the story of school finance told in this chapter will reveal.

The two quotations that open this chapter neatly summarize the reality of state finance—problems of finding adequate revenue will always be there, but, when a solution can be found, the result allows policy-makers to crow a bit. In 2003 the population had grown, many people were out of work, and the state's need to improve education and social services was increasing. Yet, many voters were in no mood to accept new revenue measures so that the governor urged caution, and the speaker of the House used the budget crisis to attack the social programs that conservatives detest (see Chapter 11 for some of the programmatic implications of these attitudes). In 2005 the economic situation was improving, and the legislature restored some of the funding slashed in 2003. However, it failed to address public school finance in a meaningful way until May of 2006.

Complicating the legislative debate on revenue and spending is the reality that the poor in Texas pay a higher proportion of their income in taxes than do the wealthy. The fairness of the Texas revenue system raises questions about how democratic the state system is and constitutes a major theme of this chapter.

This chapter looks not only at the economy but also at the ways the state gets and spends money, including how elected officials struggle to agree on what the budget will be. Because the budget is the best guide to policy priorities, it is a practical test of how well citizens' interests are accommodated in state spending. An important cautionary note is that the 2006–2007 fiscal year's budget is used as an example, but this budget was modified by the special session of 2006. However, no analysis of the changes was available at the time this book went to press. (A fiscal year [FY] is a budget period, in Texas from September 1 of one year through August 31 of the next.)

Texas had grown from just shy of 17 million people in 1990 to 22.5 million people in 2004—an increase of more than 32 percent in just 14 years. During that same period, the state budget increased from $27.2 billion for fiscal year 1991 to $68.8 billion for FY 2007—an increase of 153 percent. However, when adjusted for population growth—more people require more services—and *inflation*—that is, increases in what things cost—the Texas budget was relatively flat across this period. Budget growth has only been about 2.8 percent a year, less than the inflation rate for the period as a whole.[1]

THE TEXAS ECONOMY

The Past

Historically, the Texas economy was based on natural resources, chiefly oil, land, and water. Indeed, Texas has been characterized as the state where "money gushes from the ground in the oil fields and grows on the citrus trees in the irrigated orchards."[2] Texas is still an important producer of oil and gas, and listings of its principal products continue to include petroleum, natural gas, and natural gas liquids.[3] Chemicals, cotton, and cattle also contribute their share of wealth.

At the close of the twentieth century, slightly more than 1 percent of the state's $744 billion economy came directly from agriculture, forestry, and fisheries, and less than 10 percent came from oil and gas. The latter two resources are finite; that is, once used, they cannot be replaced. The percentages had been fairly constant throughout the 1990s.

Although the current economy is more complex than one based solely on natural resources, it is subject to national and international developments. The erosion of the natural resource-based economy meant that hundreds of thousands of Texans found themselves out of work. In June 1986 the state unemployment rate reached 9.6 percent, compared with a national rate of 7.3 percent. The collapse of financial institutions made the problem worse. In 1988–1990 Texas led the nation in the number of banks and savings-and-loans that failed. Also at that time the defense industry was depressed by the end of the Cold War in the early 1990s.

State government worked to shore up the shaky economy by consolidating economic development programs, developing aggressive marketing campaigns for farm and ranch products, and selling the high-technology capability of the state through industry–university partnerships. By 1996 the nonprofit Corporation for Enterprise Development graded the state "A" for business vitality, but "C" for development capacity, and "D" for economic performance, with criticism directed at state policies, particularly support for education.[4]

That same year, however, Development Counselors International, based on a poll of 173 executives in top firms on sites they would consider for relocation, called Texas one of the top places for business locations, running second only to North Carolina in the "business beauty pageant."[5] New and expanded corporate facilities in 1994–1996 numbered 1,968, second only to Ohio.[6] High technology, financial services, manufacturing, and communications were the economic engines for the job growth.

By the fall of 1999 Texas was creating 26,000 new jobs a month, although some concern was expressed about the number of those jobs that were in low-paying service industries. Restaurant workers and less-skilled employees in the health care industry often earn below-average wages. College-educated workers who found jobs in the growing high-technology and dot-com firms were doing well, but the economic distance between highly skilled and unskilled workers seemed to be growing.[7] In November 1999 unemployment statewide was 4.2 percent—a low that was last seen in 1979. High-technology centers such as Austin, Dallas, and Bryan–College Station had virtually full employment, with only 1.5 percent to 2.9 percent of workers unable to find work. Petrochemical centers and border cities were less fortunate; unemployment in McAllen–Edinburg–Mission stood at 13 percent.[8]

The Twenty-First Century

Beginning in the spring of 2000, the high-tech sector of the U.S. economy began to plummet. NASDAQ, the index that reflects technology stocks, lost almost three-quarters of its value, and large layoffs in telecommunications, computer, and Internet firms led to prolonged unemployment in "new economy" industries. On September 11, 2001, terrorists attacked the United States by hijacking four airliners and using them as weapons. Two of these planes brought down the twin World Trade Towers in New York; a third destroyed a section of the Pentagon in Washington, D.C.; and the fourth crashed into an open field in Pennsylvania. The horror of lost lives and the surprise of the attack coupled with actual economic damages, particularly to the travel industry, further shook confidence in the U.S. economy. (The only profitable airline in the country in 2002 and 2003 was Dallas-based Southwest.) Military action in Afghanistan beginning in 2001 and Iraq in 2003 followed the 9/11 attack, coupled with two national tax cuts, and the costs of war sent the country into significant debt and rattled the economy further. A series of corporate scandals made matters worse, especially because they involved top corporate officers growing very rich while the pensions, and ultimately the jobs, of ordinary workers were squandered. The largest scandal of all was Houston-based Enron, whose top two executives, Ken Lay and Jeffrey Skilling, were convicted of several counts of fraud in federal court in 2006.

Texas and other states were in no way immune to these national and international events.[9] Although Texas has the eighth largest economy in the world and exports more products for sale than any other state, border cities failed to realize the economic hopes they had based on the North American Free Trade Agreement (NAFTA) of 1993.[10] A prolonged drought in the southern part of the state damaged the agrarian economy and worsened the border cities' financial condition. American Airlines, headquartered in Fort Worth, came close to declaring bankruptcy, laid off thousands of employees, and gained wage concessions from the remaining ones. Tourism, important to many areas of the state, was reeling from the public's reluctance to travel, and all states were having trouble meeting new obligations for homeland security in the wake of budget deficits.[11]

Texans' confidence in the economy was steadily eroding due to the lack of job growth and the sluggish economy, and the feeling of malaise was not improved by economists indicating that economic recovery had begun in 2002, but without new jobs.[12]

The state had banked on high technology as an answer to the waning of the old natural resource-based economy, but the high-tech crash led to tens of thousands of job layoffs and foreclosures on thousands of homes; the only bright spot seemed to be the traditional oil and petrochemical industry. Texas also profited from heightened military activities because of its many defense contractors, although individual families lost ground when reservists were called up from better-paying jobs into military service. As the legislature convened in 2003, unemployment was above 6 percent. Generally, higher unemployment rates equal a demand for more government services. Thus, the economic situation that greeted the 2003 Legislature was not an encouraging one; the "bad news" had arrived with equal force in other state capitals.[13]

The economy continued to improve, however, even in the wake of hurricanes in 2005, the acceptance of many impoverished evacuees as new Texas residents, and agricultural weaknesses due to a serious drought in 2005–2006. In early 2006 job growth was running at more than 13,000 a month, and unemployment was at 5 percent. How long a more robust economy would hold up was the question. Two other issues that were becoming more and more evident were the disparity in earnings between the richest and the poorest Texans and the reliance on illegal workers, especially from Mexico.[14]

Perhaps the brightest sign of a recovering Texas economy was the state's re-emergence as No. 1 in the country for corporate relocation and expansion.[15]

Analysis

At least six reasons help to explain the ups and downs of the Texas economy and the growth in the state budget over the past quarter-century. First, over-production of oil worldwide in the early 1980s, and again in the 1990s, led to price slides that placed a strain on the Texas economy, especially in the earlier period. However, oil prices experienced resurgence in 1999, in 2003, and especially in 2006. Second, federal assistance to the states has waxed and waned over the past 25 years and is likely to decline again as a result of changes in federal social programs that first took effect in the fall of 1997 and the devolution of government, that is the passing down of authority to state and local governments from the national government, often without economic support. Third, Texans responded to the challenges posed by the economic doldrums of the 1980s and diversified the economy. However, the new technology-based economy was the hardest hit by the national economic slump that began in 2000. Fourth, at times during the 1970s, double-digit inflation prevailed; both public and private spending increased in proportion to the inflation rate. During the 1980s and 1990s, the nation continued to experience some inflation, but at a much lower rate. In the early years of the twenty-first century, the fear was that the reverse economic condition—deflation—might occur; that is, prices and wages might continue to go down, not up. Fifth, the Texas revenue system, particularly its tax structure, lacks **elasticity**, that is, it is not easily adjusted to ups and downs in the economy. The inelastic revenue structure coupled with spending demands and federal cutbacks proved to be a problem in the new century when the economy sagged. Sixth, when state government enjoyed a surplus in 1997, it chose to rebate the money to taxpayers in the form of reduced local school taxes; the 1999 surplus partly went for improved services but also included tax cuts; the 2006 surplus, along with new business and cigarette taxes, was used to reduce local property taxes and to finance public schools, but left open the question of a permanent funding mechanism. These actions were in line with strong conservative trends to reduce taxes rather than increase spending. Pent-up demands for services coupled with a reluctance to increase taxes ultimately led to extraordinary pressures on the state budget.

WHERE DOES THE MONEY COME FROM?

State finance consists of raising and spending money. For most of those who are involved in government, the budget is the bottom line, as it is for the rest of us. Policy decisions regarding state financing are made in the glaring light of political reality—what political scientist Harold Laswell called "Politics: Who Gets What, When, and How." Whenever money is raised, it comes from someone; whenever it is spent, someone gets it. Struggles over who will pay for the government and who will receive dollars from it are at the heart of politics in Texas, as it is elsewhere.

Figure 10.1 illustrates the sources of state revenue for FY 2006–2007 *before* changes were made in the special session of 2006. It shows that only 45.7 percent of revenues came from taxes. These include the sales tax, the severance tax, corporation franchise tax, vehicle sales and rental taxes, motor fuel tax, and miscellaneous other taxes such as those on alcohol and tobacco. Percentages of some taxes are dedicated to particular purposes, most notably the portion of the motor fuel tax that goes to public schools and the oil and gas lease royalties that go to the Permanent University Fund; there are about 200 funds with such particular purposes. The 2006 tax bills increased the corporation franchise tax and cigarette tax and the format of vehicle taxes so that the percentage of the budget due to taxes will rise slightly. Another 12.9 percent of Texas revenue came from fines, fees, licenses, land leases, interest, and dividends. Also, 5.9 percent came from other sources such as the lottery, bond funds, the state highway trust, inter-agency contracts, and "local" income (such as tuition and fees collected by colleges and universities). The remaining 35.5 percent came from federal receipts, especially for highways, health, and welfare.

The revenue picture of the state shows many fluctuations. In 1979 the severance tax—the oil and gas tax—produced 22 percent of state revenues. By FY 2006–2007

FIGURE 10.1

Texas State Revenues for the 2006–2007 Biennium by Fund Source (in millions)*

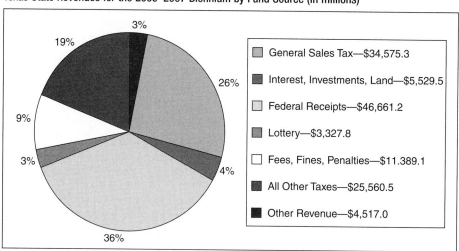

*Totals may not add upto 100% due to rounding.

SOURCE: *Fiscal Size Up 2006–2007* (Austin, TX: Legislative Budget Board, 2005), 20.

that tax produced only 5.5 percent, although this percentage was an increase from the 2.1 percent of FY 2002–2003. This huge change in revenues produced by the severance tax is testimony to the volatility of the domestic and global energy market. In contrast to the diminished contributions of the severance tax, the state has grown increasingly dependent on the U.S. government, although the percentages of federal support tend to go up and down depending on national budget initiatives. In the modern era federal funds reached a low point in FY 1984–1985 at 19.4 percent but have grown steadily over the past several years to the current 35.5 percent.

Texas hoped to solve some of its periodic money woes with a state lottery, which began in FY 1992–1993. The lottery quickly reached 5.1 percent of the state budget at the beginning of FY 1998–1999 and was called the most successful lottery in the country. Since then, it has been declining as a source of revenue, in part because of public disenchantment with the payoffs, and was only 2.1 percent in FY 2007. Lost revenues have been made up by economic growth that generated added tax revenues, by higher and more expensive fees, and sometimes by requiring local governments to fund some activities previously paid for by the state. The special session of 2006, however, lessened the local tax burden. It also made use of $2.4 billion of the budget surplus.

Nontax Sources of Revenues

Federal Grants.   The state has sources of revenue other than the checks oil producers write to the state comptroller and the pennies, nickels, and dimes that citizens dig out of their pockets to satisfy the sales tax. Monies also come to the state treasury from federal grants. In fact, beginning in the 1960s state and local governments became heavily dependent on national budgetary policies that distributed monies to the treasuries of states, cities, and other local governments. Originally, these dollars came to states in the form of **categorical grants-in-aid**, which could be used only for specific programs such as community health centers. Under President Richard Nixon, revenue sharing was enacted. Distributed by formula, general revenue-sharing funds could be used by state and local governments for whatever projects these governments wanted—police salaries, playground equipment, home care for the elderly. In addition, the federal government began to fund **block grants**, which provide money for general use in broad programs such as community development. General revenue sharing for states ended in 1979 and for cities in 1986, and block grants gained in importance.

State and local governments gained considerable flexibility under Ronald Reagan's version of "New Federalism" because more and more categorical grants were consolidated into block grants. The state gained more control because many funds were no longer channeled directly to local governments but first "passed through" a state agency. This flexibility came at a price, however; the funding for many programs, especially those affecting the poor and urban development, was reduced. For the first time in one-third of a century, states had a dollar drop in federal aid in 1982.

More recent increases in federal funding have been attributable to interstate highway construction and maintenance spending following the increase in the national motor fuels tax in 1983 and especially to the rising costs of social programs that are largely or completely funded by the national government, especially medical care for the poor, which is discussed in Chapter 11. However, critics of state policy

FIGURE 10.2

Federal Funds as Percentage of State Revenue, 1990–1991 through 2006–2007

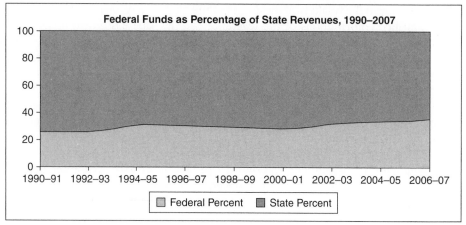

SOURCE: *Fiscal Size Up: 1990–1991 through 2006–2007 Biennums* (Austin: LBB, 1990–2005), about Figure 5 in chapter 2 in each edition.

processes have continued to chastise Texas officials for not taking full advantage of national programs and even being willing to sacrifice considerable federal funds to avoid spending a lesser amount of state funds.

Although expressing sympathy for the nation's cities and their problems, President Bill Clinton had to contend with the need for budget balancing. National welfare reform legislation signed shortly before the 1996 presidential election has resulted in the states being asked to take on new responsibilities for health benefits for the poor and to emphasize job placements instead of cash assistance as the focus of welfare programs. Figure 10.2 illustrates the fluctuations in federal funding over nine biennia. Federal funding gradually increased from FY 1990–1991 to FY 1996–1997, then tailed off for the next four years before beginning to increase again in FY 2002–2003. Each percentage point fluctuation represents a change of approximately $1 billion.

Borrowing. Governments, like private citizens, borrow money. The reasons are varied. Political expediency is one. Borrowing allows governments to implement new programs and extend existing ones without increasing taxes. A second reason is that borrowing allows future beneficiaries of a state service to pay for that service. Students who live in residence halls, for example, help pay off the bonds used to finance those halls through their room fees.

State government indebtedness is highly restricted in Texas, however. The framers of the state constitution strongly believed in "pay-as-you-go" government. A four-fifths vote of the legislature is needed to approve emergency borrowing, and the state's debt ceiling originally was limited to $200,000. A series of amendments has altered the constitution to allow the issuance of state bonds for specific programs, particularly land for veterans, university buildings, student loans, parks, prisons, and water development. At the end of FY 2005, total state indebtedness was $21.4 billion. Although this figure may seem high, Texas state debt per person is only about one-quarter of the national average, and the state typically ranks in the lowest five or six in per capita debt.[16]

Other Nontax Sources.   Because taxes are unpopular in Texas (and elsewhere), government inevitably looks to nontax revenue sources whenever possible. The budget deficits that characterized the mid-1980s and resurfaced in 2003 have led the state to raise money by increasing fees for almost everything, looking to gambling as a source of public revenue, and even manipulating state pension funds. An excellent example is college tuition, a type of user fee—that is, a sum paid in direct exchange for a service. Beginning in 2004, tuition was deregulated, and universities can charge what they need to operate—or, at least, what they think students will be willing to pay. Institutions can and do charge considerably more for graduate and professional education. Each community college district also sets its own fees because community colleges are financially supported not only by state revenues but also by local taxes. To illustrate the consequences of deregulated tuition, one need only consider that in 1985 senior college undergraduate tuition was only $4 per semester credit hour, plus miscellaneous fees. In 2005 the tuition and fee package ranged from $137 to $248 per credit hour, depending on the institution—about what the total bill was 20 years earlier. In short, state policy has shifted from the offering of a low-cost college education to considerable privatization of higher education, that is, to a steady erosion of public support in favor of students, grant givers, and donors covering more of the cost of education.

Other fees that have risen in recent years include everything from car inspections to water permits, from personal automobile tags to daycare center operator licenses, from the cost of producing court records to processing costs for a bail bond. Fines for various legal infractions have risen. Even the costs of a driver's license and a fishing license have gone up.

Other nontax sources of state revenue include the interest on bank deposits, proceeds from investments, and sales and leases of public lands. Having a surplus increases investment income. A bad stock market or low interest rates decrease revenue. The robustness in the oil industry determines income from land leases.

The 1987 Legislature proposed a constitutional amendment, approved by the voters in November of that year, that permitted parimutuel betting on horse races and, in three counties, on dog races by local option. By 1991, however, track betting had contributed virtually nothing to state coffers because the state's share of the proceeds—5 percent—was so high that track developers declined the opportunity to invest. Even though the 1991 Legislature lowered the state's share to a graduated rate beginning at 1 percent, first-class tracks have been slow to develop.

A state lottery also was debated but was not approved by the legislature in 1987, 1989, and 1991. Ann Richards and her Democratic primary opponent Jim Mattox had both campaigned on a pro-lottery platform in 1990. Once elected, Governor Richards apparently was able to work out a deal with enough legislators—allegedly supporting their redistricting concerns—to get a lottery on the November 1991 ballot. Voters approved the lottery, which began in the summer of 1992. Since then, whether the revenues were to be dedicated to education has been at issue. The 1997 Legislature did dedicate the revenues but moved other funds previously earmarked for education back to the general fund. Administrative scandals and falloff in betting have caused the lottery to fail to live up to expectations. The 2003 legislature passed a bill that allows Texas to enter a multi-state lottery such as Powerball in an effort to shore up revenues from gambling.

Taxation

Taxes are the most familiar sources of governmental revenue and the most controversial. Since colonial days and James Otis's stirring phrase, "No taxation without representation," citizens have sought justice in the tax system. Texas's conservative heritage has not always made justice easy to find.

Taxes are collected for two principal reasons. Revenue taxes—for example, the general sales tax—are the major source of state general revenue. They make it possible for government to carry out its programs. *Regulatory taxes*—for example, the taxes on tobacco and alcohol—are designed primarily to control those individuals and/or organizations who are subject to them and either punish undesired behavior or reward desired behavior. Increasingly, however, they are viewed as "easy" revenue sources because those who pay them are ill positioned to raise a fuss about increasing the rate.

Who Pays?   The question of who pays which taxes raises two issues. The first is ability to pay, and the second is whether individuals and businesses both really pay.

Ability to Pay.   A matter of some importance to taxpayers is whether their taxes are progressive or regressive. Progressive taxation is characterized by a rate that increases as the object taxed—property, income, or goods purchased—grows larger or gains in

Liberals like Ben Sargent compared the 2003 Legislature's refusal to raise taxes to meet the state's budget crisis to Emperor Nero's fiddling while Rome burned in 64 A.D.

SOURCE: Courtesy of Ben Sargent.

value. **Progressive taxation** is based on ability to pay. The best-known example is the federal income tax, which progresses from relatively low rates for those with the least income to increasingly higher rates for those with larger incomes. However, loopholes in the federal tax laws, recent tax cuts that favor the wealthy and the very poor, and ceilings on special taxes such as Social Security still result in a proportionately heavier tax burden for the middle class than for the wealthy.

Regressive Taxation.   Although technically a tax system that involves a higher rate with a declining base, **regressive taxation** has come to refer to a system in which lower-income earners spend larger percentages of their incomes on commodities subject to flat tax rates. The best example of Texas's reliance on regressive taxes is the general retail sales tax. Almost one-quarter of revenues from all sources and more than 57.5 percent of tax revenues come from this sales tax, which is assessed at 6.25 percent on a wide variety of goods and services at the time of sale, regardless of the income or wealth of the purchaser (see Figure 10.1). Municipalities can levy a 1 percent additional tax, as can mass transit districts and county economic development districts. Municipalities can also add sales tax percentages of a half-percent each for economic development and in lieu of reduced property taxes. The additional selective sales (excise) taxes—those levied on tobacco products, alcoholic beverages, and motor fuels, for example—also are regressive. The $18,000-a-year clerk and the $150,000-a-year executive who drive the same distance to work pay the same 20-cents-a-gallon tax on gasoline, but who is better able to bear the tax burden?

Citizens for Tax Justice (CTJ), a Washington, D.C.–based research and lobbying group, examined tax structures in all fifty states in 2002. The group dubbed ten states, including Texas, "the terrible 10" for the regressivity of their tax structures. Six of the 10 were states without a personal income tax; seven were states with a heavy reliance on sales and excise taxes. Only Washington, Florida, Tennessee, and South Dakota were rated as having a more regressive tax system than does Texas, and only these four states had higher tax rates for their poorest citizens than does Texas.[17] According to CTJ, in 2002 the poorest Texans paid 11.4 percent of their income in state taxes, while the richest paid only 3.5 percent. The gap, while large, had narrowed somewhat during the 1990s. Also, Texas, unlike some states, does not yet tax "lifeline items"— food purchased at a grocery store, prescription medicines, or work clothes—and holds a tax holiday just before the beginning of the school year to allow tax-free purchases of school clothes. Texas is one of only seven states with no personal income tax and one of five with no corporate income tax, although many people consider that the corporation franchise tax (to be discussed) serves as a corporate income tax.[18] Readers of its newsletter were warned by CTJ that they would not likely see more equity brought into tax systems, not only because of the strains on state budgets but also because it was evident that President George W. Bush and the congressional leadership favored tax cuts that favored the rich.[19]

At this stage, Texas cannot claim to have a progressive tax system. Yet a fair tax system is a value associated with democratic government. Many observers believe that a progressive income tax would be fairer than the general sales tax and could replace all or part of it. But the state's conservatism has thus far precluded the adoption of a progressive tax policy, either based on ability to pay or a flat percentage of income. Some business leaders have begun to advocate a state income tax, and changes in the corporation franchise tax in 1991 and 2006 were steps toward a corporate income tax.

One may also note that, while the terms *progressive* and *regressive* are most commonly applied to taxes, they can apply to other forms of revenue as well. No good example exists for a progressive revenue source that is not a tax, but a set fine for a traffic violation is regressive in that it is not based on ability to pay.

Taxes Paid by Individuals.   A number of taxes are levied directly against individuals—for example, the inheritance tax collected at the time beneficiaries inherit estates, the motor fuels tax paid each time a motorist buys gasoline, and the ad valorem property tax collected on real property, buildings, and land by local governments.[20] Businesses also pay the motor fuels tax and local property taxes, of course, but by increasing prices they let their customers pick up the tab.

Most authorities also would include all sales taxes in the category of taxes paid by individuals on the assumption that businesses pass them on to the consumer just as they do local ad valorem and state vehicle registration taxes—whether that is the intention of the law or not. There are three types of sales tax:

1. The *general sales tax* is a broadly based tax that is collected on most goods and services and must be paid by the consumer.
2. *Selective sales taxes* (excise taxes) are levied on only a few items, comparatively speaking, and consumers are often unaware that they are paying them. These taxes are included in the price of the item, not computed separately. Tobacco products, alcoholic beverages—tobacco and alcohol taxes are sometimes called "sin taxes"—automobiles, gasoline, and admission to amusements— movies, plays, nightclubs, sporting events—are among the items taxed in this category.
3. *Gross receipts taxes* are levied on the total gross revenues (sales) of certain businesses: cement producers, telegraph and telephone companies, and private clubs' and bars' sales of liquor by the drink, for example. Technically, they are business taxes that are paid directly by the business. Nonetheless, in most cases, these taxes are actually passed on to the consumer, either directly or indirectly.

Taxes Levied on Businesses.   Taxes levied on businesses in Texas produce considerable revenue for the state but are often regulatory in nature. One example is the severance taxes levied on natural resources, such as crude oil, natural gas, and sulfur, that are severed (removed) from the earth. This removal, of course, depletes irreplaceable resources, and part of the tax revenue is dedicated to conservation programs and to the regulation of production; thirty other states have similar taxes. Severance taxes once were the backbone of the state's revenue system, but the steady decline in the oil business for more than a decade has resulted in these taxes' contributing barely 5 percent of current revenues.

The major Texas business tax today is the *corporation franchise tax*, which is assessed against corporations as the price of doing business in the state. Some people regard it as a type of corporate income tax because the business pays tax on invested assets (capital) and earned surplus, which consists of federal taxable income plus compensation paid to the officers and directors of the corporation. This tax was overhauled substantially in 1991 to make it fairer, since it originally emphasized taxes on capital-intensive businesses such as manufacturing that required huge stockpiles of raw material and collected little from businesses such as computer software firms, financial institutions, and even the big downtown law firms that rely on the intellectual ability of their employees. In the 2006 special session on school finance, the corporation franchise tax was broadened further so as to apply to the gross receipts of most businesses, in essence a true corporate income tax. The tax was expected to provide about 6.4 percent of state revenue for FY 2006–2007 before it was broadened in 2006.

Another tax levied directly on businesses in Texas is the *insurance premium* tax, levied on gross premiums collected by insurance companies. Businesses also pay *special taxes and fees* for such varied activities as chartering a corporation, brewing alcoholic beverages, and selling real estate. These taxes are largely paid by consumers in the form of higher prices. Indeed, other than a corporation net profits tax, it is almost impossible to construct a tax that cannot and will not be passed on to the consumer, at least so long as consumers are willing to pay higher prices.

Who Benefits?   To address the question of who benefits from tax policies, we must consider the kinds of services the government provides. Nothing would seem to be more equitable than a tax structure resulting in an exact ratio between taxes paid and benefits received, and in Texas some taxes are levied with exactly that idea in mind.

The motor fuels tax, 20 cents per gallon on gasoline and diesel fuel, is paid by those who use motor vehicles, and three-fourths of the revenues from this tax are spent on maintaining and building highways and roads. The remainder goes to public schools. However, this same motor fuels tax also points up a paradox in the "benefit theory" of taxation: People who do not own automobiles and do not buy gasoline also benefit from those big trucks hauling goods to market over state highways.

The Tax Burden in Texas

Texas has prided itself on being a low-tax state, and the Republican leadership of the state has pushed a legislative agenda since 1997 that calls for tax relief—a popular short-term approach during a boom economy. When the *state–only* tax burden is considered, Texas ranks 48th in the country, indicating that it is, indeed, a low-tax state.[21] A further indication of the Texas tax effort is the ranking of the Tax Foundation, a Washington think tank that caters to business organizations. The foundation listed Texas as 44th in combined state and local taxes for 2006.[22] The slight difference in the state-only and combined state-local rankings indicates that the state may not be so supportive of its local governments as some other states, causing local taxes to be proportionally higher. Again, some shift in the state-local ratio of taxes will occur as the result of the 2006 revenue changes made by the legislature. The Tax Foundation ranks Texas 32nd when federal taxes are also included. That ranking is a measure not only of business activity in the state and sizeable personal wealth held by a minority of Texans but also of the population size of the state and of the fact that the state has no personal income tax so that none of the state taxes can be used to offset the federal income tax.[23]

One irony of the Texas tax situation is that the state does not fare well under many federal grant formulas, which include tax effort—the tax effort already borne by citizens—as a criterion. The state does least well on matching grants for social services and welfare. Although the state ranks second in income taxes collected from individual Texans by the national government and fourth in corporate taxes collected from Texas businesses, it ranks only 31st in per capita federal government expenditures in the state.[24] In short, Texans contribute more in federal taxes to get back a dollar in federal grants than do the citizens of most other states.

The First Decade of the Twenty-First Century

Perspectives from the Past.   For a half-century, Texas relied on oil and gas production taxes as the major source of state revenue, with most of these being paid by out-of-state purchasers. How good were the good old days? "Texas went from 1971 to 1984 . . . without an increase in state tax rates, or new taxes" while the population was growing 42 percent.[25] After the world oil market crashed, Texans were ill prepared to develop a responsible and responsive revenue policy to provide dollars for state services. As Table 10.1 shows, the state got better at revenue measures, then it benefited subsequently from a booming economy and some added federal funds.

What's Next?   Texas is no different from other states in its need to find adequate and equitable revenue sources to support the services needed by a rapidly growing citizenry and to make up for federal funding cuts in virtually everything but Medicaid and homeland security that will have a major effect on the states. Although federal spending continues to grow and Texas has become more dependent on it, national policy is still to downsize social spending wherever possible and to make the states more responsible for their own affairs. Changing the size of government is a major conservative agenda item. Many states were ill prepared to meet the challenges facing them, particularly in the face of an erratic economy.[26]

One strategy that the state will continue to pursue is *performance evaluation* and management, including funding cutbacks that are recommended in the biennial Texas Performance Review, which was initiated by the state comptroller and is now led by the Legislative Budget Board. The philosophy reflected in performance evaluation is one of maximizing tax dollars coupled with reducing the cost of state government. The performance evaluation/cutback approach is grounded in a national movement to "reinvent government."[27] This demand emerged from strategic planning and quality management movements in the private sector as sluggish industries had to downsize—or, in the new terminology, "rightsize."

Performance reviews speak not only to "smaller" but also to "smarter." *Governing* magazine published a 50-state report on taxation early in 2003. The report began with the observation that "The vast majority of state tax systems are inadequate for the task of funding a twenty-first-century government."[28] A top rating was four stars. Texas got one star on the adequacy of its revenue, one on the fairness of the system

TABLE 10.1

The Cycle of Bust and Boom: State Budgets in the FY 1986–1987 to FY 2006–2007 Period

Fiscal Year	Summary
86–87	$512 million in budget cuts, $872 million in new taxes
88–89	$5.7 billion in new taxes; intensive study by a Select Committee on Tax Equity, whose recommendations were subsequently ignored
90–91	Legislative authorization of a 12% spending increase by fiscal sleight-of-hand tricks such as using the money reserved to settle lawsuits against the state; another tax study that was ignored
92–93	Initiation of the governor's Texas Performance Review (TPR) spearheaded by Comptroller John Sharp leading to $382 million in budget cuts—not all of which materialized, leading to other cuts in agency budgets for FY 1993; 30 new revenue measures, including a major restructuring of the corporation franchise tax, totaling $2.6 billion; voter approval of a state lottery
94–95	$2 billion in increased revenues with no tax increase due to measures such as TPR savings on Medicaid and changes in tax collection schedules; voter approval of a constitutional amendment limiting the possibility of an income tax to simultaneous local property tax relief
96–97	$9.8 billion in increased revenues with no tax increase due to an improved economy, more federal contributions, more lottery revenues
98–99	Constitutional amendment to triple the homestead tax allowance for school districts, with the revenue loss to be made up with surplus state funds; more than a $7 billion spending increase due to a strong economy, federal funds; failure to produce a bill incorporating recommendations from the governor's tax study
00–01	$506 million in tax breaks, including some for business (research and development tax credits, no severance tax for small producers when prices are low) and some for consumers (the end of the sales tax on over-the-counter medicines and some Internet services plus a back-to-school tax holiday on some items of clothing); continuing pressures on local governments to raise the property tax to make up for a lack of state revenues allocated to them; also, an $11 billion spending increase due to the continuing strong economy
02–03	A session more dedicated to spending than to tax breaks, although there were minor revenue reductions; some improvement in social programs in the $12.2 billion in added spending; the last year of a surplus
04–05	A nasty legislative session because of $9.9 billion revenue shortfall, reduced at the last minute to $9.3 billion because of increased federal funds; spending up about $3 billion due to federal social program dollars; general revenue expenditures reduced for the first time since World War II; many user-fee increases but legislative resistance to a tax bill; highlight was comptroller's initial failure to certify the $117.2 billion budget
06–07	Restoration of a number of social program cuts made in the previous biennium in a record $138.2 billion budget; new business, cigarette, and used car taxes, coupled with a reduction in school property taxes, as a means of funding public education in special session of 2006

The 2006 Special Session on School Finance

"Push finally came to shove" for state policy-makers in 2006 when the state was faced with a June 1 Texas Supreme Court mandate to fix the school finance problem or risk a shutdown of the public school system (see Chapter 8). The governor and legislature had failed to reform school finance in the 2003 and 2005 regular sessions or three previous special sessions called for that purpose.

Issues included finding a replacement for the "Robin Hood" method of having wealthier school districts send money to poorer districts, gaining business support for new taxes, reducing local school property taxes, and perhaps improving the spending power of public schools. When legislators convened on April 17, armed with recommendations from a bipartisan tax commission appointed by the governor, advocacy of a plan by the governor, and a general public concern about the fate of the schools, they were able to produce a solution. To do so, they laid aside the extreme partisanship of the other legislative sessions from 2003 to 2005; the leaders agreed to agree; and they had the advantage of an $8.2 billion budget surplus. Five bills were necessary to effect a new funding system:

1. Replaced some school property taxes with $2.4 billion of the budget surplus (and the likelihood that the rest of the surplus would be absorbed over a four-year period); included teacher pay raises and some additional school funding.
2. Changed the corporate franchise tax to make it applicable to most businesses in the state through the gross receipts tax.

3. Changed the method of calculating the value of used cars in order to maximize the sales tax on them.
4. Added $1.00 to the tax on the cost of a package of cigarettes, making the tax $1.41.
5. Specified that the tax changes in the business, cigarette, and vehicles sales taxes would be used to cover the losses from reductions in local school property taxes and provided that, once the school property tax rate for maintenance and operations drops to $1 per $100 property valuation (it was $1.50), the revenue from new taxes would not only fund the difference but the rest would be used to lower property taxes further.

Almost immediately, questions began about the adequacy of the measures for the long run. Certainly, the schools would open for the 2006–2007 academic year, but the dependence on the surplus, the fact that there was some flexibility that would allow local districts to enact a small property tax rate increase, and the general dependence of the whole plan on a booming economy made analysts wonder how permanent the fix was. Public school advocates had been vocal about the emphasis placed by the governor on reducing property taxes, but the governor also understood the political reality that Texas ranked fourteenth in the nation in individual payments of property taxes.

Sources: Terrence Stutz and Christy Hoppe, "Industry Girds for Special Session," *Dallas Morning News*, March 18, 2006, 1A, 4A; Terrence Stutz, "Lawmakers Head Home Feeling Victorious," *Dallas Morning News*, May 16, 2006, 3A; Claire Cummings, "Perry: Tax Bill Aids Economy," *Dallas Morning News*, May 24, 2006, 3A; Christy Hoppe, "School 'Fix' Plan: Is It Sufficient?" *Dallas Morning News*, May 14, 2006, 1A, 2A.

---

to taxpayers, but three on management of the system. That rating echoed an earlier *Governing* report in 1999 on management practices that gave Texas a "B" for financial, human resource, and technology management, and a "B+" for managing for results, but only a "C" for capital management.[29]

Another strategy that all the states, including Texas, and the national government will use is *privatization*. Two examples are the private prisons that now serve the state and the increasing rate of tuition and fees paid by college students. The first is direct private provision of service; the second is passing along the cost to private citizens rather than burdening the revenue system.

YOU DECIDE

Should Texas Enact a Personal Income Tax?

Texas is one of seven states without a personal income tax. Should the Texas legislature enact an income tax?

Pro

The legislature should modernize the state tax structure and include an income tax because:

➪ The present tax system is regressive; an income tax could make it less so.

➪ An income tax would make billions of new dollars available for state services.

➪ Legislative sessions would be less chaotic because the revenue stream would be more flexible.

➪ The tax system would be fairer because it would be based on ability to pay.

➪ The state would probably receive more federal funds because it could meet the "tax effort" test better.

Con

The legislature should not consider an income tax because:

➪ The tax would require a constitutional amendment except under a very limited circumstance. It would be impossible to get a majority from voters.

➪ Texas does "OK" except when the economy is in a real slump.

➪ It is fair for poor people to pay a higher percentage of their income in taxes because they demand more government services.

➪ A person can control how much he pays in sales taxes by how much he spends.

➪ Texas needs to attract new businesses; a corporate income tax would drive away business.

A third strategy is to *change the revenue structure* in order to avert the **revenue shortfalls** that plagued the state in the 1980s and resurfaced in 2002–2003. The revenue system needs to be made elastic and to increase sufficiently to fund state services.[30] A significant change occurred in 2006 with the five measures passed to fund public schools (see box).

Democratic theory recognizes the equality of the citizenry, and many people think that a tax system that extracts more from the poorer people seriously compromises equality. Since 1991 business is paying a greater share of taxes but, as previously noted, the tax system in Texas is still regressive, placing a proportionately heavier burden on those with the lowest incomes. The reality is that, without an income tax, the state will always have difficulty meeting its revenue needs in anything other than a booming economy. Historically, Texas attracted businesses because they found the state's tax structure favorable. However, the experience of other states with economic development indicates that many modern industries are also concerned about stability in providing for state services. Such stability is difficult in the absence of a flexible tax structure.

Another aspect of revenue structure is the competition among governments for tax sources. National and state governments both tax motor fuels, tobacco, and alcohol, for example. Both the state and local governments have general sales taxes. The upshot is that the combined tax rates begin to vex citizens after a while. Ironically, cuts in federal income tax rates since the 1980s enhance the income tax as a logical new source of state revenue.

For tax restructuring to occur, state politics would have to change. Business has signaled some willingness to change by accepting more business taxes (though benefiting from lower property taxes). Ultimately, private citizens would have to be willing to accept a personal income tax. Only about one-third of private citizens now file an itemized federal tax return, so that one argument that in the past has favored an income tax—the ability to deduct state income taxes but not sales taxes from one's federal income tax return—may be dead, too. Changes in public attitude are critical to legislative action—the mere advocacy of an income tax is a sure ticket out of office.

WHERE DOES THE MONEY GO?

Occasionally an argument is heard in the state's legislative chambers that reflects serious concern about budgeting a particular program—who will benefit from it, does society need it, and how it will be financed. Such concerns are most likely to be evident when a deficit exists and spending has to be cut or when the courts have ordered change. Generally, however, whether funds are allocated for a proposed program depends on which interests favor it and how powerful they are, who and how powerful the opposition is, and the results of compromises and coalitions between these and "swing vote" groups. The political viewpoints of the legislators, the governor, and the state bureaucracy also have an impact on budgetary decisions. In short, decisions about spending public money, like decisions about whom and what to tax, are not made objectively. Rather, they are the result of the complex relationships among the hundreds of political actors who participate in the state's governmental system. The biases of the political system are thus reflected in the biases of state spending.

Budgetary Process

The budgetary process consists of three stages: planning and preparation, authorization and appropriation, and execution (spending). Budget planning and the preparation of the proposed budget is a function of the chief executive in the national government and in forty-four states, but Texas has a **dual budgeting system**. The constitution makes the legislature responsible for the state budget. The legislature is aided in this task by the Legislative Budget Board (LBB) and its staff, who prepare a draft budget. The LBB is made up of four senators and four representatives; it is jointly chaired by the lieutenant governor and the speaker of the House. However, modern governors have understood the importance of the budget as a political tool, and with the aid of the Division of Budget, Planning, and Policy the governor also prepares a budget. This duplicate effort is wasteful, but it does allow for different political perspectives on state spending to be heard. The LBB and governor's staffs hold joint budget hearings at which agency representatives justify their requests.

The authorization and appropriation stage consists of the authorization of programs to be provided by the state and the passage of a bill appropriating money—the state budget. The House Ways and Means (revenues), House Appropriations (spending), and Senate Finance (both revenues and spending) committees are the key legislative players. Agency representatives, the governor's staff, interest-group representatives, and private citizens testify on behalf of the particular agency or program of concern to them. There is considerable forming and re-forming of coalitions as legislators, lobbyists, and committee members bargain, compromise, trade votes, and generally endeavor to obtain as much for "their side" as possible. Past campaign contributions begin to pay off at this stage, and the relative power of different interest groups is reflected in the state budget. For example, political campaigns frequently include a call to "get tough on crime" and to build more prisons; in turn, more prison cells are built. The four main teachers' groups in the state expend considerable effort to influence legislators, and schoolteachers usually get raises, though often small ones. The success of the business lobby is the most problematic. In 1995 business got virtually everything it wanted. In 1997 business buried the tax bill it did not want but also found itself on the receiving end of a lot of negative legislation. In 2003 the business lobby was so dominant that the visitors' gallery where corporate lobbyists sat while legislators were meeting was dubbed "the owner's box." But in 2006 business agreed to accept new taxes to help fund public schools.

The authorization and appropriation stage is a lengthy one, and the Appropriations and Finance committees submit their reports—the two versions of the appropriations bill—near the end of the session. The two versions are never identical, so a 10-member conference committee made up of an equal number of senators and representatives carefully selected by the presiding officers must develop a single conference report on the budget. The two houses must accept or reject the report as it stands, including adequate revenue measures to fund the proposed spending, since Texas has a balanced-budget provision that requires the state comptroller to certify that expected revenues are sufficient to fund expenditures. For example, budget shortfalls in 2003 produced serious disagreements not only between Democrats and Republicans but also between the House and the Senate. At the proverbial eleventh hour, the two houses agreed on a spending plan, which was approved on June 1. That session was unusual also because the legislature invited the governor to play a much more active role than usual in resolving budgeting dilemmas.

The approved appropriations bill next goes to the comptroller for certification. Once the comptroller certifies the budget, it is sent to the governor for signature. Governor Rick Perry and Comptroller Carol Keeton Strayhorn, though both Republicans, were political enemies, with Strayhorn ultimately running against Perry for governor in 2006. The result of their feuding was Strayhorn's frequent threats not to certify the budget. The governor has a very powerful weapon: the line-item veto, which allows him to strike individual spending provisions from the appropriations bill if he disagrees with them. However, the governor cannot add to the budget or restore funding for a pet project that the legislature rejected.

The final budget stage, execution, is a technical one. It includes shifting money into various state funds, issuing state warrants (which are like checks), and auditing expenditures.

Major Expenditures

To the average citizen, which programs and services are funded by the budget are of far greater interest than the details of the budget process. Figure 10.3 shows that health and human services plus education account for three-fourths of the FY 2006–2007 Texas budget of $138.2 billion. The illustration is of the budget passed by the legislature in the regular session of 2005, minus gubernatorial line item vetoes. The 2006 special session increased public school spending by the state.

In 2006, after two regular sessions and four special sessions, the legislature finally produced a package of legislation to change the method of financing public schools. There was little confidence among policy analysts that the plan offered a permanent solution since it depended on the use of a large, one-time budget surplus.

SOURCE: Courtesy of Ben Sargent.

FIGURE 10.3

Texas State Spending by Function, 2006–2007 Biennium (in millions)*

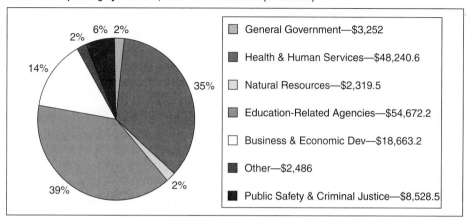

General Government—$3,252

Health & Human Services—$48,240.6

Natural Resources—$2,319.5

Education-Related Agencies—$54,672.2

Business & Economic Dev—$18,663.2

Other—$2,486

Public Safety & Criminal Justice—$8,528.5

*Totals may not add upto 100% due to rounding.

SOURCE: *Fiscal Size Up: 2006–2007* (Austin: Legislative Budget Board, 2005), 2. Total budget: $138.162 billion.

Education.   For FY 2006–2007, 39.6 percent of the state budget was slated for public schools and higher education. About 62 percent—$33.7 billion—was for elementary and secondary schools in the state's 1,090 independent school districts and for state schools for the deaf and visually impaired. The state provides textbooks as well as special services, such as programs for disabled children and vocational courses, the Texas Assessment of Knowledge and Skills (TAKS) achievement tests, school buses, operating costs, and teacher salaries. The state does not pay the total cost of public education, however.

Local school districts share the cost and also are responsible for buildings and other school facilities. Those that can afford it provide supplements to attract the best teachers, buy additional library books, develop athletic programs, and offer students enrichment opportunities. As summarized in Chapter 8, financial equality is the dominant issue affecting public schools. As of 2004, Texas ranked 36th among the states in per capita spending for public education and dead last in the percentage of students graduating from high school.[31]

The other large slice of the education dollar pie—$21 billion—supports higher education: the operations of the general academic institutions and community colleges, the technical college system, health science centers, and extension programs, plus retirement systems and debt payments for buildings. For both junior and senior colleges, a formula based on such factors as semester credit hours determines the basic level of state support, with the formula funding supplemented by special-program funding and affected by performance norms originally adopted in 1992. Local tuition and fees account for a sizeable portion of campus funding. One comparative measure of higher education in Texas is that the state ranks 35th in the number of persons age 25 or older who hold a Bachelor's degree.[32] Another measure is that of all students enrolled in higher education, in Texas 86.9 percent are in public institutions, considerably above the national average of 76.8 percent. As Chapter 11 shows, higher education funding is a continuing issue in Texas.

Health and Human Services.   Over $48 billion—34.9 percent of the budget—is allocated for human services programs, including welfare, unemployment compensation, employment services, workers' compensation, services for special groups such as the blind and the elderly, and health programs such as mental health and retardation programs, treatment of substance abuse, contagious-disease control, and treatment for catastrophic illnesses such as AIDS, cancer, and kidney failure. Of the $48.2 billion total, slightly more than 60 percent of the funding comes from the national government. Chapter 11 discusses the health and welfare systems.

Although expenditures for health and human services are the second largest segment of the state budget, Texas ranked 37th among the fifty states in per capita expenditures for welfare services and 20th in hospital services in 2003. The state has progressed in the rankings for these two service areas since FY 1990–1991, when it was 47th and 36th, respectively.

Business and Economic Development.   Texas's expenditures for business and economic development for FY 2006–2007 are almost $18.7 billion, or 13.5 percent of the budget. This category includes transportation; the Division of Economic Development and Tourism, which promotes the state's economy; the efforts of the Housing and Community Affairs Department on behalf of local governments; and employment and training services. Just under one-half of the expenditures in this category come from federal funds, particularly highway matching funds to maintain and upgrade the 3,233 miles of federal interstate highways in Texas. In 1977 the legislature capped highway expenditures, with the result that the transportation portion of the state budget has declined from 21 percent to almost 11 percent. Texas ranks 44th among the states in per capita spending on highways. Rankings are not available for other services in this category.

Other Major Expenditures.   The next largest category of expenditures is public safety, at just under $8.5 billion, or 6.1 percent of the budget. This category includes law enforcement, prisons, and related programs. Texas ranks 39th in the amount spent per inmate. The remainder of the budget, $8 billion, accounts for 5.9 percent of state expenditures. Services, programs, and agencies in this category include general government—the legislature, the judiciary, the governor, and various management offices—as well as parks, natural resources, and regulatory agencies.

SUMMARY

Economic conditions, the political climate, and power plays are all part of the game of generating revenues for state government and determining how that income will be spent. Both taxing and spending are usually incremental, with major changes rarely occurring. However, the state's boom-and-bust economy, coupled with an anti-tax attitude, has resulted in occasional tax increases and numerous fee hikes.

In comparing Texas with other states, we find that the combined state and local tax burden is relatively low, with Texas ranked in the bottom fifth of all the states. We also note the significant absence of a personal income tax, while noting that the corporate franchise tax is evolving into a corporate income tax by another name. The fundamental difference between the Texas revenue system and that of many other states is the disproportionate burden borne by the poorest citizens. This regressive system raises serious questions about how democratic the tax system is in the state.

Democracies are responsive to the citizenry. The state's spending may not meet the needs of all its citizens, particularly when one considers that Texas ranks in the lower half of the fifty states in its per capita spending for education, welfare services, and highways. It ranks in the top 10 percent only in prison spending. However, the state's rankings have been improving slightly since 1997.

The Texas budget process differs procedurally from the ones used by most other states. These differences include the dual budgeting system, the extraordinary dominance of the presiding officers in the appropriations process, and the virtually absolute veto power of the governor because of the short legislative session.

Important aspects of state finance in Texas are:

1. The reliance on taxes paid directly or indirectly by the individual.
2. The reliance on regressive taxes such as the sales tax as a major revenue source for the state.
3. The restrictions on borrowing.
4. The importance of federal funds to the state budget.
5. The extent to which the budgetary process is dominated by the legislature and the legislature, in turn, is dominated by the presiding officers.
6. The obvious need for diversified revenue sources.

The largest category of expenditure is for education, followed by health and human services, business and economic development, public safety and criminal justice, and "other," which includes everything else. Critical issues affecting some of these state service areas are discussed in the next chapter and in previous chapters.

STUDY QUESTIONS

1. What are the sources of nontax revenue in Texas? How have these changed in recent years?
2. Changing the revenue structure is one possible solution to meet the state's cash needs. Do you think business or individuals should bear the major burden of taxation? What are the consequences of relying too heavily on one or the other? Discuss.
3. This chapter criticizes both the regressiveness and the lack of elasticity in the Texas tax system. What does each of those terms mean? Give and discuss an example of each, then indicate what some of the revenue considerations are in the early years of the twenty-first century.
4. What pitfalls do you think exist because of the dual budgeting system? Do you think there are advantages to such a system?
5. If you could increase spending in any one of the categories shown in Figure 10.3, which would it be? What if the total amount available had to remain

the same? Would you still increase spending in that category? If so, in what category would you decrease expenditures to offset this increase? Discuss the likely effects on services in both the increased and the decreased categories of expenditure.

SURFING THE WEB

Visit the companion site for this book:
http://www.thomsonedu.com/politicalscience/kraemer

The site with official budget data:
http://www.lbb.state.tx.us

The comptroller's site, which includes both revenue estimates and performance data:
http://www.window.state.tx.us

Under "Tax Rates," good comparative date for all fifty states:
http://www.taxadmin.org

Another good source of analytical comparative data:
http://www.taxfoundation.org

NOTES

1. *Fiscal Size-Up 2006–2007* (Austin: Legislative Budget Board, 2005), 8.

2. Wayne King, "Despite Success, Sun Belt Oil Patch Is Finding It's Not Immune to Recession," *New York Times,* June 9, 1981, 11.

3. See, for example, "Texas, The Lone Star State: Business," *Texas Almanac and State Industrial Guide, Millennium Edition* (Dallas: *Dallas Morning News,* 1999), 5.

4. Michael Totty, "It May Be Time for Texas to Rethink Business Plan," *Wall Street Journal,* September 24, 1997, T1.

5. Steve Brown, "Texas No. 2 on List of Best Business Sites," *Dallas Morning News*, October 2, 1996, 1D, 10D.

6. "Expanding in Texas," *Fiscal Notes*, May 1997, 16.

7. See, for example, "Texas Tomorrow," the special section of the *Dallas Morning News* published on December 19, 1999.

8. Larry Bollinger, "County Jobless Rate Low," *Denton Record-Chronicle*, December 17, 1999, 16A.

9. For the budgetary plight of the states, see Robert E. Pierre, "The Budget Squeeze," *Washington Post National Weekly Edition*, March 25–31, 2002; William McKenzie, "Your Worst Nightmare Is Slithering into Your State," *Dallas Morning News*, January 14, 2003, 11A; "2002 Tax and Budget Review and 2003 Budget Preview," *State Fiscal Brief* (a publication of the Rockefeller Institute of Government at the State University of New York), March 2003.

10. Comptroller Strayhorn's e-Newsletter for Friday, March 21, 2003; Katie Fairbank, "Texas Is the Top Exporter in the U.S.," *Dallas Morning News*, March 10, 2003, 1D; Katherine Yung, "Tattered Trade Hopes," *Dallas Morning News*, April 13, 2003, 1D, 5D.

11. See, for example, John Machacek and Susan Roth, "Split Looms over $4 Billion for Security," *USA Today*, March 26, 2003, 13A.

12. Angela Shah, "Texans' Confidence in Economy Erodes," *Dallas Morning News*, March 17, 2003, 1D, 3D; "No Job Growth Seen," *Dallas Morning News*, March 7, 2003, 1D, 11D.

13. See David Broder, "Feds Turn Backs on States," *Austin American-Statesman*, November 24, 2002, G3; "State Fiscal Woes Continue," a May 16, 2002, press release of the National Governors Conference available at www.nga.org; Gene Rose and Ginger Sampson, "Putting the Squeeze On," *State Legislatures*, January 2003, 12.

14. See Angela Shaw, "Post-Storm Economy Is Taking Root in Texas," *Dallas Morning News*, January 26, 2006, 1D, 4D; Elizabeth Souder, "State's Job Growth Maintains Its Pace," *Dallas Morning News*, March 10, 2006, 1D, 5D; Asher Price and Claire Osborn, "Texas Leads Nation in Upper and Middle Income Gap," *Austin American-Statesman*, January 28, 2006, available at http://www.statesman.com/news/content/news/stories/local/01/28inequality.html; Michelle Mittelstadt, "Illegal Immigrants Make Up 5% of Workforce, Study Finds," *Dallas Morning News*, March 8, 2006, 1D, 8D.

15. Angela Shah, "Texas Ranked No. 1 for Corporate Locales," *Dallas Morning News*, March 3, 2006, 1D, 5D.

16. *Fiscal Size-Up 2006-2007*, 15.

17. "Who Pays State and Local Taxes?" *CTJ Update*, March 2003, 1–2. See also Angela Shah, "Texas Has Low Taxes—Depending on Figures," *Dallas Morning News,* January 12, 2003, 1H, 2H.

18. "2005 State Tax Collection by Source," (Washington, DC: Federation of Tax Administrators, 2006), available at http://www.taxadmin.org/fta/rate/05taxdis.html.

19. See Robert S. McIntyre, "Reading the Tea Leaves: 2003 Will Be a Tough Year for Tax Fairness," *CTJ Update*, December 2002, 1, 3; "Bush Tax Advisory Panel: A Missed Opportunity," *Just Taxes*, December 2005, 1–4.

20. The state ad valorem (property) tax was abolished by a 1982 constitutional amendment.

21. "2005 State Tax Revenues" (Washington, DC: Federation of Tax Administrators, 2006), available at http://www.taxadmin.org/fta/rate/05taxbur.html.

22. "Texas' State and Local Tax Burden, 1970–2006" (Washington, DC: Tax Foundation, 2006), available at http://www.taxfoundation.org/news/show/482.html.

23. See Rick VanderKnyff, "The Best and Worst States for Taxes," *MSN Money*, March 22, 2005, available at http://moneycentral.msn.com/content/Taxes/P111921.asp?.

24. *Texas Fact Book 2006* (Austin: Legislative Budget Board, 2006), 20. See also "Federal Taxing and Spending Benefit Some States, Leave Others Paying Bill" (Washington, DC: Tax Foundation, 2004), available at http://www.taxfoundation.org/taxingspending.html.

25. Dave McNeely, "No Texas Income Tax Means More for Feds," *Austin American-Statesman*, April 15, 1997, A11.

26. Michael Powell, "Funding Isn't Part of the Plan," *Washington Post National Weekly Edition*, May 12–18, 2003, 21, provides an excellent summary of the budgetary plight of the states in 2003 as the national government continued to pass mandates on such matters as education and homeland security and to offload the cost of social programs to the states. See also, Donald

Boyd, *State and Local Governments Face Continued Fiscal Pressure* (Albany, NY: Rockefeller Institute of Government Fiscal Studies Program, 2005).

27. See, for example, David Osborne and Ted Gaebler, *Reinventing Government* (Reading, MA: Addison-Wesley, 1992), especially chapter 5 on "Results-Oriented Government"; Jonathan Walters, "The Cult of Total Quality," *Governing*, May 1992, 38–41; and the many reports stemming from the Texas Performance Review and the National Performance Review.

28. Katherine Barrett, Richard Greene, Michele Mariani, and Anya Sostek, "The Way We Tax: A 50-State Report," available at http://www.governing.com/gpp/2003/gp3intro.htm, quotation on p. 1.

29. "Texas," *Governing*, February 1999, 80.

30. See, for example, Paul Burka, "Ten Ways to Fix Texas," *Texas Monthly*, August 2005, 185–189.

31. Comparative data are drawn from "Texas at a Glance," *Texas Fact Book 2006* (Austin: Legislative Budget Board, 2006), 18–24.

32. *Fiscal Size-Up, 2006-2007*, 51. If not otherwise specified, comparative data in the analysis of expenditures come from pp. 46–51.

11

ISSUES IN PUBLIC POLICY

. . . With growing numbers of uninsured people and costs out of control, states are looking at radical changes to Medicaid.

Kristine Goodwin
State Legislatures, February 2006

Water is like sex. Everybody thinks that there's more of it around than there really is and that everybody else is getting more than his fair share.

Old Wyoming Saying

INTRODUCTION

Texas, like all other states, must address a variety of problems and needs through an array of programs and services that constitutes the policy agenda for the state. When elected officials develop **public policy**, they are establishing priorities for programs that benefit the public. However, agreement rarely exists on what those priorities should be. People even argue, sometimes intensely, about whether government should address some problems at all. Consequently, many controversial issues confront state policy makers. This climate of disagreement and debate is part of a democratic society. Also, even when there is agreement on a particular issue, the fiscal health of the state (see Chapter 10) can complicate the policy agenda considerably. Rarely does a state have enough money to fund all the desired programs, and state finance itself becomes a major policy issue.

The development of public policy begins with the emergence of a problem that needs to be addressed. When someone in government recognizes the need to deal with a problem, it is placed on the policy agenda. One way in which a prospective program or service makes its way onto the policy agenda is through the efforts of the governor and key legislators (see Chapters 6 and 7). Often gubernatorial and legislative viewpoints conflict. In 1999 legislators of both parties were reluctant to slow down the governor's push for a presidential nomination—having a president from one's state yields all sorts of benefits. Thus, Governor Bush was successful in his social and business initiatives but still failed to get through a school voucher program. The program would have allowed students greater choice of elementary and secondary schools; however, voucher programs are complicated because they can also have a detrimental effect on the low-performing schools that most need state help, and the governor's plan died in the state senate. Between 2003 and 2006, the governor, lieutenant governor, and speaker all agreed that the Robin Hood plan of funding public schools (see Chapter 8) had to go, but they substantially disagreed on how to accomplish a new method of school finance. In May 2006, after two regular and four special sessions, the state's leadership finally came to an agreement on a school funding system (see Chapter 10), largely because the state supreme court had imposed a June 1 deadline to solve the problem.[1]

A second way in which a prospective program or service gets onto the political agenda is through the political processes described in Chapter 3. Interest groups and lobbyists make known the priorities they think the state should set. These individuals and groups work through both elected officials and the bureaucracy, but they are especially vigorous in pursuing legislative support for their demands. The water policy discussed in this chapter is an example of the coming together of legislative, bureaucratic, and interest-group concerns.

Another avenue for setting the policy agenda is through the *intergovernmental* system (the complex relationships among federal, state, and local governments) and the *intragovernmental* system (the relationships that cut across the branches of one government, whether it is federal, state, or local). Often these relationships result in a **mandate**, a term that refers to an action of one government or branch of government that requires another government to act in a certain way. National clean-air standards that must be implemented by state and local governments are an example. Intergovernmental and intragovernmental mandates help policy makers to identify and define issues even when they would prefer to ignore them. Mandates are often burdensome to the lower level of government, which is required to act even though it receives no funding to help implement the new programs.

Mandates have several possible sources. These include the courts, administrative regulations, legislative actions, and/or highly publicized shifts in national priorities. For example, changes in Texas public school finance began in 1973 with a federal court order, continued with a 1987 state court order to provide a more equitable and "efficient" system of funding public schools, and concluded with a 2006 mandate to provide a new finance system (see Chapter 8).[2] Similarly, the state prison system was tied up in a long-running court suit from 1971 until 2002, when the suit was dismissed because the state seemed headed in the right direction to correct historic problems such as over-crowding, abuse of prisoners, and poor health facilities.[3]

The welfare system in Texas is a product of the state's emphasis on efficiency, national and state budget cutting and changing national priorities, and state efforts to gain administrative approval from the federal bureaucracy. All states are struggling to provide adequate welfare services in the midst of federal changes. The transition from welfare to workfare is discussed in this chapter.

An example of intergovernmental influence through administrative regulations is environmental standards. Across the country, states are trying to deal with provisions of the Clean Water Act, the Safe Drinking Water Act, and the Clean Air Act. As this chapter notes, Texas is one of the states furthest from meeting the national standards.

Another example of how public policy gets set is the intragovernmental example of state-assisted higher education in Texas. A public university is a state agency, just as is the Department of Insurance or the Department of Parks and Wildlife. As we will see later in this chapter, the 1997 and the 2005 Legislatures, after years of ignoring higher education, mandated a number of procedures previously regarded as local business for the institutions. In doing so, the legislature was giving explicit instructions to executive-branch agencies.

Although mandates may be difficult to implement, they are not the causes of society's problems. Urbanization, industrialization, inflation, economic downturns, depletion of natural resources, the world oil market, citizen demand, and the curtailment of federal funds to state and local governments are among the causes of the policy problems that confront Texas. Because new and different problems constantly emerge, no one can conceive of all the challenges that may be on the future Texas policy agenda. Moreover, Texas's dynamic demographic changes, including the ethnic composition and average age of the population, have also contributed to the problems.

Neither is it possible to explore all the major items on the present agenda. Some issues—the fiscal crisis, campaign finance, school finance, the crisis in the courts, and civil liberties, for example—are discussed elsewhere in this book. Other issues that are not discussed here include the need for economic diversification, juvenile crime, placement of the mentally retarded in group homes, child care and child abuse, care of the elderly, the fact that many persons cannot afford health insurance, illegal aliens, substance abuse, and acquired immune deficiency syndrome (AIDS).

Simply put, this chapter samples the diverse issues on the agenda, selecting *poverty and welfare, higher education*, and *the environment* to illustrate policy-making in the nation's second-largest state.

The issues the state chooses to address and how state policy makers attempt to solve public problems once again allow an examination of how democratic the Texas political system is. Do policy makers try to deal with a wide variety of issues affecting all citizens, or do they mainly look at issues placed on the agenda by political elites? Can they solve contemporary problems in the context of a conservative political culture when many of the issues stem from the needs of the "have-nots" of society, who traditionally have been supported by liberals? Do they consider alternative viewpoints? Can their policies be implemented effectively, or are they merely "smoke and mirrors" that only *seem* to address the problem?

Overall, state policy makers have coped reasonably well. It is true that Texas, when compared with other states, tends to rank toward the bottom in many service areas. It is equally true that the state is sometimes slow to respond to emerging issues. However, state officials can proceed no faster than the public is willing to move and to fund. One of the awkward aspects of democracy is that following majority opinion does not always lead to wise or swift policy decisions.

POVERTY AND WELFARE

Conservative agendas have increasingly dominated national and state politics since 1994, and they have long shaped Texas politics. In short, for reasons discussed throughout this book, the viewpoints of individuals in upper-income brackets often dominate public policy. This political fact of life is particularly important when we examine the issues of poverty and welfare. Whenever the government attempts to improve the quality of life for the poor, it is producing *redistributive public policy*[4]— that is, policy that redistributes wealth from those who have the most to those who have the least. Inevitably, then, poverty and welfare politics produce strong emotions and sharp political divisions.

In Texas, as elsewhere, some policy makers and ordinary citizens think that poor people could be more effective at helping themselves through job training, education, and looking for work. Even when compassion exists for those too ill or infirm to work, it does not spill over into sympathy for individuals seen to be shirkers. Other people think that, in addition to well-documented reasons such as debilitating physical or mental illness, people are poor because they have never been given an opportunity to have a good education or relevant job training. In truth, all of these opinions are correct. The reasons for poverty are many. The task at hand is to determine how the state of Texas addresses poverty issues.

Any state's role in combating poverty and seeing to the welfare of its citizens is a mix of both state policy and federal programs. Because of changes in national policy, Texas, which has traditionally relied on federal funds for its welfare programs, has had to make changes in its own welfare system. However, the state continues to rely on the national government as a principal source of funding for welfare programs.

Poverty in Texas

The poverty guideline for a family of three was $16,090 in the continental United States in 2005 and $16,600 in 2006.[5] The guideline is often stated for a family of three because a typical poor family consists of a mother and two children; an additional family member increases the line by $3,400. The guideline allows for the much higher living costs in Alaska and Hawaii but makes no allowance for the higher living costs in major cities as compared with small towns and rural areas. The U.S. Bureau of the Census reports poverty statistics. The most recent figures are three-year averages for 2002–2004 reported in August 2005. At that time, 16.4 percent of Texans lived in poverty (the U.S. average was 12.4 percent). Only the District of Columbia, Mississippi, Louisiana, New Mexico, and Arkansas had higher levels of poverty.[6] Ironically, even though Texas led the country in the number of new jobs created during much of this time period, many of those jobs were low paying. As a result, the median income for a family of four in Texas in 2004 was $41,759, compared with $44,864 as the national average.[7] Seventeen of the 100 poorest counties in the country are in Texas—Starr, Brooks, Zavala, and Presidio are the poorest.[8] Slightly more than one-fifth of all the children in the state lived in poverty.[9]

A special set of public policy issues confronted Texas in 2005 and 2006 when the state absorbed as many as 373,000 Hurricane Katrina and Hurricane Rita evacuees from other states, with about half of them remaining in the state permanently. Demands on social services, transportation, and law enforcement all increased rapidly, but the state and the municipalities showed unusual compassion in dealing with the storm victims.

Sources: Nicole Gelinas, "Hero's Task," *Dallas Morning News*, April 30, 2006, 1P, 5P; "Lone Star Shelter," *Texas Observer*, September 23, 2005, 6–15; Richard Morin and Lisa Rein, "Many New Orleans Evacuees Won't Return," *Washington Post*, September 15, 2005, reported at http://www.msnbc.msn.com/id/9359357/print/1/displaymode/1098/.

Half of these poor children live in families that have at least one working parent. The reality is that the very young and the very old are the most likely to be poor. One measure of that phenomenon is that, of the 2.5 million Texas recipients of Medicaid assistance in 2004, 59 percent were children 14 years of age or younger and 14 percent were 65 years of age or older.[10] Rural south and southwest Texas and the ghettos and barrios of the largest cities have the highest number of poor people.

Texas clearly is not so rich as it likes to brag that it is. Moreover, these numbers may be *deflated* somewhat because of the difficulty of getting an accurate count of homeless people. Neither the state nor the national government has a very accurate measure of the number of homeless people because the homeless are a mix of people who sometimes have work, sometimes do not, and include a substantial number of mentally ill people. When adequate help is provided, the majority of homeless move into housing and find a job, according to the U.S. Bureau of the Census.[11] The Bureau conducted a large-scale study of homeless persons and providers of services to the homeless in 1995 and 1996 that estimated that there were almost 2 million homeless persons nationwide. It determined that "overall the homeless were deeply impoverished and most were ill." Two-thirds had some type of chronic illness, with more than half of these beset with mental illness. More than one-quarter had a childhood history of living in an institution or being in foster care. Given the population size of Texas and the entrenched poverty in some parts of the state, one can safely assume a sizable homeless population.

The Players and the Major Programs

The key players in delivering services to the needy in Texas are four large departments under the aegis of the Heath and Human Service Commission—the Department of Aging and Disability Services, the Department of State Health Services, the Department of Assistive and Rehabilitative Services, and the Department of Family and Protective Services. Overall policy setting is done by the Health and Human Services Commission (HHSC), which acts through an executive commissioner appointed by the governor. The HHSC was reorganized in 2003 and various functions from other departments and bureaus were moved to its four agencies. The HHSC has a dominant role in containing expenses for the major health and welfare programs and in preventing fraud. Employment services and benefits are handled through the Texas Workforce Commission.

In Texas, programs to help needy citizens have long been funded primarily with federal dollars supplemented by whatever additional funds the state was obligated to provide to be eligible for the federal dollars. The Texas Constitution places a ceiling on welfare expenditures. Since a 1982 amendment, that ceiling has been 1 percent of the state budget for general public assistance, so long as the state ceiling did not conflict with federal welfare program requirements. However, this provision is more flexible than the previous one, which was expressed in dollar amounts.

The national Social Security Administration provides direct case assistance for aged, disabled, and blind Texans through the Supplemental Security Income (SSI) program and channels funds to the state HHSC for the Temporary Assistance to Needy Families (TANF) program, which replaced the old Aid to Families with Dependent Children (AFDC) program. Temporary Assistance to Needy Families is a program for families with needy children under the age of 18 who have been deprived of financial support because of the absence, disability, unemployment, or underemployment of both parents. The U.S. Department of Agriculture administers the food stamp program, passing dollars through the HHSC. Medicaid, a program of medical assistance for the needy, is a joint federal–state program administered through the HHSC. Medicaid's principal programs are for children, the aged, the blind and disabled, and maternity care.

TANF, food stamps, and Medicaid are the largest welfare programs. These programs all work in conjunction with one another so that a person eligible to receive help from one program is sometimes eligible to receive help from one or more of the others. Although most states supplement these programs, Texas historically has chosen to provide "bare bones" programs. A typical welfare family of three—a mother and two children who receive no child support—received $265 for food stamps and $233 for TANF in fiscal year 2005. The complexity of the Medicaid formulas and the constant program changes make it impossible to assign a precise number in this category, but one can estimate an average of $400 per month. Thus, the typical Texas payment of approximately $998 to a qualifying family left the family $343 short of the poverty line for that year.

Table 11.1 shows the fluctuating dependence of many Texans on food stamps and TANF early in the twenty-first century. The requirements for all three programs

TABLE 11.1

Texas TANF, Food Stamp, and Medicaid Recipients, Fiscal Years 2002–2007

Program	2002	2003	2004	2005	2006*	2007*
TANF	356,765	367,893	273,520	224,284	228,427	232,171
Food stamp	1,583,000	1,885,000	2,287,000	2,449,000	2,452,000	2,459,000
Medicaid acute care	2,082,697	2,446,119	2,659,892	2,758,730	2,986,661	3,114,218

*Estimated.

SOURCE: *Fiscal Size Up: 2006–2007 Biennium* (Austin: Texas Legislative Budget Board, 2005), 166, 113.

are different. TANF is "welfare," basically for those without jobs. Recipients of both food stamps and Medicaid often include the working poor. The table indicates an overall steady increase in the number of Medicaid recipients, a fairly steady decline in recipients of welfare, and a modest increase in food stamp recipients. Changing federal and state policy, economic conditions, and population changes contribute to the variations in the numbers from year to year. Medicaid has been the subject of the most serious debate among policy makers in recent years because of the growing cost of health care.

Other social services include daycare, foster homes, energy assistance for low-income persons (to help with heating bills), and job training. Health care is, of course, a problem affecting everyone, and problems shared by persons from all social classes tend to have a higher degree of political support than problems that afflict only the poor.[12] The Texas Department of State Health Services and the Texas Department of Aging and Disability Services are the two largest agencies providing for the health needs of Texas citizens. State services range from programs for crippled children and for individuals with devastating diseases, such as cancer and tuberculosis, to rehabilitation of trainable mental retardates and the control of rabies in skunks. Although such programs are not restricted to the poor, their existence eases the burden of medical costs for less well-off Texans. Additionally, a joint state–county system of indigent health care has existed since 1985. Nationally and in Texas, almost two-thirds of all health assistance goes to children, but the highest costs are associated with the disabled and with the elderly.[13]

Another related service is unemployment compensation—that is, payments to unemployed workers administered by the Texas Workforce Commission, which also assists individuals in finding jobs and keeps records of employment in the state. Unemployment compensation is a joint federal–state effort. The basic funding method is a tax on wages paid by employers, plus any surcharge needed to make the system fiscally sound, and reimbursements from governmental units for any unemployment benefits drawn by their former employees. If a state has its own unemployment compensation program and an agency to administer it, the employers can charge off most of the tax on their federal tax returns. If the federal government administers the program directly, employers cannot take advantage of the tax write-off. In Texas, unemployment benefits vary according to previous wage and disability status.

The New "Down and Out"

The recession of 2001–2003 produced some strange side effects. Social service agencies in counties heavily populated by previously high-salaried individuals in the telecommunications industry—Collin County, for example—were receiving requests for financial assistance for out-of-work telecom executives and engineers. Caseworkers reported in the spring of 2003 that some of the applicants needed a "reality check." Unwilling to let go of their big houses, expensive cars, or club memberships, they were applying for assistance to continue their upscale life style. They were not successful.

In calendar year 2005, unemployment compensation payments ranged from a minimum of $54 to a maximum of $336 per week, depending on prior earnings.[14] Benefits are payable for a period up to 26 weeks except when the federal government extends the period, as it does in the wake of prolonged high unemployment.

Another employment-related program is workers' compensation, which provides medical support for workers injured on the job or made ill by the job environment. The workers' compensation program is administered by the Texas Department of Insurance and has been laden with problems following a 2005 legislative overhaul of the program.[15]

Recent Policy Developments

Early in the 1990s, many states including Texas had addressed the issue of welfare reform, all of them with emphases converting welfare to workfare, forcing "deadbeat dads" and "misanthrope moms" to provide child support, and employing modern electronics to aid in tracking those in the welfare system. In 1996 Congress passed and President Bill Clinton signed the Personal Responsibility and Work Opportunity Reconciliation Act, otherwise known as welfare reform. Fundamentally, this legislation followed the lead of the states in getting people off welfare and onto payrolls.

The *workfare* approach carried with it not only such positive values as helping welfare recipients regain their self-esteem by becoming better trained and gainfully employed and freeing up money for other programs but also such negatives as more rules and regulations. The federal reform allowed five years of welfare support, but the time clock begins to tick from the first date a recipient receives a check even though the person might have extensive training to undergo. Texas provides for only three years of assistance although the average time on welfare is less than two years. The federal requirement is that the individual be working within two years, without the flexibility of the earlier Texas plan that includes job training, parenting or life skills training, and education or literacy training within the definition of work.[16]

In their concern for reducing welfare fraud, putting people to work, and generally moving one step away from Big Government, the politicians initially failed to address the fundamental reality of welfare reform—namely, that the legislation forces single mothers of dependent children to go to work and may cost their children health care through Medicaid. Since workfare means that their children will either be left alone all day or placed in daycare, this consequence would seem to contradict the much-touted "family values" espoused by many politicians. Less parental care is also likely to have further consequences of more juvenile crime, poorer school performance, and thus, paradoxically, even more welfare dependency. Welfare reform illustrates how complex social issues are. In trying to fix one set of problems, it is all too easy to create another set. The health care aspect of the problem was addressed in the federal Balanced Budget Act of 1997, which created the Children's Health Insurance Program (CHIP) for low-income children. Child care has proved more elusive and is heavily dependent on local nonprofit and community programs. In fact, the administration of President George W. Bush preferred faith-based programs to solve many social problems, including child care; faith-based programs are those provided by churches and other religious organizations rather than by public agencies.

The 1996 federal act created a "cafeteria-style" welfare system for the states, with each state receiving a block grant for welfare support that a state could apportion among programs that the state judged as having the highest priority. Aid for Families with Dependent Children (AFDC), which had made welfare a right, was transformed into Temporary Assistance to Needy Families (TANF), with the stipulation that individuals have no automatic entitlement to welfare support. Proportionately less money now flows from Washington, and the states are allowed under the national legislation to slash their own welfare payments by 20 percent with no loss of federal funds.

One way to stretch a tight budget is to limit access to state services, for example, by tightening eligibility requirements for social services. Often the requirements are liberalized in a later legislative session when money is not so limited. Such was the situation in 2003, when requirements were tightened, and 2005, when they were loosened.

SOURCE: Courtesy of Ben Sargent.

Because budget surpluses in 1999 and 2001 allowed the state to fund social services, the legislature softened eligibility requirements and broadened some programs in those years. But with a faltering economy producing fewer tax revenues and more need for social services, by 2003 social service funding once again became a focal point of the legislative session. Medicaid expenses nationally were growing 7 to 8 percent a year, a major problem for Texas and many other states that were already facing deficits, as this chapter-opening quote indicates. State officials across the country found themselves having to decide among many well-deserving programs such as health care, higher education, highways, and high schools.[17] The opening ploy of the Texas legislative session was a House plan to deal with the budget shortfall via massive cuts in social services; part of this strategy was to pare back social services that House conservatives detested. That plan was unfeasible not only because it lacked Senate support but also because cutting state services meant cutting federal dollars. Nevertheless, the combination of revenue shortfalls coupled with an unwillingness to raise taxes led to significant cuts, even though the cuts were not so deep as the House wanted.

The 79th Legislature in 2005 moved to shore up the health and human services programs somewhat. Financial supplements were made to cover Medicaid and CHIP costs and the application and operations aspects of these programs were modified, although to the great confusion of clients.[18] Some of the people cut from services in 2003 were restored to the rolls in 2005.

Analysis

Signals sent during recent legislative years were not entirely clear because some years the legislature seemed to provide needed help for the poor; in other years, lawmakers found ways to cut the social services budget. One reading is that, despite a set of elected officials even more conservative than those of the past, the state had developed a social conscience with regard to the needy. An alternative interpretation is that the state was mainly interested in money—finding ways not to spend state dollars on the poor and finding ways to get a bigger piece of the federal welfare pie. Beyond dispute is the fact that Texas has a welfare problem that is tied to social divisions that rest on ethnic conflicts and struggles between the "haves" and the "have-nots."

Overall, a combination of stringent qualifications for recipients and a booming economy resulted in one effect desired by state and federal welfare reformers—namely, a sharp drop in the number of welfare recipients as, Table 11.1 shows. Although slight increases in TANF recipients were predicted for 2006 and 2007, they were very small when one considers population growth and the additional people from hurricane disaster sites. The number of food stamp recipients increased sharply in fiscal year (FY) 2004 but then leveled out. Medicaid recipients continue to grow in number, and given the costliness of health care, this rise has been alarming both for Texas policy makers and those in all other states.[19]

The second effect was that Texas, like other states, is not spending all the money to which it is entitled by federal programs. According to *State Legislatures* magazine, the states with the highest poverty rates, Texas included, were spending less than 69 percent of their allotted funds. The states as a whole were spending only 76 percent of their block grant funds.[20] This publication, which is published by the National

Conference of State Legislatures, points out two important facts about the underspending. First, those individuals who remain on welfare will be very difficult to place in jobs for reasons such as domestic violence, little training, lack of transportation, and lack of child care. Second, innovative states—Arizona, Colorado, Florida, Maine, Michigan, New York, Washington—used the federal funds not spent on TANF recipients to provide a variety of solutions to hard-core unemployment and chronic welfare-ism.

Several factors make it likely that social services will be a perennial issue in Texas politics. First, the economy swings between boom and bust, and when the economy is sluggish, the number of aid recipients increases at the same time that the state is less able to pay for the services. Second, the state's immigration rate is among the highest in the country, and many of the immigrants lack essential job skills. They often constitute the working poor. Third, early studies of the impact of the 1996 federal legislation showed that the poorest 20 percent of welfare families have lost income and become even poorer and that Texas, while moving hundreds of thousands of people off the welfare rolls, has had some trouble placing them in jobs. Subsequent national tax and spending policy intensified the phenomenon of the rich getting richer and the poor getting poorer as more cuts in social services were proposed.[21] Fourth, the conservativism of Texans is becoming even more evident in a Republican-dominated state in which many, although not all, elected officials have an inherent dislike of social programs.

HIGHER EDUCATION

Higher education in Texas includes 35 general academic teaching institutions, 3 lower-division institutions, 50 community and junior college districts, 1 technical college system, and 9 health-related institutions. The Texas Higher Education Coordinating Board is the principal regulatory authority, although each system or nonsystem independent institution has a governing board.

Higher education, more than any other policy area, seems to ride a roller coaster in Texas. In the 1970s and early 1980s, when the state was flush with funds from oil and gas taxes, Texas hired so many scholars away from out-of-state colleges that the practice inspired a rueful national joke about "locking up the faculty so a Texas school won't get them." When the state's budgetary surpluses turned to revenue shortfalls in the mid-1980s, higher education was the first program area to suffer, and it continued to suffer for a decade. Higher education received some budgetary relief in the late 1990s, but by 2003, this program area again represented one from which to seek funds for other programs. Simply put, higher education represents the largest budgeted amount available for reallocation. Public education, prisons, and mental health and retardation were all under court mandates to improve services. Welfare and highway programs were dominated by federal funding, not state dollars. In addition, few legislators really understand how colleges and universities work; thus, many of them are critical of educational spending. Too, a perennial debate exists about the extent to which higher education benefits the state as a whole versus only the college students who avail themselves of it; that debate leads to the question of who should pay for higher education. Essentially then, except as a source of funds for other programs, higher education is often ignored.[22]

The End of the Twentieth Century

1984–1996.   Some pluses did exist during the "dark decade" of the 1980s. A 1984 constitutional amendment provided a wider distribution of Permanent University Funds (PUF) to satellite campuses of the University of Texas System and the Texas A&M System and established a Higher Education Assistance Fund (HEAF) for non-UT and non-A&M institutions for capital expenditures. These expenditures include equipment, library materials, land, rehabilitation of older buildings, and new construction. In 1985 legislators created a science and high-technology research fund linked to the state's interest in attracting high-technology industries as a means of moving away from the oil-dominated economy.

The legislature also created a Select Committee on Higher Education to review higher education with a wide-sweeping agenda. The select committee report took the form of a Texas Charter for Public Higher Education, which was adopted by the 70th Legislature in 1987. Although the study and the recommendations were broad, the major outcomes were increased research funding and modest increases in operating funds following the 1987 legislative session. Two-year colleges received little benefit from the charter.

From 1989 through the 1995 legislative session, higher education received modest increases that allowed it to stay more or less even with 1985 operations—but 1985 and 1986 were the primary budget-slashing years. The legislature seemed particularly willing to give small increases if the colleges and universities supported tuition increases.

To keep pace with enrollment growth, inflation, and other factors resulting in cost increases, the institutions began to raise dollars wherever possible. Particularly at the universities, students found themselves paying fees for almost everything as the institutions sought adequate dollars to provide operating funds; state tuition began to inch up; and graduate students on most campuses were asked to pay local tuition rates above the state minimum. Some two-year colleges strove to keep tuition and fees low, but in others tuition neared the rate assessed by universities. In short, the state was moving to privatize "public" higher education by investing proportionally fewer tax dollars in its support, thus forcing colleges and universities to rely ever more heavily on contributions from alumni as well as on increases in student tuition and fees.

In other states, the same development was occurring. The fact that higher education funding was troubled in a majority of the states by the early 1990s, however, prevented another faculty drain such as Texas experienced in the mid-1980s.

In 1992 higher education had its own constitutional dilemma paralleling the *Edgewood* decision on public school finance as described in Chapter 8. The League of United Latin American Citizens (LULAC) filed suit against state officials, the Coordinating Board, and the officials of predominantly Anglo universities, claiming that South Texas institutions were discriminated against in the allocation of graduate and professional programs in the state.[23] Responding to the *LULAC* case, the state directed higher education dollars to remedy the problems. However, efforts to fix a problem once again caused other problems in that the attempt to upgrade historically Hispanic institutions merely made worse the already precarious funding situation of the non-Hispanic institutions.

As the state economy improved, higher education did receive increased funding for FY 1994–1995 and FY 1996–1997, although much of the money went to continue the South Texas initiatives mandated by the court. However, the HEAF program was re-authorized, and increasing enrollments were covered by the funding.

1997–2000.   Before the 1997 legislative session, there were four obviously problematic areas in higher education. First, higher education had an *image problem* that plagued it during legislative sessions. Elected officials often saw higher education as composed of a group of affluent institutions that salted away their private contributions and revenues from auxiliary enterprises such as student unions, bookstores, and athletics while constantly seeking more state dollars.

A second problem was *continued marginal funding.* Enrollment growth outstripped faculty and staff growth. Thus, many institutions experienced an increased reliance on part-time faculty and graduate assistants, a development that made the image problem worse. Other problems had also resulted from inadequate funding—larger classes, fewer book and journal purchases by the libraries, and some buildings continuing in poor repair despite PUF and HEAF expenditures. Community colleges had an additional problem in that their districts often coincide with those of public schools; given the massive reorganization of public school finance, the college boards were sometimes reluctant to seek a tax increase to generate more funding of the local two-year colleges. In short, while public and higher education were both vital to the state economy, higher education's consistent under-funding meant that the needed quality was almost impossible to achieve. Although higher education was not being cut in the mid-1990s, neither was it keeping pace with population growth or state spending in general.

Third, *higher education was being privatized* steadily. This phenomenon occurred in several ways. Institutions were encouraged to sell long-standing university operations such as bookstores and residence halls to private companies. They developed partnerships with private corporations to build parking garages, hotels, and residence halls, and, later, even to allow gas well–drilling on campus. Depending on the spending patterns of the institution, the state has paid less than one-third of the actual costs for some institutions but more than one-half for most. Finally, students were now constantly being asked for more dollars—that is, to support their state institutions with private dollars.

The fourth situation problem was that *higher education was rarely high on the policy agenda.* Although it is clearly linked to economic development because it provides valuable human resources trained to conduct the business of business, the legislature had not paid much attention to higher education since the Edgewood ruling invalidated public school funding. At the end of the 1995 legislative session, some key senators indicated that higher education might begin to receive attention in 1997. They proved to be prophetic.

Hopwood.   When the 75th Legislature convened in January 1997, higher education clearly had a place on the policy agenda. The political fact of life that placed it there was the difficulty of coping with an increasingly diverse state. Texas colleges and universities were heavily affected by the *Hopwood v. State* case in 1996 that struck down an *affirmative action* admissions program at the University of Texas at Austin Law School—that is, a program that gives advantages to certain classes of people, including ethnic minorities, because of historic discrimination against them. Additionally, Attorney General Dan Morales issued guidelines widely applying the court ruling beyond admissions, particularly to include scholarships and hiring unless the educational institution openly demonstrated past discrimination with ongoing effects and stipulated specific remedies to that discrimination. The case was upheld by the U.S. Fifth Circuit Court of Appeals and allowed to stand by the U.S. Supreme Court,[24] which did not hear a university affirmative action admissions case until 2003.[25]

The universities were unhappy: None wished to admit to past discrimination, and all—especially the urban ones—saw a future of sliding enrollments and an inability to serve their clientele. The ethnic minority communities were also unhappy—they saw fewer opportunities for admission and fewer opportunities for scholarship assistance. Even the U.S. Department of Education was unhappy: The short-term effects of *Hopwood* were plain to see. Black and Hispanic enrollment in professional schools dropped sharply.[26] In some cases, the students simply sought an environment in which they felt more comfortable, often out of state. In others, the students sought admission to schools where scholarship opportunities were greater. In still other cases, their place was taken by students with stronger admission credentials. The 1997 Legislature created a new admission system that required an institution to accept any student in the top 10 percent of the high school graduating class and encouraged acceptance of the top 25 percent. Shifting the admissions criterion from standardized tests to class standing allowed minority students with relatively low test scores but high grades to gain admittance to elite university campuses. Although the law helped, and was intended to help, minority students, it was not racially discriminatory because it required admission based on a measure of achievement rather than on the applicant's ethnicity. Eighteen other admissions criteria were spelled out, including first-generation-in-college and economic background, but not race or ethnicity.

The majority of Texans approved the *Hopwood* decision and its implication that race was no longer a valid criterion for university admission or financial assistance, although the decision was not as well supported by ethnic minorities as by Anglos. The case is merely symbolic of American struggles with the concept of affirmative action (AA). At its simplest, AA merely calls for ensuring that all individuals have an opportunity to be part of the "pool"—whether the pool of talent is for work or admission. At its most complex, AA results in quotas for hiring or admission based on one of the protected categories—race, ethnicity, gender, disability, age, or veteran's status. Thus, a concern for equal opportunity can be interpreted as favoritism or reverse discrimination. Issues such as affirmative action illustrate why democracy, however desirable, can be such a difficult form of government.

Back to Basics.   The other major issue confronting the 1997 Legislature was the need to address pent-up funding needs in higher education. Begun as an initiative of the chancellors of the six public university systems (University of Houston, University of Texas, Texas A&M, Texas Tech, University of North Texas, and Texas State University), who called themselves The Coalition, the back-to-basics movement became the theme of a united higher education.[27] The back-to-basics proposals laid out a strategy to achieve a competitive edge for the state by taking the following actions:

- Increase partnerships between higher education and public schools.
- Increase efforts to help at-risk students who are most likely to drop out or "stop out" (interrupt their education).
- Reverse the trend of less-experienced faculty members teaching lower-division courses.
- Provide more state financial assistance.

The information provided to legislators called attention to the need for a better-educated work force if Texas was to continue to prosper economically. The report pointed out the below-average income of the state, the growing number of unskilled workers, and the importance of a highly productive workforce to provide the state with adequate public revenues. The Coalition sought $1 billion in new funding to improve higher education and to address the state's educational problems.

Legislators were spurred by thoughts of economic decline, by the consequences of not accommodating a growing segment of the population, and by having more money to spend than usual. As a consequence, more than 1,000 bills dealing with higher education were introduced during the 1997 session. Some addressed *Hopwood*. Some addressed back-to-basics issues. Some addressed pent-up needs of institutions. Overshadowing all of the measures was a legislative desire to gain more control over the institutions, to treat them more like other state agencies. The result was typical politics—give a little, get a little. In exchange for $593 million in new funding, the universities received a number of mandates, including those establishing professorial performance reviews, tightening up on funding for credit hours generated by "professional students," dictating a statewide core curriculum, and forcing the institutions to find ways to generate more of their own funds for salaries and benefits.

1999. The issues in 1999 were little changed from those of 1997. Higher education sought more resources and got them—$940 million more. In exchange, both four-year and two-year institutions were expected to yield more control to Austin and to be especially attentive to issues of how accessible college is to anyone who wants to attend. However, not much happened during the 1999 legislative session. The 76th Legislature focused on public education, electric deregulation, tax breaks, and other issues, not higher education. Thus, following the session, Lieutenant Governor Rick Perry formed the Special Commission on 21st Century Colleges and Universities. The commission was charged with looking at workforce development (graduates), the role of technology, accessibility and affordability, the long-term role and mission of higher education in Texas, and improved accountability measures.

Beginning of the Twenty-First Century

The commission's final report bore the subtitle "Moving Every Texan Forward," a clue as to the contents.[28] The commission called on the 77th Legislature in 2001 to take six actions:

- Enhance the Texas Grant Program
- Promote a seamless PreK–16 education system
- Promote institutional excellence

- Create a college compact (less regulation in exchange for more academic and financial accountability)
- Develop priorities for higher-education facilities spending
- Support the strategic plan developed by the Texas Higher Education Coordinating Board (the agency that regulates universities and professional schools and in part regulates community colleges)

The legislature reacted by increasing funding by 10.4 percent for FY 2002–2003 over FY 2000–2001, with emphasis on taking care of enrollment growth and improving financial assistance for students. Legislators established two new research funds and created an interim Committee on Higher Education Excellence Funding. They authorized $1.1 billion in tuition revenue bonds to help institutions pay for buildings and other infrastructure. Legislators increased tuition but by adding to the available state-funded financial aid, they declared that they had responded to the Texas Higher Education Coordinating Board's plan called "Closing the Gaps,"[29] which emphasized access by more students to the educational system.

As previously noted, the 2003 Legislature opened in very different circumstances from other recent sessions. Legislators faced a $9.9 billion revenue shortfall. Meeting funding needs and increasing access to higher education are not really compatible goals. The state has struggled for a generation both to fund adequately the existing "flagship" institutions—the University of Texas at Austin and Texas A&M University at College Station—and to increase the number of flagships so as to enhance the research productivity in the state. The latter issue is not only a matter of funding but also of politics as to which institutions should be elevated. As the state becomes more diverse and as it continues to lag the nation in average income, financial support for students grows in importance. The state ranked last among the 10 most populous states in average faculty salaries in 2002,[30] and the National Center for Public Policy in Higher Education gave Texas "Cs" and "Ds" on all 5 measures it used to compare institutions nationally in 2002.[31] These facts provided the context for the 2003 session.

The legislature did not address the fundamental issues in the 2003 session. Basically, what higher education got out of that session was the ability to set tuition on an institutional basis as a means to meet expenses, with the caveat that 20 percent of the tuition increase be reserved for student financial assistance. The "catch" to that new empowerment was finding the mythical line in the sand that allowed reasonable funding for the institution without jeopardizing enrollment by putting higher education beyond the reach of many students. Legislators also relieved the institutions of having to return to the state a portion of research dollars received from the federal government and foundations, but Governor Rick Perry vetoed $45 million in excellence funds allocated for university research. Some universities came out ahead of the game by being able to keep all their federal funds even though they did not receive excellence funds; others lost in the balance. The biggest winner was the University of Texas at Dallas, which got $50 million from the governor's Texas Enterprise Fund for research connected with a new Texas Instruments microchip plant to be built adjacent to the campus.

Higher education was not a legislative focal point in 2005 either. The "10 percent law" created problems according to some of the more prestigious institutions because their available admissions slots were filling up with the top 10 percent students from all

YOU DECIDE

Should Students Pay Most of the Cost of their Education through Higher Tuition and Fees?

The 78th Legislature in 2003 deregulated tuition, at least on a temporary basis, to allow universities to charge whatever tuition they thought necessary for the operation of the institution in the wake of state cuts to higher education budgets. This development reflected both a budget reality at the time and a philosophy that the state needed to curtail its expenses for higher education.

Pro

⇨ The beneficiaries of a college education are the students themselves. Therefore, they should pay most of the cost of their education.

⇨ Texas has been on the low end of tuition and fees for years; it is only right that the state enact policies more like those of other states.

⇨ Higher education is a luxury, just like playing on a golf course. Thus, user fees should be the primary means of supporting institutions.

⇨ Privatization is a highly desirable public policy. Asking students to pay a larger share of their educational expenses is simply a logical step in making government smaller.

Con

⇨ The state as a whole benefits from having an educated populace because education is the linchpin of economic development.

⇨ Texas is somewhat poorer than most other states. Thus, the state has a special obligation to assist more in the education of its young people, at least through a Baccalaureate degree.

⇨ When good jobs are scarce and families are having a hard time making it economically, the state should pay a greater share of educational costs, not a lesser share.

⇨ Human resources are the most important resources of all. It is good public policy to invest in them.

calibers of schools while excluding, for example, someone in the top 11 percent from an excellent high school. This issue was not of paramount importance to legislators. The legislature passed H.B. 1172, which included a number of "timely graduation" provisions, including one that would limit Baccalaureate degree programs to 120 credit hours, although the coordinating board could make exceptions. It criticized the institutions for not meeting enrollment expectations and for the costs of education while putting more pressures on the institutions to raise tuition rates to pay the bills. In the 1960s, tuition was $50 a semester; during the 1980s, it was moving up from $20 to $30 a credit hour; by 2005–2006, tuition and fees at the University of Texas at Austin were $7,438 a year; at the University of Houston, $6,450; and at Sul Ross State University, $4,114. Virtually every institution raised tuition for 2006–2007, and the almost-free public community college system was also a thing of the past. In the 2006 special session, colleges did get some help with construction projects through the approval of tuition-backed revenue bonds.

Analysis

Texas has entered a new century with some genuine problems in higher education. Other states also had problems because of budget shortfalls and the lack of a comprehensive plan for delivering higher education. As one national writer noted, "The privatization of public higher education is not related to any political party, any governor, or any legislative leader, but it is happening, nonetheless."[32] Enrollments continue to grow, but institutions are not able to provide enough faculty and teaching assistants to ensure quality. Weaknesses in the public school system often produce beginning students who need individual attention, not giant classes or impersonal Web-based courses. More than a handful of universities need to be contributing to basic research. More financial assistance is needed. Affirmative action was re-introduced as an issue when the U.S. Supreme Court opened the door to some race-based consideration in 2003. From the standpoint of state policy makers, however, the institutions seemed mainly to want "more, more, more" at the same time legislators remained unconvinced that the colleges and universities were doing everything they could to meet student needs and to control expensive administrative costs. To a legislator, "excellence" comes in the classroom and through external research dollars. Thus, problems identified in the 1990s—image, funding, privatization, and finding a place on the agenda—continue well into the 2000s.

THE ENVIRONMENT

For Texans, environmental issues are particularly important. The state lived off the environment—land, water, air, and minerals—for much of its history, but that environment is deteriorating (land, water, and air) and depleting (minerals). The situation is made worse by the booming population of the state. Too, Texas is a place where nature is often hostile—tornadoes, flash floods, hurricanes, even occasional earthquakes confront its citizens, not to mention rattlesnakes, killer bees, and fire ants. Moreover, Texans, as the proud inheritors of a frontier past, remain unclear on whether to nurture the environment or conquer it. Furthermore, the national government has required a cleanup of the environment. Texas, like other states, is finding environmental cleanliness to be another well-intentioned but costly federal program. Three key pieces of national legislation are the Safe Drinking Water Act of 1996, the Clean Water Act of 1977, and the Clean Air Act of 1990. These laws include standards that are expensive to implement. The federal government was not forthcoming with funding adequate to assist state and local governments in meeting the new criteria, although these laws are examples of the mandates discussed earlier in the chapter. The twenty-first century dawned with the state facing environmental issues that affect the priority probably dearest to state policy makers—economic expansion

Is There Any Water? Is It Safe to Drink?

Texas has three basic kinds of water problems: supply, quality, and damage. All remain perennial contenders for the policy agenda.

Under average rain conditions, the rule of thumb is that for every 20 miles westward in the state, average rainfall diminishes by 1 inch. Since Texas is a very wide state indeed, by El Paso, the average rainfall is only 8 inches per year, compared with 55 inches in the southeastern part of the state. Consequently, West Texas politicians have kept the issue of *water supply* in the forefront for more than 30 years. They made water a critical issue in seven legislative sessions between 1969 and 2001, and the state produced various schemes and plans for providing water and engaged in extensive water planning. By early 2006, speculation existed that water would be a big issue in the 2007 legislative session. Texans are very conscious of that old Wyoming saying that opens this chapter. Further evidence of a likely focus on water in the 2007 sessions was the draft 2007 State Water Plan issued by the Texas Water Development Board in mid-2006, which made clear the water shortfalls facing the state in the future.[33]

Drought is a frequent Texas problem; in recent years, it plagued parts of the state in 1996, 1998–2000, 2003, and 2005–2006. The drought of 1996 made water supply a focal point of the 1997 legislative session, even though 1997 proved to be an extraordinarily wet year, with severe spring floods. Lawmakers came prepared to deal with water, and they produced a comprehensive, 220-page bill covering most aspects of water in the state. The exception was the 400 or so inadequate dams in the state. In 2001 voters approved a constitutional amendment to expand the authority of the Texas Water Development Board (TWDB) and provide additional bonding authority for the TWDB to help build water projects. In 2002, the TWDB published *Water for Texas— 2002*,[34] a three-volume, fifty-year plan for the development of water resources in the state. Texas also tried to bargain with Oklahoma, Arkansas, Louisiana, New Mexico, and Mexico at various times over water rights of shared lakes, rivers, and aquifers, although "state diplomacy" did little to solve Texas water shortages. A fundamental reality of Texas water supply is that Caddo Lake on the Louisiana border is the only natural lake in the state, thus forcing the state into a constant building program to create reservoirs to hold rain runoff.

In addition, the 2003 Legislature passed seven water conservation bills, the most notable being S.B. 1094 and H.B. 2660. The former created an ongoing task force to monitor and make recommendations about water conservation in the state; the latter spelled out five- and ten-year requirements for water savings, including percentage reductions in the average daily water use per person.

Another persistent issue is *water quality*. The oft-cited bottom line for water and for air quality in Texas is that since 1988 Texas has ranked toward the top in the country in the millions of tons of toxic **pollutants** it spewed into the air, let seep into the ground, and dumped into the water. Everything from runoff of fertilizer used in agriculture to inadequate storm water control affects water quality. A series of state agencies has overseen environmental quality. The most recent one to emerge is the Texas Commission on Environmental Quality (TCEQ) in 2002; TCEQ is the new name for the Texas Natural Resource Conservation Commission (TNRCC), which was created in 1993 as the result of a merger between the Texas Water Commission (TWC) and the Texas Air Control Board.

The TNRCC (called "Ten-Rack" or sometimes "Train-Wreck") was sometimes heavy-handed in the way it regulated Texas communities to force compliance with the standards of the Environmental Protection Agency (EPA), which administers the national policy. Consequently, in 2001 the legislature passed sunset legislation (see Chapter 7) requiring a name—and presumably an image—change. Taking the necessary steps to avoid toxic pollutants such as pesticides, heavy metals, and raw sewage is up to communities.

Water quality was not a focus of the 2003 or 2005 legislative sessions. The major water environmental bill was one prohibiting off-road vehicles from driving in or near rivers. Nevertheless, the issue remains on the policy agenda. For example, the federal Environmental Protection Agency issued a report at the end

Barton Springs, a natural swimming hole, is almost hallowed water in Austin. It has been menaced by developers for a decade. In 2003 the *Austin American-Statesman*, the City of Austin, and the state health department concluded that some clean-up was in order because the sediment at the bottom of the springs contained a carcinogen, though the three did not agree on the degree of danger in the Barton Springs mud.

SOURCE: Courtesy of Ben Sargent.

of 2005 that listed Texas among the top ten states with the most contaminated drinking water.[35] Texas was sixth on the list after California, Wisconsin, Arizona, Florida, and North Carolina.

Is the Air Safe to Breathe?

The Texas Commission on Environmental Quality also sets standards and emission limits for the abatement and control of air pollution. This agency is responsible for state compliance with the national Clean

Some of the most graphic examples of polluted black skies came in 2005–2006 as the result of the prolonged drought. Many parts of the state suffered through months of less than 50 percent of their average rainfall, and more than 1 million acres burned. People and animals died, and homes and business were destroyed in the conflagration.

Air Act. The national legislation, originally passed in December 1990 and modified in 1996, regulates emissions that cause acid rain and affect the quality of air in metropolitan areas, and it also controls the release of toxic pollutants into the air. Much work must be done to clean up the state's air, particularly in major metropolitan areas, where motor vehicles emit a large volume of toxic gases, and in areas where the petrochemical industry operates. The basic standards for clean air are set by the U.S. Environmental Protection Agency.

Although in 2002 the EPA lessened the stringent requirements it adopted in 1997,[36] Texas still had 12 million residents living in smog, and the numbers were growing. The four Texas "non-attainment areas" (areas that do not meet federal air quality standards) cover 17 counties in the heavily populated areas of Dallas-Fort Worth, Beaumont-Port Arthur, Houston-Galveston, and El Paso. Five other metropolitan areas are approaching non-attainment status; Northeast Texas (Tyler-Longview-Marshall), Austin, San Antonio, Victoria, and Corpus Christi. In addition, Texas, like everywhere else in the world, faces the various effects of global climate change, holes in the ozone layer, and the "greenhouse" effect in general. (The *greenhouse effect* is the buildup of gases that retain heat reflected from the earth's surface; this heat retention then causes climatic changes.) An emerging problem is mercury pollution.[37]

Densely populated states dependent on cars and trucks—such as Texas and California—continue to see their urban areas listed as having dirty air. Although the EPA sets standards, the national government has not wanted to be a major player in the clean-up effort, leaving that chore to the states. The 1995 Legislature, one of the least environmentally sensitive on record, shirked its responsibility for clean air by revoking the state's auto emissions testing program. This failure to comply with federal environmental standards immediately caused a $160 million lawsuit by the firm that held the contract for emissions testing.[38] Texas political leaders, however, were perceptive in reading a lack of national impetus to enforce some of the aspects of the Clean Air Act, including emissions testing, and decided to spend the state's money elsewhere regardless of any long-term consequences.

In December 1999, TNRCC published prospective air quality regulations in the *Texas Register*. These regulations stressed industrial clean-ups, a move toward California standards of motor vehicles' anti-pollution devices, and even restrictions

 When it comes to the environment, sometimes the state is its own worst enemy. In 1991 the legislature was set on encouraging an insurance company to develop a large resort on environmentally sensitive Padre Island despite a 14½-hour filibuster from Senator Carlos Truan, who represented that area. The bill finally died at the last minute, but, had it been needed, Governor Ann Richards had promised a veto. In 1995 a similar situation occurred when the legislature over-rode Austin's strict environmental regulations to allow the Freeport McMoRan corporation to develop the Circle C area in spite of potential degradation of the Barton Creek watershed. Austin Senator Gonzalo Barrientos's 21-hour filibuster went for nought, and Governor George W. Bush did not veto the law. By 2003 Barton Creek and Barton Springs were faced with a major clean-up effort.

on the times of day when heavy construction equipment could be operated. In 2001 the legislature closed a loophole that allowed older industrial plants to pollute, passed but did not fund the Texas Emissions Reductions Plan, and generally was more environmentally conscious than its immediate predecessors. By 2003 funding the emissions program was critical because the non-attainment areas faced federal sanctions in 2005 that could severely limit industrial growth and highway construction. Very late in the regular session, the 78th Legislature funded the emissions abatement plan with revenue that would come from an increase in the vehicle title transfer fee that Texans pay when they buy a car or truck. The 79th Legislature in 2005 passed legislation on administrative matters but not significant new environmental regulations.

The Land: Is It Safe to Walk Here? Is There Room?

Where does a community put solid waste, whether that waste is toxic chemicals, radioactive byproducts, or just simply the paper, plastic, bottles, and cans that are the residue of everyday living? Four possible solutions are recycling, composting, incineration, and landfill disposal. In Texas, landfills are by far the most common solution because they are also the least expensive. Consequently, the municipalities of the state are facing major problems with their landfills because of both the amount of land needed to dispose of wastes—and the resistance of citizens to having a landfill in their part of town—and the need to meet stringent new federal regulations as of 1991. The federal regulations evolved from the Resource Conservation and Recovery Act. The TCEQ has jurisdiction over solid waste disposal in the state.

One of the reasons the state has such a problem with wastes is that Texas has so many "dirty" industries. For example, Texas is a major producer of petrochemical products such as fertilizers, paints, and motor fuels, all of which produce hazardous byproducts. It is a big mining state, with the slag from mineral production being a danger in itself. These same industries intensify the water pollution problem because of the runoff of toxic materials into the storm water drains and waterways of the state.

With two nuclear power plants on line—Commanche Peak south of Dallas and South Texas near Houston—and other radioactive materials such as those from medical facilities and defense plants, the state must also be concerned about the disposal of radioactive materials. Furthermore, the national government periodically has looked to the state as a possible national storage site for radioactive wastes. Texas for years tried to deal with this problem in isolation, ignoring other states, but burying one's head in the sand does not work when an 18-wheeler carrying nuclear waste is speeding along a Texas highway. Lobbyists tried to gain passage of bills in four sessions of the legislature beginning in 1995 to open the state to private companies in the nuclear waste disposal business. They finally succeeded in 2003, when the legislature created two privately run, state-licensed disposal facilities,[39] one to

What do Willie Nelson, a private partnership in Galveston Bay, and the City of Denton with its industry partner have in common? They are all producing biodiesel fuel. Agricultural products such as soybeans and used vegetable oil from restaurants are converted to fuel; the fuel is then blended with regular diesel fuel to make a much cleaner burning fuel. In Denton, for example, the entire fleet of solid waste vehicles as well as many of the local school district buses now run on biodiesel.

handle wastes generated by states participating in an interstate compact agreement and one to handle federal wastes. One state senator protested, "This makes Texas the dumping ground of the United States and the world."[40] People in Nevada might disagree because in 2002 Congress chose Nevada's Yucca Mountain as the official disposal site for high-level waste from all the nation's nuclear reactors. President Bush signed off on the decision although he had opposed a similar nuclear waste site in Texas when he was governor. Nevada state officials promised to sue.

Analysis

Operating dirty industries and dirty municipal waste facilities is less expensive than operating clean ones, but the real problem is not a venal unwillingness to protect the environment but the very high costs of doing so. Anyone who has watched the haze settle in over Houston or Dallas or Austin in the afternoon rush hour knows that there is a problem, as does anyone who has seen dead fish floating belly-up in the state's rivers. However, environmental policy-making often tends to produce diametrically opposed views, making compromise difficult. Interests from ranches to factories that lower their costs of production by polluting air and water resist government attempts to order them to clean up their operations. And, as explained in Chapter 3, because these polluting interests tend to be organized and well represented among Austin lobbyists, they can often put up a serious resistance to pro-environmental forces. Environmental policy-making is thus an issue well suited to illustrate the difficulties encountered by democracies in achieving the public interests. In Texas, the politics of special interests often dominate land, water, and air policy to the detriment of society as a whole. Thus, Texas state environmental policy does not meet the test of democratic theory.

Nevertheless, Texas is still spending considerable money on environmental matters—an apparent reflection of its size and the magnitude of its problems. The TCEQ budget alone for FY 2006–2007 is $972 million. Local governments are also spending considerable money through their wastewater and solid waste operations.[41] However, the state's innate conservatism is unlikely to make Texas a model for environmental policy-making.

SUMMARY

This chapter does not attempt to deal with all the issues facing the state. Rather, three policy issues—poverty and welfare, higher education, and environmental quality—that illustrate the continuing and often inter-related problems of Texas and the complexity of public policy-making. These issues also point out the intergovernmental and intragovernmental aspects of modern public policy.

The resolution of each issue is important to the future of Texas, and each is linked to other significant issues not outlined in this chapter. Without addressing the considerable poverty of the state, Texas may find it difficult to resolve other policy issues such as economic diversification and sound public education. Moreover, abject poverty tends to foster crime. Education has long been seen as the key to the proverbial better future. However, Texas has allowed its higher education system to lag behind that of the nation as a whole, and its economic future depends on catching up. Everyone needs clean water, air, and land, and environmental quality also is tied to the need for economic diversity to avoid further expansion of high-pollution industries. None of the issues is new. All are costly to deal with, so much so that solving one problem may worsen another. All have implications for local as well as state governments.

Texas policy makers have dealt with all these issues to some extent, but problems remain on the public policy agenda:

1. Texas is similar to the other states in trying to meet the challenge of rising health care costs and the corresponding rise in costs of Medicaid. Changes in national philosophy and spending patterns have been both boon and bane to Texas. Texas today enjoys greater flexibility under current federal policy to make decisions on what programs to offer its neediest citizens, but the state is generally not willing to spend more of its own money for social programs. Additionally, the state continues to have one of the highest proportions of poor people in the country.

2. Higher education in Texas continues to be plagued by a bad image, under-funding, privatization, and, in most years, an inability to rank high on the policy agenda. State priorities include access to higher education for all students, providing human resources for the state's businesses, and quality control. Institutional priorities include better salaries and more money for programs. One issue bridging the two sets of interests is the ability to recruit, admit, and provide financial assistance for ethnic minority students.

3. Texas has always been proud of its resources, but it has materially damaged those resources. Now the state must find an integrated, comprehensive approach to environmental quality. It keeps trying to find a workable solution and has emphasized clean industry in its economic development efforts. In 1997 the state once again legislated a comprehensive water act (the *sixth* such effort in slightly less than 30 years), and in 2003 it addressed air pollution, although at the proverbial 11th hour.

The three issues discussed in this chapter—poverty, higher education, and pollution—affect all citizens, albeit in different ways. They bring to mind the "haves" and "have-nots" of our society, disparities among ethnic groups, and even problems of mortgaging our children's future by failing to address current problems.

Combined, these issues have major tax and quality-of-life implications for citizens. They will also help shape the future economy of Texas. They all reflect problems that will cause the governor and the legislators, as the principal policy makers of the state, many anxious moments. They are all grounded in the conservative political culture of the state and, like other issues, reflect the influence of special interests in the policy process. More participation, more concern for society as a whole, and more concern for future generations might have helped to prevent some of the problems in the first place.

The state has shown stinginess in trying to mitigate poverty, inconsistency in its approach to higher education, and, until forced into federal compliance, a cavalier attitude toward the environment. In each approach, powerful interests tended to dominate the policy arena, and the average citizen's perspective was not always considered. As we have argued elsewhere in this book, Texas, when judged by standards of democratic theory, seriously falters.

STUDY QUESTIONS

1. As we argue throughout this book, Texas public policy has often been dominated by special interests. Do you agree or disagree with this notion? Why? What effect would domination by upper-income groups have on state policy toward the poor? What effects do you think the conservative political culture has?

2. How do you think that the Texas political culture has affected Texans' attitudes toward the environment? What evidence have you seen that reflects an attitude that the environment is something to conquer or subdue? What evidence have you seen that reflects an attitude that the environment is something to be treasured and preserved?

3. Think back to what you have learned about the revenue system and revenue shortfalls in Texas. Given the revenue problems of the state, which of the issues discussed in this chapter—poverty and welfare, higher education, and the environment—would you address first? Should the state find new revenue sources to solve all the problems?

4. Consider one of the three major issues discussed in this chapter. How well do you think democratic ideals such as participation, equality, and concern for the general welfare are reflected in state policy?

5. What do you think about the legislation to end some people's practice of being "professional students?" Can you think of circumstances in which an undergraduate student might be justified in taking more than 170 hours to get a Bachelor's degree? More than 120?

SURFING THE WEB

Visit the companion site for this book:
   http://www.thomsonedu.com/politicalscience/kraemer

All about the services for needy people:
   http://www.hhsc.state.tx.us/ (families, general assistance) and
   http://www.dads.state.tx.us/ (aging and disability services)

Poverty guidelines:
    http://aspe.hhs.gov/poverty

Information on higher education in Texas:
    http://www.thecb.state.tx.us

State environmental regulations:
    http://www.tceq.state.tx.us

NOTES

1. Clay Robinson, "Deadline Sealed Deal," *Houston Chronicle*, May 14, 2006, reported at http://www.chron.com/disp/story.mpl/metropolitan/3861925.html.

2. See *Neeley v. West Orange-Cove Consolidated Independent School District et al.*, Texas Supreme Court Opinion No. 04-1144, November 22, 2005. See also *San Antonio Independent School District et al. v. Rodriguez*, 411 U.S. 1 (1973). The case was originally styled *Rodriguez v. San Antonio ISD* because Rodriguez instituted the suit. Then see *William Kirby et al. v. Edgewood Independent School District et al.*, 777 S.W. 2d 391 (1989) for the state case on appeal. Originally, the Edgewood ISD sued Kirby, who was the commissioner of education.

3. *Ruiz v. Estelle* (666 Fed. 2d 854, 1982, and 650 Fed. 2d 555, 5th Cir., 1981). Ruiz was a prisoner and Estelle was the head of the prison system. See Ed Timms, "30-Year Texas Prison Battle Ends," *Dallas Morning News*, June 9, 2002, 1A.

4. See, for example, the policy discussion in Randall B. Ripley and Grace A. Franklin, *Congress, the Bureaucracy, and Public Policy*, 5th ed. (Monterey, CA: Brooks/Cole, 1991), Chapters 1 and 6.

5. "The 2006 HHS Poverty Guidelines," published in the *Federal Register* and available online at http://aspe.hhs.gov/poverty/06poverty.shtml (use 05 for the 2005 guidelines).

6. *Income, Poverty, and Health Insurance Coverage in the United States: 2004* (Washington, DC: U.S. Census Bureau, August 2005), 25.

7. U.S. Census Bureau, "American FactFinder," found at http://factfinder.census.gov/home/saff/main.html by filling in "Texas."

8. "100 Poorest Counties by Median Household Income," *Wikipedia*, found at http:/en.wikipedia.org/wiki/ (lowest income counties in the United States).

9. "Who Are America's Poor Children?" (New York: National Center for Children in Poverty, Columbia University), found at www.nccp.org.

10. Texas Health and Human Services Commissioner, "Appendix C: Medicaid Enrollees by Age Group (as of January of 2004)," *Texas Medicaid in Perspective*, 5th ed. (Austin: Health and Human Services Commission, June 2004).

11. "Study Provides Look at Homeless," *Dallas Morning News*, December 8, 1999, 3A.

12. For an excellent discussion of the importance of middle-class attitudes in the development of social programs, see Robert Morris, *Social Policy of the American Welfare State* (New York: Harper & Row, 1979), Chapters 1 and 2. Morris, along with C. John E. Hansan, also offers useful commentary on welfare philosophy in the *United States in Welfare Reform, 1996–2000: Is There a Safety Net?* (Westport, CT: Auburn House, 1999).

13. *Fiscal Size-Up: 2006–2007 Biennium* (Austin: Legislative Budget Board, 2005), 161.

14. See Texas Unemployment Insurance Benefits at http://swz.salary.com/salarywizard/layouthtmls/swzl_unemployment_TX.html#Benefits.

15. Brett Shipp, "Workers' Comp: Medical Gridlock," WFAA-TV Channel 8 News, May 12, 2006.

16. "Welfare Reform, Part 2: A Kinder, Gentler Plan for Texas," *Texas Government News*, September 23, 1996, 2. For an excellent explanation of the federal legislation and its consequences, see Carl Tubbesing and Sheri Steisel, "Answers to Your Welfare Worries," *State Legislatures*, January 1997, 12–19.

17. Scott Pattison, executive director of the National Association of State Budget Officers, in a joint meeting of two standing panels of the National Academy of Public Administration meeting on "Social Equity Implications of Local, State, and Federal Fiscal Challenges," held in Washington, DC, Raleigh, NC, and across the country via conference telephone on June 13, 2003.

18. Robert T. Garrett, "Changes in CHIP Frustrate Families," *Dallas Morning News*, March 27, 2006, 1A, 4A.

19. See Kristine Goodwin, "Medicaid Extreme Makeover," *State Legislatures*, February 2006, 20–23.

20. Jack Tweedie et al., "Window of Opportunity for Welfare Reform," *State Legislatures*, April 1999, 22. While the specifics of the article are somewhat dated, its essential points remain unchanged.

21. Laura Meckler, "Study: Under Welfare Reform, Some of the Poor Get Poorer," *Austin American-Statesman*, August 22, 1999, A11; Christopher Lee, "Study Faults Texas' Job Help for Welfare Recipients," *Dallas Morning News*, June 28, 1998, 39A, 42A. See also Robert Greenstein and Sharon Parrot, "Cuts in House Budget Bill Aimed at Low-Income Families Reduced by only 2%; other 98% of Cuts Remain," Washington, DC: Center on Budget and Policy Priorities, December 5, 2005, reported at http://www.cbpp.org/11-17-05bud2.htm, for portents of the federal budget for FY 2007.

22. Higher education, K–12 education, Medicaid, and corrections are the "big four" of spending for state governments in the United States. See Ronald K. Snell, "The Budget Wonderland," *State Legislatures*, February 1998, 14.

23. See *LULAC et al. v. Clements et al.*, Cause No. 12-87-5242-A, in the District Court of Cameron County, 107th Judicial District; *Clements et al. v. LULAC et al.* (Appellees), Cause No. 13-90-146-CV, in the Court of Appeals, 13th Supreme Judicial District, Corpus Christi, Texas; Final Judgment, *LULAC v. Richards*, January 20, 1992. (The style, that is, the name, of the case changed when Ann Richards succeeded Bill Clements as governor.)

24. 78 F.3d 932 (5th Cir. 1996), rehearing *en banc denied*, 84 F.3d 720 (5th Cir. 1996); *certiorari denied*, 116 S. Ct. 2581 (1996).

25. See *Grutter v. Bollinger, Lee et al.*, No. 02-241, decided June 23, 2003; *Gratz et al. v. Bollinger, Lee et al.*, No. 02-516, decided June 23, 2003, by the U.S. Supreme Court.

26. A. Phillips Brooks, "Law, Medical Schools Hurting for Minorities," *Austin American-Statesman*, October 17, 1997, B1, B7.

27. This section relies heavily on *Back to Basics: The Role of Higher Education in the Economic Future of Texas*, a set of proposals for the 75th Texas Legislature prepared by The Coalition (of public university chancellors), January 1997.

28. *Higher Education in the 21st Century: Moving Every Texan Forward* (Austin: Commission on 21st Century Colleges and Universities, January 2001).

29. The plan can be accessed via http://www.thecb.state.tx.us/; click "Closing the Gaps."

30. Dave Castle, Mary Alice Baker, Joe Kemble, and Frank Fair, "State of the Profession in Texas: Compensation, Recruitment, Retention," *TACT Quarterly Bulletin*, January 17, 2003, citing information from the *Chronicle of Higher Education* for August 30, 2002.

31. "Measuring Up 2002: The State-by-State Report Card for Higher Education" (San Jose, CA: National Center for Public Policy and Higher Education, 2002), available at the time at www.highereducation.org. Texas was not among the states sampled in Margaret A. Miller and Peter T. Ewell, "Measuring Up on College-Level Learning" (San Jose, CA: National Center for Public Policy and Higher Education, 2005), available at http://www.highereducation.org./reports/mu_learning/index.shtml.

32. Graham Spanier in Stanley Ikenberry, "Higher Ed: Dangers of an Unplanned Future," *State Legislatures*, September 2005, 16–18, quotation on 17.

33. 2007 Draft State Water Plan found at http://www.twdb.state.tx.us/publications/reports/State_Water_Plan/2007/Draft_2007SWP.htm, 2007.

34. *Water for Texas–2002* is available at http://www.twdb.state.tx.us/publications/reports/state_water_plan/2002/finalwaterplan2002.asp.

35. "Texas Fares Poorly in Water Study," WFAA-TV, Channel 8 News, December 20, 2005. See also, "Study: Almost Every U.S. River Is Contaminated with Pesticides," *Austin American-Statesman*, March 4, 2006, A19; "Only 28% of Texans Definitely Know the Source of Their Drinking Water," *Lone Star Sierran*, Spring 2005, 3–5.

36. The EPA was following the lead of President George W. Bush, who wanted less stringent controls. See, for example, Terry McCarthy, "How Bush Gets His Way on the Environment," *Time magazine*, January 27, 2003, 48–50.

37. See Larry Morandi, "Staying Ahead of the Feds," *State Legislatures*, June 2005, 14–17.

38. Steve Scheibal, "Emissions Case Costs Texas $160 Million," *Austin American-Statesman*, April 5, 1997, A1, A10.

39. Natalie Gott, "Lawmakers Pass Clean Air Bill, Shoot Down other Measures," *Denton Record-Chronicle*, June 15, 2003, 4A; Amber Novak, "Up in Smoke," *Texas Observer*, May 23, 2003, 4–7, 27–31.

40. Senator Robert Duncan, a Lubbock Republican, quoted in Terrence Stutz, "Radioactive Dump Approved by Senate," *Dallas Morning News*, May 8, 2003, 5A.

41. For an indication of local water and wastewater rates, which are trending upward both to support water development projects and wastewater run-off mandates, see "Water and Wastewater Survey Results," *Texas Town & City*, reported each year in May.

GLOSSARY

administrative discretion　the freedom that administrators (bureaucrats) have to implement and interpret laws (Ch. 7)

appellate jurisdiction　the authority of a court to review the decisions of a lower court and confirm or overturn them (Ch. 8)

appointment and removal　the governor's constitutional and statutory authority to hire and fire people employed by the state (Ch. 7)

at-large elections　elections in which each candidate for any given public office must run jurisdiction-wide—in the entire city, county, or state—when several similar positions are being filled (Ch. 9)

attorney general's advisory opinion　the informal but firmly established power of the Texas attorney general to issue opinions on the constitutionality of proposed laws and government actions and to give interpretations of the Open Records Act (Ch. 8)

bicameral　for a legislative body, divided into two chambers or houses (Ch. 6)

biennial　every two years; thus, a biennial legislative session occurs every other year and a biennial budget is one that directs spending for two years (Ch. 2)

bill　a proposed law written on paper and submitted to a legislature (Ch. 6)

bill of rights　a section of a constitution, most famously that of the U.S. Constitution, that lists the civil rights and liberties of the citizens and places restrictions on the powers of government (Chs. 2, 8)

block grants　federal funds that can be used for a broad range of programs; the state or local government recipient can determine specific uses within broad guidelines (Ch. 10)

bureaucracy　a type of organization that is characterized by hierarchy, specialization, fixed and official rules, and relative freedom from outside control (Ch. 7)

campaign　the period before a democratic election in which parties and candidates attempt to persuade voters and contributors to support them (Ch. 5)

capital punishment　the death penalty for a crime; in Texas, and in all states that have it, this can be imposed only for the crime of murder (Ch. 8)

categorical grants-in-aid　federal funds allotted to the states that can be used only for specific purposes (Ch. 10)

checks and balances   an arrangement whereby each branch of government has some power to limit the actions of other branches (Ch. 2)

civil jurisdiction   the authority of a court over civil rather than criminal matters (Ch. 8)

civil liberties   the freedoms that individual citizens enjoy to be independent of government regulation and suppression; examples are freedom of speech, religion, and assembly (Ch. 8)

civil rights   rights accorded to individual citizens by a government; examples in a democracy are the right to vote and the right to equality before the law (Ch. 8)

clientele group   the interest group or groups that benefit from or are regulated by an administrative agency (Ch. 7)

co-optation   the relationship resulting from an industry's "capture" of, or intensely influencing, a regulatory agency so that instead of regulating the industry in the public interest, the agency regulates the industry for the industry's benefit (Ch. 3)

coalition   an alliance of individuals and interests who cooperate to win elections and run a government; usually the organizational basis of political parties (Ch. 4)

concurrent jurisdiction   shared authority between two or more types of courts (Ch. 8)

conference committee   a temporary joint committee consisting of members from both houses of a legislature in which representatives attempt to reconcile the differences between two versions of a bill (Ch. 6)

conservatism   the political ideology that is, in general, opposed to government regulation of the economy and redistribution of wealth but in favor of government regulation of personal life (Ch. 4)

constitution   the written law of a state or nation that takes precedence over all other laws and actions of the government (Ch. 2)

constitutional amendment   a change in a constitution that is approved by the legislative body—and, in Texas, the voters. Nationally, constitutional amendments are not approved directly by the voters (Ch. 2)

constitutional revision   the making of major changes in a constitution, often including the writing of an entirely new document (Ch. 2)

council–manager form of government   type of municipal government in which the voters elect a city council, which then appoints a professional manager to handle the executive functions of the city; there is no mayor (Ch. 9)

Court of Criminal Appeals   Texas's highest appellate court in the area of criminal law; has no civil jurisdiction (Ch. 8)

criminal jurisdiction   the authority of a court to try people accused of crime; as opposed to civil jurisdiction (Ch. 8)

democracy   the theory of governmental legitimacy that is based on the belief that the people's participation creates moral rightness and that such participation obligates the citizens to obey the laws (Ch. 1)

district elections   elections in which candidates for public office run in one geographical portion rather than the whole city or county; each district generally sends one representative (also called single-member district elections) (Ch. 9)

dual budgeting system   a system in which the executive and legislative branches of government prepare separate budget documents (Ch. 10)

elasticity   in reference to tax systems, flexibility and breadth that ensures that state revenues are not seriously disrupted even if one segment of the economy is troubled (Ch. 10)

exclusive jurisdiction   the right of a court to have sole authority over a certain area of the law (Ch. 8)

federal system   a system of government that provides for a division and sharing of authority between a national government and state or regional governments (Chs. 1, 2)

filibuster   an effort to kill a bill in a legislature by unlimited debate; it is possible in the Texas and U.S. Senates but not in the Houses of Representatives (Ch. 6)

formal qualifications   qualifications for holding public office that are specified by law or the constitution (Ch. 6)

gerrymandering   the act of drawing district boundaries so as to advantage one party or set of candidates against another; common in both state and congressional districts (Ch. 6)

home rule   in Texas, the ability of cities with a population of 5,000 or more to organize themselves as they wish within the constitution and laws of the state (Chs. 2, 9)

ideology   a system of beliefs and values that explains political legitimacy and defines appropriate political behavior for both government officials and individuals (Ch. 4)

impeachment   the process of formally accusing an official of improper behavior in office; it is followed by a trial, and if the official is convicted, the penalty is removal from office (Ch. 7)

inflation   a rise in the general price level, which is the same thing as a fall in the value of the dollar (Ch. 10)

interest   involvement in anything—economic, religious, racial, for example—that can form the basis for shared political action (Ch. 4)

item veto   the governor's constitutional power to strike out individual items in an appropriations bill (Ch. 7)

juvenile courts   courts that have jurisdiction over accused offenders who are under 17 years of age (Ch. 8)

legitimacy   the belief citizens have that their government is morally grounded and that therefore they are obligated to obey its laws (Ch. 1)

liberalism   the political ideology whose adherents generally endorse government regulation of the economy and redistribution of wealth but generally oppose government regulation of personal life (Ch. 4)

lobby   to attempt to influence government by means of personal contact rather than by voting or contributing money (Ch. 3)

mandate   any action that the national government requires state and local governments to take or that the state requires cities, counties, and special districts to take (Ch. 11)

mayor–council form   the classic form of municipal government in which the mayor and the council are elected independently, and the mayor has some executive control of the council (Ch. 9)

message power   the governor's means of formally establishing his or her priorities for legislative action by communicating with the legislature (Ch. 7)

nonpartisan election   one in which candidates on the ballot bear no party label (Ch. 9)

one-party state   a democratic polity, whether a state or nation, that is dominated by a single political party (Ch. 4)

original jurisdiction   authority over a given civil or criminal matter at the first, lowest level of the judiciary (Ch. 8)

original trial courts   courts that exercise original jurisdiction over criminal or civil matters (Ch. 8)

permanent party organization   the structures and individuals in a political party that continue to function between elections (Ch. 4)

place system   a form of at-large election in which all candidates are elected city-wide, but the seats on the council are designated Place 1, Place 2, etc., and a candidate runs only against others who have filed for the same place (Ch. 9)

plea bargain   an agreement between prosecuting and defense attorneys, in which an accused criminal pleads guilty to a lesser charge and receives a lesser punishment in return (Ch. 8)

political culture   the values, beliefs, and behaviors of a given society with regard to politics and government (Ch. 1)

political interest group   a group of people with a common interest—economic, religious, racial, etc.—that attempts to influence government, usually by means of lobbying government on behalf of their cause (Ch. 3)

political parties   organizations in democracies that attempt to win elections and thereby exercise power through government (Ch. 4)

pollutants   substances that are dumped into water supplies, landfills, and the atmosphere that are harmful to human, plant, and/or animal life (Ch. 11)

privately funded campaigns   democratic election campaigns in which candidates and parties must rely upon private sources of funding rather than government sources (Ch. 5)

progressive taxation   a tax structure that increases in rate commensurate with the wealth of those paying the tax; the richer the person or institution, the higher the tax rate (Ch. 10)

public policy   the foundational ideas that undergird individual governmental decisions and programs; policy shifts over time as public officials set priorities by creating the budget, making official decisions, and passing laws (Ch. 11)

publicly funded campaigns   democratic election campaigns in which candidates and parties are largely subsidized by government rather than private funds (Ch. 5)

re-alignment   the reshuffling of the coalitional basis of political parties in a democracy so that a party that had been in the minority becomes the majority party (Ch. 4)

re-apportionment   the re-allocation of legislative seats, adding seats to areas with heavy population growth and taking away seats from areas without growth (Ch. 6)

redistricting   the designation of geographic areas that are nearly equal in population for the purpose of electing legislators—national, state, and local (Ch. 6)

regressive taxation   a tax structure in which the rate is the same for everyone regardless of ability to pay; thus, the smaller the taxpayer's income, the larger the percentage of income that goes to the tax (Ch. 10)

revenue shortfall   a situation in which state revenues are not adequate to fund programs and services at current levels (Ch. 10)

seniority   in a legislative body, the amount of time spent in continuous service on one house or committee (Ch. 6)

separation of powers   a phrase often used to describe the U.S. political system; it refers to the assigning of powers to specific branches (in Texas, departments) of government. In reality, the powers of the branches overlap so that "separate institutions sharing powers" would be a more accurate description of the U.S. system (Ch. 2)

session power   the governor's constitutional authority to call the legislature into special session and to set the agenda of topics to be considered in that session (Ch. 7)

Supreme Court   the highest appellate court in the civil track of Texas's judicial system; has no criminal jurisdiction (Ch. 8)

tag   in the legislature, a means by which an individual senator can delay a committee hearing on a bill for at least 48 hours (Ch. 6)

temporary party organizations   the structures and individuals in a political party that function only during election campaigns (Ch. 4)

turnover   in the legislature, the proportion of it that consists of first-term members because previous members retired, died, or were defeated at the polls (Ch. 6)

veto power   the governor's constitutional authority to prevent the implementation of laws enacted by the legislature; the line-item veto allows the governor to delete individual items from an appropriations bill (Ch. 7)

voter registration   the act of making a list of eligible voters that is performed periodically by governments, the purpose of which is to prevent ballot fraud (Ch. 5)

voter turnout   the percentage of the legally eligible population that actually votes in a democratic election (Ch. 5)

INDEX